Praise f<

"This sparkling gem of a book is a riveting, breathtakingly action-packed, and fast-paced tour de force, remarkable for not only its depth and breadth but also its superlative clarity. Bar none, this eminently accessible volume is one of the most deeply satisfying and richly rewarding books on psychotherapy that I have ever read. Deceptively simple, it is actually an extraordinarily profound treatise on working with not just 'fragile' patients (whose defenses include denial, splitting, and projection) but actually all patients who have ever mobilized defenses to protect themselves from the pain in their lives—defenses that might once have enabled them to survive but that now interfere with their ability to thrive and to connect with both themselves and others.

"Seamlessly interweaving theory and practice, Frederickson offers the reader a captivating and aesthetically appealing treasure trove of theoretical and clinical pearls of wisdom garnered from his decades of experience in the field and his finely honed capacity to zero in on—always, of course, with compassion, directness, and nonjudgment—both the individual hidden behind the defenses and what the individual will need to confront to be found. Frederickson is not only a clinician extraordinaire who has mastered his art to near perfection but also a stunningly gifted thinker who, in his writings and teachings, is able to formulate his theoretical framework in a concise and compelling manner."

—Martha Stark, MD, Faculty, Harvard Medical School, and
 award-winning author of eight books, including *Relentless Hope*

"In *Co-Creating Safety: Healing the Fragile Patient,* Jon Frederickson offers the reader a valuable guide for engaging and collaborating with patients who are often the most vulnerable and challenging to treat. Jon is a master clinician and scholar who brings to bear a remarkable ability to synthesize and curate not only his substantial clinical experience but clinical gems and insights offered by many pioneering therapists and researchers. What makes this volume so useful is that Jon is also a skilled supervisor and trainer with a keen ability to describe complex clinical phenomena and treatment in clear prose. There is much here to refresh our understanding of psychotherapeutics, deepen our appreciation for the complexity, and add to our clinical efficacy when working with fragile patients. This is a must-read for all clinicians."

　—Jeffrey J. Magnavita, PhD, ABPP, founder and CEO, Strategic
　　Psychotherapeutics, LLC, and former President, Society for the
　　Advancement of Psychotherapy

"*Co-Creating Safety* is a pleasure to read at so many levels. First, we see a wise and experienced therapist working with very challenging patients. He gives the reader such extensive examples of his process that the book could be used as a workbook. Second, Frederickson integrates his approach with perspectives from neuroscience, attachment theory, varied psychoanalytic theories, and more. Third, he describes a therapy process that includes careful monitoring of the therapeutic alliance as it enables the patient to move from building a secure attachment to strengthening the patient and then toward integration. Fourth, he defines anxiety as fundamentally a relational phenomenon, and working with it in the therapy relationship, patients become more fully themselves."

　—Michael Stadter, PhD, Faculty, International Psychotherapy
　　Institute, Washington School of Psychiatry, and Center for
　　Existential Studies and Psychotherapy, and author of *Presence
　　and the Present*

"Jon Frederickson has a marvelous capacity to join with fragile patients to set the stage for a surprisingly fruitful and effective therapy experience. What makes this book so valuable to the practicing clinician are the copious and detailed clinical vignettes that include both the verbatim dialogue and very instructive explanatory comments along the way. The author draws on the best of psychodynamic and experiential traditions to help resistant patients get past their defenses, overcome fears, and become all that they can be. It is a treat to learn from a master clinician and teacher like Jon Frederickson!"

—Stanley B. Messer, PhD, Distinguished Professor Emeritus and former Dean, Graduate School of Applied and Professional Psychology, Rutgers University

"Jon Frederickson provides a thoroughly comprehensive and practical method for helping clients who experience severe anxiety symptoms and the psychological defenses that can prevent anxiety regulation. This book is packed with case examples and transcripts that illustrate how to intervene effectively with a wide variety of clinical obstacles. The theory is deep enough to benefit seasoned clinicians, and the examples are accessible and clear enough to benefit new therapists. Very highly recommended!"

—Tony Rousmaniere, PsyD, Clinical Faculty, University of Washington, author of *Deliberate Practice for Psychotherapists* and *Mastering the Inner Skills of Psychotherapy*, and co-editor of *The Cycle of Excellence*

"This magnum opus provides a jolt of clarity for clinicians seeking to enter the fragile patient's terrorized inner world. Masterful session vignettes take the therapist into the consulting room, illuminating a path for the newborn differentiated self to emerge. This delicate process walks a fine line, as Jon demonstrates how to assess the patient's capacity to take that next step toward liberation. His skillful attunement indeed creates safety for his patients and leads to success."

—Susan Warren Warshow, LCSW, founder of The DEFT Institute and author of *Master the Moment*

Co-Creating Safety

Co-Creating Safety

Healing the Fragile Patient

Jon Frederickson, MSW

Seven Leaves Press

Seven Leaves Press
sevenleavespress.com

Ordering Information

Quantity sales. Special discounts are available on quantity purchases by corporations, associations, and others. For details, contact the "Special Sales Department" at the address above.

Orders by US trade bookstores and wholesalers. Please contact BCH: (800) 431-1579 or visit www.bookch.com for details.

Printed in the United States of America

Cataloging-in-Publication Data

Names: Frederickson, Jon, author.
Title: Co-Creating safety : healing the fragile patient / Jon Frederickson.
Description: Includes bibliographical references and index. | Kensington, MD: Seven
    Leaves Press, 2020.
Identifiers: LCCN: 2020920086 ISBN: 978-0-9883788-0-3
Subjects: LCSH Psychotherapy. | Counseling. | Anxiety disorders--Treatment. |
    Psychic trauma--Patients--Counseling of. | Personality disorders--Treatment.
    | BISAC PSYCHOLOGY / Psychotherapy / Counseling | PSYCHOLOGY /
    Education & Training | PSYCHOLOGY / Reference
Classification: LCC RC480 .F745 2020 | DDC 616.89/14--dc23

First Edition
26 25 24 23 22 21   1 2 3 4 5 6 7 8 9 10

To Kath,
without whom none of this
would have been possible.

Contents

Acknowledgments

A book such as this is the summation of a life's work and apprenticeship to great supervisors and teachers. Immediately after graduate school I was blessed by the good fortune to be taught at the Washington School of Psychiatry, founded by Harry Stack Sullivan, a school linked by history, training, and knowledge to decades of work done with the severely fragile patients at Chestnut Lodge. I would like to single out among my supervisors and teachers those who helped me in working with the severely disturbed: Irv Schneider, Harold Eist, Bernardo Hirschmann, Rochelle Kainer, Gerald Perman, Sarah Pillsbury, and, most importantly, John R. Love.

I am most grateful to those who were generous enough to read parts of the book: Sanne Almeborg, Ola Berg, Thomas Brod, Linda Campbell, Lindsay Chipman, Paul Flores, Ashley Francis, Thomas Hesslow, Piotr Jeute, Maury Joseph, Robin Kay, Juliana Kunz, Mikkel Reher-Langberg, Judy Maris, Nupur Dhinga Paiva, Stanley Palombo, Niklas Rasmussen, Lenore Turner, Mark Vail, and Alexander Vaz. Special thanks go to Allan Abbass, Kessler Bickford, MaryAnn Blotzer, Diane Byster, and Ben Orlando, who critiqued the entire book. I must acknowledge the invaluable comments, suggestions, and criticisms offered by my dear friend, colleague, and mentor, F. Barton Evans, a true exemplar of the Sullivanian tradition. And I must also single out Bjorn Elwin, whose deep critiques enriched this book immeasurably.

I want to thank my trainees, whose questions teach me to think more deeply and precisely. Their questions have always helped me grow. If I have forgotten anyone who helped me, please accept my gratitude.

Of course, this book would not have been written were it not for the supervision and training I received from Habib Davanloo. I have also benefited immensely from the trainings and presentations on fragility offered by my colleagues and friends: Allan Abbass, Allen Kalpin, and Susan Warshow. And my work on moment-to-moment processing would never have become what it is today were it not for my relationships with Terry Sheldon and Beatriz Winstanley. My thanks also go to my mentor, supervisor, and colleague, Patricia Coughlin, whose work with me over years of supervision transformed my vision of what psychotherapy could be. I hope I have done justice to those who came before. The flaws in this book belong only to me.

When the Center Cannot Hold

D ashing out of the office and down the hallway, my patient raced toward the elevator. He had threatened his roommates with a knife but was afraid of me. I didn't know what I said that had scared him. So, I ran after him, stood outside the elevator, and put my foot in the door. After I calmed him down, he came back to the office.

Over the following months, we did not discuss his fear that I would invade his mind. Instead, we spoke about space invaders from other planets. We didn't talk about conflicts with his roommates. We explored the practicalities of sending up rocket ships to intercept space aliens. That way, we could make sure the extraterrestrials were safe before their spaceships came down to Earth. He stopped threatening his roommates with knives.

Another patient, a traumatized woman, described a man she had dated. She panicked and stared at the ceiling. Her cheeks puffed, and her lips closed. Her eyes widened with fright. She swallowed, then gasped, "I almost threw up." While describing her boyfriend, anxiety flooded her. Later, we learned that remembering her boyfriend evoked feelings toward a father who had beaten her and a fiancé who had betrayed her. And, on another occasion, in Rio de Janeiro, kidnappers held her at gunpoint on a bus, abducted her, drugged her, and raped her. More emotions rose than her body could bear or her words express.

A third patient, a man recently discharged from a psychiatric hospital, came to our clinic. His parents, convinced he was possessed, had him exorcised. I asked what he felt toward them. His eyes darted every which way. "What is happening?" I asked. He said, "The devil is trying to tempt me."

His parents delivered him to the clinic because he kept hallucinating the devil.

Unable to bear anger inside himself, he perceived it in a demon outside, flitting about around us. No longer a "bad" boy possessed by anger toward his parents, he could be a good son tempted by the devil. He gave up his anger to keep their love but had to lose his sanity to do so. His defense of hallucinating was "the gift of love" he offered (Benjamin 1993): "If I love you by removing my feelings, can you accept what is left?" What horrific prices patients pay to keep the people they love in their lives.

DEFINING FRAGILITY

What do we mean when we say patients are fragile? Due to past relational traumas, current relationships activate powerful, unresolved feelings. These strong emotions evoke overwhelming amounts of anxiety. Flooded by anxiety, these patients cannot hold their emotions inside. So they split off some feelings as "not-me." Then they relocate those feelings outside themselves using a strategy, or defense mechanism, called *projection*. My space invader patient, who could not bear his own anger, imagined his roommates were angry with him. Since he feared for his life, he scared them with a knife.

Sometimes people say they feel fragile. Thus, the term *fragility* is both a metaphor patients employ and a theory therapists need. Theoretically, *fragility* refers to a weakened ability to bear overwhelming feelings when clients' customary coping strategies collapse. Once these defenses break down, fragile clients drown in anxiety. They may become confused, dizzy, faint, or even run out of the office. They feel as if they are falling apart. And, in a way, they are. Their anxiety regulation fails. Their ability to put feelings into words disappears. And their capacity to differentiate fantasy from reality vanishes.

Stresses, losses, and the pain of life overwhelm these patients with unbearable affects (Garfield 1995). And for some, when the heartache is too much to bear, all that may be open to the sufferer is killing off the pain through drugs, murder, suicide, or psychosis. When a person cannot alter the world, he cannot stem his overwhelming pain, feelings, or anxiety. He can escape only through action or imagination.

He cries out for help yet slaps away the outstretched hand he fears will smack him. Dreading rejection, he conceals his need. The pain so great, he cannot bear to feel. He dares not think. And, yet, inside his heart, he yearns to be known.

The crisis causing the deluge of feelings is usually the loss of a crucial person, either through death or a severed connection. Feeling rage toward the person he loves and lost, he protects her either by attributing his rage to others, turning the rage upon himself, or turning it toward any person he meets to rebuild the missing bond. He feels helpless because he is. His higher-level defenses, having failed, have left him engulfed in anxiety. And the discovery that he is not loved by the person he loves has evoked the earliest memories of despair. Feelings from every region of his past arise, flooding over every defense he can find.

When higher-level coping strategies give way, fragile patients try to leave their pain by viewing a feeling as "not-me" (Sullivan 1953b). The suffering into reality is too much. Rather than hold an emotion inside, they split it off and experience it outside: "You are angry; not me!" Yet the implicit message is "If I can't leave the world behind, perhaps I can leave my pain behind, and depart from the heart that suffers." Splitting and projection remove their painful inner life and relocate it into the cosmos. The client sees feelings outside in others and forgets they reside in himself. But when he exports his feelings or impulses onto another person, he no longer relates to her as she is. Instead, he interacts with the picture he has projected upon her: a supposedly angry person. As a result, the fragile patient feels paralyzed in a world populated by his projections. He longs for love but perceives only the images he has placed upon people. As a result, he lives in perpetual fear or anger.

Of course, all of us at times attribute feelings or ideas to others. But when projection blinds the fragile patient, he can lose sight of the difference between the other person and his fantasy about her. Absorbed by his belief, he loses touch with the loving person he knew, and thus, reality.

When trapped by these automatic, unconscious reactions, the fragile patient cannot respond to reality because he is reacting to projections. Anxiety and projections direct his life without his conscious control.

He has no access to the acts of will (Rank 1930/1936) by which we create ourselves (Berdyaev 1944) and give meaning to our lives (Frankl 1959). Anxiety interferes with his freedom to engage in self-creation. He has become determined, in large part, by defenses—ways he protects himself and others—of which he is unaware. He longs for a different life but cannot see the projections that imprison him. His ability to survive trauma testifies to his great resilience, but his further wish to thrive is blocked by invisible obstacles.

Our task as therapists is to help fragile patients recover their freedom to love, to live, and to create a life that matters. We can mistakenly imagine that only their history, diagnoses, and genetics determine their lives. If so, we relate to dead concepts rather than living persons. Instead, we must mobilize the self-creative capacity to act.

We can create a beautiful life full of meaning or a desperate life full of suffering. At each moment in therapy, we have a choice. We can help clients see how defenses misdirect their lives so they can direct them. Then they no longer live a life on the run from their projections. Fragile people do not seek suffering, but defenses guarantee it. When we help people see how defenses cause their suffering, they can recover.

THE NATURE OF SUFFERING

To help the fragile patient, we must understand the difference between *pain* and *suffering*. In life, pain is inevitable. Everyone we love will die, and everything we have we lose, either before or at the moment of death. We can respond to the unavoidable pain of life in two ways. The person whose heart has been broken and gives up loving acts as if her heart is empty. But her heart is full of pain she fears to face or feel. She fears, "If I let myself love, you will leave me in grief. I can't awaken the pain of my past again." On the other hand, the person with a broken heart who continues to love has a full heart. And she accepts that with every love, we swallow the losses inflicted by death or desertion. Hence, our hearts are always full. The question is whether we face the fullness of a broken heart or whether we suffer by hiding our wounds with denial and projecting our pain into other people. But when we hide from the pain of life, we suffer in fear rather than live in love.

Fragile patients are no different from any of us facing the universal struggles of life. As H. S. Sullivan (1947/1966, 7) said, "We are all much more simply human than otherwise." It takes courage to face our hearts, the openness we are. Love exposes us to the pain of loss, rage, and guilt in what Keats (1891, 255) called this "vale of soul-making." When we hate the experience of life, we try to push out the inexorable pain. Defenses attempt to anaesthetize us against the losses of life. We avoid love because it opens us up to sorrow. But love embraces the pain (Symington 2006). As the poet Rumi once said, "Step into this pool of blood that is my heart, but be careful not to splash." Dare we step into the patient's pain, which, in the end, is our own?

The reality of loss and disillusionment is the very warp and woof of our web of relations. Desires arise in each of us. Yet our loved ones can meet our wants in only one of three ways. They can deliver, delay, or disappoint. They cannot always want what we want. And even if they want to give us what we wish, they may not be able. The conflict between desire and reality is ineradicable. We desire what is not here. According to the Buddha, our relationship to desire creates our suffering. Desiring what we cannot have or what does not exist makes us suffer. Our desires collide into reality. People do not want what we want. They cannot always grant us our wish. And our fantasy differs from reality. We finally admit that we cannot give them what they long for, and their fantasy of us differs from the reality of who we are. Moreover, we concede that we are not who we wish we were. We cannot become our fantasy. And as the reality of ourselves slams into our fantasy, our fantasy suffers. And, to avoid the pain of life, we ward off reality and our feelings about it by using defenses.

Reality triggers emotions. If we cannot tolerate them, we avoid the reality that triggers them. But whatever we ward off, we cannot work with. If we help patients bear the feelings reality awakens, they can face them and explore what is possible. The pain of loss, illness, and death is inherent in life. But suffering from defenses is optional—if we learn to see and let them go.

What do we mean by defenses? They are the lies we tell ourselves to avoid the pain in our lives (Meltzer 2009). We avoid feelings through maladaptive thoughts, behaviors, relational patterns, or inattention.

Every effective therapy helps us see what we avoid and how we avoid and then face what we avoided (Weinberger 1995). Once we face what we avoided, we can live into life again, walking into the unknown.

One way fragile patients avoid their feelings is by relocating them on other people. But then they become afraid of people, angry with them, or depressed. Their relationships fail. They interact with their projections instead of relating to their loved ones. The man who projected his anger onto his roommates feared they would kill him. It turns out the Buddha was right. Defenses, our resistance to what is, create our symptoms and presenting problems.

THE CAUSES OF SUFFERING

Let us examine what causes suffering. First, a rupture occurs in a relationship activating our feelings (Damasio 1999). Due to our relational history, certain feelings may make us anxious (Damasio 1999; A. Freud 1936; S. Freud 1923/1961c, 1926/1961b; LeDoux 1998). We can face our feelings and anxiety so we can live into reality (Hartmann 1964). Or, outside of our awareness, automatic defenses may arise, hiding those feelings from us. But these avoidance strategies create our symptoms and presenting problems (S. Freud 1923/1961c). For instance, a father verbally abuses his son. In response, the boy feels angry. He grew up in a fundamentalist Christian family that condemned anger toward elders. Rather than express anger toward his father, he becomes anxious. Then he projects his wish to express his anger onto a hallucination, "The devil is trying to tempt me." He remains a "good" boy with good feelings while the "bad" feeling is in the devil. But his hallucination only reinforces his family's conviction that he has a pact with the devil, no one perceiving how he protects that devil of a father. Thus, he becomes trapped in a purgatory produced by projections.

How do we help him? We offer a secure attachment (Bowlby 1969) where he can safely reveal himself. We ask about the problem for which he wants our help. And we look into his difficulties, their origin, and history. But that might prove impossible. The fragile patient may flood with anxiety before he arrives. He might already assume you are another abuser and equate you today with his perpetrator in the past.

We want to co-create a conscious alliance. But his projection created a misalliance. What happened?

He seeks a healing relationship. But relationships prepared him for pain (Bowlby 1973, 1980). From the first moments of life, the infant is "dominated . . . by the need to retain the mother—a need which, if thwarted, must produce the utmost terror and rage, since the loss of the mother is the precursor to death" (Suttie 1935/1960, 12). For the fragile patient, relational traumas led to repeated experiences of terror and rage. Even if his head has forgotten, his body and heart have not. "There is the hunger for a positive relationship, the rage from past frustrations, and the anxiety of past futilities" (Trunnell and Semrad 1967, 107). He fears you will offer an insecure attachment where he suffers pains from the past. Perhaps his words don't declare this, but his body does. It floods with anxiety. The patient cannot describe his difficulty in words, but the wordless mind of the body reveals it, silently speaking in its secret language: anxiety. Anxiety says, "It has been dangerous to share my problems, opinions, or desires." Defenses disclose how he dealt with this danger: "I must cover whatever you cannot love in me so you can care for the rest of me." In an insecure attachment, the patient adapted by adopting his parents' defenses (Bowlby 1969; Hartmann 1964). Defenses are "security operations" (Sullivan 1949, 1953a), how the patient learned to reduce anxiety in his loved ones to restore security in insecure connections. Thus, when a feeling, anxiety, or defense occur, we observe not only an event in itself but the event and the entire past of the patient (Rukeyser 1949/1996). Feelings, anxiety, and defenses are the poetry of the body, the past to which they refer, and the present enactment of that past. The facts of feelings, anxiety, and defenses are bound together in a natural yet hidden kinship, the recreated relationship with us that brings them together.

These responses of anxiety and defense in therapy are not wrong. Every response precisely expresses the patient's need in this moment. Our task is to discover why his reaction is perfect. If we perceive his need, we can respond to it optimally (Bacal 1998). Excessive anxiety exposes his need for regulation. Defenses reveal how he conceals himself to be loved. If his feelings, thoughts, and impulses were hated, he learned to hate his inner life and expel it into the external world.

If people loved his feelings, he learned to embrace life as he was embraced. So we watch moment by moment to see what elements of the patient's inner life are hated and expelled or loved and embraced (Symington 2006).

As soon as you ask about the patient's problem or his will to explore it, he becomes anxious (S. Freud 1926/1961b; A. Freud 1936). Then he uses avoidance strategies (S. Freud 1923/1961c). He wants help. But his anxiety signals that help hurts. Thus, he may avoid declaring a problem. You may think he resists you when, in fact, he is loving you.

He relates to you according to the rules of insecure attachments. He learned that if he needed help, he was punished. If he declared a separate will or desire, he was condemned. If he had an emotion, he was banished. That's why he avoids declaring a problem, a separate will, or a feeling. He learned to conceal himself to remain in a relationship (F. Evans 1996; Sullivan 1953a). He fears you cannot love him if he doesn't cover up what cannot be loved (Post and Semrad 1965). When he avoids forming a secure attachment, he shows you how he adapted in an insecure attachment (Bowlby 1969, 1973, 1980; Hartmann 1939/1958, 1964; Lyons-Ruth 1998). Hiding, his gift of love in the past (Benjamin 1993), is how he loves you today. He protects you from what he fears you cannot love. He does not resist therapy. He shows you how he learned to love—by leaving his needs behind: "If both of us hate my need, can you love what's left?"

MOVING FROM AN INSECURE ATTACHMENT TO A SECURE ATTACHMENT

These strategies, learned from the first days of life, establish attachment patterns by twelve months of age in an infant (Beebe et al. 2010). These patterns of self-erasure to preserve a relationship were never conscious or intentional. Automatic, unconscious strategies, developed from infancy, take place without the patient's knowledge in adulthood. They saved his life in the past, but they damage his relationships today.

The patient does not avoid you. He tries to avoid the thoughts, feelings, and pain evoked by depending on you. He wants your help. But the need for help and the desire for affection awaken feelings from the past. These feelings elicit anxiety, which then triggers a defense, and the defense creates his symptoms and presenting problems.

With every patient in every relationship, we find the same pattern:

1. A relationship brings out feelings based on past relationships.
2. Feelings trigger anxiety, a bodily sign that feelings were dangerous.
3. Anxiety mobilizes defenses, how he handles that danger to keep a relationship.

We call this pattern the *triangle of conflict* (Malan 1979; figure I.1). (See chapter 4 for a discussion of the triangle of conflict.)

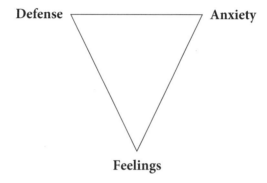

Figure I.1   The triangle of conflict

Defenses previously preserved his relationships. Today they corrupt his connections. They solved a problem in the past, but they produce his problems in the present. We help him let go of these outdated strategies so he can face the feelings he avoided. Through this new experience, we co-create a secure attachment, opening a pathway toward better relationships with others. Figure I.2 illustrates how we can understand the triangle of conflict as the unconscious memory of attachment trauma.

Everything the patient says in the session expresses this relational pattern: (1) feeling-connection, (2) anxiety, and (3) defense-avoidance. He initiates the bond by offering a problem. If he declares a problem, we encourage him to explore it to get to the bottom of his difficulties. If he is too anxious, we regulate his anxiety because it is safe to explore only when he feels safe. If he uses an avoidance strategy, we help him see it and its cost so he can let go of it and receive the help he needs. Then we help him bear together what he could not bear alone in the

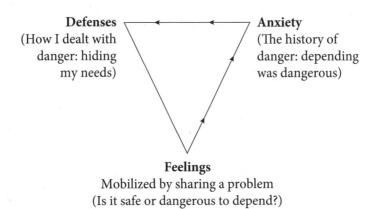

Defenses
(How I dealt with
danger: hiding
my needs)

Anxiety
(The history of
danger: depending
was dangerous)

Feelings
Mobilized by sharing a problem
(Is it safe or dangerous to depend?)

Figure I.2   The triangle of conflict as memory of attachment trauma

past. The principles are simple, but their application can be complex with fragile patients because anxiety can spike, overwhelming their capacity to function.

The three basic principles of psychotherapy are as follows:

1. Invite a healing relationship by exploring the patient's problems and feelings.
2. Regulate anxiety when it gets too high so he can feel safe. Then encourage him to explore the problems and feelings triggering his anxiety.
3. Help him see and let go of the defenses that prevent him from connecting to his inner life and other people. This helps him accept his inner life rather than reject it. Once he can bear the feelings triggered by closeness, closeness becomes possible.

As mindfulness practices have shown, we do not avoid reality or our feelings only occasionally (Safran 2003). Defenses create our suffering all day long. Thus, moment by moment, we help the patient see the defenses that inflict his suffering as they unfold in real time during the session. One might think of therapy as a form of guided heartfulness meditation. We help the client pay attention to his inner life as it arises second by second. Each time he ignores it, we invite him to pay attention to it and return to his problem, his will to work on the problem, or the feelings stirred up by depending on us. As he lets go of his defenses, they no longer cause his suffering, and the feelings he abandoned embrace him. Each time he pays attention to reality, awareness arises of the presence he is (Eigen 1998). He becomes at one with the emotional truth of this moment (Bion 1970).

Understanding causality makes the therapeutic tasks clear: (1) we help the patient present a problem, (2) we help him declare his will to work on the problem, and (3) we help him propose a positive goal for the therapy. These three steps allow us to co-create a working alliance.

In every therapy session, we see the following sequence. The therapist invites a closer relationship by inviting the patient to share the problem he wants help with. Each invitation activates feelings, which evoke anxiety, which triggers defenses. And those defenses create a symptom or presenting problem in the session. This sequence happens up to 150 times an hour. Thus, we do not say a patient has depression. Instead, his defenses create and sustain his depression. Depression is not a possession; it is a creation.

That's why we try to interrupt automatic defenses that hurt the patient. If we can help him see the defense, understand its cost, and leave each one behind, his symptoms will diminish and disappear. He tries to reveal his need, but defenses interrupt him. We interrupt the interrupters to give him a chance to reveal his inner longings and desires. Interrupting defenses shows our compassion for the patient (S. Warshow, personal communication). We do not collude with the defenses; we collaborate with the person who suffers from them. Never interrupt a person who speaks from his heart; interrupt the defenses that keep his heart from speaking. For when the heart speaks, even the silence sings.

This book will offer many ways we bear and share a person's struggles and suffering, one human meeting another. While you will learn many techniques, they serve one purpose: to encourage a secure attachment. Our interventions invite the patient to bear together what could not be borne alone. By interrupting the interrupters, we show our love and compassion for the patient's inner voice. Defenses invite us to form an insecure attachment. Instead, we invite a secure attachment by relating to the person hidden behind the defenses. Techniques are not things we do to an object but ways we relate to a person. We help him become free from the archaic strategies creating his suffering so he can take up the path of self-creation that is personality itself (Berdyaev 1944).

His defenses are the ways he learned to reject himself to make his parents less anxious (Sullivan 1953a). Now we help him surrender those defenses so he can embrace his forbidden feelings and desires. Through our compassion for him, he learns to have compassion for himself. In a letter to Carl Jung, Sigmund Freud once wrote, "Psychoanalysis is a cure through love" (Freud and Jung, 1906/1994). And that love is revealed through our faith in the patient's potential. Symptoms draw us down into the depths to the person hidden within. As one woman said to me, "You saw who I was underneath all the chaos and defenses before I knew there was a me to be found."

LOVING AND FEELING

Why didn't my patient know there was a self to be found? I asked a sculptor what she wanted me to help her with. In response, she filled with anxiety and hallucinated that the walls were moving. Later, she disclosed that her mother had tried to drown her in a bathtub. No wonder she was afraid to depend on me! Depending nearly led to her death.

I asked a painter if it was her will that we work together on her problem. She became anxious and dizzy. Later, she described a fight in which her father put a pistol to her forehead. Why did declaring her will trigger so much anxiety? Will—a separate mind—meant death.

Fragile people often suffered traumas when they counted on care-takers, declared a separate will, or had a feeling, so we help them step by step. First, we regulate high levels of anxiety. Then we help them declare a problem and their will to work on it. As they explore their problems, we help them share their feelings with us. Why?

Feelings express our primary motivations and drives (Kernberg 2001; Tomkins 1962). Without them, we lack a compass to show us where we want to go in life (P. Coughlin, personal communication). Infants do not have words, but communication still takes place. "*Emotions are* that channel of communication" (Symington 2006, 26). "[E]motions *are* the relationship," that connecting link that gathers us together (Symington 2006, 31). Yet fragile patients had to hide their feelings, the specific link that made their parents anxious (Sullivan 1953a). To survive, they let the emotions and desires of others be the compass of their lives (Lacan 1966/2007; Laing 1959/1965; Searles 1965/1986a). Sadly, they *had to* abandon themselves not to lose the one they loved. They had to conceal an emotional link to keep the emotionally stripped link their parents could bear. Instead, we help them accept their inner life, their emotions, and their link to us while we accept their inner life and our own.

In therapy, we help the patient find the truth of who she is. In the past, she had to hide the truth to be loved. Now we help her face and let go of her defenses. Then she can accept the truth she sent off to live in others that always lived in her.

Yet to help the patient embrace what others could not cradle in her, the therapist must embrace those aspects as well. We cannot help patients face issues we cannot confront in ourselves. We will help them avoid like we do. Anything a person fears and shares is part of our mutual humanity. We can embrace the patient's pain, or we can ask her to hold it alone, while we distance, judge, or try to control it. But a person is never a foreign object we observe from afar. She is a fellow human with whom we share the same feelings, longings, and struggles for connection. For "whatever we know intuitively is not an object, it is part of our own being" (Chaudhuri 1987, 32). The therapist's embodied acceptance invites the patient to accept her inner life (Symington 2006). And in our meeting, the patient's suffering—unbearable while alone—becomes bearable with us together. And that occurs through *compassion,* a word from the Latin meaning: "to suffer with." By relating, we share the pain of the patient's life so we can acknowledge, bear, and put it into perspective (Semrad 1966). And why use the word *patient?* It comes from the Latin, meaning "one who suffers." Compassion is not a cognitive skill but a mutual emotional living through (Fiscalini 2004), a co-suffering of the patient's conflicts, our universal conflicts. Our bond is the broader human perspective, where suffering becomes knowable and shareable. What was harmed in a relationship must be healed in this relationship. "What went wrong must go right" (D. Malan, personal communication). However, as we co-create this connection by bearing our shared humanity, therapy can feel dangerous to the patient due to anxiety and projection. Thus, we must first co-create a sense of safety. To do that, we regulate anxiety, the subject of chapter 1.

RECOMMENDED READINGS

Abbass, A., Town, J., and Driessen, E. (2012). Intensive short-term dynamic psychotherapy: A systematic review and meta-analysis of outcome research. *Harvard Review of Psychiatry, 20*(2), 97–108. http://www.istdpinstitute.com/resources/.

Coughlin Della Selva, P. (1996). The integration of theory and technique in Davanloo's intensive short-term dynamic psychotherapy. In *Intensive short-term dynamic psychotherapy: Theory and technique* (pp.1–25). Wiley.

Coughlin Della Selva, P., and Malan, D. (2006). Empirical support for Davanloo's ISTDP. In *Lives Transformed: A revolutionary method of dynamic psychotherapy*, (pp. 34–74). Karnac.

RECOMMENDED MATERIALS

For information on forming a therapeutic alliance presented in videos by Jon Frederickson, visit the URLs below.

Intensive short term dynamic psychotherapy part 1 (October 5, 2011). http://www.youtube.com/watch?v=cKzmk2-xnzY

Intensive short term dynamic psychotherapy part 2 (October 5, 2011). http://www.youtube.com/watch?v=dK2x906ptWA

Intensive short term dynamic psychotherapy part 3 (January 18, 2012). http://www.youtube.com/watch?v=sDmVgoKPVkw

Visit the Intensive Short Term Dynamic Psychotherapy (ISTDP) Institute for introductory skill-building exercises for working with fragile patients at http://istdpinstitute.com/resources/skills-for-working -with-fragile-patients/.

PART ONE

Building a Secure Attachment

CHAPTER ONE

Anxiety

The Signal of Danger

Listen . . . and attend with the ear of your heart.

—SAINT BENEDICT

Recently, a colleague attended a seminar on anxiety. A clinician in the audience asked, "What do you do when the patient is too anxious in the session?" The presenter replied, "I send them home. If they're too anxious, they can't do therapy."

Since when do we send people away until they no longer need our help? My oncologist did not ask me to go home until I no longer had cancer. He understood his role: to help me. At a clinic where I worked years ago, a severely disturbed man came for a consultation. The psychiatrist, Harold Eist, asked, "How can I help you?" "I'm afraid I'm going crazy." Harold replied, "Well, you came to the right place." When he said "the right place," he didn't mean the clinic but the healing relationship they would co-create.

We start therapy by asking, "What is the problem you would like me to help you with?" It seems like a simple factual request. Yet it is also a complicated question about relating: "Would you like to depend on me?" The fragile patient is not afraid of her problem. She is afraid of depending. As soon as she asks for help, her painful history of depending arises. She *wants* to depend upon you, yet her body becomes anxious. With her higher mind, she recognizes her therapist. But her lower mind may react as if you are a victimizer. And the more traumatic her past abuse, the more her anxiety rises.

ANXIETY: THE SIGN THAT RELATING WAS DANGEROUS

A few fragile patients can declare a problem without being overwhelmed with anxiety. Some flood as soon as you ask about their problem. Or they quake with terror before walking into your office! Nontraumatized people describe an inner house requiring repair. Fragile patients try to flee from an inner house on fire. Yet no matter how fast they run, they never get away from the flames because they are on fire. They first need us to douse those flames by regulating anxiety. In this way, we create a safe place for people who may never have had one. To co-create safety, however, we must know how to regulate anxiety.

Ideally, the mother cuddles the troubled baby in her arms and soothes her. The father hugs his frightened son and comforts him. We would not force a child to climb onto a carnival ride while she is screaming. Likewise, we should not explore the patient's problems if she feels scared. She is not defying you. She is drowning in anxiety. The therapist might mistakenly think, "This patient is not joining me." What if anxiety floods her *because* she is joining you? Through anxiety, her body screams, "Help me!" If you rush ahead without regulating her anxiety, you will become the cause of danger rather than the source of safety. For therapy to be safe, we help her feel safe, bodily, by regulating her anxiety.

She reaches out to a therapist because she needs relief. She tried to solve her problems on her own, but her solutions didn't work. She requires therapy, yet relying on a therapist conjures up her history of depending. Most fragile patients learned to love while enduring many traumas. People they trusted abandoned, hurt, or abused them. Depending caused pain, not pleasure. No wonder they feel fear when they seek safety. Through anxiety, the body signals that depending was not safe; it was dangerous. Anxiety tells us the history of their suffering.

Our relationship today triggers the patient's memories of past relationships, pains, and agonies. And the body offers the first memory: overwhelming anxiety (Fox and Hane 2008). Early insecure attachments repeatedly evoked so much anxiety that the toxic shock shaped the patient's brain and physiology (Jaremka et al. 2013; Landers and Sullivan 2012). And if the parent could not regulate anxiety, the child never learned self-regulation (Adam, Klimes-Dougan, and Gunnar

2007; Schore 2002). In fact, anxiety "in the mothering one, induces anxiety in the infant" (Sullivan 1953a, 41–42). Thus, the future fragile patient does not receive from the parent anxiety regulation but anxiety induction. And through this feedback loop, ever-increasing anxiety leads to somnolent detachment in the infant, the precursor to dissociative patterns later in life. (For more on the interpersonal theory of anxiety, see F. Evans [1996].)

Thus, to co-create a safe place, we regulate anxiety so the patient can depend on a therapist. But first, what is anxiety?

Anxiety Defined

Anxiety is a term widely used yet almost universally misunderstood. Fear refers to our response to an objective, external threat (A. Freud 1936): a car skids into your lane, and your foot slams on the brakes. Your heart pounds and your hands shake. Anxiety refers to our response to a subjective, internal threat: a feeling frightens us (A. Freud 1936). But why would a feeling evoke anxiety?

Many children learn that their feelings make parents anxious and frightened (Bowlby 1969). Then children become afraid of the frightened or frightening parent, fearing the loss of a relationship they require for their survival (Bowlby 1969, 1973, 1980; Main and Solomon 1990). As a result, they try to hide their feelings to decrease the caretaker's anxiety and to bring security back into their insecure connection (Sullivan 1953b). Through repeated experiences, this link between feelings and danger becomes conditioned, contaminating every invitation to love.

Anxiety is our response to feelings rising within us that endangered the security of earlier relationships. The parents or caretakers are no longer present. But anxiety rises whenever those previously dangerous feelings arise: "Love is dangerous. Stop!"

Anxiety has a specific function. It signals that feelings and impulses rising now could endanger the relationship (Freud 1926/1961b; A. Freud 1936). Fear is "induced by threat of destruction to one's physical self, and anxiety . . . by perceived threat of destruction of one's psychological self. . . . [Thus,] all anxiety is ultimately of interpersonal origin" (Cooper and Guynn 2006, 103).

To survive, animals must avoid predators; children must avoid losing relationships. Any emotion that provokes anxiety in the parent puts the child's security in peril (F. Evans 1996; Sullivan 1953a, 1953b). Therefore, the child learns to hide emotions, desires, and impulses that make parents anxious. And anxiety becomes a signal: "This feeling, thought, or impulse is dangerous."

To hold onto his parents' love, the child adopts their defenses (Geleerd 1965). He must imitate their neurotic ways to be admitted to the human community. If he cannot count on his parents to love him, he must use their defenses to cover up what they cannot love. Whatever they hate, he hides. And the ways he hides, his defenses, make him less aware of the feelings that cause anxiety—feelings he doesn't see, he can't share so his parents can care for the remainder. But the defenses corrupt his consciousness through the disowning of his inner life, leaving him psychically blinded to his being.

Not all feelings or traumatic experiences will generate anxiety in the future. The pivotal issue is whether we have a loved one with whom we can bear and share our feelings. When the child cannot depend on his caretakers for affect regulation, he has to rely on their defenses for affect dissociation (Schore 2002; Sullivan 1953a, 1953b). In fact, feelings do not fuel the child's anxiety. The parent's rejection or even hatred of his feelings fuels his anxiety: "I might lose the person I need to survive!" Thus, the font of anxiety today was fear borne in the past.

Why does anxiety cause so many difficulties? A single traumatic experience can trigger anxiety for a lifetime. Fear memories are forever (Fanselow and Gale 2003). As a result, feelings that remind us of a trauma in the past trigger anxiety and defenses in the present. What was life-threatening then feels dangerous now.

Anxiety: Understanding the Neurobiology

Having described anxiety's relational origins, let's examine how the brain produces anxiety symptoms in the body. If you can understand and observe the physical signs of anxiety, you can assess whether it is too high. You will know when to regulate it. And, when you see it, you can examine the client's previous sentence to discover what triggered anxiety in this second. With this knowledge, you can co-create safety with the fragile patient.

We have inherited our biological anxiety system from the fear system of animals. Animals don't have time to think. They must flee predators to avoid being eaten. Thus, evolution provided them with brains that nonconsciously assess risk and activate the body without a single thought involved. We have the same mammalian fear systems designed for escaping from predators (Porges 1997, 2001, 2011; Porges and Bazhenova 2006). But, in humans, those systems get activated for both external dangers that threaten our life and internal feelings that could endanger a relationship.

When a threat is perceived, such as a snake, it triggers the amygdala and hypothalamus (Damasio 1999; LeDoux 1998). They activate the autonomic nervous system, producing anxiety symptoms throughout the body. Milliseconds later, the amygdala sends a message to the cortex. The body feels anxious before the prefrontal cortex registers the signal from the amygdala. Only then does the prefrontal cortex produce the thought, "That's a stick, not a snake. You're safe." Like animals, our anxiety system gets triggered bodily before we are aware of it consciously.

First, a system prewired in the brain, inherited from prehistoric mammals (Panksepp 1998; Panksepp and Biven 2012), nonconsciously assesses danger and sends a message to the amygdala. Second, the amygdala activates the somatic and autonomic nervous systems (Goldstein 2006). These systems create the physical symptoms of anxiety in the body (Damasio 1999; Robertson et al. 2004). The somatic nervous system turns on the voluntary muscles, the ones you can move. For those muscles to act, the autonomic nervous system must provide enough blood flow and oxygen (LeDoux 1998). Then we can fight with or flee from threats (Porges 1997, 2001, 2011; Porges and Bazhenova 2006; Kennard 1947).

How does this process generate anxiety symptoms? When the somatic nervous system activates the striated, or voluntary, muscles, our bodies become tense. This tension in the striated muscles causes clenched thumbs and hands, tension headaches, and tension in the arms, abdomen, feet, legs, neck, shoulders, and back. This causes neck and back pain. Tension in the intercostal muscles in the chest wall causes sighing. Chronic tensing can also cause fibromyalgia.

The sympathetic branch of the autonomic nervous system creates the anxiety symptoms of increased pulse rate, breath rate, and blood pressure. It also withdraws blood from the extremities and redirects it to the large muscles so we can fight or flee. That makes our hands and feet cold when we are anxious. The sympathetic nervous system also creates anxiety symptoms of dry mouth, dry eyes, constipation, and dilated pupils (Goldstein 2006; Hamill and Shapiro 2004). For instance, speakers at a debate drink water when their anxiety gives them dry mouth.

The parasympathetic branch of the autonomic nervous system creates different anxiety symptoms. It causes lower pulse rate, breath rate, and blood pressure, causing blood flow to the brain to drop. It causes anxiety symptoms, including blurry vision, ringing in the ears, problems thinking, dizziness, nausea, diarrhea, and migraines. Other anxiety symptoms include increased salivation, teary eyes, constricted pupils, warm hands, cardiac arrhythmia, bodily anesthesia, and limpness (Goldstein 2006; Hamill and Shapiro 2004; McEwen, Bulloch, and Stewart 1999). This parasympathetic reaction enables animals to go limp when attacked by a predator to escape being eaten.

The somatic and autonomic nervous systems create these anxiety symptoms in our bodies (Goldstein 2006) in less than a second before we consciously see or think about a threat (Ohman and Wiens 2003). Table 1.1 lists the bodily symptoms of anxiety created by the somatic and autonomic (sympathetic and parasympathetic) nervous systems (Goldstein 2006; Hamill and Shapiro 2004).

Table 1.1   Bodily symptoms of anxiety

Part of Nervous System Activated	Anxiety Symptoms
Anxiety symptoms caused by the somatic nervous system	Sighing respiration Clenched thumbs and hands Tension headaches Tense arms, shoulders, and neck Sighing: tension in the intercostal muscles Tight stomach muscles, tension in feet and legs Fibromyalgia Chronic tensing of the pelvic muscles, resulting in painful sensations, painful menstruation, painful intercourse, menstrual irregularity, and vulvodynia Dizziness or fainting due to holding the breath

Table 1.1 (continued)

Anxiety symptoms caused by the sympathetic nervous system	Dry mouth, dry eyes, dilated pupils Cold hands Increased heart rate, blood pressure, and respiration Blushing Decreased motility of the gastrointestinal tract (constipation) Constricted bladder sphincter (urinary retention) Shivering, piloerection (hair stands on end due to muscle contraction) Hyperventilation and fainting
Anxiety symptoms caused by the parasympathetic nervous system	Salivation, teary eyes, constricted pupils Warm hands Decreased heart rate, blood pressure, and respiration Increased motility of the gastrointestinal tract (nausea, vomiting, diarrhea) Relaxed bladder sphincter (urge to urinate) Migraines (due to vasodilation) Cardiac arrhythmia Dizziness Foggy thinking Bodily anesthesia, limpness

We'll refer to three patterns of unconscious anxiety discharge in the body (see table 1.2): striated muscles, smooth muscles, and cognitive/perceptual disruption (Abbass, 2015; H. Davanloo, supervision 2002–2004; Frederickson 2013), each of which is produced by the somatic and autonomic nervous systems.

Table 1.2 Pathways of unconscious anxiety discharge

Part of Nervous System Activated	Anxiety Symptoms
Anxiety symptoms in the striated muscles	Hand clenching Tension in the intercostal muscles of the chest (sighing) Tension in arms, shoulders, neck, legs, and feet Jaw clenching, biting Tension headaches
Anxiety symptoms in the smooth muscles	Bladder urgency and frequency Gastrointestinal spasm (irritable bowel syndrome, nausea, vomiting) Vascular symptoms (migraine, hypertension) Bronchi symptoms (asthma, difficulty breathing) "Jelly legs" (unsteady gait due to lack of tension in the striated muscles)
Anxiety symptoms in cognitive/perceptual disruption	Drifting, dissociation, confusion, losing track of thoughts, poor memory Visual blurring, tunnel vision, blindness Anesthesia (sudden loss of feeling in areas of the body) Fainting, freezing, fugue states, dizziness, ringing in the ears Hallucinations Projection, projective identification

And when we begin therapy with the fragile patient, anxiety is triggered by declaring a problem: the issue of depending. See figure 1.1.

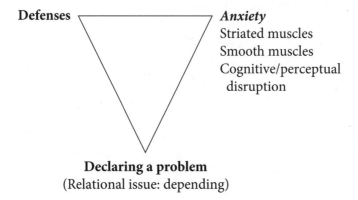

Defenses

Anxiety
Striated muscles
Smooth muscles
Cognitive/perceptual
  disruption

Declaring a problem
(Relational issue: depending)

Figure 1.1   Anxiety and depending

In summary, nonconscious threat detection in the brain produces a biophysiological activation in the body (Damasio 1999). Fear is the bodily reaction triggered by an external danger. Anxiety is the bodily reaction triggered by forbidden feelings, impulses, and wishes (A. Freud 1936). Fear prepares the body to fight off physical threats. Anxiety triggers the mind to ward off psychological threats: feelings.

The therapy relationship triggers feelings based on past relationships. Those feelings can trigger overwhelming anxiety in the fragile patient. The brain activates the nervous system, which creates anxiety symptoms in the body. And the anxiety symptoms are discharged in the striated muscles, smooth muscles, and cognitive/perceptual disruption. When the fragile patient feels unsafe due to anxiety, we must regulate it to co-create a sense of safety.

HOW TO IDENTIFY AND ASSESS ANXIETY

In this section, we will look at how to identify the relational triggers for anxiety and how to assess where it is discharged in the body. In "How to Regulate Anxiety," we will look at how to regulate anxiety. And in "When Defenses Prevent Anxiety Regulation," we will look at what to do when anxiety regulation does not work.

First, let's look at the four steps in identifying, assessing, and regulating anxiety:

Step one: Identify the relational issue that triggers anxiety (declaring a problem, declaring will to work on the problem, declaring a positive goal, declaring a specific example, or declaring one's feelings). See "Step One: Identify the Relational Triggers for Anxiety," pp. 11–17.

Step two: Assess where anxiety is discharged in the body (striated muscles, smooth muscles, or cognitive/perceptual disruption). See "Step Two: Assess Anxiety: The Bodily Symptoms," pp. 17–22.

Step three: Regulate anxiety by inviting the patient to observe and pay attention to anxiety symptoms while cognizing about the sequence of causality: trigger, anxiety, and symptoms. See "How to Regulate Anxiety," pp. 22–44.

Step four: When anxiety regulation does not work, identify the defenses that prevent anxiety regulation or perpetuate anxiety. See "When Defenses Prevent Anxiety Regulation," pp. 44–75.

Step One: Identify the Relational Triggers for Anxiety

When children's feelings make a parent anxious, the calm carer disappears, replaced by a frightened or even frightening figure. Children learn that their feelings trigger anxiety in people, leading to loss (Sullivan 1953a). The mothering one who should regulate anxiety induces it. Feelings and fear become a conditioned reaction. Then, children, and later, adults, feel anxiety automatically in the body whenever previously dangerous feelings arise in other relationships or in therapy.

In the initial session, anxiety may flood the fragile patient. But he has no idea what triggers it. When you point out the trigger, he can see it, and his experience makes sense to him. That brings his anxiety down, making him feel more secure. Before we learn how to assess and regulate anxiety, let's consider its relational triggers.

Stage One in Alliance Building: Anxiety Triggered by Declaring One Has a Problem

The therapist invites the patient to declare what he would like help with to ensure that treatment focuses on a problem that motivates him to seek therapy.

Therapist (Th): What is the problem you would like me to help you with?

Patient (Pt): [*Patient looks frightened, and her eyes are darting around. Anxiety.*]

Th: You look a bit anxious. Are you feeling anxious right now?

Pt: I'm always like this.

Th: To help you with your anxiety, could we look at your anxiety symptoms and see if we can help you bring your anxiety down? [*Invite her to pay attention to and regulate anxiety.*]

Pt: Okay.

Th: Where do you notice feeling anxiety in your body right now?

She may need several minutes to observe and pay attention to her anxiety until it is regulated. Then the therapist continues.

Th: You became anxious when I asked you about the problem you would like me to help you with. Something about having a problem you want help with triggers some anxiety. Do you notice that too? [*Point out causality: declaring a problem triggers anxiety.*]

Pt: Yes.

Th: The anxiety came in and attacked you as if it was against the law to get some help with a problem. [*Differentiate the patient from the anxiety she experiences so she won't blame herself for being anxious.*] Do you see that too?

Pt: I hadn't thought of it that way before.

Th: Wouldn't it be nice to get some help with your problem without this anxiety giving you such a hard time? [*Mobilize her will to the task: to be able to depend without getting anxious.*]

Pt: Yes, it would because this anxiety bothers me all the time.

Th: You must be very upset with this anxiety for the way it attacks you for having a problem. [*By describing it as an "attacker," the therapist differentiates the patient from the anxiety. Instead of being anxious, she can observe her anxiety. Now it comes down.*]

Many fragile patients learned that it was dangerous to depend. Thus, feelings and anxiety will rise when you invite them to describe a problem to work on. If you recognize this relational trigger, you can help regulate the patient's anxiety provoked by depending on you.

Stage Two in Alliance Building: Anxiety Triggered by Asking for Help with the Problem

In this example, the therapist helps the patient with her anxiety about asking for help. If asking for help makes her too anxious, she cannot let us help her.

A woman has declared a problem hesitantly.

Th: And is this the problem you would like me to help you with? [*Invite the patient's will to work on her problem.*]

Pt: Do you think this is the problem I should work with? [*Projection: she invites the therapist to declare what he wants rather than declare her own desire. Through this unconscious strategy, the patient hides what she wants and submits to the desires of others.*]

Th: Only you can know if you should work on this problem. That is not for me to say. [*Deactivate the projection.*] That's why I have to ask you. In your opinion, is this the problem you want help with?

Pt: [*Touches her stomach.*]

Th: Are you feeling something in your stomach right now? [*Assess anxiety.*]

Pt: I feel nauseated. [*Anxiety in the smooth muscles: too high.*]

Th: That's a sign of anxiety. Something about saying that you want my help on this problem seems to trigger your anxiety. Do you notice that too? [*Causality: wanting help triggers anxiety.*]

Pt: I don't like asking for help.

Th: Of course. Is it possible that asking me for help is triggering this anxiety in your stomach right now? [*Make the link between depending on the therapist and anxiety.*]

Pt: I'm afraid. [*Anxiety is now becoming conscious.*]

Th: Right. Is it possible that asking for help with your problem triggers this anxiety?

Pt: I'm afraid of how you will react. [*Projection.*]

Th: Right. Something about asking me for help with your problem triggers this anxiety in your stomach. And then a thought comes up that a therapist would react badly if you asked him to do what therapists are supposed to do: help you. [*Describe her conflict: asking for help, anxiety, and the defense of projection.*]

Pt: It sounds silly when you put it that way. [*She can think about her projection instead of projecting.*]

Th: Sure. With your higher mind, you know that a therapist is supposed to help you with a problem. But your lower mind is operating with some old information. Your lower mind has the idea that if you ask for help, a therapist would react badly. Am I understanding your thoughts accurately? [*Refer to "lower mind" and "thoughts" so she can observe and reflect on a projection rather than just believe it. Now she can think about her lower mind and her thoughts. This builds her self-reflective functioning.*]

Pt: [*Sighs.*] Yes. [*Anxiety returns to the striated muscles.*]

Th: With your higher mind, you know that therapists help you with a problem. To make sure that this is what you want for yourself, do you want me to help you with your problem? [*Deactivate the projection of judgment. Then ask the same question again to see if she can declare her wish for help.*]

Pt: Yes. [*No sigh.*]

Th: What do you notice feeling when you say that? [*Intervene before she can use a defense.*]

Pt: [*Sighs.*] Anxious.

Th: Isn't that interesting? Isn't that fascinating? [*Hold her attention on the anxiety to build her affect tolerance.*] Something about asking me for help triggers some anxiety in your body. What is it like to see how your body reacts when you ask for help? [*Help her see causality: forming a helping relationship where she asks for help triggers anxiety. The question "What is it like?" invites her to step back and reflect on the process. This builds her capacity for meta-cognition: to think about her thinking.*]

Many fragile patients learned that it was risky to ask for help. Thus, this wish triggers feelings and anxiety. Regulate the patient's anxiety so she can reclaim her right to ask for help.

Stage Three in Alliance Building: Anxiety Triggered by Declaring One's Will to Work on the Problem

Once the patient declares a problem to work on, we ask if it is her will to work on it. We have no right to explore anything unless she wants to.

Th: Is it your will to work on this problem?

Pt: I feel like you are pushing me. [*Projection.*]

Th: I have no right to push you to do anything. [*Deactivate the projection.*] That's why we have to find out if you want to work on your problem for your benefit. [*Invite him to become aware of his will.*]

Pt: I'm afraid of what you are looking for. [*Projection: the patient believes the therapist is looking for something when the patient came to therapy looking for help.*]

Th: I have no right to look for anything unless it is something you want to look for inside yourself. [*Deactivate the projection.*] That's why we have to find out if you want to look inside yourself to get better information so you can make better decisions for yourself. [*Invite him to notice his will.*]

Pt: I think so. [*Defense: hesitating. His will is not online.*]

Th: I have no right to explore something unless you are sure that is what you want to do for your own benefit. [*Deactivate the projection.*] That's why I have to ask you, are you sure you want to look inside yourself to get better information so you can make better decisions for yourself? [*Invite him to become aware of his wish to look inside himself.*]

Pt: Yes. [*No sigh. Since no anxiety rises, his will may not be online yet. So the therapist inquires further into the patient's will.*]

Th: What do you notice feeling as soon as you say that you want to look inside yourself to get the information you want that you think would be helpful for you? [*As soon as he expresses his will, anxiety will rise. Bring his attention to his anxiety before he avoids it by projecting again. This builds affect tolerance.*]

Pt: Uncomfortable. [*Anxiety.*]

Th: Good you notice. Something about saying that you want to look inside yourself triggers some discomfort. Where do you notice that discomfort physically in your body right now? [*The longer we keep his attention on the anxiety aroused by his will, the more affect tolerance we build before he resorts to projection.*]

Many fragile patients learned that it was dangerous to declare their desires so they submitted to the will of others. Thus, declaring their desire triggers feelings and anxiety. If you regulate patients' anxiety, therapy can be based on their desires.

Stage Four in Alliance Building: Anxiety Triggered by Declaring One's Goal for the Therapy

We help the patient declare positive goals so he will feel motivated to do the hard work of therapy. Without positive goals, he will feel no motivation.

> Th: Wouldn't it be nice to assert yourself with your boss so you wouldn't have to be anxious instead? [*Invitation to work toward a positive goal.*]
>
> Pt: Everybody is telling me to talk to my boss. [*Projection.*] They don't realize how difficult he is.
>
> Th: If we leave everyone else out of this [*block the projection*], would you like to be able to assert yourself without getting anxious instead? Is that a goal you would like to achieve in therapy for your benefit? [*Invite her to declare her positive goals.*]
>
> Pt: I get dizzy just thinking about it. [*Cognitive/perceptual disruption: anxiety too high.*]
>
> Th: That's a sign of anxiety. Having a thought about asserting yourself triggers this anxiety. Do you notice that too? [*Cognize about causality: declaring a goal triggers anxiety.*]
>
> Pt: I can't think about it.
>
> Th: Of course not. The anxiety makes it impossible to think. Isn't it a shame how this anxiety attacks you as if it is against the law for you to have a thought about asserting yourself? Almost like a policeman coming in to tell you to stop having that thought. [*Differentiate the patient from her anxiety and the defense of self-attack so she won't blame herself for being anxious.*]
>
> Pt: That's it. "No. Don't do that."
>
> Th: Wouldn't it be nice to be able to have a thought without this anxiety attacking you for having a thought? [*Invite her to declare a positive goal at a lower dosage ("having a thought") instead*

of "asserting herself," which triggered more anxiety than she could tolerate.]

Pt: Yes. Because when I'm with the boss, I get so anxious I can't think. [*First, regulate anxiety. Cognize about causality. Then invite her to declare a positive goal at a lower dosage. Now she can declare a positive goal.*]

Some patients learned that it was perilous to declare a positive goal they wanted. Thus, declaring a positive goal will trigger feelings and anxiety. If you regulate the patient's anxiety, you can co-create a relationship designed to achieve those positive goals. Then he can take these relational steps while feeling safe. (See table 1.3.)

Table 1.3   Stages in building the alliance that trigger anxiety

Stages in Building the Alliance with the Fragile Patient	Response: Anxiety	Therapeutic Task
Declaring a problem	Cognitive/perceptual disruption	Regulate anxiety so the patient can declare a problem without anxiety.
Declaring one's will to work on the problem	Cognitive/perceptual disruption	Regulate anxiety so he can declare his will without anxiety.
Declaring a positive goal to work toward	Cognitive/perceptual disruption	Regulate anxiety so he can declare a positive goal without anxiety.

Having reviewed the steps in alliance building that can trigger anxiety, let's look at how to assess anxiety when it becomes too high.

Step Two: Assess Anxiety: The Bodily Symptoms

When we propose to the patient that we form a therapeutic alliance, we invite her to depend on us. Depending triggers feelings and anxiety based on her past. After each intervention, we assess the following:

1. What are the patient's bodily symptoms of anxiety? If anxiety is in the striated muscles, explore feelings and address defenses. If it is in the smooth muscles or cognitive/perceptual disruption, regulate it until it returns to the striated muscles. Then return to the focus (problem, will, or feelings).

2. How rapidly does the anxiety rise and fall? If it rises slowly when you explore feelings and drops quickly when you pay attention to it, the patient regulates it well. You can explore feelings. A rapid rise and slow fall of anxiety indicate poor regulation,

defenses that perpetuate anxiety, and lingering effects of neuro-endocrine discharge (described on pp. 38–40). For instance, a woman becomes sick to her stomach as soon as the session begins. Regulate anxiety until it returns to the striated muscles before exploring feelings.

3. Can she observe and pay attention to her anxiety? If so, explore the feeling under the anxiety. If not, help her observe and regulate it. This can take time. The more dysregulated the patient, the longer it takes for her to become regulated.

4. Does anxiety regulation work? If not, identify the defenses that prevent her from observing, paying attention to, and regulating it.

We can assess the patient's anxiety as soon as she enters the room by noticing her gait. A woman with striated muscle tension walks energetically. She has an erect posture and an expressive or tense face. In contrast, a fragile man whose anxiety goes into his smooth muscles or cognitive/perceptual disruption may walk slowly. He may wobble on his feet because he lacks tension in his muscles ("jelly legs"). He sits in a slumped and tired posture, his face expressionless. When interventions trigger no tension or sighing, assess his anxiety.

Now, let's look at how to assess anxiety by paying attention to the patient's bodily responses to our interventions.

Anxiety in the Striated Muscles

The first transcript illustrates striated muscle discharge created by the somatic nervous system.

Th: Could we look at an example of when this is a problem for you?

Pt: [*Sighs.*] A couple days ago she said she wanted to dump me.

Th: What is your feeling toward her for saying that?

Pt: [*Sighs.*] Well, I didn't like it. [*Defense: intellectualization.*]

Th: Of course. What is the feeling toward her for saying that?

Pt: [*Sighs. Clenches his hands.*] I was angry.

Each time the therapist asks about feelings, the patient becomes tense, sighs, and clenches his hands. These are signs of anxiety in the striated muscles. With such a person, you can explore high levels of feeling (H. Davanloo, supervision 2002–2004).

Anxiety in the Smooth Muscles and Cognitive/Perceptual Disruption

A fragile patient may experience anxiety in the striated muscles when feelings are not intense. As mixed emotions rise, however, anxiety moves into the smooth muscles or cognitive/perceptual disruption. Here's an example of a fragile woman recovering from drug addiction.

Th: What you would like me to help you with?

Pt: [*Small sigh.*] My anxiety and depression. I have both. [*Anxiety in the striated muscles.*]

Th: Okay. Are you feeling anxious right now?

Pt: Uh-huh.

Th: Wonderful you notice. Where do you notice the anxiety physically?

Pt: In my stomach.

Th: What do you notice in your stomach?

Pt: I get nauseous, but the thing is that I have more control over it now than I used to. I used to just go and throw up. [*Smooth muscle discharge of anxiety. When higher-level defenses fail, anxiety can shift into the smooth muscles quickly. Also, the patient ignores her anxiety by moving her attention out of the moment.*]

Th: Just go and throw up, uh-huh. You are feeling the nausea right now in your stomach? [*Invite her to pay attention to anxiety in the moment.*]

Pt: But I can control it a little more now.

Th: Wonderful. You are feeling nausea right now in your stomach. I'm going to invite you to pay really close attention to your anxiety, particularly to how you experience your body; we are going to try to do that together. And this anxiety that you are feeling, this nausea, can you describe how you experience the nausea in your belly? [*Mobilize her will to the therapeutic task: paying attention to anxiety to regulate it.*]

Pt: Just when I'm nervous. [*No attention to this moment.*]

Th: And right now, you are nervous, and you're feeling it; right now, you are feeling nausea. [*Return her attention to anxiety in the body in this moment.*]

Pt: It doesn't have to be just when I'm nervous, it's when I feel anything.

Th: Uh-huh.

Pt: When I feel anything—when I'm too happy or sad or excited or anything. [*She sees that her feelings trigger anxiety.*]

Th: Any emotions can trigger it. So there is something about emotions that triggers a lot of anxiety, and you experience it in your gut, and right now, there's anxiety in your gut, right?

Pt: Uh-huh. It goes away, like right now, when I'm fidgeting around, but it goes away.

Th: So, let's keep our attention right now here because you are feeling anxious right now. We're going to pay close attention to any feelings, any anxiety in your body, any shifts so we can see what is happening internally that's creating this bodily problem. [*She nods.*] Aside from the nausea in your belly, are you feeling anxiety anywhere else in your body? [*Keep returning her attention to anxiety until it is regulated.*]

Pt: All over, and I think I know why because I think you are going to ask me personal questions, things I don't want to talk about. [*Projection of will.*]

When she feels anxious all over, her higher-level defenses have failed. And now a more primitive defense appears, the projection of will: "It is not my will to get answers to my questions. You want answers to your questions." People come to therapy because they have questions: for instance, "Why am I depressed?" But when anxiety is high, the patient forgets that this is *her* question. She attributes her questions and need for an answer to me. Projection makes her afraid of me, keeping anxiety elevated and unregulated. Thus, we could not regulate her anxiety yet. Later excerpts will show how we deactivate projections to bring anxiety down.

Assessing Unconscious Signaling in the Body: The Sigh

The therapist's invitation to a secure attachment triggers unconscious feelings in an insecurely attached patient. And these unconscious feelings trigger unconscious anxiety in the body (H. Davanloo, supervision 2002–2004) within one second. That means anxiety rises in the body even though the patient may not be aware of those symptoms. Anxiety symptoms are signals that point to rising unconscious feelings. Therefore, any intervention that mobilizes unconscious feelings will trigger unconscious anxiety in the patient's body.

The primary unconscious signal of anxiety we look for is the sigh. If an intervention triggers a sighing respiration, it mobilized mixed feelings and anxiety. Therefore, it was effective. The sigh also indicates that anxiety is in the striated muscles. Thus, it is regulated, and we can safely explore feelings. When we see a sigh, we know we are working within the window of tolerance (Siegel 1999). Other signals of anxiety in the striated muscles include clenching or wringing of the hands or tension in the back and neck before we see a sigh.

Interventions do not trigger unconscious anxiety if we avoid feelings or problems the patient needs to face. But if anxiety is too high, the patient cannot bear the emerging emotions. The optimal level of anxiety is signaled by sighing and tension in the striated muscles. When we see sighs, we are headed in the right direction, and anxiety is at an optimal level. If you don't see sighs but change the focus to feelings, and sighs resume, you are back on track.

If a fragile patient's anxiety is too high, we will not see sighs or tension because anxiety is discharged into the smooth muscles or cognitive/perceptual disruption. Then we can regulate anxiety until it returns to the striated muscles. From this position of bodily safety, we can explore.

If defenses ward off feelings, feelings cannot rise to trigger anxiety, and we will see no unconscious signaling in the body. When defenses stop the signaling, help the patient see and let go of those defenses. Then feelings will rise, and anxiety signals will resume.

Suppose a man curses his girlfriend and calls her vile names. If you explore his anger, no tension or sighing will occur. Why? Since he perceives her as completely bad, he feels only hatred toward her, no love. This defense is called splitting. Pure rage will not cause anxiety. If I asked if you hate Hitler, no anxiety would rise because you don't have mixed emotions toward him. But when you are angry toward someone you love, anxiety rises. Our fragile man here splits off his love, denies it, and claims to feel only rage. Remind him of his mixed feelings so he can see himself and his girlfriend more realistically.

> *Th:* You say you are enraged with her. And isn't she the same girlfriend who sat next to your bed all night when you were in the hospital? [*Invite him to face and experience his mixed feelings.*]

Pt: I don't think it meant anything. [*Denial.*]

Th: You think it didn't mean anything. Yet it meant something to you when you were in the hospital fighting for your life. [*Invite him to face and experience his mixed feelings.*]

Pt: She's a bitch. [*He splits off and denies his positive feelings, leaving an all-bad image.*]

Th: A bitch who sat next to your bed in the hospital and held your hand. [*Invite him to face and experience his mixed feelings.*]

Pt: [*Becomes dizzy.*] What did you say? [*As he tolerates his mixed feelings, anxiety rises, causing cognitive/perceptual disruption.*]

Unconscious signaling allows us to assess the pathways of unconscious anxiety discharge. We see no signaling in the striated muscles (tension, sighing, or clenching of the hands) in the fragile patient when (1) anxiety is discharged into the smooth muscles or cognitive/perceptual disruption or (2) defenses prevent the experience of mixed feelings. When the fragile patient experiences anxiety symptoms in the striated muscles, smooth muscles, or cognitive/perceptual disruption, anxiety signals that the previous intervention mobilized unconscious feelings.

HOW TO REGULATE ANXIETY

At the beginning of this chapter, I defined anxiety and then we looked at the sequence of relational needs that trigger anxiety when co-creating an alliance. Then we learned how to assess the patient's anxiety in the body. Here, we will focus on anxiety regulation. Figure 1.2 illustrates the steps for regulating anxiety when it becomes too high.

The steps for regulating anxiety when it becomes too high are as follows:

1. Stop exploring more feelings.
2. Regulate anxiety. If necessary, note symptoms of anxiety the patient ignores and invite her to observe them in her body. Keep doing this while reminding her about her feelings.
3. Keep the patient's feelings at this level while regulating anxiety until she starts sighing again, intellectualizes, or shows signs of muscle tension, such as clenching hands. Now anxiety is in the striated muscles, and she can tolerate this higher level of

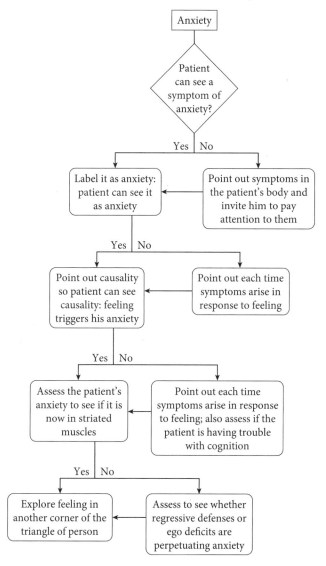

Figure 1.2   Decision tree: Inviting the problem and response of anxiety

feelings without anxiety moving out of the striated muscles. Her anxiety tolerance has increased.

4. Shift to a new example to explore feelings. Once she bears feelings at this slightly higher level, she will spontaneously mention another relationship where you can explore feelings again. Or introduce a higher-level defense, changing topics, by asking for another example where she would like to explore her feelings.

Principles of Anxiety Regulation

The following list describes the principles of anxiety regulation we use to co-create safety with the fragile patient. Listen to the patient's body as it speaks to us in its secret language: anxiety.

1. *Emphasize the present moment:* Mixed feelings in this moment trigger anxiety now, not thoughts about the past or future. Punitive thoughts may perpetuate anxiety, but find out what feelings trigger it now.

   Th: Since you are anxious now, could we look underneath the thoughts and see what feelings are triggering this anxiety now?

Principle: *Feelings now cause unconscious anxiety, not thoughts about the past or future.*

---

2. *Invite the patient to observe and pay attention to anxiety symptoms in the body in this moment:* When the therapist and patient pay close attention to the patient's bodily anxiety symptoms, they co-create safety. The patient does not have to ignore her anxiety to calm the other person in an insecure attachment. Instead, she and the therapist pay attention to her anxiety to calm her within a secure attachment.

   Th: Since you are feeling anxious, could we take a look at these anxiety symptoms in your body and see if we can help you regulate it?

Principle: *Paying attention together to bodily anxiety symptoms in this moment regulates anxiety and co-creates a secure attachment. The patient must feel safe in her body to feel safe in therapy.*

---

3. *Block insecure attachment patterns that prevent anxiety regulation:* When the patient ignores her anxiety, point out those behaviors. Then invite her to pay attention to her anxiety and regulate it.

   Th: My concern is that if you ignore your anxiety, it will get worse. And I don't want this to be an uncomfortable experience for you. Could we pay attention to this anxiety and see if we can help you regulate it?

Principle:	*Ignoring anxiety symptoms perpetuates anxiety and co-creates an insecure attachment. Encourage a relationship that regulates her anxiety: a secure attachment.*

4. *Notice patterns of unconscious anxiety:* Unconscious feelings make unconscious anxiety rise in the body, triggering a sigh. Explore whatever triggers a sigh to find what the patient is hiding, what she feared no one could love.

Th: What is the problem you would like me to help you with?

Pt: [*Sighs.*] I'm not sure what you think I should work on. [*Defense: projection. The invitation to declare a problem triggers anxiety in the patient, her sigh. Then she invites the therapist to declare the problem. We see a pattern: declaring a problem, anxiety, and hiding a problem. All of this occurs outside of her awareness and without her intent.*]

Principle:	*Unconscious feelings trigger unconscious anxiety in the body. Defenses do not.*

5. *Notice patterns of defense:* Feelings trigger anxiety first, and then a defense. An unconscious defense tells you that unconscious feelings rose. We explore whatever emotions defenses ward off. We see four patterns: (a) relating triggers feelings, (b) feelings trigger anxiety, (c) anxiety triggers defenses, and (d) anxiety drops after a defense. For instance, a woman feels grief over the loss of a fiancé who died. She becomes anxious. To avoid her mixed emotions, she may split off and deny her love and claim to feel only rage. When she splits her feelings of love and rage apart, they no longer trigger anxiety. Remind her of her love for her boyfriend (block her splitting). Then her mixed emotions will trigger unconscious anxiety in her body.

Principle:	*Notice the sequence—relating triggers feelings, feelings evoke anxiety, anxiety triggers defenses, and defenses ward off feelings, decreasing anxiety.*

6. *Pay attention to the process:*
   a. The therapist invites a secure attachment.
   b. Mixed feelings rise immediately.
   c. Anxiety rises in the body in a split second.
   d. A defense occurs in the next split second.
   e. Anxiety drops and a symptom often occurs in the next second (e.g., depression or a somatic symptom).

This sequence repeatedly occurs in every session. If not, the therapist is avoiding the patient's feelings.

Principle: *Unconscious feelings trigger anxiety, followed by a defense.*

---

7. *Help the patient see causality:* When his anxiety rises, ask, "If we look under the anxiety, what feelings are making you anxious?" When he experiences a symptom, help him see the defense, which is creating the symptom.

Th: Notice when a critical thought went out toward your teacher, it came back onto you just now? [*Point out the defense.*] Could that critical thought be making you depressed? [*Point out how the defense causes his symptom.*]

Principle: *Help the patient see the stimulus triggering his feelings and how they trigger anxiety in the body. Then help him see the defenses, which create his symptoms. By seeing how defenses cause his suffering, he feels more motivated to let go of them.*

Examples of Anxiety Regulation with Fragile Patients

Every therapy "should be conducted on as high an emotional level as the patient . . . can stand without diminishing [his] capacity for insight" (Alexander and French 1946, 30). Anxiety in the striated muscles is the physiological marker for that emotional level: the window of tolerance (Siegel 1999). If anxiety is too low, we are not facing what the patient usually avoids, and no new learning can take place. If anxiety is in the striated muscles, the patient is facing her feelings at her highest level while anxiety is regulated. If anxiety is too high, the brain malfunctions, preventing new learning, and the patient will experience suffering rather than healing. Anxiety is often too high when we begin therapy with fragile patients. Let's review the continuum of unconscious anxiety discharge.

Example A: Anxiety Pathway—Smooth Muscles

Regulation strategy: Focus attention on bodily symptoms of anxiety.

A woman describes her problems but with elevated anxiety. She first exhibits a dry mouth, some tension, and an elevated heart and breathing rate. But as her feelings rise, anxiety shifts out of the striated muscles into the smooth muscles. She experiences nausea or a migraine headache. She becomes weepy, her tension drops, her sighing stops, and she looks limp. Her anxiety is too high. Rather than explore her problem, we regulate her anxiety immediately by inviting her to pay attention to her bodily symptoms.

Th: Notice how your anxiety shot up? When I asked about the problem you wanted help with, you became anxious. And your anxiety caused a stomachache. Do you see that too? [*Point out causality: describing a problem brings up feelings and triggers anxiety symptoms. Cognizing about causality in the moment helps her regulate her anxiety and understand what causes it.*]

Pt: Yes.

Example B: Anxiety Pathway—Cognitive/Perceptual Disruption

Regulation strategy: Focus attention on bodily symptoms of anxiety.

A fragile woman enters the office, collapses into the chair, sitting slumped without tension in her body. She does not sigh or clench her hands. She describes her difficulties in a confusing fashion. Her vocal tone is flat. Her face is affectless. Her anxiety is too high. When she neither sighs nor shows signs of tension, anxiety is not going into the striated muscles. We need to assess where it is discharged in the body.

Th: As we begin today, are you aware of feeling anxiety in your body?

Pt: No. I just feel tired. [*When anxiety goes into the parasympathetic nervous system, tension, blood pressure, heart rate, and breathing rate drop. This makes people feel tired.*]

Th: Does it feel like a healthy tired after exercising or a sick kind of tired?

Pt: It's like a sick tired. I'm always exhausted. [*A sign of anxiety going into the parasympathetic nervous system.*]

Th: That can be a sign of anxiety. Could we take a moment and see if we could help you regulate it? [*Invite her to regulate her anxiety.*]

Pt: Okay.

Th: What do you notice feeling in your stomach? [*Assess anxiety.*]

Pt: I'm sick to my stomach, but I think it's because of something I ate. [*She sees the symptom but does not realize it is a sign of anxiety. People who were ignored as children often ignore their anxiety.*]

Th: Good. That's a sign of anxiety. Anytime that comes up in our session today, let me know because that's a sign anxiety is too high. As you let yourself pay attention to your stomach, what changes do you notice happening there? [*Encourage her to pay attention to an anxiety symptom until it decreases to co-create a sense of safety.*]

Pt: [*Pays attention for twenty seconds.*] It's coming down. [*The fragile patient, when flooded, cannot pay attention to her anxiety by herself. She will avoid it. Support her by reminding her every few seconds: "Notice what is happening in your stomach."*]

Th: What do you notice sensing in your stomach now? [*Invite her to pay attention to her anxiety.*]

Pt: It's calm now.

Th: Notice how paying attention to an anxiety symptom can bring it down? [*Point out causality.*]

Pt: It's weird.

Th: It is, isn't it? Anytime you feel sick to your stomach, let me know so we can regulate your anxiety together. [*Offer an anxiety regulating relationship: a secure attachment.*]

When you ask the fragile patient if she feels anxious, she may say no. She does not realize that her limpness, dizziness, blurry vision, and cognitive confusion are anxiety symptoms. The absence of tension or flatness makes her appear relaxed, but it indicates high anxiety discharged into cognitive/perceptual disruption. Regulate it immediately. If it rises more, she will need to use defenses such as splitting and projection. And, once she projects, she may lose the ability to differentiate you from her projection (Eissler 1954; Fonagy et al. 2002; Marcus 1992/2017; Segal 1981).

When parents induced anxiety rather than regulated it, fragile patients never learned to pay attention to their anxiety and regulate it. They need your support. Help them pay attention to their anxiety symptoms, and see what triggers their anxiety until it returns to the striated muscles. Patients must feel safe in the body to feel safe in therapy.

Example C: Anxiety Pathway—Cognitive/Perceptual Disruption with Projection

Regulation strategy: Focus attention on bodily symptoms of anxiety. Then deactivate a projection, and invite the patient to bear his desire inside rather than project it outside.

Each step in building the alliance can trigger excessive anxiety. But some people suffer from chronic free-floating anxiety. Their social engagement system (eye gaze, gesture, facial affect, vocal tone, control of the middle ear, and orienting reflex) remains neurologically unavailable (Porges 2001, 2011). To regulate anxiety, focus on his body. Describe the triangle of conflict (feeling, anxiety, and defense) several times. Then invite him to repeat back what he heard. Anxiety in the smooth muscles or cognitive/perceptual disruption may drop slowly because the body needs time to metabolize the neurohormones released by the parasympathetic nervous system (Franchini and Cowley 2004). Give your patient and his physiology the time necessary to become regulated.

When feelings trigger excessive anxiety, the patient may also project onto others the feelings that make him anxious. For instance, he may project his awareness of a problem: "My sponsor thinks I have a problem." When you ask if he wants to work on the problem, he may project his will: "My parents want me to be here." When you ask what he feels, he may project his feelings: "You are angry with me." In response, help him recognize inside himself what he projects onto others. By deactivating projections that make therapy seem dangerous, we help him bear inside the feelings that endangered his early relationships. Then therapy becomes a safe place to explore his inner life. The patient must feel safe with you rather than unsafe with a projection.

A middle-aged man shuffles into the office and falls into the chair. He makes no eye contact and looks limp. [*No signs of striated muscle tension.*]

   Th: What's the problem you would like me to help you with?

   Pt: [*Pauses.*] Well, the first thing I should tell you, [*pauses*] I first entered psychoanalysis when I was thirteen years old. [*He doesn't answer the question: defense against presenting a problem. He does not reveal his need to the therapist. However, he may have trouble thinking due to rising anxiety.*]

   Th: I would like to hear more about your history later. [*Block the defense. Then invite him to engage in the therapeutic task.*] But first, to be helpful to you, what's the problem you would like me to help you with?

   Pt: I have problems with anxiety.

   Th: Are you aware of feeling anxious right now? [*Immediately assess.*]

   Pt: Yes. [*Ability to observe his anxiety.*]

   Th: Where do you notice feeling anxious in your body? [*Assess the pathway of unconscious anxiety discharge.*]

   Pt: All over. [*Anxiety spreads rapidly in the body when higher-level defenses fail.*]

   Th: Specifically where in your body? [*Invite him to pay close attention to anxiety in his body.*]

   Pt: I'm often sick in my stomach. [*Anxiety often goes into his smooth muscles. He moves out of the present moment, a defense that prevents anxiety regulation now.*]

   Th: Are you feeling sick in your stomach now? [*Block the defense of moving out of the present moment. Return his attention to his anxiety now.*]

   Pt: Yes, I threw up before the session. [*Anxiety discharged into the smooth muscles. It was already too high before the session. Regulation is imperative. He moves out of the present moment, which shows he cannot pay attention to his anxiety now.*]

   Th: Are you feeling like throwing up now? [*Draw attention to this moment.*]

   Pt: Yes, but not as much. [*His speech is very slow, often a sign of cognitive/perceptual disruption. Speak as slowly as the patient to match the speed at which he can process your speech. If you talk too quickly when he is cognitively disrupted, he may not comprehend what you say. And the information overload you provide may increase his anxiety.*]

Th: You are feeling intense anxiety here today.

Pt: Not just today. I've been feeling this way for a couple of weeks [*when he called for the appointment*].

Th: You are feeling anxious here with me today. And you have been feeling intense anxiety ever since you called my office. [*Link his request for help to the resulting anxiety.*]

Pt: Yes.

Th: We see that you have a problem with anxiety, and it is coming up here with me. Can we take a look at this anxiety in your body to help you with it? [*Invite him to observe and pay attention to his anxiety to regulate it.*]

Pt: Yes. [*Tears up, a sign of high anxiety. His anxiety is in the smooth muscles. Exploring feelings now would trigger more anxiety when it is too high, so regulate it.*]

Th: You mention feeling anxious in your stomach. Where else do you notice feeling anxiety in your body?

Pt: I have a migraine right now. [*Smooth muscles. People often get migraine headaches when anxiety shifts into the smooth muscles.*]

Th: That's another sign of anxiety. What's another sign of anxiety that you notice in your body?

Pt: What did you say? [*Problem with hearing: a sign of cognitive/perceptual disruption.*]

Th: I was wondering where else you notice this anxiety. Are you having some trouble with your hearing right now? [*Assess his anxiety.*]

Pt: I don't think so.

Th: Is there any ringing in your ears? [*Assess his anxiety.*]

Pt: Yes. [*Cognitive/perceptual disruption.*]

Th: That's another sign of anxiety. How is your vision? Is it clear or blurry?

Pt: I can see you, but it's a little blurry. [*Cognitive/perceptual disruption.*]

Th: That's another sign of anxiety. How is your thinking right now? Is it clear, or are you having trouble forming your thoughts?

Pt: I think it is clear, but people tell me that I seem slow. [*Anxiety impairs his thinking and hearing: signs of cognitive/perceptual disruption.*]

Th: We see that you are very anxious. You have anxiety in your stomach, blurred vision, ringing ears, and difficulty forming your thoughts. All of this is anxiety, and it has to do with coming here to see me today. [*Summarize the anxiety symptoms and link them with feelings toward the therapist to help the patient see causality.*] There must be a lot of feeling underneath that is triggering all this anxiety. [*Direct his attention to the feelings that trigger his anxiety. But I made a mistake. His anxiety needs to be lower, in the striated muscles, before I ask for feelings.*]

Pt: Yes. [*Wave of tears. Anxiety overwhelms him.*]

Th: As these tears come up, there's another wave of anxiety. Do you notice that? [*Return to anxiety regulation.*]

Pt: Yes. I'm afraid of what you want. [*With a high rise of anxiety, a new defense arises: projection. He wants something from therapy. But through projection, he believes I want something from him. I deactivate his projection. Otherwise, he will ward off a "persecutory" therapist who wants something from him. That projection would produce a misalliance.*]

Th: Let's clarify something. Who called me for this meeting? [*Remind him of his desire for therapy, which he has located in the therapist. This deactivates his projection.*]

Pt: I did.

Th: And who thought he had a problem? [*These questions remind him of his will, which he relocated in the therapist.*]

Pt: Me.

Th: And who asked me to help him with this problem?

Pt: Me.

Th: So who wants something out of this?

Pt: Me, but I'm wondering what you want. [*He still believes his projection, so deactivate it. Otherwise, we will have a paranoid transference where he wards off a therapist's "desires."*]

Th: But who wants something out of this?

Pt: Me.

Th: Right. Let me offer you something to think about. You are the one who wants something out of this. Right? [*Invite him to notice his desire.*]

Pt: Yeah.

Th: And you are the one who wants to reveal something about himself to this therapist. Right? [*Invite him to notice his desire.*]

Pt: Right.

Th: I wonder if you find it scary how much you want to reveal yourself here. [*Establish an internal focus. His desire, not the therapist's, triggers his anxiety.*]

Pt: That's true because I've been hurt before. [*Once he tolerates his desire inside himself, we learn why he placed it outside of himself. He thought that if he revealed his wish for help, I would hurt him as he was hurt in the past. Deactivate his projection so he can have an alliance with the therapist instead of a misalliance with a projection.*]

Th: As you and I sit here together, it's like there's an image of someone in the past that comes between you and me. And when this image comes between you and me, you can lose touch with me and feel more in touch with this image instead. [*Differentiate me from the image he projects onto me.*]

Pt: Yes. [*Relaxes in his chair. The projection triggered projective anxiety, anxiety caused by the projection. The decreased anxiety shows that the projection has dropped.*]

Principles in the Opening Phase of Work with Fragile Patients:

Principle 1: *Assess and regulate anxiety.*

Principle 2: *When defenses such as projection and splitting prevent anxiety regulation, address those defenses until anxiety returns to the striated muscles.*

Principle 3: *Each time the patient accepts inside what he previously projected outside, that increased amount of feelings inside will cause anxiety to rise. Regulate anxiety or deactivate the next projection to build affect tolerance.*

Example D: Anxiety Pathway—Shifting from Striated to Smooth Muscles

Regulation strategy: Remind the patient of the feelings triggering her anxiety while cognizing about causality to regulate her anxiety. This combination of inviting feelings plus anxiety regulation is called bracing (Abbass 2015).

In this example, we'll see how to regulate anxiety and learn what causes it.

Th: You mentioned a family problem. Would you like to look at that?

Pt: I've got a conflict with my son. He's been mentally ill for some years, and it wouldn't be a problem except that he's living with me. And I told him he would have to leave if he kept drinking. He told me he stopped drinking, but I keep finding empty bottles in the cabinets. [*She describes what her son does, not how it poses an emotional problem for her.*]

Th: How is that a problem for you?

Pt: I don't know what to do about it. My friends say I should kick him out, but then I don't know where he would go. [*Clear statement of the problem. She wards off her anger by worrying and ruminating ("I don't know where he would go"). These defenses keep her stuck, preventing her from using her feelings for effective thinking and action.*]

Th: There's some feelings you have toward your son. But then you seem paralyzed [*defense*], as if you don't know what to do with your feelings.

Pt: That's true. I don't know what to do. [*Price of the defense.*]

Th: Would you like to look at these feelings toward your son so we could help you get unstuck? [*Mobilize her will to the therapeutic task.*]

Pt: [*Sighs.*] Yes. [*Anxiety goes into the striated muscles: clear wish to collaborate.*]

Th: What's the feeling toward your son who lied to you about his drinking?

Pt: [*Sighs. Clenched hands—striated muscles.*] I feel he should have told me the truth. [*Defense: intellectualization.*]

Th: That says what you think. [*Defense.*] What is the feeling toward him? [*Differentiate the feeling from the defense. Then invite her to face her feelings.*]

Pt: Upset. [*Defense: vagueness.*]

Th: Clearly, he upset you. What's the emotion toward him for lying to you? [*Differentiate the stimulus, what he did, from her feeling toward him for doing it.*]

Pt: My stomach is starting to cramp. [*After I ask about her feelings three times, her anxiety moves from the striated muscles into the smooth muscles. Since her anxiety has gone over the threshold for anxiety tolerance, we will do some bracing.*]

For *bracing* (Abbass 2015), support her feelings at this level while regulating anxiety until she sighs or intellectualizes. Once anxiety returns to the striated muscles, the higher level of feelings will be her new threshold of anxiety tolerance (i.e., the amount of feelings she can bear before her anxiety moves out of the striated muscles). We raise that threshold gradually until she can bear 100 percent of her feelings without anxiety shifting out of the striated muscles.

Th: As soon as we touch on these feelings toward your son, notice how this anxiety comes in to attack you as if it's against the law for you to have feelings toward him? That something about feelings triggers this anxiety? Feelings rise, you get anxious, then the stomach problems start. Notice how the feelings do that? [*Point out the anxiety's function: to attack and punish her. Differentiate her as an observer from the anxiety she observes. Regulate anxiety while sustaining her feelings at the same intensity level.*]

Pt: I hadn't thought of it that way before. Do you think these cramps are related to my anxiety? [*Intellectualization: a sign her anxiety is returning to the striated muscles.*]

Th: What's the sequence we saw here? Feelings toward your son, then stomach cramps. [*Draw her attention to causality: anger triggers anxiety. Don't ask her to believe you. If the same pattern repeats in the session, she will see the evidence for herself. It's not her job to agree with the therapist. It's our task to see if our hypotheses fit the facts.*]

Pt: That's true. [*Her hands start clenching: a sign her anxiety is returning to the striated muscles.*]

She can tolerate her desire for therapy without projecting. She has a higher capacity for affect tolerance than the previous patient. She tolerates her feelings briefly while anxiety is in the striated muscles, but it shifts into the smooth muscles. The therapist reminds her of her emotions while regulating her anxiety until it returns to the striated muscles, and she sighs or intellectualizes.

Example E: Anxiety Pathway—Cognitive/Perceptual Disruption Leading to Mild Thought Disorder

Regulation strategy: Focus on bodily symptoms of anxiety.

The following example illustrates *thought disorder,* a sign that anxiety has become too high. Then we'll look at how to address it and regulate the anxiety that causes it.

Th: What's the problem you would like me to help you with?

Pt: Yeah, well, a lot of reflection on what's going on and everything. She's in New Orleans at the moment. [*She has not declared a problem. And her second sentence doesn't follow logically from the first, a common sign of soft thought disorder. Her anxiety is too high.*]

Th: Your grandson's mother. [*The therapist tries to guess who she is referring to. In this section, I will mark with an asterisk instances where the patient's thoughts don't link together.*]

Pt: Yeah. I haven't gotten to. Sit her down. * Look they've taken my money. They're taking the insurance out of my check. * "You took my money. Where's my insurance?" "I have to pay a hundred dollars a month." [*After the last asterisk, she shifts from describing a situation to enacting a conversation she had.*]

Th: This is going on in your negotiations with her?

Pt: Right. I tried to speak to her. I went down to see her. She called me a liar. * My grandson's mother is not my blood relative. She's a friend. I'm trying to work through to be friends for my grandson's sake. But she's not a blood relative. And she knows she's not supporting me. * But they call me a liar.

Th: Who's they?

Pt: Down at the social security office. * She has issues herself. She can't see what's going on with my body, and I don't think she knows more than the doctor. She's not a doctor. So she sits down there in judgment.

Th: This is the person at social security? [*The therapist guesses to compensate for the thought disorder.*]

Thoughts connect facts. Those connections evoke feelings. When fragile patients cannot bear those feelings, they break the links between one idea and another (Bion 1959) to keep them from connecting, causing experience, and then anxiety. The resulting chopped up bits create thought disorder. To help her see the defense, we can point it out (Sullivan 1953b).

Pt: I don't appreciate being called a liar. * I was getting a check for Alabama and got called a liar again and then called them a liar.

Th: I'm sorry. I'm a bit confused. You said you didn't appreciate being called a liar. And then you said you were getting a check for Alabama. Could you help me see how those two thoughts are connected? [*Stop after each instance of thought disorder. Do not say she is confusing. Own the confusion as yours so she won't feel ashamed. Then invite her to provide the missing link.*]

Pt: She said I was a liar, taking this money from Alabama.

Th: You didn't appreciate her calling you a liar. That makes sense. How is that related to taking money from Alabama? [*Invite the patient to provide the missing link in her thoughts.*]

Pt: She said I was a liar because I was taking money from Alabama when I'm living in Virginia. [*Now she can provide the link that will allow feelings to rise.*]

In another case, a woman who had been hospitalized over thirty times talked in a scattered fashion. In each session, I interrupted her after each example of thought disorder so we could get clear about her thoughts. A month later, she said, "For some reason, people are talking to me more." She didn't realize that as her thought disorder decreased, she spoke more clearly, and people could understand her. And when her thinking became disordered, she could clarify what she was trying to say.

Cognitive work can help, but we also need to regulate anxiety.

Th: What's the problem you would like me to help you with?

Pt: I wasn't even sure I was going to stay here. I was trying to be a law-abiding citizen. You know I don't know. You have a grace period before you change it over. [*Thought disorder: a sign of anxiety in cognitive/perceptual disruption.*]

Th: That sounds really uncomfortable. Could we check on your anxiety? Are you aware of feeling anxious right now? [*Invite her to pay attention to her anxiety to regulate it. Don't mention the thought disorder. Use it as a signal to regulate her anxiety.*]

Pt: No. It's the grace period. That's the problem. [*She cannot pay attention to her anxiety.*]

Th: And I'd be glad to help you with that. [*Use her concern to bridge back to anxiety regulation.*] First, let's look at your anxiety. How is your vision? Is it clear or a little blurry? [*Invite the patient to pay attention to her anxiety.*]

Pt: It's blurry. But it's always that way. I think I need some glasses. [*Cognitive/perceptual disruption.*]

Help her pay attention to and regulate her anxiety. Once the anxiety is regulated, her thinking may improve. Indicate when you are confused by what she says so she can observe the disjointed thoughts. Then you can explore her problems in more detail.

Why Does High Anxiety Create Cognitive/Perceptual Disruption?

It can be hard to believe that anxiety creates cognitive/perceptual disruption. Yet, the research is clear. As soon as anxiety goes over the threshold of anxiety tolerance, the parasympathetic branch of the autonomic nervous system gets activated. It affects numerous aspects of our physiology, which impair cognitive functioning in our patients:

- *Blood flow:* The parasympathetic nervous system causes a sudden drop in blood flow to the brainstem, the frontal lobe, and Broca's area, and it causes a fall in the heart rate (the heart may stop beating for a few seconds) (Arnsten 1997, 1998, 1999; Birnbaum et al. 1999; Goldstein 2004, 2006; Rauch et al. 1996). In response, the patient faints, has trouble finding words to describe his experience, and loses postural tone in sessions (Goldstein 2004, 103; Kaufmann 2004; Ziegler 2004). The prefrontal cortex can no longer inhibit the amygdala and the fear response (Grawe 2006; Wehrenberg and Prinz 2007). As a

result, the patient becomes less capable of executive functioning (Austin 2006) and has trouble thinking, and fears and projection worsen in session.

- *Neuroendocrine discharge:* People with depression, anxiety disorders, and personality disorders suffer from disturbed autonomic
  nervous system functioning (Beauchaine 2001; Porges 2011;
  Prins, Kaloupek, and Keane 1995). The adrenal gland discharges
  norepinephrine, keeping the patient's anxiety symptoms high
  for long periods (Goldstein 2006; Rosen and Schulkin 2004,
  176). The discharge of adrenaline and other neurohormones
  interferes with the functioning of the prefrontal cortex, impairing the patient's ability to reflect and make rational decisions.
  As a result, the patient acts impulsively and inappropriately.
  He is distractible, inattentive, disorganized, and hyperactive
  (Arnsten 1999; Porges and Bazhenova 2006). His reasoning
  cannot influence his behavior. Defenses emerge automatically,
  but the ability to reflect on them disappears.

High levels of endorphins impair the patient's short-term memory
for several hours, preventing explicit, declarative memory from forming and consolidating (Newcomer et al. 1999; Scaer 2001). Thus, he
cannot remember what you say in therapy (Joels and Karst 2009;
Southwick et al. 2005). Stress hormones redirect blood glucose away
from the hippocampus to the striated muscles. This prevents the
fragile patient from forming new memories or retrieving long-term
memories in therapy. Thus, anxiety regulation is the precondition for
the patient to be able to remember important insights in therapy and
to progress.

- *Developmental physiology:* The repeated experience of severe
  anxiety during childhood increases the frequency of cortisol
  releases, damaging the hippocampus. Physiologically, it shrinks,
  and the amygdala enlarges (Bremner et al. 1995, 2000; McEwen
  and Sapolsky 2000, 182; Sheline et al. 1996; Sheline, Gado, and
  Kraemer 2003), impairing learning, executive functioning, and
  self-regulation (Blair, Granger, and Razza 2005; Lupien et al.
  1998; Sapolsky et al. 1990). This compromises brain development, creating the neurological basis for anxiety disorders.

The altered development impairs the capacity for storing and retrieving new learning in therapy (Sapolsky 2004). It also reduces the ability to inhibit the amygdala. The conditioned fear responses become stronger. As a result, the patient may have trouble thinking or regulating herself in session (Perry 2004). Attachment trauma influences brain development resulting in wide-ranging neurocognitive deficits in traumatized children (Almas et al. 2012; Bos et al. 2009). As a result, fragile patients, as adults, often suffer from neurocognitive deficits that amplify fear responses and impair the capacity for anxiety regulation (Etkin, Gyurak, O'Hara, 2013).

These factors create the symptom of poor heart rate variability, now recognized as a transdiagnostic biomarker of psychopathology (Beauchaine and Thayer 2015). Symptoms of cognitive/perceptual disruption result when neurohormones shut down the hippocampus and prefrontal cortex. Thus, the patient cannot remember what happened or what you said in the session. The patient cannot reflect on his thinking or projections because his mind cannot function properly. Therapy cannot succeed if anxiety shuts one mind down. Without anxiety assessment and regulation, we ask patients to do the impossible: work with a mind disabled by neurohormones and reduced blood flow.

With this understanding of the neurobiological causes of cognitive/perceptual disruption, the importance of anxiety regulation becomes obvious. We regulate anxiety as soon as it moves out of the striated muscles to restore biophysiological functioning and to reverse cognitive deficits. Then we can gradually build the patient's capacity to bear feelings without excessive anxiety.

The Graded Format: When Anxiety Moves Out of the Striated Muscles

We use a gradual approach for exploring when patients' anxiety goes into the smooth muscles or cognitive/perceptual disruption (H. Davanloo, supervision 2002–2004; Whittemore 1996). In this *empathic diagnosis*, we explore the patient's desires to discover which interventions will be helpful (Semrad 1969). To build affect tolerance when anxiety goes too high, do the following:

1. *Stop exploring more feelings when anxiety is too high*: Otherwise, more feelings will trigger more anxiety, cognitive/perceptual disruption, projection, and then loss of reality testing. Put the fire out before you rebuild the house.

2. *Regulate anxiety*: If necessary, note anxiety symptoms the patient ignores and invite her to pay attention to them.

3. *Keep the patient's feelings at this level while regulating anxiety*: Maintain this level of feelings until she sighs, signs of muscle tension return, such as clenching hands, or she intellectualizes. When she can tolerate this higher level of feelings while anxiety remains in the striated muscles, her affect tolerance has increased.

4. *Shift to a new example to explore feelings*: Once she bears feelings at this slightly higher level, she may spontaneously mention another relationship where you can explore feelings again. Or you can introduce a higher-level defense by changing topics and ask for another example where she would like to explore her feelings.

The Graded Format in Action

The next vignette shows how to assess and regulate anxiety. A depressed woman's daughter lied about her drug use.

Th: What are the feelings toward her for doing that?

Pt: I'm getting a migraine. [*Her anxiety just became too high. Stop exploring the feeling; regulate the anxiety.*]

Th: It's good you notice. This headache is a sign of anxiety. Are you aware of feeling anxious right now? [*Draw attention to the anxiety.*]

Pt: Not really. I'm aware of feeling this headache. [*She is not aware of her anxiety.*]

Th: You notice the headache. What do you feel in your stomach right now? [*Help her see other anxiety symptoms.*]

Pt: A little queasy.

Th: That's another sign of anxiety. You've got a headache and a sick stomach, and those are signs of anxiety. [*Draw her attention to her anxiety.*]

Pt: I didn't know that was anxiety. I feel that a lot.

Th: You have these symptoms of anxiety a lot. It's important to notice that you had some feelings toward your daughter for lying to you. Then those feelings triggered this anxiety, which took the form of your headache and a queasy stomach. Do you see that now? [*Draw her attention to causality: feeling triggers anxiety.*]

Pt: I see it now, but I didn't see it before.

Th: You saw the headache. But now we see you felt something toward your daughter for lying to you. And that triggered anxiety, which went into your headache and your stomach. [*Causality.*] How are your headache and stomach now? [*Assess if anxiety has dropped.*]

Pt: The headache is gone, and the stomach is okay. [*Her anxiety has decreased. Ask about the feeling again.*]

Th: Would you like to look at this feeling you had toward your daughter so we can help you feel your feeling instead of anxiety? [*Mobilize her will to the task.*]

Pt: Yes.

Th: What is the feeling toward your daughter for lying to you?

Pt: Frustrated. [*She confuses the stimulus (what her daughter did) with the feeling toward her.*]

Th: Sure. She frustrated you by lying to you. What is your feeling toward her for doing that? [*Differentiate the stimulus from her reactive feeling.*]

Pt: [*Sighs.*] I feel angry.

Her anxiety shifted from the smooth muscles back into the striated muscles: her sigh. Now the therapist can explore feelings again to build affect tolerance. When anxiety shifts into the smooth muscles or cognitive/perceptual disruption, regulate it. Once tension returns to the striated muscles, you can explore feelings again.

Raising the Threshold of Anxiety Tolerance

The threshold of anxiety tolerance refers to the maximum amount of mixed feelings a person can bear while anxiety stays in the striated muscles. When it shifts into the smooth muscles, he has gone over the threshold of anxiety tolerance. If feelings rise higher, anxiety can move into cognitive/perceptual disruption.

Why does he flood with anxiety? His higher-level defenses collapsed, which kept his feelings out of awareness. Thus, he is drowned by these emotions and the anxiety they trigger. He can no longer bear or channel feelings into effective action (Jacobson 1953). We help him build this capacity for anxiety tolerance until he can bear 100 percent of his mixed feelings while anxiety remains in the striated muscles. Table 1.4 illustrates the thresholds for an imaginary fragile patient.

Table 1.4   Thresholds of affect tolerance in a sample fragile patient

Percentage of Affect Activation	Pathway of Anxiety Discharge in the Body
30–100 percent of mixed feelings	Cognitive/perceptual disruption
10–30 percent of mixed feelings	Smooth muscles
0–10 percent of mixed feelings	Striated muscles

He functions well under 10 percent of his feelings, but over 10 percent his anxiety shifts into the smooth muscles. Over 30 percent, he floods with anxiety and has trouble thinking. Now his functioning deteriorates. At 35 percent, perhaps he projects and his reality testing becomes weakened so that he misperceives his boss, his wife, and his therapist. Each higher level of anxiety will further impair his functioning.

When anxiety is too high, he cannot collaborate optimally in therapy. Anxiety impairs his brain functioning. He will have physical symptoms. We would not work with him at 15, 20, or 30 percent of his feelings because he would regress and become worse. If he crosses the threshold of anxiety tolerance at 10 percent, we work at that level. Then we gradually raise his threshold to 100 percent of his mixed feelings. We have no empirical measure for affect intensity. I use these numbers only metaphorically. However, we can recognize the empirical biophysiological thresholds of striated muscles, smooth muscles, and cognitive/perceptual disruption.

The fragile patient can tolerate only a little of his mixed feelings. As a result, we explore the mixed feelings until anxiety moves out of the striated muscles. Then we regulate anxiety while holding feelings at this higher level until he sighs or intellectualizes. That level turns into a new threshold for anxiety tolerance. We repeat that process at successively greater levels of feeling in the *graded format* (Whittemore 1996), as shown in figure 1.3.

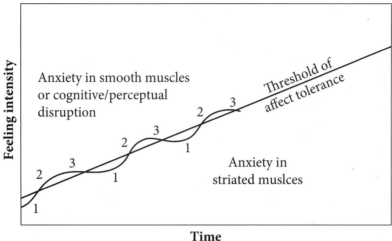

1 Therapist explores feelings
2 Patient goes over the threshold of affect tolerance
3 Therapist regulates anxiety or braces

Figure 1.3   The graded format

Principle: *When anxiety goes into the smooth muscles or cognitive/ perceptual disruption, stop exploring feelings. Instead, hold feelings at this level while regulating anxiety. Continue until anxiety returns to the striated muscles at the higher feeling level. Then explore feelings again.*

WHEN DEFENSES PREVENT ANXIETY REGULATION

Regulating anxiety in the body is the precondition for a therapeutic alliance (Schore 2002) and any successful therapy. When anxiety regulation does not work, assess the patient's defenses that prevent her from observing, paying attention to, and regulating her anxiety. These defenses include ignoring one's anxiety, shifting attention to other topics or people, self-dismissal, and minimization. Block these defenses to make anxiety regulation possible. (See figure 1.4.)

Principle: *If anxiety regulation does not work, assess the defenses that prevent the patient from paying attention to and regulating her anxiety.*

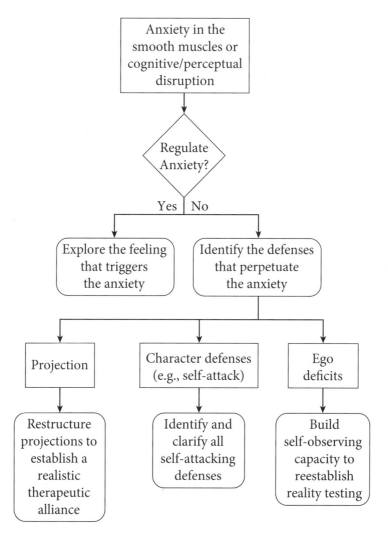

Figure 1.4   Regulating anxiety when it goes into the smooth muscles or cognitive/perceptual disruption

Here are a few interventions to help the patient pay attention to anxiety to regulate it:

- *Ask about her problem, her will to work on it, or her feelings.* Keep asking until her anxiety goes into the smooth muscles or cognitive/perceptual disruption.

- *Invite her to observe her anxiety:* "Are you aware of feeling anxious right now?"

- *Help her observe and pay attention to her anxiety to regulate it:* "Can we pay attention to your anxiety and see if we can help you bring it down together?" Exploring feelings while anxiety is too high will trigger more anxiety and make her feel worse.
- *If she is not aware of her anxiety, point out the anxiety symptoms in her body until she recognizes them:* "The stomachache is a sign of anxiety."
- *Help her observe and pay attention to her anxiety and her defenses against doing so, then point out causality:* "Letting me know about your problem is triggering your anxiety as if it is against the law for you to get help. Would you like to break that law so you can get the help you need?"
- *If she is aware of her anxiety but ignores it, clarify the price of her defense and invite her to engage in better self-care:* "If you shift topics now, we would ignore your anxiety. Shall we pay attention to it instead so we can help you bring it down?" Once she lets go of these defenses, she can learn to pay attention to and regulate her anxiety.
- *Continue to link her feelings and anxiety until she sighs or intellectualizes:* "Letting me know about your problem made you anxious, and the anxiety gave you an upset stomach. Do you notice this too?" As you and the patient intellectualize about her anxiety, it will shift into the striated muscles. When she tolerates this higher level of feelings without cognitive/perceptual disruption, you will have raised her threshold of anxiety tolerance.

Defenses That Prevent Anxiety Regulation

To regulate anxiety, the patient must observe and pay attention to it. If she ignores her anxiety, she cannot regulate it. If she uses defenses that make anxiety worse, they would prevent anxiety regulation. Help the patient see those defenses so she can regulate her anxiety and find safety in therapy.

Vignette One: The Defenses of Self-Dismissal and Ignoring

This excerpt shows how to interrupt defenses that prevent anxiety regulation. Then we help the patient pay attention to her anxiety. A woman enters the office with her eyes darting about—often a sign of projection. She shows no tension. Her body is limp as she shuffles to the chair. With such symptoms of high anxiety, we regulate it.

Th: As we begin today, I'm going to invite you to check in on your anxiety. Are you aware of feeling anxious?

Pt: No. [*No observing ability.*]

Th: Are you aware of feeling tired? You look really tired. [*A sign of anxiety.*]

Pt: I'm exhausted. I can't get a good night's sleep. [*People who look tired and flat, with no muscle tension, may experience anxiety in the smooth muscles or cognitive/perceptual disruption.*]

Th: That's often a sign of anxiety. Could we take a moment to check on your anxiety? [*Invite her to engage in self-care.*]

Pt: Okay. But I'm always anxious. [*Defense: self-dismissal, which prevents her from observing and paying attention to her anxiety. Chronic anxiety often results from chronic projection. She may fear people on whom she projects.*]

Th: That makes sense. If you weren't anxious, you wouldn't be here. How is your stomach? Does it feel tense, or are you sick to your stomach? [*Invite her to pay attention to her anxiety.*]

Pt: But I didn't come here to talk about my anxiety. [*Defense: ignoring her anxiety.*]

Th: Of course. You came here to get help. But if we don't bring your anxiety down, we won't be able to help you with your problem. Would it make sense that we help you with your anxiety first so this could be a more comfortable experience for you? [*Block the defense and clarify its price: unregulated anxiety will keep her from solving her problems. Patients may invite the therapist to ignore their anxiety. Instead, offer a secure attachment where we pay attention to anxiety to regulate it together.*]

Pt: But there are other things that are more important to me. [*Defense: ignoring her anxiety by shifting to other topics. Her defense enacts an insecure attachment: "Ignore my anxiety and pay attention to something else."*]

Th: Sure. But if we ignore your anxiety, we won't be able to bring it down. And then this would be very uncomfortable for you. Would it make sense to bring this anxiety down so we could help you deal with your problems more easily? [*Block the defense and clarify its price: unregulated anxiety. Then invite her to work together to regulate it.*]

Pt: Okay.

Th: To bring your anxiety down, what do you notice sensing in your stomach? [*Block the defense of ignoring and enlist her will to regulate her anxiety.*]

Pt: I get nauseated down there. [*Defense: moving out of the present moment. When she doesn't focus on her anxiety, we cannot regulate it. Return her attention to her body.*]

Th: And now? What do you notice sensing in your stomach as you keep your attention focused right there? [*Return her attention to the present moment.*] Yeah. What do you notice sensing in your stomach? [*She has trouble paying attention to her anxiety. The therapist speaks slowly to keep the patient's attention on her anxiety.*]

Pt: Do you want me to pay attention to my stomach? [*Defense: projection of her wish to pay attention to herself. Deactivate the projection so she can recognize her wish to pay attention to herself.*]

Th: Do you want to pay attention to your stomach so you can regulate your anxiety and so you don't have to suffer these symptoms? Is that what you want for yourself? [*Deactivate her projection: help her notice her desire to care for herself.*]

Pt: Yes, I think so. [*She does not sigh, and she hesitates. Her will is not online. Defense: she may be projecting her will onto the therapist.*]

Th: What tells you inside that this is what you want? How do you know that you want to pay attention to yourself so you can feel less anxious? [*Invite her to become aware of her will to deactivate the projection.*]

Pt: I know it would help me. [*Unconscious therapeutic alliance. Her new words "help me" inform our next invitation.*]

Th: And do you want to help yourself by regulating your anxiety? Is this something you want to do for yourself? [*Focus on her relationship to herself first. Once that is solid, we can talk about her relationship with the therapist.*]

Pt: I have a hard time doing something good for myself. [*Unconscious therapeutic alliance. Her new words "doing something good for myself" inform our next invitation.*]

Th: And do you want to do something good for yourself by regulating your anxiety? Is that what you want to do for yourself? [*Invite her to become aware of her desire.*]

Pt: I'm getting a little dizzy. [*The wish to do something good for herself makes her anxiety go into cognitive/perceptual disruption. Remind her of her wish while regulating her anxiety. Help her accept her wish without excessive anxiety.*]

Th: That's a sign of anxiety. This anxiety attacks you when you want to do something good for yourself. You must be upset at that anxiety for doing that. Would you like to have the freedom to do something good for yourself without getting so anxious? [*Remind her of the forbidden wish while regulating her anxiety. Help her differentiate herself from the anxiety by talking about how it attacks her.*]

Pt: That would be nice. I haven't been able to do that before. [*She can intellectualize: a higher-level system of resistance. Intellectualization suggests that her anxiety is in the striated muscles. Thus, her anxiety tolerance has increased.*]

Th: And you would like to do something good for yourself in this therapy? [*Invite her will to do something good for herself.*]

Pt: [*Sighs.*] Yes. [*With a sigh and her "yes," we can explore feelings safely.*]

Principle: *When a patient ignores her anxiety, point out the defense. Then invite her to pay attention to her anxiety to regulate it.*

Why does the patient become anxious over the prospect of paying attention to her anxiety? Perhaps her anxiety made her mother anxious, making her relationship unsafe. If ignoring her anxiety regulated her mother, she could reestablish an insecure attachment. Once she lets go of the defense of ignoring, the feelings her mothering ones could not tolerate will surface. Those feelings in turn trigger anxiety. But if the therapist and patient regulate anxiety, they can build a secure attachment where those feelings can be faced.

Vignette Two: The Defense of Avoiding the Present Moment

To regulate her anxiety, she must pay attention to it. Defenses that distract her will prevent her from regulating her anxiety. All anxiety regulation happens in this moment.

Th: I notice you are anxious. Do you notice that?

Pt: Yes, but I'm afraid of what we are going to get into here. [*Projection: she attributes her wish to get into something. We cannot regulate her anxiety when projection sustains it. First, deactivate the projection.*]

Th: I have no right to get into anything here unless there is something you want to get into. Let me check with you: do you have a problem you want to get into so you can get the results you want for yourself? [*Block the projection of her desire onto you. Then deactivate it by inviting her to declare her problem and positive goals.*]

Pt: I am anxious. It feels fast to look at it. I don't know you yet. [*Projection: she wants to get help fast, a wish she cannot yet tolerate inside herself.*]

Th: Of course. That's why we have to check with you if you want help with this anxiety now. I have no right to help you with it unless you think it would be in your best interest. [*Deactivate the projection of will again.*]

Pt: Okay. But I don't know if I can do it. [*Fragile patients don't take a helpless stance. They describe genuine deficits from which they suffer.*]

Th: Would you like us to help you build that capacity so you could regulate this anxiety? [*Turn the deficit into a positive goal for the therapy.*]

Pt: Yes.

Th: If we take a minute, let's see what sensations you notice in your body now. What do you notice in your stomach? [*Help her pay attention to her body so she can become regulated.*]

Pt: In my stomach?

Th: Yes. What sensations you notice in your stomach? What do you notice sensing in your stomach? [*Help her pay attention to her anxiety symptoms until they disappear.*]

Pt: Lots of times, I get nauseated. [*Defense: her attention goes out of the moment.*]

Th: And now? What do you notice now in your stomach? As you let yourself focus there. [*Return her attention to signs of anxiety in her body in this moment.*]

Pt: I'm a little sick to my stomach, but I think that has to do with—

Th: [*To regulate anxiety, interrupt a defense that will worsen the patient's anxiety. While affect dissociation can preserve an insecure attachment, it prevents anxiety regulation through mutual attention and care.*] And the sickness in your stomach? What do you notice there as you let yourself pay attention to it? What sensations do you notice there? [*Interrupt the defense, then help her pay attention to the anxiety symptom.*]

Principle: To regulate anxiety, keep bringing attention back to the current moment. Fantasies of future dangers or past memories prevent anxiety regulation. Focus on experience in the moment to calm the patient. Then help the patient see the sequence of causality: depending on the therapist evokes feelings that trigger anxiety in the body.

Principle for All Defense Work:
Point out defenses and how they hurt the patient. Then invite patients to engage in the healing task of facing what they usually avoid. At this stage, we help them face their anxiety so we can regulate it.

Defenses That Perpetuate Anxiety

Anxiety regulation is not possible when defenses such as self-attack, splitting, and projection perpetuate the anxiety. Differentiate what causes anxiety from the defenses that sustain it.

Symptoms in the somatic and autonomic nervous systems are triggered by the following:

- Objective dangers (A. Freud 1936)
- Unconscious cues (Freud 1926/1961b; A. Freud 1936), which are paired through conditioning with autonomic nervous system

arousal (H. Davanloo, supervision 2002–2004; LeDoux 1998, 2000, 2002; Panksepp 1998; Panksepp and Biven 2012; Schore 1994, 2003a, 2003b). Mixed feelings trigger anxiety. If you cannot regulate the anxiety, assess the defenses and weaknesses sustaining it. Once you address them, you can regulate anxiety.

Vignette: The Defense of Self-Attack

Suppose a depressed college student feels anger toward his father.

Th: How do you experience this anger toward your father?

Pt: He's right. I'm a terrible son. [*Cries. Self-attack. He feels anger toward his critical father, but he turns the anger on himself to protect the father he loves.*]

Suppose a fragile patient feels anger toward his critical father.

Th: How do you experience this anger toward your father?

Pt: I think he's really angry with me. I'm afraid to visit now. [*Projection: he feels anger, but he projects it on his father and fears it there.*]

The defense of projection keeps him from experiencing his anger inside himself, but there is a price. Rather than feel his anger and strength, he fears his father's "anger."

Here's the same pattern with a more fragile patient.

Th: How do you experience this anger toward your mother?

Pt: The voice is yelling at me now. [*Projection: feeling anger toward her mother makes her too anxious. Rather than yell at her mother, she relocates her rage onto a voice that yells at her.*]

In the first example, the patient feels as if he is being attacked. But he does not realize that self-attack attacks him. In the second and third examples, projection increases the patient's fear of a father or a voice. Since the defenses of self-attack and projection increase anxiety, we must interrupt them before we can regulate anxiety.

Interrupting the Defense of Self-Attack

Some patients feel anxious, as if they are under attack, because the defense of self-attack occurs outside of their awareness. Feeling angry toward a person they love, their unconscious defense protects that loved one by turning the anger back onto themselves.

Pt: I feel like a failure.

Th: Could that be a critical thought? [*Defense identification.*] Could that critical thought be getting you depressed? [*Clarify the defense's price.*] If we look under that thought, could we see what feelings are coming up here with me? What feelings are coming up here with me? [*Invite the patient to feel his feelings toward the therapist so the anger does not go back onto him through self-attack.*]

Interrupt self-attacks immediately. Otherwise, anxiety will shift into the smooth muscles. Depression will worsen. And reality testing can collapse if the patient equates himself with the image of a failure. Once he can feel mixed feelings toward the therapist, anxiety will return to the striated muscles. The patient protects the therapist he loves by turning anger upon himself. Perhaps he did this to keep an insecure attachment in the past. Instead, we offer a secure attachment where his mixed feelings can be accepted.

Examining causality allows us to understand what causes anxiety. Cognitive therapy points out a relationship between rumination and anxiety (A. Beck et al. 1979; A. Beck and Emery 1985). However, it is not a causal relationship. In psychotherapy sessions, unconscious feelings trigger anxiety, and defenses ward them off. Cognitive therapy focuses on the defenses that perpetuate the preexisting anxiety such as rumination, catastrophizing, and projection. As we see in these examples and in figure 1.5, defenses of self-attack and projection perpetuate the anxiety. This feedback loop activates the autonomic nervous system (McEwen and Lasley 2002).

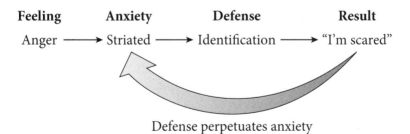

Feeling	Anxiety	Defense	Result
Anger ⟶	Striated ⟶	Identification ⟶	"I'm scared"

Defense perpetuates anxiety

Figure 1.5   Feedback loop to be broken for anxiety regulation

Our anxiety rises when a perceived threat appears and falls when it disappears. When the anxiety drops, the body returns to a state of homeostasis. However, when defenses such as projection persist, chronic projection creates chronic fear of the people on whom the patient projects. Then anxiety remains elevated in the body, a condition known as *allostasis* (Schulkin 2004).

For instance, we must be vigilant regarding dangers. However, fragile patients have to be hypervigilant because they focus on real dangers *plus* the imaginary dangers created by their projections. When vigilant, we relate to reality. If we are hypervigilant, we interact with projections, and safety cannot be found. Interrupt defenses such as self-attack and projection to stop the feedback loop so the patient can feel safe again. From safety, we can explore the feelings triggering anxiety. As we build the patient's capacity to bear those feelings inside without projecting them outside, the risk of relapse will drop.

Principle: *When defenses perpetuate anxiety, help the patient see and let go of these defenses first to make anxiety regulation possible.*

Ego Deficits and Regressive Defenses That Perpetuate Anxiety

Patients become flooded with anxiety when they lose specific capacities for bearing feelings. Restore or build those capacities so anxiety can become regulated.

Lack of Differentiation between the Observing Ego and the Experiencing Self

Some patients become flooded when they lose the *mental boundary* between themselves and their anxiety (Hartmann 1939/1958, 1964; E. Marcus 2017). (See chapter 8 for more on restoring capacities.) They feel as if anxiety is who they are rather than a symptom they can observe in the body. Help the patient differentiate himself from the anxiety he experiences, for instance, through the use of metaphor.

> *Th:* Let's see if we can bring your head up above the anxiety water so we can look and see what's going on down there.

Motion with your hands, as if you are pushing the water down from above your head to below your shoulders to illustrate how to get his head above the anxiety (B. Winstanley, personal communication).

Use language that emphasizes observation to strengthen his ability to differentiate from and observe his anxiety.

> *Th:* Let's *step back* for a moment and see if we can *notice and observe* some bodily symptoms. If we take a moment to *look*, let's *see* where you *notice* symptoms of anxiety happening *in your body.*

When saying this, you might point toward and look at the wall at your side, as if his anxiety is there where you can observe it at a distance. Sometimes a visual metaphor helps patients observe anxiety rather than be flooded by it.

> *Th:* Let's put the anxiety *out here* for a moment [*gesture with your hand from your chest out to the other side of the room*] where we can *look* at it (A. Sheldon, personal communication).

> *Th:* Let's see if we can get you up on the riverbank and on the shore so you can dry off while we observe the anxiety water flowing by.

Projective Anxiety

When anxious, the fragile patient may project aspects of herself onto the therapist, such as feelings, self-critical thoughts, or wishes. Then she experiences those facets as if they are coming back at her. For instance, if she is angry, she figures the therapist is angry with her. If she criticizes herself, she thinks the clinician criticizes her. And she becomes afraid of the projection she imputes to the therapist. This fear of the projection is referred to as *projective anxiety* (H. Davanloo, supervision 2002–2004). We cannot regulate anxiety when projection perpetuates it. We need to deactivate anxiety caused by projections before regulating anxiety triggered by feelings.

- *Projection of declaring a problem:* "What should I work on?"

> *Th:* I don't know since I'm not you. What would you like to work on that you think would be helpful for you? [*Deactivate the projection.*]

- *Projection of positive goals:* "Where are we going here?"

> *Th:* I don't know because this is not my therapy. Since it is your therapy, where would you like the therapy to go that you think would be good for you? [*Deactivate the projection.*]

- *Projection of the ability to think:* "I don't know what to think about this. What do you think?"

Th: I can't know what you should think about this because I'm not you. If you give yourself a moment, what do you think? [*Deactivate the projection.*]

- *Projection of feeling:* An angry man says, "I think you are angry at me." When he projects his anger onto you and believes you are angry, he will fear you. In the following vignette, the therapist helps him see the difference between the therapist and the projection.

Pt: I think you are angry with me.

Th: What's the evidence for that?

Pt: It's the way I feel. [*"If I feel it, that makes it so": failure of reality testing.*]

Th: That's the way you feel. So we need to ask, what is the evidence?

Pt: I just think you are. [*Failure of reality testing.*]

Th: Given you think and feel that, we need to check out whether that is the case. I'm not aware of feeling angry, so I need to ask what the evidence is that you see.

Pt: I don't have any evidence. It's just a feeling. [*Progress in reality testing.*]

Th: It's a feeling. I'm not aware of feeling angry toward you, and you mention you don't have any evidence that I am angry with you.

Pt: What is your point?

Th: My point is this: you were talking about being angry with me for taking a vacation next month. Remember that?

Pt: Yes.

Th: As soon as you felt this anger toward me, you got anxious. And it's as if you asked me to hold your anger because it felt risky to feel it toward me. [*Remind the patient of the triangle of conflict: feeling, anxiety, and defense.*]

Pt: [*Relaxes in his chair: drop of projective anxiety.*] Yes, it did feel risky.

Th: There's no reason you should like my vacation. Shall we take a look at this anger toward me?

Here, the patient projected his anger onto the therapist. It may be useful to differentiate projection from transference:

Projection: The patient attributes a feeling, urge, thought, or capacity to the therapist. Then he denies that it exists in himself.

Neurotic transference: The patient projects an image of another person onto the therapist (Freud 1912/1958c, 1914/1958g, 1915/1958e). For instance, he might view the therapist as if he is like a detached, withholding father. But he can differentiate his therapist from this image. His reality testing remains intact.

Borderline transference: The patient projects an entire relationship onto the therapist. One moment, he feels as if he is being abused by his father. The next moment, he acts like his abusive father toward the therapist. For an instant, he feels and acts like the child. Later, he feels and acts like the father. The roles oscillate (Kernberg et al. 1989). He temporarily loses reality testing.

Psychotic transference: A patient projects onto the therapist and believes his projection is true. The loss of reality testing is permanent (Kernberg 1975, 1977b; Kleiger and Khadivi 2015; E. Marcus 2017).

In the following vignette, a woman has lost her reality testing. She entered the room, sat down trembling, glanced at the therapist, and then gazed at the floor, her legs jumping up and down. If the therapist deactivates the projections she places on him, she can relate to him rather than interact with her projections.

Th: You seem anxious today. What thoughts and ideas are you having about the therapy that could be making you anxious? [*Invite the patient to share her projections so the therapist can deactivate them.*]

Pt: About the therapy?

Th: Yes. What thoughts and ideas are you having about the therapy that could be making you anxious? [*Do not ask for thoughts about the therapist. That could trigger more anxiety when the patient is already overwhelmed. And she might regress.*]

Pt: I feel like I need to be near the door.

Th: What thoughts and ideas are you having about the therapy that make you want to be near the door? [*Inquire into the projections she wants to control. Patients do not try to control you. They try to control a projection they have placed on you.*]

Pt: This room doesn't feel safe.

Th: What thoughts and ideas do you have about the room that make it seem not safe? [*Let the dosage of the patient's words guide interventions. She refers to the "room," displacement from the therapist, so explore her thoughts within her defense.*]

Pt: I like to know that I can get out quickly if I need to. [*A sign of projection. Walking out signals that she equates the therapist with a dangerous projection.*]

Th: Okay. What thoughts and ideas are you having about the room that make your legs feel like getting out? [*Inquire into the projections onto the therapist within the patient's defense: displacement onto the room. Since the legs have an urge, not her, she can observe an urge and reflect on it.*]

Pt: Are you saying I don't have the right to leave the room? [*Projection.*]

Th: You can enter and leave the room whenever you think is best for you. I have no right to ask you to do anything you don't want to do. [*Deactivate the projection.*] Does that make sense to you?

Pt: Yes. I don't want anyone trying to control me. [*She projects onto the therapist, not the room. Progress in affect tolerance.*]

Th: Of course. None of us like that. I have no right to control you. This is your therapy, and, for it to work for you, it has to be under your control. [*Deactivate the projection.*]

Pt: [*Relaxes, a sign I can take the next step and address the transference more directly.*]

Th: With your higher mind, you know that you came here to see this Frederickson guy. And we are here at 3000 Connecticut Avenue. But there's a part of your mind that forgets you are with Frederickson. It's as if there is an image of someone else who comes in here between you and me. [*I take a book and place it in front of my face.*] And then you see this image, but then you have trouble seeing me. [*I pull the book away from my face so she can see me.*] Does that make sense to you?

Pt: I don't know if I can trust you. [*She can tolerate looking at our relationship: progress. However, she still equates me with her projection.*]

Th: Right. Given that you are here, the higher part of your mind trusts Frederickson, the therapist. But the lower part of your mind is operating on some old information. And it relates to an image of some controlling person. [*I place a book in front of my face.*] Could we look at that image [*I tap on the book*] so you and I could work together? And then you wouldn't have to live in so much fear. [*I pull the book away from my face. Speak to the patient's longings to deactivate the projection.*]

Pt: Yes. I don't know why this is coming up, but I'm having a memory about my father.

Th: Before you say more about that, could we check on your anxiety first? [*A memory can quickly trigger overwhelming feelings and anxiety. Each time a new memory or feeling arises, regulate anxiety before exploring it. We want to explore while she feels safe. We are climbing a stairway while building it. Make sure the next step is stable before she puts her foot on it.*]

Pt: [*Small sigh.*] Yes.

Principle: *When the patient cannot differentiate you from the projection, deactivate the projection first before trying to regulate the anxiety. If she views you as dangerous, she cannot trust you to regulate her anxiety.*

When the fragile patient projects, deactivate projections to dissolve the misalliance. We frequently deactivate projections in the sequence seen in table 1.5 to build the alliance.

Table 1.5   Steps in building the alliance and projections to be deactivated

Steps in Building the Alliance	Response: Defense	Therapeutic Task
Declaring a problem	Projection: "You think I have a problem."	Deactivate the projection so the patient can declare his problem.
Declaring one's will to work on the problem	Projection: "You want me to do this."	Deactivate the projection so he can declare his will to work on his problem.
Declaring a positive goal to work toward	Projection: "You want me to work toward a positive goal."	Deactivate the projection so he can declare a positive goal he wants to work toward.

Symbolic Equation

The traumatized patient may equate a memory in the past with reality today. He relives the trauma rather than remembers it. He equates a symbol (memory or fantasy) with reality (Segal 1981). He may equate a feeling today with an experience in the past (reliving a memory or having a flashback). Or he may equate the therapist with a projection.

Some people offer a verbal projection that we need to deactivate. Others may not tell us when they project, but we can see the result: a *freeze reaction*. In a freeze reaction, patients are tense from head to toe. Tension without sighing or wringing of the hands may be a freeze reaction, not a striated muscle discharge of anxiety. These patients engage in thoracic rather than abdominal breathing and suffer from cognitive/perceptual disruption. They project a frightening image onto the therapist. When they fear the therapist whom they equate with the projection, they freeze or go limp (Scaer 2001). A fearful look, shifting gaze, or angry glare are signs of projection.

During the freeze reaction, patients have symptoms of para-sympathetic dominance. Their blood pressure drops, tension goes out of their muscles, and the body is immobilized. Plus, they have symptoms of sympathetic activation: a racing heart. High levels of endorphins cause numbness, amnesia, and impaired memory (Scaer 2001, 17, 2005). To regulate the anxiety, deactivate the projections (see pp. 55-59) and restructure time-space distortion (see pp. 65–72).

As the patient differentiates the therapist from the projection, the freeze response drops, and sighing respiration and hand clenching return. Then you can explore feelings. Reptiles freeze when they cannot flee from a predator. Likewise, children freeze when they cannot break away from an abuser (Scaer 2001, 2005). When patients relive a trauma, they relive the terror and the former freeze response. They cannot separate the past from the present.

Understanding Dissociation

The freeze reaction can also result from a kind of splitting called *dissociation*. Through splitting, an aspect of our experience is isolated and treated as "not-me" (Fairbairn 1952/1969; Freud 1938/1963b; M. Klein 1975b; Sullivan 1953b). Splitting creates dissociation, a separation from our emotional experience.

A relationship with a frightening or frightened caretaker can trigger dissociation (Liotti 1992, 2004) when the child experiences unregulated terror. But the person who should cure the terror is the cause. Unable to escape physically from the parent causing her panic, the child disappears mentally through dissociation, the escape where there is no escape.

The unbearable affect is split up and distributed among diverse "selves" within a story of multiplicity, which implicitly holds together what the client cannot bear inside. She is no longer overwhelmed by the unbearable trauma because the splitting has divided up the feelings and sent them off to live in symbolic selves. However, the more her inner life is split off, the less alive she feels. Dissociation saves her life but at the cost of her aliveness. She no longer feels real.

Later relational experiences trigger memories of early traumas and feelings. When they rise, overwhelming anxiety results. When the fragile patient relives a memory, she cannot think about affects symbolically. For her, a feeling does not remind her of a trauma in her past. Instead, she relives a trauma in the present. She experiences an emotional memory rather than a memory of emotions. To deal with the overwhelming anxiety that arises, she *has* to split those feelings apart.

In *primary dissociation*, split-off somatosensory fragments of an early experience arise, taking the form of flashbacks, nightmares, or intrusive memories (Howell 2005; Nijenhuis 2004; Perry 2005; Schore 2002; Van der Hart, Nijenhuis, and Steele 2006). Primary dissociation keeps experiences split off so that the patient cannot think about or process the trauma. In this form of splitting, she does not recognize her feelings as hers, but as alien elements in her awareness.

Pt: [*Trembling.*] It's like I'm there, and he is coming toward me. [*Reliving a memory when her father abused her.*]

Th: Would that be a memory coming up now? [*Remind the patient of the present moment.*]

Pt: It feels real. [*Reliving rather than remembering a memory of her father's abuse.*]

Th: Of course. It really happened then. And, today [*pause*], as you sit here with me and are looking at me [*pause*], is that a memory that is coming up now in your mind that you are aware of?

[*Ground her in the present moment. Then encourage her to see a memory in her mind, differentiating her as an observer from the memory she observes.*]

Pt: Yes.

Th: As we step back to observe and notice that memory, as you and I sit here in my office on Connecticut Avenue [*ground her in the present*], what is it like to see that memory from the past? [*Differentiate past and present.*]

Pt: [*Freeze reaction in the body drops.*] That is so weird. It felt so real. [*She can observe and intellectualize about the experience.*]

Th: Of course! When a real memory comes up with real feelings, it can feel like the past is alive now when it is just a memory coming up in the present.

Here, the dissociation results from anxiety and can be dealt with by restoring the patient's reality testing.

In *secondary dissociation*, the patient experiences himself as having left his body and observing the trauma from afar. Splitting distances him from his feelings, anaesthetizing them so he cannot experience or process his emotional experience. As a result, he suffers from an altered sense of time, out-of-body experiences, changed pain perception or numbness, disorientation, and depersonalization. With pain split off, what remains seems unreal.

Pt: I'm not here. I'm back on the wall here. [*Dissociation.*]

Th: Wonderful you notice. And as you give yourself permission to be back on the wall, what do you notice feeling? [*Encourage the defense to reduce the fragile patient's anxiety.*]

Pt: I'm still there.

Th: Good. As you let yourself be on the wall as long as you need to, what do you notice feeling as you let yourself be on the wall? [*Encourage the defense to reduce the fragile patient's anxiety.*]

Pt: I feel calmer now.

Th: How do you experience that calm? [*Ground the patient in his new experience of decreased anxiety.*]

Pt: Not so anxious.

Th: What's that like?

Pt: Feels good.

Th: And what feelings come up here that might have made your body go onto the wall? [*Once anxiety is regulated, explore the feelings that triggered the defense of dissociation.*]

Pt: For some reason, I'm feeling irritated. [*Feeling.*]

Th: For some reason, irritation comes up here. You became anxious. Then it was as if you left your body. [*Describe the triangle of conflict: feeling, anxiety, and the defense of dissociation.*] Do you notice that too?

Pt: I didn't. But I see what you are saying.

Th: Wouldn't it be nice to be able to feel this irritation without leaving your body so you could assert yourself more effectively? [*Invite the patient's will to work toward a positive goal.*]

Pt: Yes. That would be nice.

Th: Let's take a look. How do you experience that irritation here toward me? [*Invite his mixed feelings toward me.*]

Pt: I'm getting dizzy. [*Anxiety going into cognitive/perceptual disruption.*]

By reinforcing the defense, the therapist reduces the patient's anxiety, making it safer for him to feel his forbidden feelings. These mixed feelings derive from the patient's past traumas. We are dealing with a memory of the past and his affect tolerance in the present. As we keep building his affect tolerance, he will be able to face and bear his affect-laden memories without suffering from excessive anxiety. Then he will no longer need to split off those feelings and dissociate.

Principle: *When the patient dissociates, regulate anxiety first. Then help the patient face the mixed feelings toward you he split off through dissociation. Build his affect tolerance until splitting and dissociation are no longer necessary.*

In *tertiary dissociation*, the patient splits apart her feelings and her abilities to think, feel, and perceive. She relocates these capacities in distinct states that contain parts of the trauma experience. Each state contains different cognitive, affective, and behavioral patterns. And she may regard these split-off states as selves.

Pt: Jane thinks I shouldn't be here. [*Referring to a split-off self.*]

Th: I wonder what feelings Jane has about therapy that make her think you shouldn't be here? [*Explore feelings within the defense of splitting.*]

Pt: She says she is angry with you. [*Feeling within the defense of splitting.*]

Th: How does she experience this anger toward me? [*Explore feelings within the defense of splitting.*]

Pt: She doesn't want to talk about it. [*Defense.*]

Th: That would be a way for Jane to avoid talking about her anger. Why is she afraid to talk about her anger? After all, it's only an emotion. [*Explore the patient's fear of anger within the defense of splitting.*]

When primitive splitting creates a split-off personality, the therapist can explore feelings within the defense. As the patient's affect tolerance increases, she will be able to accept her feelings directly without splitting them off and projecting them onto a split-off self. (See "Graded Invitation to Feelings within Dissociation" on pp. 214–215 and 221–222 for an example of exploring within the defense of dissociation.)

The patient may equate herself with each self that emerges. This is symbolic equation (Segal 1981). She equates the whole of herself as a person with a fragment of her experience she labels as a "self." The term *self* is a concept, and no patient is a concept. She is the awareness in which concepts appear. But, as a child, neither she nor her parents could bear her experience. The fewer feelings they could bear, the more she had to split off and project—hoping they could accept what was left.

If a dropped plate shattered into fragments, we would not equate any piece with the plate. Likewise, in therapy, we put together split-apart and projected feelings and experiences. The patient can gradually bear her inner life inside rather than split off and project it outside. All the chapters in this book show different ways to address splitting and dissociation. Here, we will focus on how to regulate anxiety before splitting and dissociation occur. And we need to differentiate anxiety symptoms of cognitive/perceptual disruption (blanking out, trouble thinking, or dizziness) that precede the defense of splitting, which creates the symptoms of dissociation (flashbacks, out of body experiences, or multiple personalities). [For more on the confusion between the person and selves or parts, see Frederickson (2000, 2003, 2005).]

Vignette One: Equating a Memory of the Past with Reality in the Present

When the patient relives a past trauma with an abuser, she loses contact with the therapist. We do not want her to relive a past trauma but to rewrite it. Help her remember and work through feelings from the past while anxiety is regulated. Then she can differentiate the present from the past. In the following vignette, the therapist has asked the patient what she feels toward her abusive mother. She hides her hands, freezes, and braces herself.

Th: You seem to be bracing yourself. What is happening inside?

Pt: I feel anxious.

Th: I see that. How do you experience this anxiety in your body?

Pt: I see her coming at me with the knife. [*Primary dissociation: she loses the distinction between reality in the present and a memory from the past.*]

Th: Would that be a memory that comes up in your mind right now? [*Ask a question to mobilize her thinking and capacity to reflect. Differentiate the past from the present.*]

Pt: She's coming toward me. [*She is still reliving the memory.*]

Th: As you look here at me, could you tell me when this memory occurred? How old were you? [*Orient her to the present by inviting her to look at the therapist. Then invite her to think about the past.*]

Pt: [*Looks at the therapist.*] The date? [*She is confused, still in the flashback.*]

Th: Yes. As we step back for a moment, you and I together here, what date would that have taken place? Would that be 1995, do you think? [*Orient her to the present, and invite her to observe the past from the present. Ask a question to help her think about the past rather than relive it.*]

Pt: I'm not sure. I would have been about five, so that would have been about 1990, I think. [*She can reflect on the memory rather than relive it. From this point of safety, we can explore her memory. When a patient is drowning in anxiety, pull her out of the river. Invite her to cognize in the present about the past.*]

Th: About 1990. Okay. *Let's step back and look* at what happened. When you started to remember your mom, you began to relive the memory. Do you see that now too? [*Invite the patient to reflect and summarize what happened in the therapy. The italicized words help her differentiate herself as an observer from the experience she observes.*]

Pt: Yes. That happens a lot. [*Rising feelings and anxiety overwhelms her reality testing.*]

Th: Would it make sense that we explore your feelings slowly so you can process what you feel without having these flashbacks? [*Orient her to the therapeutic task and get her will online. This deactivates the projection that the therapist will come after her like her mother did.*]

Pt: [*Sighs.*] Yes. I don't like it when they come at me like that.

Vignette Two: Equating an Image from the Past with the Therapist

When the patient relives a past trauma, anxiety overwhelms him. To prevent retraumatization, we help him differentiate the past image from the present therapist. A middle-aged man in his third session describes his reactions to learning that he dissociates in therapy. He suffered massive physical abuse as a child.

Th: What are you feeling right now?

Pt: Anxious.

Th: That's what I thought. Where do you notice that anxiety in your body right now?

Pt: In my chest and in my legs.

Th: What do you notice in your legs?

Pt: They're jumpy. [*Patients do not want to run from the therapist but from the projection they place on the therapist. The previous invitations to feeling triggered no sighs. This is consistent with cognitive/perceptual disruption.*]

Th: They are jumpy. You have a connection with me in the present, and then we see anxiety come up. And we know we have been talking about how you and your wife can be even more connected. And we're trying to help you with anxiety because we saw last time that there's connection, anxiety, and then blip [*secondary dissociation*], right?

Pt: Yes.

Th: This is progress because you're present with me, and you are feeling anxiety without a blip.

Pt: Yes.

Th: That's progress. Right now, you're feeling this anxiety as a jumpiness in your legs? [*The "jumpiness" in his legs is the wish to run from a projection. Help him observe his impulse rather than act on it.*]

Pt: Yeah.

Th: How do you experience the jumpiness in your legs?

Pt: It's like a pressure in my legs. Yesterday I felt that same thing, and I had to keep moving my legs. I kept—they didn't feel comfortable in any position I put them.

Th: When you say that the legs feel jumpy. What are your legs wanting to do? [*That phrase allows him to observe the impulse rather than act on it.*]

Pt: Move.

Th: Are they wanting to jump? Are they wanting to run? If they did what they wanted to do, what would they do?

Pt: If they were doing like last time I was here, they'd want to jump and then run.

Th: They'd want to jump. What do you notice feeling right now?

Pt: Tension. [*We have tension but no sighs. Anxiety is not yet in the striated muscles.*]

Th: What do you notice feeling in your arms? [*An unconscious impulse has arisen in his arms.*] Because you notice your arms are like this. [*Grabbing position.*] What's that? What are those arms wanting to do?

Pt: Not sure. They're—they're kind of locked into position.

Th: They're locking into position. What are those arms wanting to do?

Pt: Well, the most comfortable position is like this. [*Places arms to his side at rest—defense.*]

Th: Yes, but they were doing something else, weren't they? There was this jumpiness in the legs and the arms. What do you notice in those arms?

Pt: They want to do something.

Th: What is that? What is it they want to do?

Pt: Protect myself. I felt comfortable protecting myself like this. [*Crosses arms across his chest: defense against the grabbing impulse.*] And I think I was saying to myself, I don't want to protect myself. I want to move forward, and if I protect myself, I'm not going to be able to. [*Defense against the grabbing impulse.*]

Th: But you know what? Your body is telling us at some point in your life you had to protect yourself, or you couldn't, right?

Pt: Mm-hmm.

Th: And it's telling me that right now. I want us to listen to your body because at some point you apparently had to not listen to it. I don't know when that was. Maybe you'll figure that out. But right now, I'm seeing your body's having this reaction as we have this connection because you know you're sitting here with me, a mild-mannered therapist on Connecticut Avenue. But we're seeing your body is having a different experience. Your body's not here with me. Your body is with someone else. Your body is with somebody where you're feeling like you've got to jump and protect yourself or jump and run. [*Address time-space distortion. The present is not the past (Rothschild 2003). Differentiate the real relationship from the projection.*]

Pt: Okay.

Th: It's sort of like we're having a relationship in stereo.

Pt: Okay.

Th: We've got two tracks right now. We've got a good connection. You're wanting to connect with me. And I'm wanting to connect with you. But your body is telling me you're having a relationship with someone who's apparently dangerous, whom you want to protect yourself from or run away from. [*Distinguish the therapeutic alliance in the here and now from a projection based on the past (Bateman and Fonagy 2004; Fonagy et al. 2002).*]

Pt: Right.

Th: And that's getting in the way because you've been talking about how you and your wife have trouble making love. It's hard if this protecting and running and jumping urge is coming up in bed, right?

Pt: That's true.

Th: It's impossible, right? We're trying to help you with what your body does. I want us to really listen because you're here wanting to connect with me. But your body is doing something different. And we have to listen to what happens because in connecting here with me, you got jumpy. [*His anxiety drops as we differentiate the therapist from the projection.*]

Pt: Okay.

Th: Then there's this urge to jump, and then the arms are wanting to protect you. How are the arms wanting to protect you?

Pt: More like—more like this. [*Crosses his arms in front of himself—defense.*]

Th: There's this, and then there's this. [*The therapist imitates the two defensive gestures.*] But I also saw your hands are doing this. [*The therapist imitates the impulse gesture.*] And I want to pay attention. What's that? What are the arms wanting to do when they're like that [*in the grabbing position*]?

Pt: The thing that comes to mind that doesn't make any sense is that I want to put my hands around my father's neck and choke the life out of him. [*A murderous impulse toward his father emerges. He holds his hands in front of his face as if strangling his father.*]

Th: Okay.

Pt: But that's with my hands in this position.

Th: Do I have your permission for us to go there? [*Invite the patient's will.*]

Pt: [*Nods.*]

His jumpy legs reveal his anxiety *and* his projection. He mistakes the therapist for his abusive father. He is not conscious of his projection, but his body reacts as if he is in danger. To reduce the risk of his acting out, invite him to observe the urge to run and put it into words. Next, help him see the difference between present and past, here and there, the therapist and someone else, the therapeutic alliance and a past relationship. As those distinctions become clear to him, his anxiety drops, and his body relaxes. And murderous rage emerges toward his father.

Principle: *When the patient dissociates and is about to act out in response to a projection, (1) identify the sequence of closeness, anxiety, and dissociation, (2) invite the patient to notice the urge without enacting it, and (3) build his capacity to notice feelings without enacting them until a memory emerges. Then remembering in words replaces reliving a trauma.*

Vignette Three: Equating Fantasy with Reality

Some fragile patients, especially those with panic disorder, equate their fantasies with reality. Their conflicts often involve rage toward people they love, which triggers anxiety. But equating a fantasy with reality can perpetuate their anxiety.

In the following vignette, a woman has called the therapist's office crying hysterically. She arrives at her session twenty minutes later, hyperventilating. She had a panic attack in the car and got lost on her way to the appointment. Her daughter had recently gotten into legal trouble due to alcoholism. And the patient fears her daughter could lose her job.

Pt: I'm afraid she could die if she does not get into rehab. [*Speech races. Anxiety rises.*] Do you mind if I call her right now to find out if she is still alive? [*She feels murderous rage toward her daughter. But she wards off her anger by turning her wish into a fear her daughter is dead. Often, a conscious fear is an unconscious wish. She calls the daughter to reassure herself that her unconscious wish has not come true. She cannot distinguish fantasy from reality. First, we regulate her anxiety.*]

Th: You seem anxious right now. Do you notice that too? [*Interrupt her defense of rumination to draw her attention to her anxiety.*]

Pt: Yes, do you mind if I call?

Th: Before you do that, can we pay attention to this anxiety? [*Block the defense and return her attention to her anxiety.*] You were so anxious before you got here that you said your eyes were blurry. Right? [*Identify her anxiety symptoms.*]

Pt: Yes.

Th: That's a serious sign of anxiety. Then you got lost, which means your anxiety was so high that your mind wasn't working right. Would you agree?

Pt: Yes, I was terribly anxious. [*Intervene immediately before a defense distracts her from her anxiety. Then keep her attention on it until we regulate it. Rapid intervention supports her when defenses would dysregulate her. Flooded with anxiety, she can barely think about one thing (anxiety), much less two things (anxiety and defense). Tailor interventions to the patient's capacity when anxiety impairs thinking. Block her defenses and focus on only her anxiety.*]

Th: Let's pay attention to this anxiety that has been so torturous to you today. Where do you notice feeling tension in your body? [*Mobilize her attention to symptoms of anxiety in her body. Invite her to pay attention to one symptom until the symptom decreases or disappears. Then invite her to pay attention to another symptom. Five minutes later, she is calmer.*] How is your vision now?

Pt: My vision is fine now.

Th: And how is your thinking?

Pt: Much better—it's not racing so much.

Th: That's another sign your anxiety has dropped. How is your breathing?

Pt: It's much better now. I was having trouble breathing, like I was choking.

Th: But now, in this moment?

Pt: Now the breathing is fine.

Th: We see that your anxiety was extremely high, your vision was blurry. Your thinking was racing, your breathing was difficult, but now your vision is fine. Your thinking is fine, and your breathing is easy. You are calm now. I assume you were not anxious when you began driving here today.

Pt: No, I was fine. I was looking forward to seeing you today.

Th: I wonder, what happened on the way to my office that triggered so much anxiety? [*Her anxiety has dropped, and she can intellectualize. Now we can safely explore what triggered her panic attack.*]

Pt: Nothing. [*Unconscious denial.*] I talked to my husband. And he told me that my daughter did not follow the judge's instructions, so she could end up in jail. [*She does not see that this stimulus triggered her feelings and panic attack.*]

Th: Even though the judge had told her, and you had told her.

Pt: Yes!

Th: What are you feeling toward your daughter for sabotaging herself like that? [*Invite feelings.*]

Pt: I was angry.

Th: You were angry with your daughter. The anger made you anxious, and then you had a panic attack. [*Describe her conflict.*]

Pt: To punish myself.

Th: You were angry. You became anxious. Then you punished your-self with a panic attack, punishing yourself with a horrible fantasy that she would die. [*Describe her conflict.*]

Pt: But she could.

Th: That's not the point. The point is you have punished yourself many times for your anger by imagining her dead. [*Help her see how anger toward her daughter triggered her imaginary fantasies and panic attacks.*]

Pt: I see. It's a way to hurt myself.

Th: Right. Suppose a friend of yours had a problem with her daugh-ter. Would you torture her by whispering in her ear all day long, "Your daughter could die!"

Pt: Of course not.

Th: Why not?

Pt: Because it would be cruel and not true.

Th: And the same is true if you do it to yourself.

Pt: I see. [*She is much calmer because she can distinguish fantasy from reality and no longer punishes herself in the session.*]

Regulate her anxiety. Describe causality: rising feelings trigger anxiety, and she uses a defense that causes her symptoms. When her mind can function again, explore her feelings. Later, she explored her rage toward her daughter.

Vignette Four: Transient Pseudodelusion

When flooded by anxiety, severely fragile patients may experi-ence a pseudodelusion, a fixed belief contrary to evidence that has a defensive function. Pseudodelusions resolve when we address splitting and projection in patients with a borderline level of character structure (Kernberg 1975, 1977a, 1977b; E. Marcus 2017).

A *transient pseudodelusion* can heighten anxiety. In the following vignette, a woman suffers from panic attacks and frequent problems in reality testing. The therapist explores her anxiety after she felt angry with her son.

Th: Where do you notice this anxiety in your belly? [*Explore her symptoms and mobilize her attention to her anxiety.*]

Pt: Right here, like acid in my stomach. [*Anxiety in the smooth muscles.*]

Th: Where else do you notice anxiety in your body?

Pt: [*Becomes weepy and more anxious.*] I feel like maybe I have my babies in my belly. Pregnant.

Her rage triggers anxiety and the defense of a delusion. In effect, she says, "I am not a mother who feels rage toward my children. I want to give birth to them." The breakdown of the boundary between reality and fantasy triggers more anxiety. To improve her reality testing, remind her of concrete facts that contradict the delusion and regulate her anxiety.

Th: It's like your babies are in your belly.

Pt: Uh-huh, and I am trying to keep them from being—[*Rise in anxiety and weepiness. She does not distinguish between reality and her delusion.*]

Th: As you look at your belly, are you pregnant? [*Draw attention to reality.*]

Pt: [*Looks at her belly.*] No, but it feels that way. [*Cries.*]

Th: But are you pregnant, as you look there? [*Remind her of reality.*]

Pt: [*Looks at her belly.*] No. [*Cries.*]

Th: Are Jim and Jane [her children] in your belly right now? [*Remind her of reality.*]

Pt: But it reminds me of Jim. [*Still does not differentiate reality from fantasy.*]

Th: But are Jim and Jane in your belly? [*Remind her of reality.*]

Pt: No, they are not. [*She calms down and takes off her coat. With the clear differentiation between reality and delusion, her anxiety drops.*]

Th: They're not in your belly. What do you notice feeling in your belly now?

Pt: [*Sighs.*] A little better there. [*The return of sighing signals a drop in her anxiety.*]

Th: Are you pregnant as you look there? [*Remind her of reality.*]

Pt: [*Calmly.*] No.

Th: Are Jim and Jane in your belly? [*Remind her of reality.*]

Pt: [*Calmly*] No. They are not here.

Th: Would you agree they are probably too big to be in your belly now? [*Remind her of reality.*]

Pt: [*Laughs and smiles.*] Yes. [*Her children are adults. As she differentiates reality from delusion, her anxiety drops further.*]

Th: How is your belly now?

Pt: The pain is still there, but it is smaller.

Later, the therapist can point out causality: "You felt rage toward your son, and it made you anxious. And you tried to hide your rage toward him since you love him. So your mind imagined that you want only to be pregnant with him."

Transient delusions occur when anxiety goes into cognitive/perceptual disruption. First, address reality testing. Then regulate anxiety and point out the causality of feelings, anxiety, and defense. Do not explore the content of delusions when anxiety is too high for her to distinguish between reality and fantasy. Instead, help reflect on her delusion and think about it. She cannot think about the raging river when she is drowning in it.

The delusion's content is not as important initially as its function: to ward off feelings. Pay attention not to the delusion but to the person who has it. Since her loss of reality testing was temporary, this was a pseudodelusion (E. Marcus 2017). (See figure 1.6 and chapter 12 on severe fragility.)

Principle: *To address reality-testing problems, first try to regulate the anxiety. If this does not help, address ego weaknesses or projections perpetuating it.*

To address the ego deficits or projections, do one of the following:
- *Pseudodelusions:* Remind the patient of reality to deactivate a pseudodelusion: "As you look at your belly, are you pregnant?"

Principle: *When unconscious feelings cause excessive anxiety, regulate it. Then help the patient face the feelings to build her affect tolerance. Restructure defenses or weaknesses that perpetuate anxiety. When projective anxiety or anxiety resulting from defenses drops, regulate anxiety resulting from feelings.*

- *Weaknesses:* Regulate anxiety, show causality, and then explore feelings. (See chapter 8 on restoring capacities.)

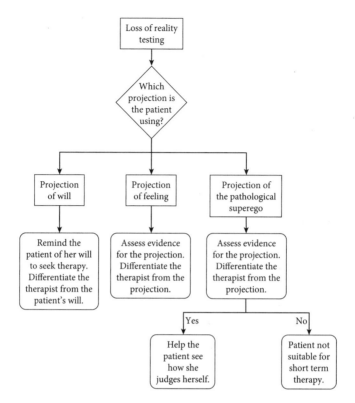

Figure 1.6   Decision tree for restructuring the loss of reality testing

- *Self-attack*: Help the patient differentiate herself from and let go of the defense. Then explore the feelings she warded off.
- *Projection*: Deactivate the projection and the resulting projective anxiety. Regulate anxiety due to feelings. Then explore feelings. (See chapters 11 on projection and 12 on severe fragility.)
- *Splitting*: Draw the patient's attention to contradictory realities to build the capacity to bear mixed feelings while anxiety is regulated. (See chapters 10 on splitting and 12 on severe fragility.)

WHY DON'T I SEE ANXIETY SIGNALING? COMMON PROBLEMS IN ANXIETY REGULATION

Fragile patients show no anxiety in the striated muscles when anxiety goes into cognitive/perceptual disruption or a feeling is projected onto someone else. And anxiety will not rise if the therapist does not explore feelings. However, the lack of unconscious signaling of anxiety can occur for other reasons (Abbass 2004; Abbass, Lovas, and Purdy 2008; Abbass 2015, chap. 7; Frederickson 2013):

- *Involuntary referral:* If the patient does not want to do therapy or share his feelings, he will feel no anxiety.

  Solution: Explore his lack of desire. Accept him as he is: a man who doesn't want to be in therapy finds himself in a therapist's office. Invite him to talk about this. If necessary, leave the door open for him to return when he is in a different stage of the change process (W. Miller and Rollnick 2002; Prochaska and Norcross 2007). (See chapter 3 on will and chapter 9 on denial.)

Pt: I don't want to be in therapy.

Th: I have no right to ask you to do something if you don't want to.

- *Ambivalence:* The patient has one foot in and one foot out. If she does not want therapy, no feelings or anxiety will rise.

  Solution: Accept and explore ambivalence.

Th: Is it your will to look at this problem?

Pt: Yes, but I don't know if now is the best time.

Th: I have no right to ask you to work on this problem before you are ready to do so.

If you bypass her ambivalence, she will become more resistant. Instead, accept and explore her ambivalence. Avoid a conflict with her so she can experience the conflict between her wish for help and her avoidance of it.

- *Projection of the wish for therapy:* If the patient reacts to your imagined desire, therapy will not be based on his desire.

  Solution: Deactivate the projection and find out if the patient wants to do something good for himself in therapy.

Pt: I don't know if now is the best time.

Th: Since this is not my problem, I cannot know either. That's why I have to ask you if it is your wish to be here to do something good for yourself.

- *Hesitation:* The patient hesitates to engage in therapy.

  Solution: Help her experience her internal conflict.

Pt: I'm not sure I want to do this.

Th: You come to therapy, and you're not sure you want to do therapy. It's good you notice that. How do you experience this struggle inside yourself? [*There is no conflict between you and her. Her reluctance conflicts with her wish for help. Accept her conflict as it is so she can see it in herself.*]

- *Compliance:* If she does therapy to please someone else, she projects her will to do therapy onto that person.
  Solution: Deactivate the projection until she declares a problem she wants to work on for her benefit.

Pt: My mom thought I should come here.

Th: But therapy is not something we can do to please her. Our task is to find out what you want out of your therapy that would please you. What do you want to work on here that you think would help you and achieve your goals?

- *No need for therapy:* If you work in a hospital or a large office building, a person may have come to the wrong office while seeking a different professional.
  Solution: Refer the patient to the correct treatment or nontreatment. For example, a man came to me for short-term therapy. But he had suffered a serious head injury in a recent automobile accident. This caused problems of executive functioning, balance, proprioception, and physical pain. He did not need psychotherapy yet. He needed physical therapy, neurofeedback, and psychoeducation to recover from brain injury.

- *Organic or brain factors:* The patient may experience genuine confusion about the therapeutic process. This could result from brain injury, below-average intelligence, neurodevelopmental deficits, or physical illness and exhaustion.
  Solution: Explain the therapeutic task clearly for people with below-average intelligence to get a conscious therapeutic alliance. Do supportive psychotherapy with physically ill patients until they recover the strength to engage in exploratory therapy.

- *Discharge of anxiety into the smooth muscles or cognitive/perceptual disruption:* The patient may appear calm because her anxiety is discharged into the smooth muscles and cognitive/perceptual disruption instead of tension.
  Solution: Regulate anxiety until it returns to the striated muscles.

- *Discharge of anxiety through subtle tensing or hiding the tension consciously:* The patient can get rid of his anxiety by chewing gum, so it does not show up elsewhere in the body.

  Solution: Ask him to take out the gum. Then, anxiety will appear in the body, becoming more palpable to him and more visible to the therapist. However, if a severely fragile patient chews gum in the initial session, it may be best to ignore the gum chewing for the first session. First, regulate his anxiety and deactivate his projections. Once he sighs, you can ask him to take his gum out. Without this defense, his anxiety will rise again, so regulate it. If you ask him to take out the gum while he is experiencing cognitive/perceptual disruption, his anxiety will rise even more, possibly causing projection and a loss of reality testing.

- *Hiding of unconscious feelings through character defenses:* Character defenses can manifest as defiance, compliance, passivity, helplessness, hyperintellectualization, denial, splitting, projection, or projective identification. For instance, the patient can defy or comply with a projection he places on you. Or he may remain passive while projecting his will upon you. If he projects that you will criticize him, he may talk over you to prevent the criticism he expects. These defenses are all secondary to the primary defense of projection. He is not reacting to you but to the projection he places upon you.

  Solution: Once you deactivate projections to which he is reacting, he will become less afraid of you. As his anxiety shifts back into the striated muscles, signaling will resume in the body.

- *Repression:* Sighing stops when the patient turns anger onto himself to protect someone he loves. He can do this through weepiness, self-attack, somatization, or character defenses. When he turns anger onto himself, he will become depressed and, perhaps, suicidal. The defense of self-attack can prevent anxiety from rising in the striated muscles. He feels only love toward the other, not the mixed feelings of love and rage that would trigger anxiety.

  Solution: Help him see and let go of his defenses. As he lets go of self-attack, he will feel mixed feelings toward the therapist. Invite him to share these mixed feelings toward you when sighing occurs. Then anxiety will move into the striated muscles.

- *Errors in technique:* No unconscious anxiety will rise if the therapist supports the patient's defenses. Agreeing that others are all-good or all-bad supports splitting and projection, preventing the rise of mixed feelings and anxiety. Exploring pure rage toward an all-bad person reinforces splitting and projection. Likewise, idealizing the therapist supports splitting, preventing him from developing the capacity to bear mixed emotions toward people. Challenging the fragile patient's defenses prematurely will cause feelings and anxiety to spike. That may cause cognitive/perceptual disruption or projection, and he will feel attacked. This misalliance will trigger conscious, split-off anger but not unconscious anxiety due to mixed feelings.
  Solution: Rather than challenge unhelpful defenses, encourage patients to do the opposite: to face what they usually avoid.

- *Splitting:* Fragile patients who split may not exhibit any anxiety because their mixed feelings cannot come together to trigger it.
  Solution: Remind people of contradictory facts to build the capacity to bear mixed feelings. As they let go of splitting, anxiety will rise in the striated muscles. (See chapter 10 on splitting.)

- *Projection:* Desire projected onto others will not trigger anxiety in the patient.
  Solution: Help patients bear their desires inside without projecting them outside. As their capacity grows, anxiety will rise again in the striated muscles. (See chapter 3 on will and chapter 11 on projection.)

- *Low affect tolerance while restructuring the pathway of anxiety discharge:* Fragile patients bearing mixed feelings at very low levels may not sigh or show tension.
  Solution: Help them bear mixed feelings while cognizing rather than engage in splitting and projection. As their affect tolerance increases, they will tense up and intellectualize, and small sighs will occur.

- *Overmedication:* Patients may appear emotionally flat if they are taking psychotropic or pain medications. They show no sighing or tension.

Solution: Consult with the psychiatrist. Reducing medications can help overmedicated fragile people experience their anxiety and learn what triggers it.

- *Illegal substances:* Patients under the influence of drugs may fidget, squirm in the chair, and speak in a pressured manner. However, they do not sigh systematically when we explore feelings.

  Solution: Explore feelings to see if anxiety rises. If there is no shift in anxiety, inquire about drug use. If he denies using, do a drug screen. A positive urine test indicates that he may require a higher level of care.

- *Reality stressors:* Fragile patients may face overwhelming circumstances such as eviction, abusive partners, unemployment, and poverty. Facing the fear of survival, the patient does not have the free space to think about lesser priorities.

  Solution: Regulate the patient's anxiety while recognizing the stressors the patient faces. Help her cope with her situation by asking how she has dealt with past stressors. When the patient feels hopeless, she is temporarily overwhelmed. Hold onto your perspective even when she has lost hers. Your calm will calm her. You might empathize while offering a covert hope, "I can understand how it looks that way right now." "Right now" implies that it may not always be this bad. To help her reflect, ask her, "If you were talking to someone else who has this problem, what would you suggest to her?" When working with severely ill patients suffering under reality stressors, sometimes we have to let go of our usual therapeutic focus. Help her with her crisis until her life has stabilized, her fear of survival has abated, and her anxiety is regulated again. Basic needs come first. Freud's (1909/1955) session notes for one of his unemployed patients read, "He was hungry and was fed." Never forget the violence of poverty and the devastation it inflicts on our patients (Azzi-Lessing 2017). One of the strongest predictive factors for psychotic symptoms is relative poverty (Pickett and Wilkinson 2009).

Common Misconceptions: Anxiety Is Not a Stimulus

We cannot deal effectively with anxiety if misconceptions hamper us. For instance, psychotherapy literature has described anxiety in terms of stimuli: separation anxiety, fear of losing a loved one; castration anxiety, fear of damage to your body or genitals; moral anxiety, fear of transgressing one's values; annihilation anxiety, fear of being invaded and destroyed; fragmentation anxiety, fear of self-disintegration; and persecutory anxiety, fear that others want to hurt you (Waelder 1960). If someone threatens to abandon you, you will feel anxiety. However, the threat is the external stimulus, not the internal anxiety it triggers in the body.

Anxiety is a feeling that has a specific and unique function: to signal when potentially dangerous feelings rise in a relationship. Thus, we explore the feelings toward which the anxiety points. Just as fear points to an objective danger, anxiety points toward a relational danger.

Th: What is the feeling toward your boyfriend?

Pt: I feel abandoned.

Th: Of course! He abandoned you. That's what he did. What is the feeling toward him for doing that? [*Differentiate the stimulus (the boyfriend's deed) from her feeling.*]

Common Misconceptions: Anxiety Is Not a Thought

Anxiety is not a thought in the head; it is an experience in the body. (See table 1.6.) A student is furious with a professor who gave him a poor grade. Afterward, he imagines that the professor is angry with him. Then he fears the teacher's anger. Anger triggers his anxiety. However, once he relocates his feeling, he believes the angry professor makes him anxious. In fact, the patient's anger causes his anxiety; projection creates his thought about the professor.

Table 1.6   The causality of anxiety

Sequence in Time	Element of Conflict	Description
1	Feeling	"I am angry with him."
2	Anxiety (bodily experience)	Blurry vision, ringing in the ears, and nausea
3	Defense (projection)	"I am not angry. My professor is angry with me."
4	Consequence (thought)	"I fear him." The patient fears the projection he has placed on the professor.

Common Mistakes When Assessing Anxiety

Since most therapists have not been taught how to assess anxiety signals in the body, it's very easy to make mistakes. (See figure 1.7.) The following list illustrates the most common ones.

- *Failing to assess all the anxiety pathways:* A patient exhibits striated muscle tension. However, the therapist does not assess all the anxiety pathways. Mildly fragile patients will experience anxiety in striated muscles at very low levels of feeling. But it shifts into the smooth muscles at a moderate level of feeling. That is the first threshold. Then they experience cognitive/perceptual disruption at a higher level of feelings. Thus, we might find three different pathways of anxiety discharge at three levels of affect intensity. Assess for the threshold when anxiety shifts out of the striated muscles.

- *Not remembering that symptoms of smooth muscle discharge or cognitive/perceptual disruption can disguise anxiety:* A woman appears calm and limp. The therapist might assume she has no anxiety. As a result, he might miss invisible symptoms of anxiety in the smooth muscles or cognitive/perceptual disruption. Explore those symptoms and ask the patient to tell you whenever they occur.

Th: I'm pretty good at assessing anxiety, but these symptoms in your stomach, vision, hearing, and head are invisible to me. So I need you to help me. Any time you have those symptoms, let me know right away so we can regulate your anxiety as soon as possible.

- *Forgetting to explore feelings and observe causality:* A man appears calm. The therapist might assume he has anxiety in the smooth muscles or cognitive/perceptual disruption. But without exploring issues, we cannot assess how the patient responds as feelings rise. We need that information to assess the pathways of anxiety discharge and to find the level of feelings where anxiety moves out of the striated muscles. Once we find that threshold of anxiety tolerance, we know where to build the patient's capacity.

- *Rushing ahead with fragile patients:* A patient can observe her anxiety. But the therapist might rush ahead without assessing

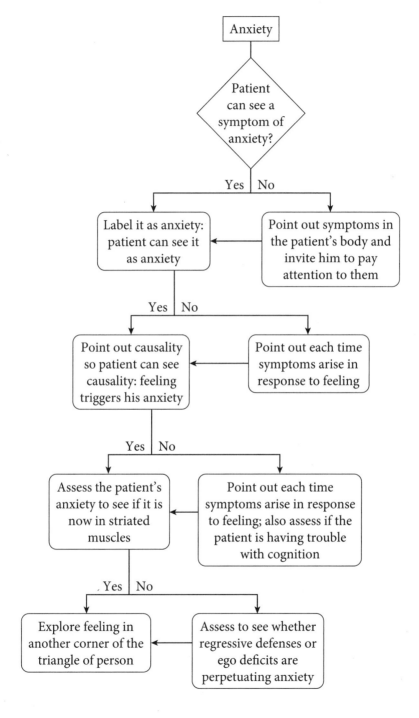

Figure 1.7   Decision tree for regulating anxiety

whether she can pay attention to and regulate it. She may observe her anxiety but then ignore it, preventing anxiety regulation. Until she can pay attention to and regulate her anxiety, inviting feelings will make her too anxious. Go slow with fragile patients to build their capacity.

- *Prematurely exploring feelings before anxiety is regulated:* Pursuing feelings when anxiety goes into the smooth muscles or cognitive/perceptual disruption results in stomachaches, headaches, increasing depression, dissociation, and projection. The patient suffers from excessive anxiety. The therapeutic goal is not to face one's feelings while paralyzed with anxiety. The goal is to experience one's feelings deeply while anxiety stays in the striated muscles—the *window of tolerance* (Siegel 1999).

- *Mistaking weepiness for genuine grief:* Inviting feelings when the patient becomes weepy and depressed takes her further over the threshold of anxiety tolerance. Several signals tell us that her defense of weepiness is not grief. Weepiness does not trigger anxiety in the form of sighs. Nor do defenses block the weepiness because weepiness is a defense. Further, after a passage of weepiness, the patient feels no relief or increased cognitive clarity. Instead, she feels more depressed. (See Frederickson 2013, 329–336.) In contrast, grief triggers anxiety and defense. And, after grieving, the patient feels greater relief, clarity, and insight about her life.

- *Assuming anxiety is in striated muscles without substantial evidence:* Therapists can mistake a freeze or immobilization response for striated muscle activation. A patient may have a hypervigilant or vacant stare. His breathing is barely noticeable in the upper chest. We see no abdominal breathing. He has racing thoughts or brain "fog" (Levine and Frederick 1997; P. Ogden, Minton, and Pain 2006; Scaer 2001, 2005). Do not assume his anxiety is going into the striated muscles. See if he has clenched hands and abdominal breathing and is sighing. Deactivate projections to undo a freeze reaction.

- *Failing to explore feelings when fragile patients' anxiety is in the striated muscles:* When therapists avoid exploring feelings, the fragile patient cannot gain the capacity to bear them. As a result, her suffering will continue. To build her capacity, we explore gradually.

- *Exploring feelings before projections are cleared up:* If we explore rage based on a projection on the therapist, we risk reinforcing the projection. Then reality testing decreases until a misalliance develops. Clear up the projection and restore reality testing to reestablish a conscious therapeutic alliance. Then explore feelings.

Principle: *Deactivate projections so the patient can feel safe with you rather than unsafe with a projection. Then we can explore the patient's inner life.*

- *Misunderstanding anxiety signals, resulting in improper interventions:* Therapists may misinterpret trembling as a discharge of the patient's rage. Instead, it often indicates excessive anxiety requiring regulation.
- *Misdiagnosing anxiety in a panic attack:* Fainting resulting from hyperventilation can be confused with fainting in cognitive/perceptual disruption. When the patient hyperventilates, carbon dioxide levels drop, the blood becomes alkaline, and blood vessels constrict. That causes lightheadedness and fainting. These techniques can help regulate hyperventilation.
  - Slow the patient's breathing. Count out loud to her, "Inhale for 1-2-3. Pause at the top of the inhale. Exhale for five seconds, 5-4-3-2-1." Repeat three times, then check on the patient's anxiety. The short inhale and longer exhale can correct the low carbon dioxide levels in the blood resulting from hyperventilation.
  - A second technique invites the patient to hold her breath for fifteen seconds while she makes a fist. Carbon dioxide levels will return to normal, and vasoconstriction will stop. Help her see that feelings triggered anxiety, which triggered her symptoms. Then resume exploring feelings.
  - A third technique invites the patient to inhale while she presses her palms together and flexes her biceps. Say, "Inhale and

press your palms together and flex your biceps. Now hold the breath at the top of the inhalation. Pause. Now exhale and release the grip." Repeat three times. Regulating anxiety together helps the patient feel better immediately, building the alliance.

- *Not regulating anxiety soon enough when it is discharged into the smooth muscles:* Fainting due to the parasympathetic discharge of anxiety occurs after symptoms of nausea, jelly legs, and lightheadedness. With smooth muscle activation, blood vessels dilate and blood pressure drops, leading to cerebral hypoperfusion. As soon as you see any signs of nausea, regulate anxiety to prevent lightheadedness and fainting from occurring at higher levels of anxiety. If faintness still occurs, you can do one of the following:
  - Summarize what has happened by describing the triangle of conflict.

Th: As we looked at the feelings toward your mother, anxiety made you lightheaded and faint. Do you see how that happened here as well? What's that like to see that?

  - Or encourage the patient to tense the muscles in her hands and arms. Invite the patient to press her palms together for thirty seconds. This activates the sympathetic nervous system, decreasing symptoms resulting from the parasympathetic nervous system.
  - Or invite the patient to inhale while extending her arms out to the side, lifting them overhead, and then bring her palms together. Invite her to exhale and bring the pressed palms to her chest. Repeat three times. Pair inhalations with tensing muscles, and pair exhalations with muscle relaxing and resting (Gaynor and Egan 2011).
  - Or you can invite the patient to stand up slowly and descend into a squatting position with bent knees for fifteen seconds and then slowly stand up (Rothschild 2003). Repeat three times. Then check on her anxiety. Regulating anxiety to calm the body builds the therapeutic alliance. Patients can also use these tools outside of therapy to self-regulate.

■ *Forgetting that anxiety can activate in multiple pathways simultaneously:* Some patients can experience anxiety in several pathways. Traditionally, many believed that the parasympathetic nervous system had a "braking" effect on the sympathetic nervous system (Gellhorn 1967; P. Ogden, Minton, and Pain 2006; Scaer 2001, 2005). However, recent research has shown this not to be true (Jänig 2003, 142, 2006). Symptoms of anxiety vary because the sympathetic and parasympathetic branches can activate independently and antagonistically rather than in homeostatic balance (Berntson, Cacioppo, and Quigley 1991, 1994). This helps explain the spectrum of anxiety symptoms described by Abbass (2004, 2007, 2015) and Folkow (2000).

SUMMARY

Our animal brain detects threats nonconsciously. Next, the amygdala mobilizes the body nonconsciously (Damasio 1999; Panksepp 1998). Finally, the amygdala sends a message to the prefrontal cortex. The cortex is responsible for thinking and decision making and can send corrective feedback. Only now can we become conscious of feelings and anxiety. Thus, helping patients become aware of anxiety is essential for self-regulation.

Depending on the therapist is the first relational trigger for anxiety. As an infant, the fragile patient learned that depending made her caretakers anxious. The mothering one induced anxiety in the infant who had no one else to depend on for anxiety regulation. The potential loss of the relationship meant the possible threat of death. Depending sometimes endangered her security (Benjamin 1993; Bowlby 1969; Sullivan 1953a). Hiding the desire to depend becomes an unconscious, automatic habit triggered by unconscious anxiety, the signal of danger. As an adult, the fragile patient's longing to depend rises as soon as she asks for help. Her body becomes anxious, and her mind does not realize why. "The heart has its reasons, which reason does not know" (Pascal 1670/1995).

The fragile patient's conflict has a pattern: To depend means danger.

Wish: She needs to depend.

Anxiety: Dizziness ensues.

Defense: She hides her need to depend.

This relational memory of feelings, anxiety, and defenses is neither conscious nor verbal. It was stored in the brain from the earliest years of life before the infant could speak or store verbal memories. Until the third or fourth year of the child's life, the hippocampus remembers only the quality of her experiences—the somatic sensations and behaviors (DeRijk, Kitraki, and De Kloet 2009, 142; O'Keefe and Nadel 1978). Thus, the right hemisphere of the brain stores our memories of relationships in the form of feelings, anxiety, and relational behaviors.

Before we have words for our experiences, "feelings are the relationship" (Symington 2002). Feelings are our emotional memories of relationships (Bowlby 1969; Kernberg 1975; Symington 2002). Anxiety is the bodily memory of danger in relationships (Schore 2002). And defenses enact relational memories, how we adapted to those dangers (Benjamin 1993; Sullivan 1953b). Thus, feelings, anxiety, and defenses are how the past speaks to the present. They represent our implicit relational knowledge, our experience of how relationships work (Lyons-Ruth 1998). Unconscious feelings, unconscious anxiety, and unconscious defenses reveal the past nonverbally, the silent language of our inner life.

Since these embodied memories form the basis for all emotional growth, we focus on the physical experiences of feelings and anxiety in the body. Then the patient can observe her previously unconscious relational reactions. As a result, she gains greater freedom to respond from her feelings rather than react from anxiety and defenses.

To help her, assess symptoms to discover the level of mixed feelings that makes anxiety shift out of the striated muscles. Regulate anxiety when it goes into the smooth muscles or cognitive/perceptual disruption. If you cannot regulate the anxiety, address the defenses or weaknesses that perpetuate it so regulation becomes possible.

The therapist actively addresses projection. If he remains silent, the fragile patient's anxiety increases, her projections will fill the silence, and the alliance will be lost. The patient needs enough activity and presence from the therapist to keep projections from filling the room. By actively addressing projections, the therapist prevents them from dominating the therapy. And the patient's projective anxiety can drop.

Once anxiety is regulated, we can explore other problems for which the patient seeks our help—the subject of the next chapter.

RECOMMENDED MATERIALS

The ability to regulate anxiety depends on how well you, as a therapist, regulate your own. Personal psychotherapy is essential for any practicing therapist. Recognizing your anxiety will help you recognize it in others. To develop your anxiety regulation to the highest levels, consider using a biofeedback device such as those offered by Unyte (https://support.unyte.com/hc/en-us/articles/115015711867--Relaxing-Rhythms). It will help you become better physiologically regulated. Improved self-attunement will help you attune better to your patients. Also, reviewing videotapes of your work will allow you to see when your anxiety is driving your interventions.

If you would like to study a videotaped session that shows how to assess and regulate anxiety in a fragile patient, see https://istdpinstitute .com/dvds/treatment-fragile-patient/. There you will find a DVD of an actual session, a teaching DVD on fragility, and an analyzed transcript of the session on a CD.

If you would like to review the basic points of anxiety assessment and regulation on videos by Jon Frederickson, you can visit the URLs below.

Anxiety assessment part 1 (May 24, 2012). http://www.youtube.com
/watch?v=22yLR49VUeM

Anxiety assessment part 2 (May 24, 2012). http://www.youtube.com
/watch?v=FBZF-Ni4rNo

Anxiety assessment part 3: Anxiety regulation (November 12, 2012).
http://www.youtube.com/watch?v=Vo62ZMGl6ew

CHAPTER TWO

Declaring a Problem

Is It Safe to Depend?

We take it for granted that, when a relationship to a special loved person is endangered, we are not only anxious but are usually angry as well. As responses to the risk of loss, anxiety and anger go hand in hand. It is not for nothing that they have the same etymological root.

—John Bowlby, *A Secure Base: Parent-Child Attachment and Healthy Human Development*

A colleague was contacted by a potential client whose recurrent long-term depression had returned with a vengeance. Her current therapist, with whom she had worked for decades, encouraged the patient to ask my colleague to call her before the consultation. When the colleague called, the therapist warned her, "Don't do any deep work." The patient was "too fragile" and needed only "supportive" therapy, meaning chitchat and some advice. Sadly, the former therapist was afraid of her fragile patient, and fear—not a realistic assessment—directed her work. She would never have dared to ask this fragile patient, "What's the problem you would like us to work on?" For that clinician, such a question seemed confrontational and not supportive.

Yet we should not start therapy by assuming the patient cannot do it. Instead, we should find out what she can do. We expand our working alliance by exploring what is possible. In every therapy, we walk into the unknown. We cannot know the patient's potential before we explore. That is what therapy is designed to discover. As soon as we make an assumption, we equate the patient with our concept. But no person is an idea. In fact, her being is the surplus that overflows any notion you have. She is unknowable (Berdyaev 1944).

The therapist had given up hope and called it "compassion." She was not directed by capacities in the patient but by fantasies in her mind. By offering so-called advice, she regarded the patient as incapable rather than develop her capacities. The "supportive" therapy the patient was offered was not support but despair.

Sadly, the patient seeks therapy after the descent into despair. To a degree, she learned that there was no hope to be loved as she was. Whatever others could not love, she had to reject so they could love what was left. And through this self-rejection, she could find partial acceptance within an insecure connection. She regained membership in a bond but lost the hope for a better life, and that loss is the most tragic (Bloch 1954/1995). She lost hope that her insecure attachment could be secure. The child lost hope that life could be different since her family was her life. Thus, the therapist will help her bury the hopes that died so together they can find the hopes that could be lived.

For therapy to help, we can be guided neither by irrational optimism nor irrational despair (Fromm 1973). These are attitudes, not assessments derived from evidence. Rather than guess, we explore to discern where her anxiety is discharged and what defenses she uses. We discover what causes her problems. And we can develop a plan to help her overcome them using abilities we build during therapy. If we do not explore, improvement remains impossible. We explore to find out what is possible by asking, "What is the problem you would like me to help you with?"

With this question, the patient confronts her first psychological conflict: "Do I have the right to depend on you?" The fragile patient floods with anxiety, a sign from the past that depending was dangerous. Or she may use defenses to hide her wish to depend: "This is how I survived in an insecure attachment." For instance, she might deny that she wants anything (denial). Or she declares that she can meet her needs on her own (omnipotence). A recovering alcoholic claims he knows everything he needs to know (omniscience). Or a client assumes that you want something out of him (projection). An addict may split off his wish for health and identify with the defense of self-destruction (splitting and projection). Why?

When a patient declares a problem, his wish to depend elicits his relational history (Bowlby 1969, 1973, 1980). For most fragile patients, depending led to pain. Therefore, anxiety signals, "Depending was dangerous." Defenses signal, "I hid my needs to avoid danger."

Sometimes parents punished children for wanting to depend, so children learned to deny their needs or project them onto others to avoid being punished for depending. Previously, we learned how to identify and regulate anxiety that arises when you ask about the patient's problem. Now we will learn how to address defenses fragile patients use to avoid declaring a problem. In this chapter, we will focus on the defense pole of the triangle of conflict. (See figure 2.1.)

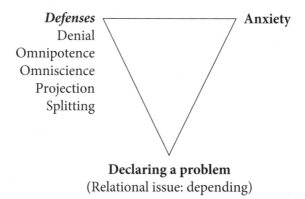

Defenses
Denial
Omnipotence
Omniscience
Projection
Splitting

Anxiety

Declaring a problem
(Relational issue: depending)

Figure 2.1   The triangle of conflict regarding declaring a problem

DENIAL OF A PROBLEM

When fragile patients deny that they have a problem, they show us their problem: their fear of depending.

Th: What is the problem you would like me to help you with?

Pt: I don't have a problem. [*Denial.*]

Th: And yet you are here. So what is the problem you would like me to help you with?

Pt: Everything is fine. I don't know what I'm doing here. [*Denial.*]

Th: Neither do I. Which is why I have to ask, what is the problem you would like me to help you with?

Pt: I don't know. What do you think my problem is? [*Projection: "You think I have a problem." By projecting, he hides his need and his wish to depend.*]

Th: I don't know. Since I'm not you, I can't know what your problem is. [*Deactivate projections by reminding patients of reality.*] That's why I have to ask you what the problem is you would like to work on. [*Invite him to declare his problem.*]

Pt: Isn't that what you are supposed to do? Tell me what my problem is? [*Projection.*]

Th: Oh, no. That's not my job. My job is to help you with a problem. [*Block the projection.*] Your job is to say what problem you want help with. What is the problem you would like help with?

Pt: I can't think of anything. Everything is going well. [*Denial: omnipotence.*]

Th: That's wonderful. A lot of people would like to be in your position. [*Mirror the denial.*]

Pt: I can't think of anything you could tell me that I haven't already figured out. [*Denial: omniscience.*]

Th: Always possible. [*Mirror denial.*] And yet, for some reason, you find yourself in a therapist's office. [*Remind him of evidence that conflicts with his denial. A man who doesn't need therapy came to a therapist.*] So what is the problem you would like me to help you with?

Pt: Can you help me?

Th: That's why we are here to find out. And so far, we don't know if you have a problem that requires the help of a therapist. [*Remind him of reality. We can't resolve a problem if there isn't one.*]

Pt: I'm getting dizzy. [*Anxiety in cognitive/perceptual disruption.*]

Th: This dizziness is a sign of anxiety. Something about coming here is triggering your anxiety, and you get dizzy. Do you see that connection too? [*Point out causality: depending triggers anxiety.*]

Pt: I get dizzy a lot. [*He frequently suffers from cognitive/perceptual disruption.*]

Th: You get anxious a lot. Is that a problem you would like me to help you with? [*Invite him to declare his will to work together on his problem.*]

Pt: If you think you can help. [*No sigh. His will is not online.*]

Th: That's what we could find out. But first, do you want me to help you with this anxiety? [*Invite him to declare his will to work together.*]

Pt: [*Sighs.*] Yes.

Denial often stuns the therapist: "Why is he here?" You offer a secure attachment, but the fragile patient follows the first commandment of an insecure attachment: "Thou shalt not depend." This is his internal working model for how relationships work. He does not resist you or the therapy. He collaborates according to the rules of an insecure attachment: "Hide your needs." Instead, we help him reveal his needs to co-create a new relationship that meets them.

To address his denial, we must avoid two mistakes. First, we might mistakenly argue with his denial.

Pt: I don't have a problem. [*Denial.*]

Th: But didn't you say you are recovering from alcoholism? [*Mistake: arguing with the patient's defense.*]

Pt: No. That's already taken care of. [*Patient denies that he has a problem or claims he has resolved it.*]

He believes he is in conflict with you. Instead, help him experience his internal conflict: he wants to depend and is afraid to do so.

Another mistake we make is fishing for problems. "How is your marriage?" or "Are you satisfied with your career?" After our fishing, he gives nothing. He loves his wife. His job is fine. Exasperated, we may blurt out, "So why are you here?" In response to a premature confrontation, he replies, "Beats me. I told you I don't have a problem." Again, the patient is in conflict with you instead of with his denial.

So how do we deal with denial? We mirror it.

Th: What's the problem you would like me to help you with?

Pt: I don't have a problem. [*Denial.*]

Th: Wonderful. And yet you are here. [*Mirror denial and a fact that contradicts his denial.*]

We mirror the fragile patient's denial so it conflicts with his wish to depend instead of with you. In the previous vignette, the therapist has no conflict with the patient's denial. The therapist doesn't need anything from the patient because the therapist's need does not drive the patient's therapy. The patient came because of his need. Do not argue with him. Mirror the patient's denial and a fact that conflicts with it: he is in a therapist's office.

When mirroring, offer a neutral tone, adding nothing. When the mirror reflects my face in the morning, it adds no commentary or emotion—no matter how I look at 6:30 a.m. It merely reflects what is there. If we express any sarcasm, we reject the patient. And our judgment will trigger anger, anxiety, and defenses. Then he will be in conflict with our judgment rather than with his denial. Mirror his denial and a fact he denies: he is in a therapist's office. Express no disbelief. Without a struggle between you and him, conflict arises within him, creating the conditions where he can reveal his needs to you.

Therapists can have trouble mirroring the patient's denial. Why? Mirroring denial requires us to face our own defenses. How can we judge anyone for using a defense? To mirror any patient, radically accept him as he is. By doing so, we accept ourselves as fellow defense users. When mirroring the patient, we see our reflection in the mirror. If you cannot identify with the patient as another person flawed like you, work on that before you try mirroring. Then you can mirror from a position of radical acceptance.

Principle: *Mirror denial and remind the patient of evidence he denies.*

One form denial takes is omnipotence: "I can handle this myself." The inner message is "I have learned that I cannot depend on others, so I depend on only myself." But none of us is an island. Each of us lives in a web of interdependency. Without the experience of a helpful relationship, the patient cannot sacrifice his omnipotence, for his imaginary power is preferable to depending on a powerless person who cannot help: the history of his suffering.

PROJECTION OF AWARENESS OF THE PROBLEM

Patients avoid depending by denying that they have a problem while believing that others think they do: "My wife thinks I have a problem." In effect, the patient says, "I'm not aware. My wife is." He has not declared a problem or a wish to do therapy yet, so we have no right to comment on his avoidance strategy. Instead, remind him of reality: "Since your wife is not here, I can't help her." Return to the focus: "What is the problem you would like me to help you with?"

He might ask the therapist what she thinks he should work on. He says he is not aware, but he imagines she is.

Th: What is the problem you would like me to help you with? [*Invite the patient to declare a problem, his wish to depend.*]

Pt: What do you think I should focus on? [*Projection of awareness.*]

Th: Only you can know what you should focus on. So what is the problem you would like me to help you with? [*Block the projection by reminding him of reality and return the focus to an internal problem.*]

Pt: Where should I start? [*Projection of awareness.*]

Th: I can't know where you should start. That's why I have to ask you, what is the problem you would like me to help you with? [*Block the projection by reminding him of reality. Invite the patient to declare a problem, his wish to depend.*]

Pt: I was hoping you could tell me what to work on. [*Projection of awareness.*]

Th: I have no right to tell you what to work on. Only you have the right to make that decision for yourself. So what is the problem you would like me to help you with? [*Block the projection by reminding him of reality. We have no right to tell patients what to do. If you tell them what to do, they will comply with you or defy you. Either choice creates a misalliance.*]

Pt: So what are we supposed to do here? [*Projection of awareness.*]

Th: We don't *have* to do anything. If you have a problem you would like me to help you with, we can work on that. If you don't have a problem to work on, we don't have to do anything. So what is the problem you would like me to help you with? [*Block the projection by reminding him of reality. Invite the patient to declare a problem, his wish to depend.*]

Pt: My mom thinks I have a drug problem. [*Projection of awareness.*]

Th: And you? In your opinion, what is the problem you want help with? [*Invite the patient to declare a problem, his wish to depend.*]

Pt: I just can't get my life together.

Th: And is that the problem you want me to help you with? [*Invite the patient to declare a problem, his wish to depend.*]

Pt: [*Sighs.*] Yes.

Principle: *Block the projection of awareness. Then invite the patient to declare the problem he wants to work on in therapy.*

PROJECTION: SUSPICIOUSNESS

Fragile patients often begin therapy fearing you will hurt them. You might mistakenly hear the mistrust as the whole story. But if it were, the patient would not be in your office. He is in conflict.

Th: What's the problem you would like me to help you with?

Pt: How do I know if you can help me? [*Suspicion.*]

Th: We can't know that yet. That's why we are here, to find out if we can work well enough together to help you. [*Remind the patient of reality.*]

Pt: I don't trust you yet. [*Projection: he trusts that I will harm him.*]

Th: Okay. There must be a good reason for that. [*Deactivate defiance.*] We notice that you don't trust me yet, and you came here. What is it like to notice these mixed reactions as we begin here today? Coming here and not trusting me yet. [*Invite consciousness of splitting.*]

Pt: You are trying to trick me into trusting you. But I won't. [*Projection: he wants to trust me but ascribes the desire to me.*]

Th: Make sure you distrust me as much as you need to so you can feel safe here. [*Deactivate the projection.*] What happens as you let yourself distrust me as much as you need to? [*Invite him to notice the feelings inside himself as he experiences that I do not encourage him to trust me.*]

Later, he said he was getting paranoid. I invited him to be as paranoid as he needed to be to feel safe with me. After about five minutes of this stance, he said, "Okay. That's enough. You can ask about my feelings now." I did, and he experienced cognitive/perceptual disruption but without projecting—an important piece of progress.

SPLITTING

Some people cannot bear the conflict between the wish for help and the fear of it, so they engage in splitting. A patient may split off and deny his wish for health and identify with an urge for self-destruction. A fragile drug addict came for treatment.

Th: What is the problem you would like me to help you with?

Pt: I don't know. The counselors want me to stop taking drugs, but I don't want to. [*Projection of the wish to stop taking fentanyl. Denial of the wish.*]

Th: Not wanting to stop taking drugs and meeting with a therapist in a rehab facility. What's it like to notice these two urges? [*Invite him to become aware of his split-apart conflict: the wish to take drugs (conscious) and the wish to get help, since he is with a therapist (unconscious, split-off, yet enacted). Help the patient observe his conflict to build his capacity to bear it.*]

Pt: Yeah. I want to keep using the drugs. [*Denial of the wish to stop taking drugs.*]

Th: Yeah. Wanting to keep using the drugs and meeting with a therapist in a rehab facility. What's it like to notice these two urges, this complexity inside you? [*Invite him to notice his split-apart conflict, to harm himself through drugs and heal himself through therapy to build the capacity to bear conflict.*]

Pt: Uh. I'm feeling a little dizzy. [*Cognitive/perceptual disruption.*]

Th: Something about wanting to use drugs and talking to a therapist, something about this complexity triggers some anxiety. What's it like to notice how these contradictory urges trigger this anxiety? [*Cognize about causality to regulate his anxiety.*]

Pt: I mean, I'd like to get off drugs eventually but not right now. [*Progress: emergent wish.*]

Th: You'd like to get off drugs. And you would like to use. How do you experience that struggle inside yourself as you let it be there? [*Invite him to see his conflict to build the capacity to bear it.*]

Pt: I'm feeling a little sick to my stomach. [*Anxiety in the smooth muscles.*]

Th: Wanting to get off drugs and wanting to stay on drugs, something about those mixed urges triggers some anxiety in your stomach now. What's it like to see that? [*Invite him to notice his conflict to build the capacity to bear it.*]

Pt: I know it doesn't make sense. [*The ability to reflect reveals increasing affect tolerance.*]

Th: It doesn't make sense. And yet wanting to give up drugs and not wanting to give up drugs—how do you experience this struggle inside you as you let these contradictory urges be there? [*Invite him to notice his conflict to build the capacity to bear it.*]

Pt: I feel uncomfortable. [*He can intellectualize about his anxiety now while tolerating conflict at a low level of affect. His affect tolerance has increased.*]

We reflect both sides of the split to build the patient's capacity to bear conflict. Initially, bearing contradictory urges triggers cognitive/perceptual disruption in this patient. As his affect tolerance increases, anxiety goes into the smooth muscles. At a higher level of affect tolerance, his anxiety will go into the striated muscles, and he will be able to intellectualize. Do not take sides with one part of the conflict. If you praise him for not using or tell him to stop using, you encourage more splitting.

Observing the wish to get off drugs and the defense of using drugs builds the patient's affect tolerance, increasing his impulse control. If he cannot bear the conflict inside himself, he may split off and project his motivation to recover onto other people or the therapist.

Principle: *Invite the consciousness of splitting when patients split off their awareness of the problem or their desire to work on it. Help them bear both sides of their conflict so they can form a conscious therapeutic alliance.*

FORMING AN ALLIANCE WHEN ASKING FOR
THE PROBLEM WITH A FRAGILE PATIENT

A fragile middle-aged man was in recovery at a drug rehabilitation center. He had been homeless, imprisoned, and diagnosed as bipolar, and was now on antipsychotic medication.

Th: What is the problem you would like me to help you with?

Pt: My process of coming out. [*Clear answer without hesitation.*]

Th: Uh-huh.

Pt: Being, uh, just accepting the fact that I am gay.

Th: Uh-huh.

Pt: Um, there was a lot of childhood stuff that went on in my life, molestation, uh, abandonment, my friends have moved on.

Th: Uh-huh.

Pt: I had a buddy of mine, he told me they went on to the spirit world and that they are okay. I miss them. I miss them a lot. They were gay. They told me to be proud. To hell with what everybody else thinks about me. Just be proud. My family is not supportive at all. I had a lot of people tell me I'm going to hell. It scares me a lot.

His speech is now disjointed: he brings up people in the "spirit world." Then he shifts: "My family is not supportive at all." Then he switches again without preparation: "I had a lot of people tell me I'm going to hell." These sudden shifts between logically unconnected thoughts are signs of thought disorder resulting from cognitive/perceptual disruption. He avoids looking at me while his eyes dart around, a sign of projection. The patient who projects hate-filled eyes onto me will avoid those eyes. I explore his projections onto me by asking for his thoughts about other people.

Th: What exactly scares you?

Pt: Being told I'm going to hell. That I'm a freak, a fag. A lot of times I go to church, every time I go to church, the pastor says how sinful my life is, I'm going to hell. He doesn't say it to me, per se, but he says that it is wrong. It's just, sometimes, I'm all right with it. And other times, I'm just, like, you know, I don't want to go to hell when I die, so I've got to do the right thing. So now I do stuff for people. I volunteer for a program. Like alcoholics, the program, and when I see homeless people on the street or something, I talk to them. I kind of like pay it forward because when I was in the street [*clears throat*], a lot of people were good to me. And, um, there was one lady that was really nice to me, and we are friends now. [*Disjointed speech: excessive anxiety.*]

Th: If we don't go off to the lady [*block defense*], I want to make sure that I'm understanding you so that I can be of most help to you with the time we have. You say you want some help coming out. You say you have no problem with coming out, per se, but you say what you are struggling with is that there are people who judge you. [*He projects his internal judgment onto others and worries about "their" judgments.*]

Pt: What other people think. [*He validates the therapist's intervention.*]

Th: People are calling you names, call you fag and freak.

Pt: Yeah.

Th: You say there is a minister who says you are going to hell.

Pt: Always.

Th: It sounds like you have a lot of feelings toward people who are judging you. You say that some of this judging is happening in your family as well.

Pt: Yeah.

Th: And this is the main kind of conflict that you want my help with? [*Summarize what he has said to see if we have consensus on what to work on.*]

Pt: If you can, yeah. I don't know how it is going to work, but if there was a pill I could take that would make it all right.

Th: And that is what you would like me to help you with here today? [*Invite his will to engage in the therapeutic task.*]

Pt: Yeah.

Th: With that in mind, can we look at a specific example of that? [*Explore a specific example to get a clearer picture of his conflict and to assess his anxiety and defenses.*]

He then describes a situation with his sister. However, his gaze avoidance suggests that he fears my judgment, as with everyone else. If so, he cannot feel safe enough to share his inner life. I deactivate his projection onto me to establish a therapeutic alliance.

Th: You mention that you were afraid of what people will think of you, how they will judge you. I'm wondering as we are sitting here, how are you perceiving me? [*Explore projection in the therapy relationship.*]

Pt: I feel comfortable. I do.

His darting eyes and cognitive/perceptual disruption suggest that he is anxious. But he is not aware of it. We help him observe what he senses in his body to help him regulate his anxiety.

Th: Uh-huh.

Pt: Yeah, I feel comfortable.

Th: I have to say that you look a little anxious right now. I'm wondering if you are aware of that? [*Anxiety regulation.*]

Pt: I'm okay. I have a counselor. [*Talking about his counselor prevents him from paying attention to and regulating his anxiety in the moment. Bring his attention back to his anxiety.*]

Th: Right now, are you aware of feeling anxious now as you are talking to me?

Pt: I feel kind of uncomfortable. [*Notices anxiety.*]

Th: Good to know, it's good for us to notice that. It's really important for you to notice any discomfort, any anxiety, any reactions that you are having here as we are talking so we can help you get more comfortable in the world.

Since his anxiety is too high, we pay close attention to it so he can regulate it. I remind him of the task. Then he knows what to do. That orients and calms him.

Th: We need to check in because we notice as we are talking here that you are feeling a little uncomfortable. How do you experience that discomfort right now physically in your body? [*Invite him to pay attention to the anxiety in his body to regulate it.*]

Pt: Nervous.

Th: How do you experience that anxiety right now, physically in your body?

Pt: Um.

Th: Just in your body, physically in your body?

Pt: How am I experiencing it?

Th: Yeah.

Pt: That's what you are telling me to do. [*Projection: he forgets what we agreed to work on.*]

Th: Just wondering how you are experiencing that anxiety in your body right now. Do you feel tense anywhere? [*He has trouble describing his anxiety. Ask more specific questions that are easier to answer.*]

Pt: Yeah, in the shoulders. [*Striated muscle tension.*]

Th: How is your stomach? [*Invite him to pay attention to symptoms of anxiety in his body.*]

Pt: Queasy, butterflies. People call them butterflies. [*Anxiety in the sympathetic nervous system pulls blood from the stomach to the large muscles for fight or flight responses.*]

Th: That is a sign of anxiety. [*Regulate anxiety by helping him identify signs of it.*]

Pt: Yeah.

Th: A little queasy in your stomach. Does it feel like you are a little sick, a little nauseated?

Pt: No, just like nerves.

Th: So just kind of queasy down there. You are feeling a little queasy in your stomach. I'm going to ask you another question—this may seem a little more personal—so that we can assess your nervousness. Do you ever suffer from diarrhea? [*Assess the level of his anxiety.*]

Pt: Yeah, I do, a lot. I usually go, like, twice a day. [*Anxiety in the smooth muscles.*]

Th: Uh-huh. Yeah, that is another form of anxiety. [*Regulate anxiety by identifying anxiety symptoms.*]

Pt: Is it?

Th: Yeah, that is another form of anxiety.

Pt: I thought it was something I ate. [*When parents ignored patients' anxiety in the past, patients ignore it today. Thus, he mistakes an anxiety symptom for a digestive problem.*]

Th: Since it is happening chronically, that is a sign of anxiety. You are letting me know that when you get anxious, you get a little queasy in your stomach and a little shaky in your bowels, you get diarrhea. [*Regulate his anxiety by showing how it causes his bodily symptoms.*]

Pt: I get scared a lot. [*If he gets scared a lot, he projects onto people a lot.*]

Th: Uh-huh. You get scared a lot. We want to notice right here any time you feel a little scared, any time you have these physical symptoms here, so we can help you with this problem of getting scared. [*Outline the therapeutic task.*]

Pt: Yeah.

Th: Yeah, so you are saying you get a little anxious here in your stomach. You've got this bit of butterflies. [*Draw his attention to his anxiety.*]

Pt: I do.

Th: And then you get this queasiness, a little bit of shakiness in the bowels, a little bit of diarrhea. Do you ever get migraines? [*Patients whose anxiety takes the form of diarrhea often suffer from migraines.*]

Pt: No.

Th: And right now? [*Bring his attention to his anxiety to regulate it.*]

Pt: I get headaches but not severe. I think once or twice, maybe a couple of months ago. The light was really bright, and I was wearing shades in the house, and people were asking me, what's wrong with you? I had a headache. The light was really bothering me. [*Migraine headaches, anxiety in the smooth muscles.*]

Th: Yeah. Right now, how is your vision?

Pt: It's good.

This focus on anxiety regulation has finally brought his anxiety down. He no longer experiences cognitive/perceptual disruption. That's why I can point out the triangle of conflict, knowing he will be able to understand me.

Th: It's clear. Good. So right now, we are noticing that you and I are talking, and you said you are wanting my help with this conflict. You've come out and let people know you are gay, and you are afraid of how people could judge you or criticize you. And we notice as you are telling me about this, it triggered some anxiety, and you are having anxiety in your stomach and in your bowels. [*Depending triggers mixed feelings toward me based on his experience. Those feelings trigger anxiety in the smooth muscles and cognitive/perceptual disruption. And his primary defense so far is projection.*]

Pt: Uh-huh.

Th: And there is something about letting me get to know you, letting me learn about you, that triggers this anxiety in your body. [*Point out causality: depending triggers his anxiety.*]

Pt: It does.

Th: It feels a little scary to let me get to know you. As you are about to let me get to know you, there is this anxiety. You are aware of that too? [*Relationship triggers feelings and anxiety.*]

Pt: Yeah.

Th: Wonderful. Well, it's wonderful that you can notice that, right? We notice that anxiety about other people, fear about other people is coming up right here.

Pt: Uh-huh.

Th: It gives us a chance, it's not wonderful that it is happening, not that you have this anxiety, because it is terrible to have all this anxiety. But it's wonderful that it is happening here because you and I together can look at this anxiety and see what gets stirred up in you. [*Remind him of the therapeutic task.*]

Pt: I had a counselor tell me. I had another counselor tell me one time that I need to learn to take a shot to the gut. I need to not worry so much about what other people say or what people think. [*Projection 1: "I must let you attack me (take a shot to the gut)." Projection 2: "You will tell me not to think what I think" and "Rather than listen to me, you will try to control me."*]

Th: What I would suggest is, since you do worry about what people think, we should take a close look at that. [*Remind him of the therapeutic task (pay attention to his projections) to deactivate his second projection.*]

Pt: Okay.

Th: Because you are saying this is a problem. There are a lot of people who come out and are gay, and that's not a problem. But if you come out, and you are always worried about what other people think, that is a problem. [*Get an internal focus.*]

Pt: Yeah.

Th: So being gay is not a problem. But constantly worrying about what other people think is a real problem, right?

Pt: Yeah.

Th: Yeah, so being gay is not a problem. A lot of people come out and are gay and don't worry about what other people think. But being worried all the time what other people think, that sounds like the problem that you're needing me to help you with, would that be fair to say? [*Consensus on what he wants to work on.*]

Pt: Yeah.

Th: Let's check in, how are you feeling that anxiety in your body right now?

Pt: It's kind of subsiding; it's going away a little bit. [*Sighs: anxiety in the striated muscles.*]

Th: Okay. As we're getting to know you here right now, are you aware of having any thoughts about what I might think about you? [*Explore projections onto the therapist.*]

Pt: Yeah.

Th: Good. Let's get really clear about those thoughts you're having right now. Can we pay really close attention to them right now? [*Invite him to intellectualize about his projections.*]

Pt: Yeah.

Th: Because this is probably the only relationship where you sit down and find out what really happens because you know you're worried about whether people think, right? [*Therapeutic task.*]

Pt: Yeah, I do.

Th: Because this is happening, right?

Pt: Yeah.

Th: Let's notice that as well. We can learn about it. Does that make sense? [*Mobilize his will to the task.*]

Pt: Yeah.

Th: You are aware you have some thoughts about me right now, right? [*Task: observe projections.*]

Pt: Yeah.

Th: What are those thoughts you have about me? [*Do not ask, "What do you think about me?" Instead, ask, "What thoughts come up about me?" Differentiate him as an observer separate from thoughts he observes.*]

Pt: [*Sighs.*] I don't know. Honestly? [*His sigh is a signal of rising feelings.*]

Th: Let's be totally honest about whatever thoughts you have because this is what you're needing help with, right? [*Mobilize his will to the task.*]

Pt: I'm like, I'm like, you know. Honestly?

Th: Yeah.

Pt: That you don't want to be bothered with this shit. That you have a lot of your own stuff going on and, ah, I'm just taking up your time. [*Projection.*]

Th: Good, good. I appreciate you're being so honest. And this is kind of like the thoughts that come up with other people, isn't it? [*Show him his pattern of thinking.*]

Pt: Yeah, I don't know about other people, but with you, I mean.

Th: But you are letting me know that when you are with people, you've got a lot of thoughts about what they're thinking, right, and so we're trying to get that problem on the table here. You're saying one of the thoughts is, he doesn't want to be bothered with my shit. He doesn't want to hear what I am thinking and feeling, right? [*Identify projections. Don't say, "One of the thoughts is like I don't want to be bothered." Why? He will remember, "I don't want to be bothered." Instead, differentiate the therapist from his projection. Together, we explore his inner life as if it is on a screen on the wall "over there" (Havens 1976, 1986; Sullivan 1953b).*]

Pt: Sure.

Th: And what other thoughts are coming up here about me? [*Find the other projections.*]

Pt: There are so many of them.

Th: Well, let's get them on the table because this is the problem you need help with, right? [*Mobilize his will to the task.*]

Pt: Yeah.

Th: There is this tendency to think that people are criticizing you. [*Identify projections.*]

Pt: Like, where's the best place I could start to help him, what could I possibly do?

Th: That I would be thinking that I can't help. [*Identify projections.*]

Pt: Make his life easier.

Th: Uh-huh.

Pt: Or this guy doesn't stand a chance. I'm forty-eight years old; you know, I should've dealt with this years ago. [*Projection of internal judgment.*]

Th: Let's pause. You're saying the first thought that comes to mind is Frederickson doesn't want to be bothered with my shit. Then there is the thought: Frederickson doesn't want to hear this. And there is the thought: Frederickson thinks that I'm hopeless. I couldn't get better. It's too late, or something like that, right? [*Identify projections. Again, differentiate the therapist from the projection by using a last name: "Frederickson doesn't want to be bothered with my shit." Help him relate to the therapist while he reflects on his projection.*]

Pt: Yeah.

Th: Are there any thoughts you're thinking I might have about your gayness here? [*Explore projections.*]

Pt: Yeah.

Th: Let's get that out on the table, too, right?

Pt: I don't know. It's kind of like, how could I possibly help him see the good in him and not worry about what other people think? [*Projection: belief I would feel despair about his prospects for change. But he can intellectualize about his projection—a significant move forward.*]

Th: There is this sense I would be criticizing you. That you are not worth listening to. That you are hopeless, nobody could help. I would be kind of critical of you, right? [*First, I used the word "he" to refer to myself. Then "Frederickson." And now, I use the word "I," hoping his affect tolerance has increased enough to tolerate these higher dosage words. The patient's affect tolerance is higher because he can intellectualize about the projections now.*]

Pt: Yeah.

Th: And are there any thoughts about how I would criticize your gayness? Does that come up as we look at these critical thoughts? [*Remind him of the task while differentiating him as an observer from the thoughts we observe.*]

Pt: Um, I mean, with you being a professional and all of that, I, like, you know, I guess, I think it's your job, and you're supposed to say stuff like, "it's okay." [*If fragile patients were punished for having critical thoughts, they protect us by denying them.*]

Th: Yeah, yeah, and you're thinking something else about me, though, right? [*Block his denial.*]

Principle: Bring all projections out into the open, so he can establish a therapeutic alliance. Otherwise, he'll have a misalliance with the projection.

Pt: No, no, I'm not.

Th: Because I'm wondering, with your higher mind you know I'm a therapist and I'm listening to you, but you're letting me know that your lower mind has some other thoughts about me. Right? [*Remind fragile patients of their ability to see reality when they also believe their projection.*]

Pt: Yeah. [*Smiles.*]

Th: Because you are letting me know your higher mind thinks, "Frederickson, oh, he's a therapist, he's a trained professional," but your lower mind is letting me know you are having these other thoughts about me. It's kind of turning around. It's coming up with something else. What's your lower mind thinking? [*Differentiate fantasy and reality. Then invite him to describe his projections so we can examine them together. By referring to his "lower mind," we enlist his "higher" mind as an ally.*]

Pt: It is, it is.

Th: What's your lower mind saying about me? [*Invite more projections.*]

Pt: "What's he going to do with this information? What's he going to do with this stuff?" [*New projection.*] Um, I, I had an experience years ago with a lady who was a therapist, and I, uh, the issue was the same. [*With the deactivation of several projections, a memory emerges.*]

Th: Uh-huh.

Pt: And she and I talked only to find that she wasn't a therapist. She wasn't certified, and she took a lot of my information, everything. She put it down in the computer and did all that. And once my program found out she wasn't a certified therapist, she wasn't official, they fired her. And a lot of things since then, you know, I just have been really afraid to talk to people and the things that I say because I don't know, I don't know what's right now. . . .

Th: Well, let's hang on a second. You are letting me know that you've had this thought that "Frederickson doesn't want to listen to me." That "Frederickson thinks I'm hopeless," right? "Frederickson has judged me, criticized me"; and the sense that "Frederickson might misuse what I tell him in some way." [*Projections.*]

Pt: Yeah.

Th: Right. Although you are also letting me know that there is this wish to depend on me, right?

Pt: Uh-huh.

Th: There is this other thought that Frederickson might hurt me. [*His conflict.*]

Pt: Yeah.

Th: Right?

Pt: Right.

Th: "Frederickson might hurt me. Frederickson might hurt me, criticize me." Then you are making this link to a previous therapist who actually did lie to you. She said she was a trained professional, and it turned out she wasn't. [*Link his projection in the therapy to a reality in the past.*]

Pt: She hurt me, and she hurt a lot of other people.

Th: Yeah, but she claimed she was a professional, and she wasn't.

Pt: I—I—I confided in her. I told her everything. She knew everything about me.

Th: Wow.

Pt: And it hurt. It hurt like hell.

Th: Because you trusted this woman who turned out wasn't a real mental health professional, right? [*His fear about therapy.*]

Pt: Right.

Th: So it is important as you and I begin working here, right, it looks like Jon Frederickson here, but a part of your mind brings this image of this previous therapist in front of me, right? [*Differentiate the therapist from his transference: he was projecting the image of another person onto me.*]

Pt: Right. I see her.

Th: You see her, right?

Pt: Yeah. I see her.

Th: You see this woman. It's kind of like we have to get rid of that image so you can relate to Jon. It's not like you are doing it on purpose, but you're telling me it's like your body was telling us the history of your suffering, right? [*Differentiate me from his projection.*]

Pt: Right.

Th: It's like you got all nervous. You were here with Jon Frederickson. But it's like your body was with this woman and reminding you of this woman who was lying to you and going to hurt you. [*Differentiate me from his projection.*]

Pt: When I walked in the door, the first thing I said to myself, I thought, "Here I go again. I don't know what he's going to do. I don't know what we are going to talk about, but I'm trusting somebody one more time." [*Link of past and present. He can differentiate me from his projection, which he couldn't do twenty minutes earlier. Now we can explore feelings toward his former therapist.*]

Th: Exactly. And it sounds like that triggered some feelings, doesn't it?

Pt: It does because I get—I get angry. I get sad, it hurts.

Th: That's right. It hurts.

Pt: It hurts.

Th: Can we put this together? You come here. You are depending on me, right?

Pt: Uh-huh.

Th: Right, and this stirs up a lot of feelings, right? Because it reminds you of this person you trusted.

Pt: Of her.

Th: Who lied to you, who betrayed you, right?

Pt: Yeah, right.

Th: And you are learning that when she lied to you, and she betrayed you, right? [*Stimulus.*]

Pt: Uh-huh.

Th: You find yourself feeling really angry at this woman. [*Describe the triangle of conflict in the past and today. He depended on a fake therapist who lied to him. Anger arose toward me (as the former therapist), and he became anxious. Then he projected his anger,*

*thinking I wanted to hurt him. Now he feels his anger toward her,
and we can explore it to build his affect tolerance.*]

Pt: Yeah, yeah.

Th: Can we look at the anger toward this woman who lied to you?
[*Explore feeling.*]

Pt: Okay.

HIGHER-LEVEL DEFENSES TO AVOID DECLARING A PROBLEM

Fragile patients rely on splitting, denial, and projection to avoid
declaring what they want to work on. However, sometimes they use
higher-level defenses to avoid declaring a problem.

Diversification

The patient changes topics as a defense. Return to the topic.

Th: What's the problem you would like me to help you with?

Pt: I should first tell you about my childhood. [*Defense: diversification.*]

Th: I would be glad to hear about that, but, first, what is the problem
you would like me to help you with? [*Interrupt the defense and
return to the problem.*]

Vagueness

Rather than offer a clear problem, the patient hides her need behind
vagueness.

Th: What's the problem you would like me to help you with?

Pt: It's hard to say. I guess a lot of things. It's just, I don't know. [*Defense:
vagueness.*]

Th: "A lot of things" is vague. Could you be more specific about your
problem so we could get a clear idea of how to help you? [*Point out
the vague words. Then invite him to state the problem more clearly.*]

Rationalization

Rather than offer a problem to work on, the patient offers reasons
for the problem.

Th: What's the problem you would like me to help you with?

Pt: I think it is because my parents got divorced when I was a kid.
[*Defense: rationalization. He offers a reason but not the problem
itself.*]

Th: That may be the reason for your problem. But what is the problem itself you would like me to help you with? [*Differentiate the defense from the problem. Then return to the focus.*]

Intellectualization

Rather than offer a problem, the patient offers thoughts.

Th: What's the problem you would like me to help you with?

Pt: I've been thinking about a lot of things lately, about some philosophy books and alienation. [*Defense: intellectualization. He offers a thought instead of a problem.*]

Th: These are some thoughts. If we look underneath the thoughts, what is the problem you would like me to help you with here today? [*Identify the defense. Then return to the focus.*]

Self-Attack

The patient turns anger toward others back on herself. This protects them and the relationship, but she suffers depression as a result.

Th: What's the problem you would like me to help you with?

Pt: I'm such a mess. I can't seem to do anything right. [*She starts to cry. Defense: self-attack.*]

Th: Coming back here, could those be critical thoughts coming up in your mind? [*Identify the defense.*] Could they be getting you down, do you think? [*Clarify the price of the defense.*]

Pt: I guess so.

Th: Are those the kinds of thoughts you would like me to help you with? [*Get consensus on the therapeutic task.*]

Pt: Yes, because I have them all the time. [*Cries again.*]

Th: Could we look underneath those thoughts and see what they are covering up? [*Invite her to engage in the therapeutic task.*] Could we look underneath those thoughts and see if we can find the rest of you? [*Invite her to pursue a positive goal.*]

Pt: [*Nods. Tears clearing up.*]

Th: If we look underneath those tears, what feelings are coming up here toward me? If we look under the tears, what feelings are coming up here toward me?

This patient did not describe her problem in words; she enacted it through defenses: her self-attack. Usually, patients do this to protect others from feelings. It's a learned behavior from the past. Interrupt any defense that makes her depressed. Block any self-damaging behavior, and invite her to explore the feelings the defense is covering up. Then she learns that she does not have to hurt herself to protect us from her feelings.

You may wonder if the therapist is interrupting rather than listening to the patient. The therapist always listens to the patient's problems. But defenses prevent the patient from telling us her problem. She does not do this on purpose. Nor does she even know when defenses happen. But if they keep occurring, she will not get the help she needs. Interrupt the defenses when they interrupt him. You can defend the patient from defenses when you block and interrupt them.

SUMMARY

To establish a therapeutic alliance, the patient must declare a problem she wants to work on. However, earlier traumas may have taught her that it is dangerous to depend. To avoid depending, she uses defenses such as denial, projection, omnipotence, or omniscience. Address these defenses until she describes a problem. Then ask if she wants to work on it together. That brings us to the next chapter.

RECOMMENDED MATERIALS

To get a DVD of the initial session with the patient whose projections linked to a previous therapist, go to https://istdpinstitute.com/dvds/restructuring-projection-borderline-patient-instructional-video-bundle/. Included are a two-hour session with the patient, a presentation on projection, and a CD with the complete transcript analyzed.

CHAPTER THREE

Declaring One's Will

Is It Safe to Have a Separate Will?

All conceivable nonsense,
All evil
Stems from our struggle to dominate our neighbor.

—CZESŁAW MIŁOSZ

A patient whose therapist was retiring sought a consultation with another clinician. Upon walking into his office, she looked around and paused, unsure which chair was hers. The therapist suggested, "You're wondering where to sit. The little chair is for you. The big chair is for me because I'll be the captain."

No therapist should act as the captain. Our task is to help the patient become the skipper of her own ship. His proposed domination would have replicated the patient's experiences with a domineering patriarch. Fortunately, with a twinkle in her eye, she said to her retiring therapist, "I don't think I'll be going back."

The therapist forgot that the patient's will drives her therapy. We work to resolve *her* problem and achieve *her* goals. For the therapist is not the master but the servant of the patient's will to health.

When the therapist asks, "Is it your will to work on this problem?" the patient confronts a crucial psychological conflict: "Do I have the right to say what I want?" and "May I have a separate mind in our relationship?" Anxiety tells us that declaring her will was dangerous. Defenses show how she hid it. She may deny her desire, or she may project it onto other people: "My daughter told me to come here."

But the problem is even worse. Not only was it dangerous for her to declare her will, it may have been dangerous even to know it. For the child who knows her will might divulge it and be punished for having a separate mind. Thus, her will becomes a secret she cannot allow herself to feel. To protect her true self, she cannot know she has one (Winnicott 1960/1965a). Buried so deeply, it appears to have died. But it always rests within, waiting to be called forth from its premature grave.

Why emphasize will? Each of us has an inherent will to recover (Nunberg 1955), a principle of restoring our integrity (Symington 2002) that is deeply unconscious (Bion 1957). The will is the key to recovery such that any healing therapy needs to be a will therapy (Rank 1930/1936; Schulkin 2004), for the patient's will to health is the engine of therapy (H. Davanloo, supervision 2002–2004). We have no right to explore anything in psychotherapy unless she wants to explore it. We must ask if it is her will to work toward her goals for her benefit.

If we don't ask, then therapy may be based on the therapist's agenda, not the patient's desire. At best, this leads to pseudocompliance. At worst, the patient drops out because we ignore what she wants, as others did in the past.

THE ROLE OF WILL IN BECOMING A PERSON

Will is an expression of the life force that drives the universe and, thus, the patient in her life task of self-creation (Rank 1930/1936). At birth, every infant's will rises as a natural force. Yet, to be born psychologically, someone must say "yes" to the child's will. Then she learns through relating how to reveal herself as a separate person.

Why, then, does the patient become anxious when declaring her will? A parent abandoned her when she declared it: "Get rid of your will, and I'll accept what is left." Thus, she thinks, "Will my therapist abandon me too if I reveal a separate will, mind, or desire?" (Rank 1930/1936, 1929/1978). As a result, she lets go of her will to hold onto a love that left.

But if the therapist accepts her will, she can too. By listening to her will, she discovers herself as a separate person. And when she and the therapist embrace her differences, she can "find the creativity and strength to change" (Menaker 1986, xv). The "I" cannot exist in a relationship unless someone accepts her will. Thus, the therapist must create a climate that recognizes the patient's right to will. Then she can accept herself as a separate person. To interpret her fear is not enough. She needs you to welcome her will.

"No one else can want for me. No one can substitute his act of will for mine. It does happen sometimes that someone very much wants me to want what he wants. This is the moment when the impassable frontier between him and me, which is drawn by free will, becomes most obvious. I may not want what he wants me to want—and in this precisely I am incommunicable. I am, and I must be, independent in my actions. All human relationships are posited on this fact" (Wojtyla 1960/1993, 24).

THE HISTORY OF A CRUSHED WILL

Many fragile patients suffered verbal, physical, or sexual abuse. That crime communicated these messages: "Your will does not matter. You must serve my will," "It's my way or the highway," "If you don't like it here, there's the door," "When I want to hear from you, I'll let you know," or "Quit crying, or I'll give you something to cry about." The patient's choice was to fuse with the abuser's will or lose his love. This soul murder (Shengold 1991) could also be called will murder. Through the "poisonous pedagogy" of abuse (A. Miller 1990), the child learns to hide her separate mind. The tyrant crushes her will, so she makes her will invisible to avoid more emotional violence. Since she hides her true self (Winnicott 1960/1965a), inviting her will triggers her relational past.

When asked, "Is it your will to work on this problem?" a few people can say "yes" and mean it. But, due to traumas, most fragile patients flood with anxiety. With their higher mind, they hope we can embrace their will. With their lower mind, however, they fear we will abuse them.

The fragile patient's history of suffering may rise in other ways. He may comply with the therapist, like he did with his abusers. Or he may defy the desires he imagines the therapist has. These defenses reveal his inner conflict: "Can I declare my will, or must I satisfy yours?" "May I declare my goal, or must I pursue yours?" or "Can I want what I want? Or am I supposed to want what you want?" On an even deeper level, he asks, "Can I even know my desires in your presence?" "Can I have a goal in our relationship?" or "Can I want anything at all when I am with you?"

WILL AND THE MASTER-SLAVE DISCOURSE

The problem of will begins at the beginning. Every child starts life as the slave of the mother's desire: "How can I become what she wants?" (Lacan 1966/2007). Powerless, the child as a slave suffers at the hands of a mother she regards as a master. Yet, the master-slave discourse goes both ways. The child experiences itself as the helpless slave of a mother who can go away. And the mother may perceive herself as the slave of a baby who has stolen her prematernal life. The powerless infant is a slave to the mother's demands. And the mother is a slave to the infant's needs. The infant learns that she cannot be loved as a subject but as only an object of the mother's desire. Thus, she becomes fixated on discerning and incarnating the mother's desire. For the child, loving means, "I must become whatever you want. To manifest your will, I must forget about mine."

The fragile patient may enter treatment, wondering, "If I hide my desire and become the slave of yours, will you love me?" She begins therapy by projecting her will. Emptied of her will, she hopes to become loved as a vessel filled with the therapist's desire: "My will vanishes in the presence of your desire, and I make your desire appear to be mine." The therapist, unaware of this dynamic, may state what he wants or what he thinks the patient wants. He becomes the master, the patient the slave, and the master-slave discourse continues unexamined. Suppose the therapist claims to have superior knowledge of the patient's unconscious. Now the patient becomes a slave filled with pseudoknowledge: "To incarnate your desire, I can know myself through only your eyes. If you do not see me, I don't exist." She hides her desires by projecting them onto others. And the therapist hides from the patient's inner life by claiming to "know" her unknowable depths. Then, the therapist's desire for omniscience drives their deal. He talks at a fantasy, a conceptual replica he has of the patient. Instead, he should speak to the patient's unknowable depths so that her desire can guide the therapy. (For more on the Lacanian concept of the master-slave discourse, see Fink [1999], P. Hill [2002], and Lacan [1966/2007].)

Having addressed anxiety earlier, in this chapter we will focus on the defense pole of the triangle of conflict when inviting the patient's will. (See figure 3.1.)

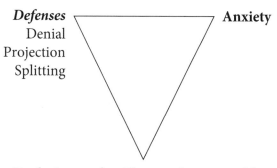

Declaring one's will to work on a problem
(Relational issue: having a separate will)

Figure 3.1   The triangle of conflict regarding declaring one's will

DEACTIVATING PROJECTION OF WILL

To avoid the anxiety over declaring his will, the patient may project his will onto the therapist (Rank 1930/1936, 17).

Th: Is this the problem you want to work on?

Pt: If you think it's a good idea. [*Projection of will.*]

To deactivate his projection, remind him of reality: therapy can be based only on his will, not yours. Then ask him what he wants for himself out of his therapy.

Th: I can't know if this is a good idea for you because I'm not you. Only you can know what would be best for you. [*Remind him of reality.*] That's why I have to ask you if you want to work on your problem for your benefit. [*Invite him to declare his will.*]

Remind him of what he has forgotten. He came to therapy to work on his problem to achieve his positive goals. Through these reminders, the therapist invites him to reveal his separate will. The patient no longer submits to the other's will. Instead, he expresses his own. Otherwise, he will get better at pretending to be a ghost, a host for the desires of others (Rank 1930/1936): "How much of me do you need me to lose so I will never lose you?"

These will conflicts begin in childhood during the phase of separation-individuation. In that phase, we become autonomous, differentiated persons within relationships (Mahler 1972; Mahler, Pine, and Bergman 1975; J. Marcus 1973; Rank 1930/1936). By learning to declare their will, patients can differentiate from—while connecting to—those they love.

But declaring her desire will trigger her guilt. Why? She becomes different from those she loves and on whom she depended. To discover herself as a separate person, she must face her guilt over differentiating. Whenever we say what we want, we reveal that we don't want what the other person wants. We step forward. The word *aggression* derives from the Latin *ad-gradus*, "to step forward." To declare our will is an act of aggression that triggers guilt.

To avoid her guilt, she may project her will. She might blame others, God, or fate for being the guilty ones guiding her life. Or she can judge those who express their will and accuse them of being guilty. In this way, she flees from the inevitable guilt we feel as people who create our lives through willing, lives not always to our liking: "I didn't create my problems in adulthood; they did!" In therapy, we help the patient accept her will rather than project it onto others. By accepting her will, she can become a person who acts rather than remain the victim of others' actions (Rank 1930/1936).

Th: Your parents may have created the mess in the past, but only you can clean up the mess today.

Pt: You're saying it's all my fault?

Th: No, of course not. From what you have said, it's clear that in many ways your parents ruined your childhood. You mention that they abused you and at times rejected you. They did their dirty work then. But if you carry on their dirty work today by criticizing yourself and not supporting yourself, you will keep suffering. We can't change them. Would it make sense for us to focus on what you are doing today that's hurting you? That way you don't have to wait for anyone else to change first. We could help you change now.

Only the patient can change the problems her defenses create today. If she focuses on only how others inflicted suffering in the past, she won't see how her defenses create her suffering in the present. Of course, we empathize with her history of suffering. But that is never enough. We must also help her see and let go of the defenses providing her pain today.

In the following example, a fragile patient projects his will to work on his problem. The therapist blocks the projection of will. And he invites the patient to declare what he wants for himself from the treatment.

Th: Is this a problem you would like to work on here with me?

Pt: [*No sigh. Diffident voice.*] Sure.

Th: What tells you inside that you know you want to do this for yourself? [*There is no sigh, no unconscious anxiety: his will is not online. If he wants to work on his problem, feelings and anxiety will rise. Why? Declaring his will forms a more intimate relationship. Ask about will until you see an unconscious "yes," the patient's sigh.*]

Pt: If you think I should. [*Projection of will onto the therapist.*]

Th: But do you want to for yourself? [*Block the projection by inviting his will.*]

Pt: [*No sigh.*] Okay. [*The absence of a sigh reveals the defense of compliance. He complies with the therapist's will rather than declare his own.*]

Th: What tells you inside that you know you want to do this for yourself? [*Block the projection by inviting his will.*]

Pt: I know I should. [*Projection onto the therapist.*]

Th: The question isn't whether you should but whether you *want* to work on your problem. Is that what *you* want for yourself? [*Block the projection by inviting his will.*]

Pt: Mm-hmm. [*No sigh.*]

Th: What tells you inside that you know you want to do this for yourself? [*Block the projection by inviting his will.*]

Pt: I'm here. I know that's what we're supposed to do. [*Projection onto the therapist.*]

Th: There's nothing here that you are *supposed* to do. That's why we need to find out what tells you inside that you know you *want* to do this for yourself? [*Block the projection by inviting his will.*]

Pt: [*Flat voice, no sigh.*] I want to work on my problems.

Th: What tells you inside that you know you want to do this for your-self? [*Block the projection by inviting his will.*]

Pt: I have to. [*Projection onto the therapist.*]

Th: That's not true. You don't *have* to work on any problem. The question is whether you *want* to work on your problem for your benefit. [*Deactivate the projection onto the therapist, and then invite his will.*]

Pt: What do you think I should do? [*Projection onto the therapist.*]

Th: I don't know. [*Block the projection by reminding him of reality.*] That's why I have to ask you if you want to work on your problem for your benefit. [*Invite him to see his desire.*]

Pt: Maybe I don't want to. [*If he projects his will on me, he will defy me as if I want something from him.*]

Th: Okay. If you don't want to, I have to respect your wish. [*Deactivate the projection by reminding him of reality.*] It just means we won't be able to help you with your problem. [*Remind him of the price of the defense.*]

Pt: I feel like you are wanting something from me. [*Projection onto the therapist.*]

Th: I don't need anything from you because this isn't my therapy. [*Remind him of reality.*] The question is, what do you want from your therapy that you think would be good for you? [*Block the projection by reminding him of reality.*] If you don't want to work on your problem, I can accept that.

Pt: I don't want to be stuck. I'm feeling dizzy. [*As he expresses his will, his anxiety rises and shifts into cognitive/perceptual disruption.*]

Th: Something about saying what you want makes you anxious, and then you get dizzy. It's as if it is a bit risky to say what you want out of the therapy. Do you notice that too? [*Cognize about causality: declaring his will triggers high anxiety. Now he understands why he became anxious.*]

Pt: I'm not good at saying what I want for myself. [*He reveals a potential problem to work on.*]

Th: Is that something you would like to be better at? [*Invite him to declare a positive goal for the therapy.*]

Pt: [*Sighs.*] Yes. I think that would be good for me. [*With this unconscious sigh, we know that he is declaring his will in therapy.*]

The therapist has no right to explore until the patient wants to. Focus on his will until he declares that he wants to work on his problem and sighs when he says so. If he does not sigh, he is complying with what he surmises you desire. Consciously, he says yes. Unconsciously, he says no through his actions. We see no sighing, emotion, or energy in the body indicating true desire.

If the patient does not sigh when he declares his will, he does not feel a desire in himself. Instead, he follows a longing he attributes to you. You will have pseudocompliance or defiance. He will react to the will that he has projected onto you.

Declaring his will triggers anxiety in the patient. He is breaking a commandment of his insecure attachment: "Thou shalt not declare a separate will or mind." Thus, the expression of will can trigger the following responses: (1) a sigh, anxiety in the striated muscles; (2) nausea, anxiety in the smooth muscles, or dizziness, anxiety in cognitive/perceptual disruption; (3) dizziness, then projection; or (4) projection of will. A sigh tells us that we can proceed because his will is online. Nausea or cognitive/perceptual disruption reveal that we need to cognize with him about how his will triggers anxiety until he sighs. When he projects, we deactivate the projection of will, then we encourage him to declare his will until he sighs.

PROBLEMS CAUSED BY PROJECTION OF WILL: DEFIANCE AND COMPLIANCE

When the patient projects his will on the therapist, he reacts to his projection in one of two ways. He either defies the therapist's "will" or complies with it. To prevent defiance and compliance, deactivate the underlying projection of will.

The defiant patient does not defy the therapy or the therapist. He opposes the will he has projected onto the therapist. He is convinced he has an outer conflict with you when he has an inner conflict within himself. He wants to do therapy and is afraid to. Unable to bear this inner conflict, he projects his will onto the therapist. He then assumes you want him to do therapy while he doesn't. Once you deactivate his projection of will onto you, he can experience his will to health inside himself, and anxiety will rise. Once he sighs, his will is online for the next step: exploring a specific example.

Principle: *When the patient defies you, remind him of reality. His defiance conflicts with the demands of reality, not with you.*

Deactivate defiance through a stance of radical acceptance. Every defense has its history and wisdom. Accept all the patient's inner life so he can too. Let patience, acceptance, and persistence guide your work. Never defy defiance. Accept it unconditionally so the patient can experience the conflict between his wish for help and fear of pain. In the following vignette, a fragile patient has declared a problem but not his will to work on it. Then defiance emerges, which the therapist deactivates.

Th: Would you like to work on this problem?

Pt: I'm not sure. [*By not being sure, he invites the therapist to make him work. Instead, ask if he wants to work on his problem.*]

Th: If you're not sure, I have no right to ask you to work on something you don't want to work on. [*Remind him of reality.*]

Pt: I'm afraid to face what's underneath. [*He invites the therapist to make him face what he fears.*]

Th: Of course. Everyone is. You can face what you fear so you can be in charge. Or you can avoid what you fear, and then fear will be in charge of you. But the choice is yours. [*Remind him of reality: working on his problem is his choice to make, not the therapist's.*]

Pt: No. I don't want to look at it. [*Defiance: he opposes the will he attributes to the therapist.*]

Th: Okay. [*The therapist does not defy the patient's defiance.*]

Pt: I like feeling in control, and I don't want to get into something I don't understand. [*Defiance: he opposes the will he attributes to the therapist.*]

Th: If you don't want to get into something, I have no right to ask you to get into it. [*Remind him of reality.*]

Pt: I don't want to work on it. [*Defiance: he opposes the will he attributes to the therapist.*]

Th: Okay. [*The therapist does not defy the defiance.*]

Pt: You probably think I should work on this, but I don't want to. [*Defiance: he opposes the will he attributes to the therapist.*]

Th: Why work on a problem if you don't want to? [*The therapist accepts the defiance.*]

Pt: What if I don't want to work on this?

Th: Then I have to respect your wish. But then you would get no help for your problem. [*Remind him of reality.*]

Pt: So can I go? [*Invites the therapist to agree with the defiance.*]

Th: You can have as little help as you want. [*Point out the price of his defense: he will get no help if he leaves.*] I have no right to ask you to work on a problem if you don't want to work on a problem for your benefit. [*Remind him of reality.*]

Pt: Are you kicking me out? [*Projection: by not declaring his will, he kicked himself out of therapy. Sitting in a therapist's office doesn't make a person a patient nor would sitting beside a barbell make him a weightlifter. He becomes a patient when he works on his problem.*]

Th: No. You said you don't want to work on your problem, so you haven't entered therapy yet. And that's okay. This may not be the right time to do therapy for you. [*Remind him of reality.*]

Pt: Maybe it's not the right time. [*Defiance.*]

Th: It may not be the right time for you to work on your problems. Maybe a later time would be better. [*Mirror his defiance.*]

Pt: I'd like to wait until later. [*Defiance based on projection of his will.*]

Th: You have a right to wait as long as you want before you work on your problems. Why rush yourself? [*Remind him of reality to deactivate the projection.*]

Pt: I feel like you are putting the ball back in my court. [*I cannot put his will in him because it has always been in him.*]

Th: But whose problem are we talking about? [*Remind him of reality.*]

Pt: Mine.

Th: Right. I can't put your problem back into you. It's been there all along. [*Remind him of reality to block the projection.*] The only question is whether it's a problem for you that you want to work on now. And it may not be something you want to work on right now.

Pt: Right. I don't see it as a problem I need to work on. [*Denial.*]

Th: Good, you are so clear. Why work on a problem you don't think you need to work on? [*Remind him of reality.*]

Pt: Are you saying I have to leave? [*Projection: he has been saying he should leave.*]

Th: No. Since you said you don't want to work on your problem, you haven't entered therapy yet. You can't leave a therapy you haven't entered. [*Remind him of reality.*]

Pt: But I'm here. [*Denial: sitting in a workplace doesn't make one a worker. He needs to declare an internal problem and his will to work on it. Until then, he is a tourist, not a patient.*]

Th: But being here isn't enough. We would have to work together on your problem to achieve your goals. And if you don't want to do that right now, I have to respect your wish to wait. [*Remind him of reality.*]

Pt: Aren't you supposed to try to convince me to do therapy? [*Projection: he assumes that the therapist should make him do what he doesn't want to do. The conflict would be between the patient and therapist. Instead, the conflict is between his will to health and his resistance.*]

Th: I have no right to convince you to do something you don't want to do. [*Remind him of reality.*] Why look at your problem if that is not what you want for yourself?

Pt: I thought that's what therapists did: convince patients. [*Projection.*]

Th: No. If you are not convinced that you should look at your problems, I have no right to convince you to do something you don't want to do. [*Remind him of reality.*]

Pt: You're not going to make me work on my problem?

Th: No. I can't make you work on anything. Only you can make yourself work on your problems. If you don't want to, I have to respect the facts: you may not want to right now. [*Remind him of reality.*]

Pt: What if we look at a problem later and not now?

Th: Then we would have a nontherapy now while waiting for an imaginary therapy in the future. Why waste your time doing that? [*Remind him of reality.*]

Pt: So you are okay with me not working on a problem? [*Projection: he has been okay not working on a problem.*]

Th: Absolutely. If you don't want to work on a problem, I have no right to ask you to do what you don't want to do. [*Remind him of reality.*]

Pt: Don't you care whether your patients get better? [*Projection: he doesn't care. His self-neglect is now conscious but within the defense of projection. This is a whisper from his unconscious will to health. He has revealed his key problem.*]

Th: Apparently, you don't care whether your problems get resolved now. [*Block the projection.*] If so, I have to accept that you don't care about yourself. [*Remind him of reality.*]

Pt: What if I don't care? [*Defiance.*]

Th: Then we would have to accept that at this point in your life, you don't care enough about yourself to work on your problems. And we would have to wait until you do. [*Remind him of reality.*]

Pt: Okay. I guess I have to work on this problem. [*Projection: "I guess" and "have to" show that this is not his will.*]

Th: No. There's no law that says you have to work on your problem. [*Remind him of reality.*] The question is, do you want to work on your problem for *your* benefit? And, if you don't, that's okay. It may not be the time to get help.

Pt: If I don't get help now, I'll just keep making the same mistakes. [*He speaks realistically about his plight.*]

Th: So is it your will to work on your problem? [*Invite his will.*]

Pt: [*Sighs.*] Yes. [*The sigh tells us his will is online.*]

Th: What would be a specific example of your problem you would like us to look at?

Do not explore a specific example until he declares his will and sighs. Only then is his will online. It must be his will to do therapy. If you give 100 percent of your effort, and he gives only 10 percent of his, he will get a 10 percent result. We might try to give 190 percent to make up for the 90 percent he withholds. That never works. You can offer only 100 percent. But you can never give what the patient withholds from himself. Only he can give what he withholds. Deactivate his defiance by reminding him of reality. His defiance is not in conflict with you. His defiance conflicts with his desire and the demands of reality.

Do not try to be the patient's will to health by giving advice, direction, or approval. His will to health can rise only in him (Rank 1930/1936, 17). No patient became better because you tried to be his will to health. Patients become well only when they declare their will.

MOBILIZING THE PATIENT'S WILL TO ENGAGE IN THE THERAPEUTIC TASK

In the following example, the patient describes her problem but not her will to work on it. The therapist invites her to declare her will to work on her problem to achieve a positive goal. Help her see the purpose of therapy: to achieve her positive goals.

Principle: *Propose a positive goal and ask if it is her will to work on it.*

Pt: I'm a people pleaser.

Th: Is that a problem you would like me to help you with? [*Invite her will to work toward a positive goal.*]

Pt: I feel uncomfortable with this. [*Anxiety.*]

Th: Of course. Would you like help regulating your anxiety so you wouldn't have to feel so uncomfortable? [*Invite her will to work toward a positive goal.*]

Pt: I can't get past that anxiousness. [*She hasn't declared her will.*]

Th: Would you like to find out what is driving your anxiety so you wouldn't have to feel anxious instead? [*Invite her will to work toward a positive goal.*]

Pt: I feel like you are looking for something. [*Projection.*]

Th: I don't need to look for anything because this isn't my problem. The question is, what are you looking for from therapy that would be good for you? [*Remind her of reality.*]

Pt: I guess we could look at my being a people pleaser. [*"I guess" indicates compliance, not her will.*]

Th: But do you want to? [*Invite her will to work toward a positive goal.*]

Pt: Being a people pleaser isn't working for me. [*She hasn't declared her will.*]

Th: Would you like the therapy to help you to please yourself? [*Invite her will to work toward a positive goal.*]

Pt: A guy approached me at the AA meeting and said he wanted to take me out for a date. I agreed. I didn't feel like I could say no. [*She presents a possible problem.*]

Th: Would you like the therapy to help you say no to others so you could say yes to yourself? [*Invite her will to work toward a positive goal.*]

Pt: Helping me say yes to myself? I hadn't thought of that.

Th: Would you like the therapy to help you say no to others so you could say yes to yourself? [*Invite her will to work toward a positive goal.*]

Pt: I think I would like that. [*No sigh. Her will is still not online.*]

Th: And is that what you want? [*Invite her will to work toward a positive goal.*]

Pt: Yes. I feel anxious now. [*Will is coming online. Hence, her anxiety rises.*]

Th: Isn't that interesting? Just wanting to say yes to yourself triggers this anxiety. It's as if a policeman came in and Tasered you with anxiety as if it was against the law to say yes to yourself. Do you see how that happened here?

Pt: Yes. That's weird.

Th: Is that a law you'd like to break? [*Invite her will to work toward a positive goal.*]

Pt: [*Laughs.*] Yes.

DEACTIVATING PROJECTIONS IN THE FRAGILE PATIENT BY MOBILIZING WILL TO THE TASK

The fragile patient often becomes frightened when she declares her wish to get well. So she projects her wish to become well on the therapist, her sponsor, or the rehab unit. As long as she projects her will, she will oppose therapy or recovery. Thus, deactivating the projection of will is essential if she is to recover.

Principle: *Patients don't become well because of your will. They become well because of their will to health.*

Therapy expresses our faith that the patient wants to become well. Yet when treatment starts, that wish may be imperceptible to her even if perceivable in her projections. As you deactivate the projection of will onto you, she will experience her will. This force, her will, drives all recovery.

Pt: I'm afraid you will get too close. [*Projection: she wants to get close.*]

Th: I have no right to get closer to you than you want me to. [*Remind her of reality to deactivate the projection.*] The question is, do you want to get close to your own issues so you can get to the bottom of your problems? [*Invite her will to engage in the therapeutic task.*]

Pt: I'm afraid all this stuff will come out. [*Projection: she wants to share her inner life.*]

Th: Do you want this stuff to come out so you have the information you need to overcome your problems? [*Inviting her will to engage in the therapeutic task.*]

Pt: I'm afraid you will take this stuff out of me. [*Projection: she wishes I could bring her inner life out of her.*]

Th: That's not possible. No one can take anything out of you. [*Remind her of reality to deactivate the projection.*] That's why I have to ask you. Do *you* want to let some stuff out of yourself so you have the information *you* need to feel more in control of *your* life? [*Invite her will to engage in the therapeutic task.*]

Pt: I feel like you are trying to get into my head. [*Projection: she wants to get into her head so she can understand herself.*]

Th: The good news is that I can't. Only you can get into your head. [*Remind her of reality to deactivate the projection.*] Do you want to know what is going on inside yourself so you have better information about yourself and can make better decisions for yourself? [*Invite her will to engage in the therapeutic task.*]

Pt: I'm not sure what the program is here. [*Projection: she projects her desire and agenda onto me.*]

Th: Neither do I. [*Remind her of reality to deactivate the projection.*] That's why I have to ask you. What program would you like to have here in therapy? What goal do you want to achieve? [*Inviting her will to engage in the therapeutic task.*]

Pt: You don't have a program?

Th: No. Because this is not my therapy. [*Remind her of reality to deactivate the projection.*] Since this is *your* therapy to achieve *your* goals, we need to find out what goals *you* want to achieve. Then we can make sure the therapy gives you what you are looking for. [*Invite her will to engage in the therapeutic task.*]

Pt: I hadn't thought of therapy that way before.

Th: As we think about therapy that way, what goals would you like to achieve here so we can make sure the therapy program gives you what you are looking for? [*Invite her will to engage in the therapeutic task.*]

In this example, I never referred to our relationship. Since she was projecting, her first problem was not with me but with her inner life. She split off her desires and projected them outward. Thus, I deactivated each projection. Then I invited her to recognize inside what she had relocated outside. Once she accepts her projections, we have "collected" a person. Only when we have collected a person, only then can we talk about a relationship between her and the therapist.

For example, when she projects her wish to be close, focus first on her wish to be close to her inner life.

Th: Do you want to pay attention to yourself?

Th: Do you want to listen to yourself?

Th: Do you want to look inside yourself?

First, help the patient build her relationship with herself. Then build the relationship with the therapist. The following questions illustrate that shift.

Th: Do I have your permission to help you work toward your goal?

Th: Do you want us to work together toward your goal?

Th: If I notice a mechanism that is hurting you, do I have your permission to point that out so you can be in control rather than those mechanisms controlling you?

We do not have a person in the room if she locates her feelings, desires, and goals in other people. We have only the absence left after her inner life has been banished. As we help her accept the projections she rejected, we invite her orphaned feelings and urges to return home. Gradually, she gains the affect tolerance to bear all her inner life inside herself. Once we achieve that first step, she becomes a person with her own will. And as a separate person, she and the therapist can work together toward her goals.

One intervention is not enough to undo the projection of will. Projection has been habitual and unconscious. In an insecure attachment, she learned to love others by concealing her will. Your persistence alters the way she relates to herself, her will, and other people. Each time she projects her will, she asks you to pass a test: "Can you love my will?" You may have to pass her test many times before her true self emerges (Winnicott 1960/1965a). This is not a cognitive test for her but a relational test for you (Sampson and Weiss 1986).

SUPPORTING THE PATIENT IN BEARING INTERNAL EXPERIENCE

When the patient begins to voice her will, a previously forbidden act, her anxiety will rise. As soon as it rises, help her bear her will and feelings inside so she does not have to send them outside through projection. Support her as soon as anxiety rises so she can depend on you rather than rely on a projection.

Vignette One

We can support the patient in bearing his will by keeping his attention on it for a longer time. This helps him bear his will longer without having to project it outside. The longer he can bear his will, the greater his affect tolerance.

Pt: I know you think I should work on this.

Th: Only you can know if working on this problem would be in your best interest. [*Deactivate the projection onto the therapist.*] That's why we have to find out if you think working on this problem would be good for you. Is this a problem you want to resolve for your benefit to achieve your goals?

I used the pronoun "you" five times in that intervention to help the patient pay attention to his inner experience for twenty seconds. That increases his ability to bear his will inside without projecting it back outside. Patients with less reality testing need more support to do this.

Vignette Two

In the face of her anxiety, the patient may forget that it was her will to seek therapy. Gentle reminders can help her accept her will inside after she projected it.

Th: Is it your will to work on this problem?

Pt: I'm just afraid of the questions you are going to ask me. [*Projection of will.*]

Th: Just to be sure, was it your will to come here today?

Pt: Yes.

Th: And are there problems you want to resolve?

Pt: Yes.

Th: And are there questions you want answers to so you have better information about yourself?

Pt: Yes.

Th: And do you want to ask yourself those questions so you can make better decisions for yourself?

Pt: [*Sighs.*] Yes.

The therapist's questions remind the patient of her will, which she had forgotten when anxiety rose. The more she accepts her will, the less she projects, and the more her projective anxiety drops.

Principle: *To eliminate projective anxiety, remind the patient of reality, and invite her to observe her will inside herself. Once she accepts her will inside, she will not place it outside. Her anxiety will drop, returning to the striated muscles, and she will sigh and intellectualize.*

Vignette Three

Let's review common projections of will that can prevent a therapeutic alliance. In each case, the therapist reminds the patient of reality to deactivate the projection. Then the therapist invites him to become aware of his inner life.

The underlined words outline the exact projection the therapist can deactivate. The unconscious will to health provides the precise words to use when inviting the patient to bear his projections inside. Help him accept tiny projections inside, one at a time, without overwhelming him with anxiety.

Pt: I'm unable to do <u>what you want me to do</u>. [*Projection.*]

Th: There's nothing I need you to do because this isn't my problem. [*Deactivate the projection onto the therapist by reminding him of reality.*] The question is, what do you want to do for yourself here that you think would be good for you? [*Invite him to accept his will to do something good for himself.*]

Pt: If <u>you think this is the solution</u>, I'll do it. [*Projection.*]

Th: I can't know what the best solution is for you. Only you can make that decision. [*Deactivate the projection onto the therapist.*] Do you want to work on your problem to find a solution that works for you? [*Invite him to recognize his wish to work on his problem.*]

Pt: You're asking me for something I can't give you. [*Projection.*]

Th: The good news is, I don't need to ask for anything because this isn't my therapy. [*Deactivate the projection onto the therapist.*] The question is, what do *you* want to ask of the therapy that *you* want it to give *you* that would be good for *you*? [*Invite him to declare his desire.*]

TIMING OF INTERVENTIONS

Inviting the fragile patient to recognize his desires triggers mixed feelings and anxiety. Once he becomes anxious, notice how long he can bear it before projecting. Then you know how quickly to support him before he projects. As soon as the patient declares his will, help him observe and tolerate his desire and anxiety without using projection. If you wait a few seconds, anxiety will rise until he has to project. Instead, immediately help him bear a higher level of his desire just before he projects. Then you can support him at the moment of his greatest need.

Vignette One

Recognizing her will inside herself will trigger anxiety within a second, and often a projection. Intervene as soon as the patient becomes anxious and before the projection. Then you can build her capacity to bear her will inside before she projects. Support her at the point of greatest need: just before she projects.

In the following vignette, the therapist intervenes before or as soon as projection starts. Block the projection and build the capacity to bear will inside.

Pt: I'm just afraid of where this therapy is going. [*Projection: fear of the therapist's imagined will.*]

Th: The good news is, that's not my decision. Only you have the right to decide where the therapy is going. [*Deactivate the projection.*] That's why I have to check in with you. Where would you like therapy to go so it would help you achieve the goals you think would be in your best interests? [*Invite her to bear her desire inside without projecting it outside.*]

Pt: I want to get help with my marriage, but I'm afraid that—[*She declares her goal, but her anxiety rises rapidly. Interrupt before her anxiety and projection escalate.*]

Th: Let's pause. [*Introducing a defense.*] You just said you want help with your marriage. What do you notice feeling now when you say what you want for yourself? [*Invite her to pause. This provides a higher-level defense to keep feelings from rising higher. Then invite her to notice her anxiety before she projects.*]

Pt: Anxious. [*Now she can observe her anxiety rather than be flooded by it. As a result, she no longer needs to project her will onto the therapist to get rid of her anxiety.*]

Th: [*Immediately.*] Okay. Let's pause. Something about noticing that you want to look at this problem makes you anxious. Do you see that too? [*Help her see the link between declaring her will and anxiety.*]

Pt: Yes. [*She relaxes in the chair. Since she can declare her will, she does not have to fear the therapist's "will." Reality testing has improved. Now she can get clearer about her goal and her will to work on it.*]

Due to anxiety, she projected her awareness of a goal. As soon as she recognizes her goal, anxiety will rise, and she may project again. The therapist helps her accept her goal before she projects again. Otherwise, she would fear "his" agenda.

Build the capacity to bear her will inside without projecting. Then she can form a conscious therapeutic alliance. If she projects her will, she will have a misalliance with her projection, not an alliance with the clinician.

Do not ask for feelings toward the therapist while the patient projects her will. Suppose she believes you want to make her do something against her will. She will be angry not at you but at the projection of a dominating figure. Exploring split-off anger toward a projection will only strengthen her projection, decrease her reality testing, and create a misalliance.

Likewise, do not confront the apparent resistance in the fragile patient. People who project may become passive, avoid your gaze, or hesitate. They do not resist you as the therapist. They oppose the projection they have placed on you. For instance, they fear the therapist's "will." "What is he going to do to me?" Confrontation will cause feelings to spike, resulting in splitting, projection, and a loss of reality testing. Instead, deactivate the projection with which the patient is interacting.

When a fragile patient avoids your gaze, ask what ideas she has about the therapy that make her look away. If you ask her to look at you, you may reinforce her belief that you want to control her. Help her intellectualize about her projection. Then you can invite her to look at you to find out if what she sees matches what she thinks. If she looks at your face and sees what she believes, she is relating to her hallucination, not to you. Thus, deactivate the projection. As projection decreases, eye gaze will increase. In this context, gaze avoidance is a secondary defense, resulting from the primary defense of projection. Thus, we address projection first.

Vignette Two

When deactivating the projection of will, remind the patient of therapy's purpose: to achieve his positive goals. Then his will to achieve his goals drives the therapy.

> Pt: I'm afraid you are going to make me feel something. [*Projection of will.*]
>
> Th: The good news is that I have no right to make you feel anything you don't want to feel. Only you can make yourself face your feelings. [*Deactivate the projection.*] The question here is, do you want to face the feelings that have been making you anxious so you can feel your feelings instead of getting anxious? [*Invite him to bear his will inside without projecting it outside. Remind him of positive goals to mobilize his will to the task: "feel your feelings instead of getting anxious."*]

DEACTIVATING LATENT PROJECTIONS OF WILL

When fragile patients describe their conscious fears about other people, they symbolically describe their unconscious fears of the therapist. They claim to feel fine about therapy, yet their latent projections reveal their unconscious fear of it.

A young woman came to a clinic complaining of friends, relatives, and executives who were hostile and cruel. The consistently all-bad characterizations indicated that she was splitting. And the perpetual portrayal of herself as a victim intimated that the patient was projecting her anger onto others. Thus, she began therapy with a conscious belief that people were hostile and an unconscious fear that the therapist would be too. The therapist did not hear this fear, however. Instead, she explored the patient's anger toward these apparently hateful people. As the patient's feelings rose in therapy, the defense of displacement collapsed. Instead of thinking others didn't care, now she believed the therapist didn't care either. And, believing these projections, she abandoned therapy as she had before.

When feelings rise in therapy, higher-level defenses such as displacement dissolve. Then the fragile patient's latent, unconscious projections suddenly become conscious. She becomes convinced the therapist is evil, just like the others. She loses reality testing, equates the therapist with the projection (psychotic transference), and acts out or leaves therapy to escape from the projection.

Since conscious concerns about others can reveal unconscious fears about the therapist, deactivate latent projections before they become conscious. In the following example, a fragile patient in her second session has declared a problem. She has angry outbursts that frighten her family. Ten years of therapy gave no benefit, and she fired her last therapist.

> Pt: People are always telling me what to do. [*Latent projection: you will tell me what to do.*]
>
> Th: And no one likes that. [*Deactivate the projection onto the therapist by working within the defense of displacement: the therapist does not refer to himself, only to a universal theme—no one likes to be told what to do.*] To make sure that we are doing only what you want to do, what is the problem you want us to focus on here today that you think would be helpful to you? [*Remind her of her will. Deactivate the projection that the therapist will be another person telling her what to do.*]
>
> Pt: I don't know. I hate it when people are always trying to control me. [*Latent projection: "You will try to control me in therapy."*]
>
> Th: Of course. Nobody likes that. And nobody has the right to control you. [*Deactivate the projection by working within the defense*

of displacement: "nobody likes that." Remind her of reality.] To make sure you are in control here, what is the problem you would like us to work on so we can help you feel more in control of your life? [*Remind her of her will to deactivate the projection that the therapist will try to control her.*]

Pt: It's just that my last therapist made me talk about my parents. [*Latent projection: "You will make me talk about things I don't want to talk about."*]

Th: I'm sorry to hear that. We therapists have no right to ask you to talk about anything you don't want to talk about. [*Deactivate the projection by working within the defense of displacement: "we therapists have no right." Remind the patient of reality.*] To make sure we talk about only what you want to talk about, what is the problem you want us to focus on that you think would be helpful to you? [*Remind her of her will. This deactivates the projection that the therapist will make her talk against her will.*]

Pt: Anger. I explode all the time over little things. [*The problem. We check on the patient's will.*]

Th: And is this tendency to explode the problem you want us to focus on? [*Invite her will to work on her problem.*]

Pt: It happens all the time. I blow up, and I can't control it. [*She hasn't declared her will, so invite her will again.*]

Th: And would you like us to help you with this tendency to blow up so you could be in control instead of the blow-up habit taking control of you? [*Frame the therapeutic task in terms of her projected wish: to be in control. Differentiate her from the defense that creates her problems.*]

Pt: I just feel so bad because after I yell and scream, everybody is angry with me.

Th: Sure. Because when you yell, the yelling urge gets what it wants, but you don't. You end up having to clean up the mess the yelling habit created. [*Differentiate her from her defense of yelling.*] Would you like us to help you with this yelling habit so we could help you be in control instead of the yelling habit being in control of you? [*Invite her will to engage in the therapeutic task to achieve a positive goal.*]

Pt: [*Sighs.*] Yes. That would help me a lot.

With low affect tolerance, fragile patients have to relocate their will onto others. Thus, therapists (1) explore will according to the patient's capacity, and (2) provide and strengthen higher-level defenses to make exploration possible. In these previous examples, the therapist strengthens the patient's defense of displacement to prevent a rapid rise of anxiety, conscious projection, and loss of reality testing. The therapist works within the defense of displacement by never referring to himself and only referring to the theme in the patient's projections. If he talked about the patient's unconscious fears about him, the projection would become conscious, the patient would lose reality testing, and she would leave. Thus, the therapist deactivates the projections within the defense of displacement to strengthen the only higher-level defense she has at this stage of therapy.

Deactivating the projection helps the patient retain the therapist as a safe ally. Meanwhile, the therapist also helps the patient bear feelings and urges inside without projecting them outside onto other people. Deactivating the projection while supporting the defense of displacement is a counterprojective maneuver (Havens 1976, 1986; Sullivan 1953a). We counter unconscious projections onto the therapist to preserve a conscious alliance. Meanwhile, we build affect tolerance in the patient so she does not cross the threshold of anxiety tolerance and have to project her will onto the therapist.

Principle: *Deactivate latent, unconscious projections before they become conscious by working within the defense of displacement.*

The fragile patient's bad experiences with other people tell you what she unconsciously expects from you. As feelings rise, latent projections may become conscious, and we can lose a realistic alliance. Deactivate latent projections before they become conscious. Then you can establish a therapeutic alliance and avoid misalliance problems later.

SUMMARY

The patient's will is the engine of therapy (H. Davanloo, supervision 2002–2004). Unconscious forces do not entirely determine our lives (Rank 1930/1936). The will to health, being unknowable and unpredictable, offers a different form of causality. The person is both determined and indeterminable, creation and creator.

But the fragile patient's loved ones often abandoned him when he declared his will. As a result, inviting his will triggers anxiety and defenses. Regulate his anxiety, help him let go of his defenses, and invite his will. When he projects his will, deactivate the projection by reminding him of reality. Next, invite him to recognize his will to health inside. Build his ability to accept his will by observing it and the anxiety it triggers. Then therapy can proceed based on his will, goals, and desires. And we can explore a specific example of his problem. As we explore a specific example, feelings will rise. That phase, building capacity, will be the topic of part 2 of the book.

RECOMMENDED MATERIALS

Rank, O. (1936). *Will therapy* (J. Taft, Trans.). Norton. (Original work published 1930)

Projection (December 20, 2012). https://www.youtube.com /watch?v=pPY2wKhiSWA&t=17s.

CHAPTER FOUR

Psychodiagnosis
Co-Creating an Effective Focus

We are never so defenseless against suffering as when we love, never so helplessly unhappy as when we have lost our loved object or its love.

—SIGMUND FREUD, *CIVILIZATION AND ITS DISCONTENTS*

Working with the wide range of fragile patients is complex. Thus, we need to understand the simple principles underlying that complexity. We will illustrate two principles in this chapter: (1) how to use the triangle of conflict to assess the patient's need and (2) how to do this assessment at each stage of developing the therapeutic alliance. This process of assessment, known as psychodiagnosis (H. Davanloo, supervision 2002–2004), determines every intervention by the therapist.

To know what to say, we need to know what is going on. To find that out, we assess each patient's response moment by moment. In theory, the therapeutic process appears simple:

- You ask what problem the patient wants help with, and he answers you clearly.
- You ask if he would like to explore a specific example, and he offers one.
- You ask if he would like to take a look at his feelings, and he says he would.
- You ask, "What is your feeling toward X?" He says what he feels.

- You ask, "How do you experience that anger/sadness in your body?" He tells you.
- You ask, "What is the impulse with that feeling?" He tells you and faces his feelings deeply, achieving insights along the way.

But therapy never goes this way. Each of your questions invites the patient to depend on you, but fragile patients have learned that depending leads to pain, not help. As a result, rather than offer a problem, their will to work on a problem, a specific example, or a feeling, these patients respond with anxiety and defenses. Often, the fragile patient floods with anxiety at the mere prospect of depending on the therapist. Or he may claim that he has no problem (defense). Or he describes his problem but does not declare his will to work on it (defense). Rather than explore his problems and feelings (the therapeutic task), the detours of anxiety and defense arise instead.

Each step in building the alliance triggers only three possible patient responses, which we refer to as the *triangle of conflict* (Malan 1979).

Step one: Declaring a problem to work on

Responses: Problem, anxiety, or defense

Step two: Declaring the will to work on the problem

Responses: Will, anxiety, or defense

Step three: Declaring a specific example to explore

Responses: Example, anxiety, or defense

Step four: Declaring a feeling in that example

Responses: Feeling, anxiety, or defense

Anxiety and defenses are not obstacles but opportunities to help the patient. They reveal the patient's attachment needs in each moment. If he responds with anxiety that is too high, regulate his anxiety and then find out what the problem is for which he wants your help. If he responds with a defense, help him see and let go of that defense and then explore to find out the problem for which he wants your help. When the patient takes a detour, help him see it so he can return to the therapeutic task: working on his problem so he can achieve his goals. By identifying these detours, his anxiety and defenses, you will discover what causes his problems and symptoms.

This internal conflict between feelings, anxiety, and defenses always occurs within a relationship: relating, anxiety/danger, and defenses (how patients adapted to the dangers of relating). Internal conflicts tell the history of past external conflicts. Thus, we always need to look at the triangle of conflict and the interpersonal context within which it occurs: the triangle of person. (See figure 4.1.)

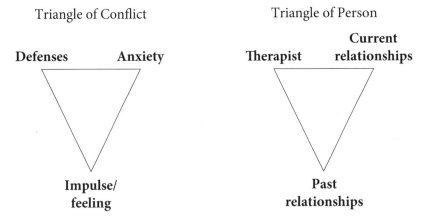

Figure 4.1 The triangle of conflict and the triangle of persons

Anxiety and defenses tell the history of the patient's relational past as it awakens in our relationship. Anxiety is not just a fact in the present but an indicator of what was dangerous in his past. Likewise, a defense is not just a fact but a relationship, how the patient enacts his history of loving: "How do you need me to protect you from my being?" When the patient cuts off a feeling and sends it off to live in others, he commits an act of psychic erasure to become the shadow he hopes you could love. In each relationship, whether in the past, his current life, or in therapy, anxiety reveals what is dangerous, and defenses show how he deals with those dangers.

The following steps illustrate how the patient's internal conflict between feelings, anxiety, and defenses reflects his external conflict: how he manages his relationship with you.

Step one: Declaring a problem to work on

Responses: Depending, anxiety, or protecting you from his need

Step two: Declaring the will to work on the problem

Responses: Revealing his will, anxiety, or protecting you from his will

Step three: Declaring a specific example to explore

Responses: Exploring, anxiety, or protecting you from his need

Step four: Declaring a feeling in that example

Responses: Feeling, anxiety, or protecting you from his feelings

Thus, our psychodiagnosis assesses his internal conflict (feelings, anxiety, and defenses), where unconscious anxiety is discharged in the body, and which unconscious defenses are causing the presenting problems and symptoms.

Then psychodiagnosis also assesses the unconscious relationship with us, within which anxiety and defenses arise. Since anxiety is a sign of danger, whom do I represent where sharing a problem, will, or feeling would be dangerous? And since defenses show how the patient dealt with this danger, whom do I represent where these defenses would have been adaptive? Thus, psychodiagnosis initially assesses the patient through two perspectives: (1) the internal conflict of unconscious feeling, unconscious anxiety, and unconscious defense; and (2) the unconscious interpersonal relationship within which conflict occurs.

PSYCHODIAGNOSIS OF THE TRIANGLE OF CONFLICT

All patient responses are perfect. They perfectly show us where the patient needs help in this moment:

- If the patient declares a problem, we ask if it is his will to work on it.
- If the patient becomes too anxious, we regulate his anxiety and return to the problem.
- If the patient uses a defense, we help him see it, and invite him to declare his problem.

This is how we maintain an effective therapeutic focus at each stage of developing the alliance, addressing his relational needs moment by moment. Every time we regulate anxiety or address a fragile patient's defense, we meet his need and learn what causes his problems. Thus, treating and assessing go hand in hand. To assess what causes the patient's problems, follow these three principles:

- *Assess each patient response:* Is it a feeling, anxiety, or a defense?
- *Assess the patient's capacity for self-observation in this moment:* Can he observe his response and reflect on it?
- *Help the patient with that specific problem:* Do you need to (1) invite a healing relationship, (2) regulate anxiety, or (3) identify

or block a defense to help the patient maintain an effective therapeutic focus?

Through this process of *psychodiagnosis*, we diagnose what causes the patient's difficulties. In psychotherapy, diagnosis usually refers to a label that describes the patient's directly observable symptoms (e.g., depression). A phenomenological diagnosis tells us the patient's symptoms but not what causes them. For instance, if you went to a physician and he said, "Your diagnosis is fever," you would become irritated. "I know, doctor. But what is *causing* my fever? A cold, flu, or an infection?" If we don't know the cause, we cannot treat it. For instance, the term *depression* describes a symptom but does not diagnose the cause. A description is not an explanation (Bateson 1969/2000). Genuine clinical thinking requires that we diagnose the cause. Our current model of "diagnosis" does not do that (Verhaeghe 2004).

Once we know the cause, we know what to treat. When we *psychodiagnose*, we ask, "What causes the patient's symptoms?" Moment to moment, the therapist assesses the patient's responses to each intervention: feeling, anxiety, or defense. (See figure 4.1.) This constant analysis reveals the feelings with which the patient struggles, the anxiety discharge pattern in the body, and the defenses that cause the symptoms. Now the therapist knows what feelings to explore, how to address the anxiety, and the defenses the patient needs help with. Now we know what to focus on, what to treat, and how to treat. To analyze each patient's response, we use the triangle of conflict.

If the patient responds with feeling, we can explore it. However, the fragile patient usually responds with anxiety or defense. Thus, the therapist must assess the pathway of anxiety discharge and the defenses to know how to help the patient in each moment.

Psychodiagnosis of Anxiety

Each time the patient responds to an intervention, watch the patient's body to assess the pathways of unconscious anxiety discharge. Focus on the following areas:

- Striated muscles
- Smooth muscles
- Cognitive/perceptual disruption

We explore feelings when the patient's anxiety goes into the striated muscles. Anxiety in the striated muscles is a good sign, indicating that the patient is facing feelings he previously avoided. If we avoid conflictual feelings, the patient's anxiety will remain low, but he will not learn to face the feelings and issues he usually avoids. Work at the highest level of feeling the patient can bear while his anxiety is discharged into the striated muscles.

As feelings rise, anxiety shifts out of the striated muscles into the smooth muscles or cognitive/perceptual disruption. That is the patient's threshold of anxiety tolerance, the maximum level of affect he can bear before anxiety shifts out of the striated muscles. We try to work at that level to build his affect tolerance. If anxiety shoots over that threshold, it is too high, and we regulate it.

Psychodiagnosis of Defense

To learn what causes the fragile patient's symptoms and presenting problems, we identify the defenses he uses. We also assess his ability to observe and let go of defenses and his capacity to bear mixed feelings. For fragile patients, we focus primarily on denial, splitting, projection, and projective identification. Hallucinations, delusions, idealization, devaluation, and dissociation all result from these first four defenses.

Fragile Character Structure

All fragile patients go over the threshold of anxiety tolerance into cognitive/perceptual disruption. And they use the defenses of splitting and projection. Their capacity to detach from feelings (isolation of affect) is weak or nonexistent. When isolation of affect collapses, primitive defenses emerge such as weepiness, compliance, somatization, turning on the self, depression, projection, splitting, externalization, dissociation, and, finally, hallucinations and delusions.

Fragile patients exist on a spectrum. Mildly fragile patients can intellectualize and rationalize to detach from feelings at low levels. However, as feelings rise, they experience cognitive/perceptual disruption. Moderately fragile patients may be able to intellectualize a little bit, but, as feelings rise, they experience cognitive/perceptual disruption and use the defenses of splitting and projection. Severely fragile patients rely almost exclusively on primitive forms of denial, splitting, and projection.

Ability to Observe and Let Go of Defenses

Fragile patients cannot see their defenses initially. Splitting and projection lead to a loss in reality testing, so patients cannot differentiate the therapist from a projection. We need to deactivate their projections to establish an internal focus in therapy. Then patients can see that defenses, not other people, cause their symptoms.

Capacity to Bear Feelings

Fragile patients can bear only low levels of feeling before their anxiety shifts into the smooth muscles or cognitive/perceptual disruption. Able to bear only a small amount of feeling inside, they have to project the excess outside. To do so, they try to get rid of their feelings through splitting, denial, and projection.

Psychodiagnosis of Self-Observing Capacity

A patient needs to be able to observe and pay attention to her feelings to feel them deeply. To regulate her anxiety, a patient must be able to observe and pay attention to it. To see and turn against her defenses, a patient needs to be able to observe and pay attention to them and the suffering they cause. The patient must be able to observe and pay attention to feelings, anxiety, and defenses moment by moment to get well. The following is a list of the self-observing capacities we need to mobilize in patients:

1. *Ability to observe*
   - Feelings
   - Unconscious anxiety in the body
   - Defenses
   - The difference between the observing ego and experiencing self
   - The difference between other people and projections
2. *Ability to pay attention to*
   - Feelings
   - Anxiety
   - Defenses

- The relations among feeling, anxiety, and defenses
- The therapeutic relationship

3. *Ability to differentiate*
   - Stimuli from feelings
   - Feelings from anxiety
   - Feelings from defenses

4. *Ability to see causality*
   - A stimulus triggers a feeling; a feeling triggers anxiety; and anxiety triggers defenses, which create the presenting problems.

5. *Dystonicity* (Can the patient see the defense, see its price, see that the defense is a behavior and not him, and can he let go of the defense?)
   - Ability to differentiate oneself from the defenses one uses
   - Ability to see the price of the defenses
   - Ability to experience grief and guilt over the price paid for the defenses

THE CYCLE OF PSYCHODIAGNOSIS

After every intervention, the patient will respond with a feeling (which the therapist will explore), excessive anxiety (which the therapist will regulate so they can establish a secure attachment), or a defense (which the therapist will help the patient see and let go of so they can build a secure attachment). Thus, the therapist assesses each patient response to develop the next intervention:

- The patient's response to intervention. [*Feeling, anxiety, or defense.*]
- Psychodiagnosis by the therapist. Where is the patient's response on the triangle of conflict? Should you explore a feeling, regulate anxiety, or address a defense?
- Intervention to address the patient's need in this moment.
- The patient's next response to intervention. [*Feeling, anxiety, or defense.*]
- Psychodiagnosis by the therapist.

Principle of Psychodiagnosis:
> *Assess the patient's response to each intervention.*

This cycle of intervention, response, assessment of the response, and intervention allows us to continually assess and respond to the patient's needs moment by moment. Now we will review common responses by patients, their psychodiagnostic implications, and interventions to address them. When the patient answers the therapist's question or offers a feeling, continue exploring. If he responds with a detour to anxiety or defense, help him see the detour and return to an effective therapeutic focus.

Interventions for Detours when Asking for a Problem to Work On

To co-create a therapeutic alliance, we need to know what problem motivates the patient to seek therapy. Thus, we begin by asking about the problem for which he seeks our help. When patients have been hurt in relationships, they fear depending on us. Thus, rather than describe a problem, the fragile patient may offer a detour.

Anxiety Detours

The patient, rather than offer a presenting problem, may present with anxiety instead. This section shows common detours to anxiety, how to assess them, and how to intervene.

Intervention: "What is the problem with which you would like me to help you?"

Response One: "I'm nervous. There are so many things going wrong." [*The patient begins to talk rapidly.*]

Psychodiagnosis: The patient experiences a fast rise of anxiety, which he ignores by talking over it.

Intervention: Mobilize attention to the anxiety, assess it, and point out the destructive consequences of talking over and ignoring it.

Th: [*Speaking slowly.*] This nervousness is a sign of anxiety. I notice you are talking rapidly over your anxiety. Do you notice that too?

Pt: [*Defense: rushing speech.*] I always do.

Th: When you talk over your anxiety, that can be a way to ignore it. [*Identify the defense.*]

Pt: If I ignore my anxiety, it will go away. [*Defense: rationalization and denial.*]

Th: But has it ever gone away? [*Contrast the denial with reality.*]

Pt: No.

Th: Ignoring the anxiety may make you less aware of it, but your body is still anxious.

Pt: Yes.

Th: Could we pay attention to your anxiety and see if we can bring it down? [*Help the patient let go of the defense of ignoring so we can regulate his anxiety.*]

Response Two: "I'm feeling a pain in my stomach."

Psychodiagnosis: The patient experiences a fast rise of anxiety in the smooth muscles.

Intervention: Stop the inquiry into the problem and mobilize attention to the anxiety to regulate it, and then invite feeling.

Th: You are aware of pain in your stomach. That's a sign of anxiety. Are you aware of feeling anxious right now? Where else do you notice anxiety in your body right now? [*Go through the complete list of symptoms to assess his pathways of unconscious anxiety discharge.*]

Intervention: Once the patient can observe his symptoms of anxiety, regulate it by promoting higher-level defenses, such as isolation of affect and intellectualization.

Th: You have come here of your own free will to tell me about your problem. You want help; this makes you anxious, and the anxiety goes to your gut. Do you see that sequence too? [*Help the patient see causality to regulate his anxiety.*]

Response Three: "I'm sorry. What did you say?"

Psychodiagnosis: The patient exhibits no tension anywhere in his body. Assessment reveals that he is experiencing cognitive/perceptual disruption; he cannot think or remember what you said.

Intervention: Regulate the anxiety immediately by mobilizing attention to the experience of anxiety.

Th: Before we get into that, how is your thinking right now? Is it a little cloudy? Are you feeling a little confused? How is your vision? Are your ears ringing? Okay. I noticed that as soon as I asked what you would like me to help you with, your anxiety went straight up, and your mind blanked out. Did you notice that? How is your thinking now? [*Talk about the triangle of conflict and mobilize attention to the body until the symptoms of cognitive/perceptual disruption disappear.*] Is this problem of anxiety and your mind blanking out something you would like me to help you with?

Defense Detours

Sometimes the patient will avoid presenting a problem. This section shows common detours to defense, how to assess them, and how to intervene.

Intervention: "What is the problem with which you would like me to help you?"

Response One: "Do you think I have a problem?"

Psychodiagnosis: Projection.

Intervention: The patient projects his awareness of a problem onto the therapist. But therapy can be based only on a problem the patient wants to work on. Thus, the therapist will deactivate the projection and then invite the patient to declare the problem he wants to work on.

Th: I can't know if you have a problem because I'm not you. That's something only you can know. So what is the problem you would like me to help you with?

Response Two: "I don't have a problem."

Psychodiagnosis: Denial.

Intervention: Since the patient says he has no problem, you have no agreement to explore. Instead, make noninterpretive interventions to address his denial. Point out the contradiction between what he says (he has no problem) and does (he is sitting in a therapist's office).

Th: And yet I'm sure you wouldn't come here for no reason at all.

Th: Although your *lips* say you have no problem, your *feet* brought you here.

Response Three: "The problem is my wife and the way she handles our money." The patient is fidgeting.

Psychodiagnosis: Externalization. He does not see the defenses that cause his problems, so he assumes someone else causes them. If we agree that his wife is the problem, we help him blame others for his problems. He invites us to study his wife rather than his inner life. But then therapy would not have an internal focus.

Intervention: Block the projection and invite an internal focus.

Th: Since she's not here, I can't help her. So I wonder what *internal* problem you would like me to help you with?

Response Four: "I don't know what you are looking for."

Psychodiagnosis: Projection. The patient projects his will to look into himself onto you.

Intervention: Deactivate the projection of his will to avoid a misalliance. Remind him of his will to look inside himself, which he has forgotten.

Th: I don't need to look at anything because this isn't my therapy. The question is, what do you want to look into so that you get better information and can make better decisions for yourself?

Interventions for Detours when Inviting a Specific Example of the Problem

Once the patient describes the problems for which she seeks help, we ask for a specific example of the problem. By exploring that example, we can find out what the triangle of conflict is that creates the patient's problems and symptoms.

Intervention: "Can we take a look at a specific example?"

Response: "My husband told me he is having an affair."

Psychodiagnosis: The patient gives a clear answer. She exhibits no defenses, so the therapist can explore feelings in that example.

Th: What feelings do you have toward him?

Anxiety Detours

When the therapist asks for a specific example of the problem, the patient may offer a detour of anxiety that requires anxiety regulation before exploring a specific example.

Intervention: "Can we take a look at a specific example?"

Response: "I'm getting sick to my stomach just thinking about it."

Psychodiagnosis: The patient's anxiety is discharged in the smooth muscles.

Intervention: Regulate the anxiety before exploring a specific example of the problem.

Th: That's a sign of anxiety. Are you aware of feeling anxious right now? [*Identify and label the symptom as anxiety.*]

Pt: Yes.

Th: As soon as I invited you to look at a specific example of this conflict, you became anxious, and the anxiety gave you a stomach-ache. Do you see that too? [*Point out causality: stimulus, anxiety, and symptom.*]

Pt: Yes. It feels scary to look at this.

Th: I'm sure it does. Would you like to face this conflict so we can help you overcome your anxiety? [*Invite the patient to face what she fears to achieve a positive goal.*]

Pt: [*Sighs.*] Yes. I have to get rid of this anxiety. [*The patient's anxiety is back in the striated muscles. Now it is safe to explore a specific example of the problem.*]

Th: Can we take a look at a specific example of where you and he were in conflict?

Defense Detours

When the therapist asks for a specific example of the problem, the patient may offer defenses rather than a specific example. Address those defenses until the patient offers a specific example.

Intervention: "Can we take a look at a specific example?"

Response One: "I can't remember one."

Psychodiagnosis: Forgetting. This defense prevents the patient and therapist from exploring the problem.

Intervention: Point out the price of the defense to help the patient get the help she needs.

Th: If we don't have a specific example, we won't be able to get a clear picture of your problem, and we won't be able to help you with it. So could we look at a specific example of where this problem comes up for you?

Response Two: "There are so many, I can't think of a place to start."

Psychodiagnosis: Generalizing.

Intervention: Block the defense, draw the patient's attention to the price of the defense, and then invite a specific example.

Th: Notice how you are having a hard time coming up with a specific example? That's going to be a problem because if we don't have a specific example, we won't be able to get a clear picture of your difficulties. What would be a specific example of your problem?

Interventions for Detours when Inviting Feelings

Once the patient offers a specific example of the problem, we explore her feelings in that example to find out the triangle of conflict that causes her problems. However, the patient usually offers detours of anxiety and defense rather than describe her feeling.

Intervention: "What is your feeling toward her for doing that?"

Response: "I was angry."

Psychodiagnosis: The patient gives a clear answer to the question.

Intervention: Explore how the patient experiences his feeling in his body.

Th: How do you experience that anger right now, physically in your body?

Anxiety Detours

When the therapist invites the patient to label his feeling, anxiety will rise. The pathway of anxiety discharge determines the therapist's interventions as we see in the following examples.

Intervention: "She told you she wants a divorce and doesn't want you to have any contact with her?"

Response One: "I feel tense."

Psychodiagnosis: The patient's anxiety goes into the striated muscles. Since the patient cannot distinguish his feeling from anxiety, he can observe his anxiety but not the feeling.

Intervention: Differentiate anxiety from the feeling.

Th: The tension is your anxiety. If we look under the anxiety, what is the feeling that makes you so anxious?"

Response Two: "I feel sick to my stomach."

Psychodiagnosis: The patient's anxiety is discharged into the smooth muscles. Since the patient cannot distinguish his feeling from anxiety, he can observe his anxiety but not the feeling.

Intervention: Regulate the anxiety by mobilizing self-observation, and then point out causality.

Th: Where do you notice that symptom in your stomach? Do you notice any other symptoms of anxiety in your body right now? So we notice that when I asked about your feeling, you became anxious, and then got sick to your stomach. [*Differentiate his feeling from anxiety and point out causality.*]

Th: As you looked at your feeling toward your wife, this anxiety comes in and attacks your gut. Do you see that?

After drawing the patient's attention to causality, you can also regulate the anxiety by switching the focus to the patient's feeling in another relationship.

Th: Does anxiety attack you as soon as you face your anger in other relationships? Could we look at an example?

Defense Detours

The therapist invites the patient to label his feeling, which triggers anxiety and defenses. Thus, the therapist must help the patient see the defenses he uses. Once the patient sees the defenses he uses, he can make a different choice and face the feelings he previously avoided.

Intervention: "She yelled and spit at you, called you names, and threw the ring into the street. What is your feeling toward her for doing that?"

Response One: "I feel hurt."

Psychodiagnosis: The patient confuses his feeling with what the other person did (the stimulus). That is why he cannot see his feeling of anger.

Intervention: Help the patient differentiate the stimulus from the feeling.

Th: Absolutely! She hurt you! [*Point out the stimulus.*] That's what she did. What is your feeling toward her for doing that? [*Differentiate the stimulus from the feeling.*]

Response Two: "I feel sad."

Psychodiagnosis: The patient cannot distinguish his feeling from a defensive affect. Since his wife threw the ring away, the patient will feel sad. But what function does the sadness serve now? Does sadness mobilize or paralyze the patient? Does his sadness help him face or avoid his complex emotions? Here, the patient's sadness has a defensive function. It covers his anger.

Intervention: Differentiate the feeling from a defensive affect.

Th: Right. Of course, you feel sad. This sadness is between you and you. But I'm asking you something different: What is the feeling *toward* her for hurting you?

Response Three: "I think she was wrong to do that."

Psychodiagnosis: The patient does not distinguish his feeling from the defense of intellectualization.

Intervention: Help the patient distinguish between the feeling and the defense, and then invite the feeling.

Th: That's your thought. If we look under the thought, what's the feeling toward her for doing that?

Response Four: "She hates me."

Psychodiagnosis: The patient does not distinguish his feeling from the defense of projection.

Intervention: Help the patient distinguish between his feeling and the defense, and then invite the feeling.

Th: We can only speculate about what she feels, but we could get absolutely clear about how you feel. If we leave her mind to the side, what's the feeling toward her for doing that?

Response Five: "I was so stupid to trust her."

Psychodiagnosis: Self-attack. Address this defense immediately. Otherwise, it will make him depressed in the session.

Intervention for a depressed patient with low observing capacity: Help the patient see the defense of self-attack.

Th: Could that be a critical thought? Could that thought be hurting you? Shall we take a look underneath that thought so we can see the feelings underneath? If we look under that thought, what are the feelings toward her?

Response Six: [*Sighs.*] "I feel confused."

Psychodiagnosis: Intellectualization. Anxiety goes into the striated muscles. The patient offers a thought instead of a feeling.

Intervention: Differentiate the feeling from the defense.

Th: Confusion is a thought. If we look under the thought, what's the feeling toward her?

Response Seven: [*The patient's body goes limp.*] "What did you say? I feel confused."

Psychodiagnosis: The patient's anxiety is discharged into cognitive/perceptual disruption. The patient's anxiety has become too high.

Intervention: Regulate the anxiety and show the causality of feeling, anxiety, and symptoms.

Th: You are confused? How is your thinking now?

Pt: Not good.

Th: Is it cloudy?

Pt: Yes.

Th: That's a sign of anxiety. Did you just blank out?

Pt: It's like my mind emptied.

Th: That's another sign of anxiety. How is your vision and hearing?

Pt: My vision is a bit blurry.

Th: That's another sign of anxiety. Are you feeling faint or dizzy?

Pt: No. [*Anxiety is no longer in cognitive/perceptual disruption. As a result, the therapist can describe the triangle of conflict.*]

Th: When I ask about your feelings, your anxiety goes up rapidly, your mind starts not working right, and you become confused. Do you see that sequence?

Response Eight: [*The patient sighs.*] "I don't feel anything."

Psychodiagnosis: The patient denied his feelings right away without looking inside himself.

Intervention: Point out the defense.

Th: Do you notice you said that right away before you even looked inside to see what you feel?

To better understand this defense, imagine that you asked a friend if she had any coffee in her pantry and she replied, "I don't know." You would be perturbed because she didn't even bother to look in the cupboard to see what was there.

Response Nine: "I'm embarrassed. I feel so bad."

Psychodiagnosis: Rather than describe a feeling toward his fiancée who hurt him, the patient describes a feeling toward himself. In effect, he "borrows" her shame (Nathanson 1996), identifying with her, rather than face his feelings toward her. Here, shame functions as a defensive affect to hide his anger.

Intervention: Point out the defensive function of shame. Differentiate the patient and his feeling from the defensive affect of shame.

Th: Notice how this embarrassment attacks you just when I ask you what you feel toward her? It's like the shame police come in to Taser you before you tell me how you feel toward her. Do you see that? Could we take a look underneath the shame [*differentiate the defensive affect (shame) from the underlying feeling*] and see what the feeling is toward her that the shame has been covering up? What's the feeling toward her?

Interventions for Detours when Inviting the Physical Experience of Feeling

Once the patient has correctly labeled her feeling, ask her how she experiences that feeling physically in her body. In response, the patient may use detours of anxiety and defense. The following vignettes show how to address these detours and maintain an effective therapeutic focus.

Intervention: "You felt angry with him. How do you experience this anger physically in your body right now?"

Response: "I feel some heat coming up from my belly, and my hands want to grab something."

Psychodiagnosis: The patient is aware of the experience of her feeling.

Intervention: Explore how she experiences that impulse physically in his body.

Th: If you let that heat come up through your body, what impulse comes up with that rage?

Anxiety Detours

Rather than describe how she experiences the anger in her body, the patient may report the experience of anxiety instead. The therapist differentiates the patient's feeling from anxiety, regulates the anxiety if it is too high, and then invites the patient to face the feeling that triggered her anxiety.

Intervention: "You felt angry with him. How do you experience this anger physically in your body right now?"

Response: "I'm really afraid." [*Patient starts shaking.*]

Psychodiagnosis: The patient's anxiety starts to rise rapidly.

Intervention: Differentiate the anxiety from the feeling, and encourage the patient to face her anger.

Th: Of course, you are afraid of your anger. That's why you are here. Wouldn't it be nice to be able to feel your anger so you could assert yourself with power instead of being paralyzed with fear?

Pt: Yes.

Th: Shall we take a look at this anger so you can be in charge instead of the anxiety being in charge of you?

Defense Detours

Rather than describe how she experiences her anger physically in her body, the patient may use defenses. The therapist can help the patient see and let go of her defenses so she can face the warded-off feeling.

Intervention: "You felt angry with him. How do you experience this anger physically in your body right now?"

Response: "I feel like walking away from him."

Psychodiagnosis: The patient does not differentiate his feeling of anger from her defense against it. She wants to walk away from him and her feelings.

Intervention: Differentiate the feeling from the defense, and invite the feeling.

Th: Of course, you want to walk away from him and your anger. But no matter where you go, the anger follows you. Would you like to turn around and face this anger so you can embrace your power and no longer have to live a life on the run?

PSYCHODIAGNOSIS WHILE BUILDING THE ALLIANCE

Anxiety and defense can occur at each phase of developing a therapeutic alliance. Thus, fragile patients can respond with anxiety in cognitive/perceptual disruption, the defenses of splitting and projection, or both.

Declaring an Internal Problem

Declaring an internal problem brings up anxiety and defenses triggered by depending.

Projection: "My probation officer said I have a drinking problem."

Th: That's what he thinks. What is the problem you want to work on? [*Block the projection and return to the focus.*]

Denial: "I don't have a problem."

Th: And yet you are here. [*Remind him of a fact that contradicts his denial.*]

Splitting: "Maybe I have a problem. I don't think so."

Th: You think maybe you have a problem and maybe you don't. What's it like to notice that complexity? [*Bring together the conflictual motivations that he splits apart.*]

Declaring One's Will to Work on the Problem

Declaring one's will to work on a problem brings up anxiety and defenses triggered by the act of revealing a separate mind and will in a relationship.

Projection: "My wife thinks I should."

Th: That's what she wants. What about you? [*Block the projection and invite him to declare his will.*]

Denial: "I don't want to work on this."

Th: Okay. I have no right to ask you to want something you don't want. [*Deactivate a battle of will by reminding him that his therapy can be based only on his will and desire.*]

Splitting: "I want to, but, no, not now."

Th: You want to and you don't want to. What's it like to notice that complexity inside you? [*Bring together the conflictual motivations that he splits apart.*]

Declaring a Positive Goal

Declaring a positive goal can bring up anxiety and feelings.

Projection: "My sponsor said I should try to get sober."

Th: That's his goal. What is yours? [*Block the projection and invite him to declare his positive goal.*]

Denial: "I can't think of anything to work toward."

Th: Okay. Then we'll just have to wait until you can. After all, without a goal that is positive to you, why do this? [*Deactivate a battle of will by reminding him that his therapy can be based only on his will and desire.*]

Splitting: "I don't want to stop using drugs." [*Negation plus splitting, since he is in a therapist's office.*]

Th: A man who doesn't want to stop using drugs finds himself in a drug counselor's office. [*Bring together the conflictual motivations that he splits apart.*]

At each stage of building the alliance with fragile patients, the same defenses of splitting and projection may occur. Once you perceive this pattern, dealing with defenses becomes easier. Patiently block projections, remind him of facts that contradict his denial, and remind him of his complex motivations when he engages in splitting. By doing so, you can build his capacity to ask for help, declare his will, and declare a positive goal. These steps will build his affect tolerance as you form an alliance. Then you can explore specific examples of his problems and help him with his feelings. See figure 4.2 for an illustration of this sequence.

SELF-SUPERVISION

To supervise yourself, assess each of your sentences to see if your interventions matched the patient's need and if you consistently returned to a therapeutic focus. Then the self-supervision can help you maintain a healing focus in therapy.

To assess your alliance, use the following outline for self-supervision. *Phase One in Alliance Building: The Problem*—Analyze each sentence you offered using the following questions:

1. Did you ask the patient about the problem for which he needs help?

2. If the patient became too anxious, did you regulate anxiety and ask about the problem again?

3. If the patient used a defense, did you identify the defense and then ask about the problem again?

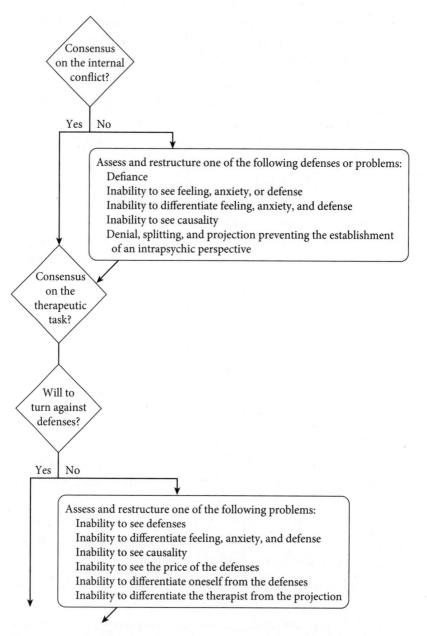

Figure 4.2 Decision tree for a conscious therapeutic alliance

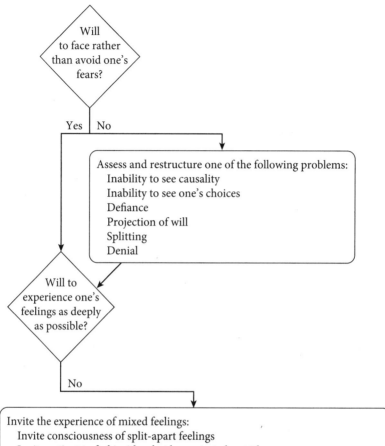

Figure 4.2 (continued)

4. Or did you block the process by offering a defense, such as explaining, giving advice, or intellectualizing?

Phase Two in Alliance Building: A Will to Work on the Problem

1. Once the patient declared a problem, did you ask if it was his will to work on it?

2. If the patient became too anxious, did you regulate anxiety and ask about his will again?

3. If the patient used a defense, did you address the defense and ask about his will again?

4. Or, did you block the process by offering a defense, such as explaining, giving advice, or intellectualizing?

Phase Three in Alliance Building: Consensus on a Positive Goal

1. Once the patient declared his will, did you ask about a positive goal the patient wants to work toward?
2. If the patient became too anxious, did you regulate anxiety and ask about his positive goal again?
3. If the patient used a defense, did you address the defense and ask about his positive goal again?
4. Or, did you block the process by offering a defense, such as explaining, giving advice, or intellectualizing?

Phase Four in Alliance Building: A Specific Example to Explore

1. Following the previous three steps, did you ask about a specific example of his problem the patient wants to explore?
2. If the patient became too anxious, did you regulate anxiety and ask about a specific example of his problem again?
3. If the patient used a defense, did you address the defense and ask about a specific example of his problem again?
4. Or, did you block the process by offering a defense, such as explaining, giving advice, or intellectualizing?

Phase Five in Alliance Building: Exploring Feelings

1. Following the previous four steps, did you ask about his feelings toward a person in a specific example?
2. If the patient became too anxious, did you regulate anxiety and ask about his feelings again?
3. If the patient used a defense, did you address the defense and ask about his feelings again?
4. Or, did you block the process by offering a defense, such as explaining, giving advice, or intellectualizing?

Each time you leave the therapeutic focus by offering a defense, such as explaining, giving advice, or intellectualizing, your defenses block the process. Next session, analyze your transcript to help yourself maintain a better therapeutic focus.

PSYCHODIAGNOSIS OF THE PATIENT'S NEEDS

To assess your understanding of the patient, analyze each sentence the patient says. Did the patient describe any of the following?

- A stimulus that would trigger a feeling
- A problem, will to work on the problem, an example of the problem, or a feeling
- Anxiety in the body
- A defense

Her responses tell you her needs. You will know where to focus to develop the alliance, whether to regulate anxiety or to help her with the defenses creating her problems. Since you understand the detours, you will know when and how to return to the therapeutic focus.

We need certain ingredients for therapy to succeed. If you do not find out the problem the patient has, therapy can have no focus. If you do not find out if it is the patient's will to work on the problem, you cannot have a partnership. If you do not find a positive goal the patient wants to work toward, he will have no motivation to do therapy. Without a specific example, you cannot explore the feelings the patient has avoided.

If you invite the alliance in the steps above, regulate anxiety when necessary, and block alliance-defeating defenses, you will co-create a therapeutic alliance. However, if you do not consistently invite the alliance (problem, will, positive goal, specific example, and feelings), the therapy will become stalled. And if you offer defenses or go along with patient defenses, your behavior will create a misalliance.

Analyzing your sessions can help your interventions be more focused, helpful, and targeted to the patient's needs. Week by week, this analysis can give you accurate feedback on how to improve your therapeutic focus.

SUMMARY

Each patient's response to intervention will be a feeling, anxiety, or a defense. Psychodiagnosis allows us to assess those responses so we can offer targeted interventions moment by moment.

Principle: *Assess each patient response so your intervention will address the patient's need in this moment.*

Principle: *Assess each therapist response to see if your intervention matched the patient's need.*

Metaprinciple: *When therapy is stuck, your behaviors are keeping it stuck. Assess each of your interventions to see which ones are meeting a patient's need or offering a defense.*

RECOMMENDED READINGS

To build your capacity to psychodiagnose the triangle of conflict, see the chapters "Theory of the analysis of conflict" and "Conflict analysis studies," in J. Frederickson (1999), *Psychodynamic psychotherapy: Learning to listen from multiple perspectives* (pp. 51–110), Taylor and Francis. These readings will help you listen to a session in terms of the triangle of conflict.

Frederickson, J. (2012). *Maintaining an effective focus on feeling.* https://istdpinstitute.com/maintaining-a-focus-on-feeling/. This is a private download only for purchasers of this book.

Frederickson, J. (2018). *Self-supervision for therapists.* https://deliberate practiceinpsychotherapy.com/wp-content/uploads/2019/04/ Self-Supervision-in-ISTDP.pdf

RECOMMENDED MATERIALS

For three videos on psychodiagnosis presented by Jon Frederickson, you can visit the URLs below.

Intensive short term dynamic psychotherapy part 1 (October 5, 2011). http://www.youtube.com/watch?v=cKzmk2-xnzY

Intensive short term dynamic psychotherapy part 2 (October 5, 2011). http://www.youtube.com/watch?v=dK2x906ptWA

Intensive short term dynamic psychotherapy part 3 (January 18, 2012). http://www.youtube.com/watch?v=sDmVgoKPVkw

CHAPTER FIVE

Co-Creating a Therapeutic Alliance

Making the Unconscious Will to Health Conscious

The sole purpose of human existence is to kindle a light in the darkness of mere being.

—CARL JUNG, *MEMORIES, DREAMS, REFLECTIONS*

For therapy to be effective, the patient needs to declare a problem to work on, his will to work on it, a positive goal he wants to achieve, and a specific example of his problem. Then we can explore the feelings, anxiety, and conflicts that create his problems. As we explore his problems and help him see his conflicts, we can develop a consensus on what causes his difficulties. Then we can develop a consensus on how to work together to resolve them. At that point, we have a conscious therapeutic alliance.

Some patients readily declare their wish to work together. Others, however, are not conscious of a wish to do therapy. They tell us that other people think they need therapy, people like parents, spouses, and parole boards. Since the wish to do therapy is projected onto other people, the patient sees the wish in them but not in himself, yet he sits in a therapist's office. The less affect tolerance the patient has, the more his will to health must be projected. Thus, it remains unconscious.

Nearly every patient who enters a therapist's office wants to be there. The question becomes how much of his desire is conscious and how much is unconscious because it is projected onto others. Therefore, we need to pay attention to two dimensions of the therapeutic alliance: the conscious alliance and the unconscious will to health (Nunberg 1955; Rank 1930/1936).

INVITATIONS TO THE CONSCIOUS THERAPEUTIC ALLIANCE

We invite people to form a healing relationship to achieve their positive goals. We invite them to declare a problem and their will to work on the problem—the stages of alliance building outlined in chapters 1, 2, and 3. Next, we invite them to declare a positive goal they would like to work toward in therapy.

Declaring a Positive Goal

There is no reason to work hard unless the patient will get a positive result. To mobilize hope, we invite the patient to declare a positive goal. Yet he may present as if he has no motivation. Perceiving himself through past failures or current depression, he may see no reason to try. We must help the patient find positive goals to work toward. Otherwise, he has no reason to do therapy.

Turn a Negative Symptom into a Positive Goal

When patients offer a negative symptom, reverse it into its opposite, and then propose a positive goal to work toward in therapy.

Principle: *Turn each negative symptom into a positive goal that mobilizes the patient.*

Pt: I just feel anxious.

Th: Would you like to look at the feelings underneath the anxiety so you wouldn't have to feel anxious instead? [*Turn the negative symptom into a positive goal.*]

Pt: I feel depressed.

Th: Would you like to look at the feelings underneath the depression so you wouldn't have to feel depressed instead? [*Turn the negative symptom into a positive goal.*]

Pt: I'm so tired.

Th: Would you like to look at the feelings underneath the tiredness so we could find your energy? [*Turn the negative symptom into a positive goal.*]

Pt: I feel hopeless.

Th: Of course. That's how we feel when we're depressed. Could we look under the hopelessness, see what it is covering up, and try to find the rest of you? [*Validate the symptom. Then turn the negative symptom into a positive goal.*]

Pt: I am not sure I'm able to.

Th: Sure. It sounds like you haven't been able to alone. Shall we join forces together and see if we can help you discover your true potential? [*Validate the deficit. Then turn the negative symptom into a positive goal.*]

A depressed patient sees himself through the lens of depression. It's how a depressed brain works. Nothing personal about you. Your gentle, persistent encouragement to work toward a positive goal will not transform him after one magical intervention. He will gradually shift as he experiences your persistence—enacted faith in his potential.

Turn an Avoidance Strategy into a Positive Goal

Fragile patients may present ways they hurt themselves. If the therapist focuses only on destructive defenses, the patient will become hopeless. He will feel criticized for having a problem. Instead, reframe each defense as a positive goal for the therapy.

Principle: *Turn the avoidance strategy into a positive goal the patient might want to pursue in therapy.*

Pt: I'm too hard on myself.

Th: Would you like to be a little kinder to yourself? [*Turn the avoidance strategy into a positive goal.*]

Pt: I always say yes to what other people want.

Th: And would you like to be able to say yes to what you want too? [*Turn the avoidance strategy into a positive goal.*]

Pt: I'd like to, but I don't seem to be able to help myself.

Th: Would you like to learn to help yourself? [*Turn the avoidance strategy into a positive goal.*]

Pt: I'm not sure I can.

Th: Of course. That's why you are here. Would you like us to work together and find out if you can be better to yourself? [*Validate his deficit. Then invite him to build the capacity.*]

Pt: I've tried to do things differently.

Th: And it sounds like you couldn't when you did it alone. Shall we see if we could have a different result if we work together? [*Invite him to work together for a "different result." We don't promise the moon. We explore to see what is possible.*]

A depressed patient reveals a defense to show you where he needs help. By turning his problem into a positive goal, you show him how therapy could help.

Turn a Negative Goal into a Positive Goal

When asked for a positive goal, a depressed patient might say, "I don't want to feel depressed." He proposes a negative goal: what he does not want. Negative goals prime avoidance. Positive goals prime approach. The psychotherapy researcher Klaus Grawe (2006) said that if the patient cannot offer a positive goal, you should not attempt therapy. Instead, reframe negative goals into positive goals that will motivate him to do therapy.

Principle: *Turn each negative goal into a positive goal for therapy.*

A depressed and anxious man has not responded to previous therapies because he has never had a positive goal.

Pt: I don't want to feel depressed. [*Negative goal.*]

Th: Sure. What would you like to feel instead? [*Invite a positive goal.*]

Pt: I don't want to feel so anxious. [*Negative goal.*]

Th: Of course. Would you like to find out what the anxiety is hiding so you could feel calm instead? [*Invite a positive goal.*]

Pt: I don't want to feel so shut down. [*Negative goal.*]

Th: Would you like to look under the shutdown so you could feel your feelings instead? [*Invitation to a positive goal.*]

Pt: I feel overwhelmed.

Th: Would you like to look under the overwhelm so we could find out what it is covering up? Wouldn't it be nice to know what you feel so you don't have to feel overwhelmed instead? [*Invite a positive goal.*]

Pt: I don't want to feel like a failure. [*Negative goal.*]

Th: Sure. No one does. Would you like to find out what is driving your anxiety so we can help you succeed? [*Invite a positive goal.*]

Pt: [*Sighs.*] If we can. [*The sigh indicates that his will is online. Mixed feelings and anxiety are mobilized by his work together with the therapist.*]

No one wants to work hard for a bad result. Thus, help the depressed patient find a positive goal for us to work toward.

Turn a Lack of Capacity into a Capacity We Can Build

Patients may believe that if they lack a capacity, therapy cannot work. It's a legacy of an insecure attachment: "If I have a need, an insecure attachment cannot work." In fact, the so-called obstacle reveals the need for treatment. If she lacks a capacity, together, we can build it. In a secure attachment, we accept her need and try to meet it.

Principle: *Turn a lack of capacity into the task of building that capacity.*

Pt: I don't know what I feel.

Th: Would you like us to help you build that capacity? [*Invitation to build a capacity.*]

Pt: I can't do this.

Th: Of course. That's why you're here. You couldn't do it alone. Shall we work together to see if we can help you build that capacity? [*Invitation to build a capacity.*]

None of our patients want to do therapy if they think they can't do it. Acknowledge the problem and turn it into a positive goal.

At each stage of building the conscious alliance, you can combine your invitations with an invitation to achieve a positive goal:

- "Wouldn't it be nice to know what you feel so you wouldn't have to be depressed instead?"
- "Wouldn't it be nice to know what you feel so you wouldn't have to have these symptoms?"
- "Shall we look at these feelings so you don't have to feel anxious instead?"

- "Would you like us to look at these mechanisms so we can help you have a closer marriage?"

Micro-invitations to a Conscious Alliance

So far we have focused on invitations to build the alliance in stages: declaring a problem, declaring one's will to work on the problem, and declaring a positive goal to work toward. However, at each stage, we need to help the patient see what he has not seen before (e.g., feelings, anxiety, defenses, or causality). By helping him see what he has not seen before, his anxiety becomes regulated, and he sees how defenses are causing his problems. But since his experience in insecure attachments taught him to ignore himself and his inner life, we may need to help him engage in secure attachment behavior. The following micro-invitations show how we encourage a secure attachment in the early phases of building the therapeutic alliance.

Invitations to Pay Attention to One's Inner Life

To know his inner life, he must look and listen. Since looking inside himself may be new to the patient, we can help him through specific interventions.

- "Would you be willing to listen to yourself so you could know what you want for yourself?"
- "Would you like to look at your feelings so we could find out what is driving this anxiety?"
- "Would you be willing to look at the anxiety so we can help you regulate it?"
- "Could we look under those critical thoughts and see what they are hiding?"
- "Shall we look under these symptoms and see if we can find the rest of you?"
- "Can we take a look underneath this shame and see what it is covering up?"
- "Could we look underneath the depression to see who you really are?"

Invitations to Collaborate

Therapy is not something a therapist does to a patient. It is a relationship. The therapist and patient work together to accomplish the patient's goals. Specific interventions help the patient form a collaborative alliance.

- "Could we do this together?"
- "I know you couldn't face this alone. Shall we see what we can do if we face it together?"
- "Shall we look at this anxiety so we can help you regulate it?"
- "Do I have your permission to point out any behaviors here that might prevent you from having the marriage you want so you could be in control instead of those automatic mechanisms being in control of your marriage?"

Invitations to Reflect

We help patients see anxiety and defenses they never saw before, the mechanisms that cause their difficulties outside of their awareness. When they can see what they never saw, reflecting on this can give them new insights and freedom. Specific interventions can help patients reflect.

- "You want to be here, and you don't want to be here. What is it like to notice that complexity inside you right now?" [*Reflect on splitting.*]
- "What's it like to see that these feelings are triggering your anxiety?"
- "If we pause and go no further, what do you notice feeling in your body?"
- "As you step back and observe those thoughts, what other thoughts are coming up about the therapy?" [*Reflect on and intellectualize about one's projections.*]
- "Could that thought be hurting you?" [*Price of the defense.*]
- "What's it like to see how the tears come in to wash away your anger?"
- "What's it like to notice this calm in your body after you faced your feelings?"

Invitations to Experience Emotional Closeness

When the patient shares feelings, he becomes emotionally closer to the therapist. And the more he shares emotionally, the closer he becomes to his inner life, shifting from an insecure to a secure attachment. Specific interventions can help patients become emotionally closer to themselves and others.

- "What feelings are coming up here toward me?"
- "What feelings do you have toward your husband?"
- "How do you experience that anger physically in your body?"
- "What do you notice feeling now that you have shared what you were afraid to share?"

Our constant invitations encourage the patient, expressing our faith that a different future is possible when he faces his feelings. Hope is for the soul what air is for the lungs.

Building Conscious Capacity

Since infants and children rely on relationships to survive, any feeling that threatens the security of the relationship must be hidden. These unconscious patterns of assessment were never conscious and remain unconscious today. Therefore, we face a surprising situation: feelings can rise, of which the patient is unaware. Anxiety rises in the body, which the patient may or may not observe. Defenses happen automatically without the patient's intention. And symptoms result from defenses, which patients do not see. They do not see the unconscious mechanisms causing their suffering.

Thus, we help the patient see what he has never seen: his unconscious feelings, unconscious anxiety, and unconscious defenses. When unconscious defenses cause the patient's symptoms and problems, he can't do anything about them. Defenses operate, he doesn't know it, and he suffers. That's why we help the patient see the defenses causing his problems. We help him notice his anxiety so he can regulate it rather than suffer from physical problems. And we help him see his feelings so he can feel and deal rather than avoid and suffer. If he sees his defenses, he can face feelings rather than suffer from symptoms. We build the patient's capacity to become conscious of previously unconscious feelings, unconscious anxiety, and unconscious defenses.

(See table 5.1.) Then he can face feelings rather than unconsciously use defenses.

Table 5.1 Conscious capacities for anxiety and how we build them

Conscious Capacities We Need to Build	How We Build Them
Ability to observe anxiety and regulate it in the moment	*Th:* That dizziness is a sign of anxiety. Can we pay attention to your anxiety for a moment so we can help you regulate it?
Ability to observe what triggers anxiety	*Th:* You said that you want help with your marriage, and then you became dizzy. Notice how asking for help and letting yourself rely on me triggers some anxiety?

We also help patients become aware of their defenses so that feelings can rise to the surface. (See table 5.2.)

Table 5.2 Conscious capacities for defenses and how we build them

Conscious Capacities We Need to Build	How We Build Them
Ability to observe a defense and its function	*Th:* You want help with a problem, you got anxious, and then you wondered what I wanted from you. Notice how your desire traveled over here?
Ability to observe a defense and its price	*Th:* If you cannot declare what you want, then you won't get the help that you came here for.
Ability to let go of a defense to face what is avoided	*Th:* If you let your desire go back to you, what do you want out of the therapy that you think would be good for you?
Ability to differentiate the corners of the triangle of conflict	*Pt:* I feel anxious. *Th:* Can we look at the feeling underneath, triggering that anxiety? [*Differentiate feeling from anxiety.*] *Pt:* He is an idiot. *Th:* That is your thought. Can we look at the feeling underneath that thought? [*Differentiate feeling from the defense of intellectualization.*] *Pt:* I feel depressed. *Th:* Can we look underneath the depression and see what the feeling is that the depression is covering up? [*Differentiate feeling from a symptom.*]
Ability to differentiate the therapist from a projection	*Pt:* I feel like you want something from me. *Th:* I don't need anything because this isn't my problem, and it's not my therapy. The question is, what do you want out of the therapy that you think would be good for you?

While necessary, these conscious capacities are not sufficient for change. We also need to build the patient's unconscious affect tolerance: (1) the ability to bear 100 percent of his feelings while anxiety is in the striated muscles, and (2) the ability to bear 100 percent of his feelings inside without splitting or projecting those feelings outside. These are unconscious capacities, much like the ability to lift heavier weights following a period of muscle building.

As the patient bears more feelings inside without projecting them outside, anxiety will rise that he previously avoided through splitting, projection, and denial. Then the question becomes how high anxiety rises, and how he deals with it. The fragile patient splits his mixed feelings apart and projects again. Projection is not primarily a problem of cognition but affect tolerance. Thus, cognitive restructuring addresses a cognitive problem, but it does not clear up the affect tolerance problem that creates the need for projection.

When the intensity of feelings rises too much, the patient projects the excess amount of feeling outside again. If he can tolerate only 10 percent of his feelings and 15 percent are triggered, he has to project the excess 5 percent onto others. When he can tolerate 45 percent of his feelings and 50 percent are triggered, he still has to project the excess 5 percent onto others. But his projection occurs at a higher threshold of affect tolerance. This is progress. Projection still occurs while affect tolerance increases during the initial phase of treatment. Thus, we build conscious, cognitive understanding and unconscious affect tolerance. This brings us up to the second part of the therapeutic alliance: our relationship to the patient's unconscious will to health.

INVITATIONS TO THE UNCONSCIOUS THERAPEUTIC ALLIANCE

Each of us has an inherent will to recover (Nunberg 1955), a principle of restoring our integrity (Symington 2002) that is deeply unconscious (Bion 1957). We have an inherent instinct to become at one with the truth of our lives (Bion 1970). Any healing therapy must be a will therapy (Rank 1930/1936) since the patient's will to health is the engine of therapy (H. Davanloo, supervision 2002–2004). In chapter 3, we addressed conscious will. However, we also learned that experiencing one's will to health can trigger so much anxiety that the patient may project his will onto others. Although he is no longer conscious of his will, he sees it in others: "My wife thinks I need therapy." And yet if there were no will to health rising in him, he would have no need to project it onto others.

The addict who says he is delighted with drugs becomes preoccupied with parents who are scared he will kill himself. He relocates his will to health in them. If we do not know about projection, we might mistakenly believe he is fulfilled by fentanyl. After all, unaware of his will to health, he talks about only his apparent will to death. We could not have a conscious alliance because he has no conscious will to recover. As a result, we might have to form an alliance with his unconscious will to health—unconscious because it is denied, split off, and projected onto others. Thus, we have to deactivate denial, splitting, and projection so the will to health rises within the patient instead of within other people. To speak to the will to health, however, we must first hear it.

Hearing the Unconscious Will to Health in Defenses

We often first hear the will to health in the fragile patient's defenses. Each defense represents a compromise between the unconscious will to health and the resistance to it. If we hear the will to health hidden within the defense, we can reach through the defense to the patient's longing to become well. To illustrate this principle, let's examine some common defenses to show how to listen to the unconscious.

Projection: "I sense you are looking for some answer. I don't know what you are looking for."

Unconscious will to health: "I am looking for an answer. But it makes me anxious, so I attribute my search for an answer to you."

Projection: "I'm fine with drugs. It's my parents who are afraid I'm going to die."

Unconscious will to health: "I'm afraid I'm going to die."

Splitting and denial: "I'm anxious, and I don't know what I'm doing here. I don't want to be here."

Unconscious will to health: "I want to be here."

The unconscious will to health is always present but frequently relocated in other people or the therapist. If the therapist hears the denied and projected will to health, she can speak to it. The following examples illustrate how to hear and then mobilize the unconscious therapeutic alliance hidden within the defenses of projection, denial, and splitting.

Projection: Projection relocates an aspect of the patient's unconscious will to health that he cannot bear inside. Help him bear it.

Pt: I sense you are looking for some answer. I don't know what <u>you
are looking</u> for. [*Projection of his wish to look for an answer to his
questions.*]

Th: Since this is not my therapy, I don't need to look for anything
out of this. The question is what you are looking for out of the
therapy? [*Deactivate the projection and invite the patient to accept
his projected will to health: his wish to look for an answer.*]

Denial: The content of denial reveals the aspect of the unconscious therapeutic alliance the patient cannot yet bear. Help him
bear it.

Pt: I'm fine with drugs. It's my parents who are <u>afraid I'm going to
die</u>. [*He denies his own fear that he will die from drug abuse.*]

Th: You're fine with drugs. It's your parents who are afraid drugs could
kill you. [*Flat mirroring of his denial. Now he is not in conflict with
the therapist but with his denial.*]

Splitting and denial: Whatever the patient splits off is the aspect of
the unconscious therapeutic alliance he cannot yet bear. Help him
bear it.

Pt: I'm anxious. <u>I</u> don't <u>want to be here</u>. [*Denial of will: awareness of
will is split off from the fact that he is in a therapist's office.*]

Th: Don't want to be here and being here—what's it like to notice that
complexity? [*Invite the patient to notice these contradictory facts,
consciousness of splitting.*]

The therapist hears the denial and splitting. However, she also
hears a concrete fact that the patient has split off and denied through
silence: the patient is in the office. As a result, she mirrors his splitting
and mentions the split-off, denied fact. Splitting and denial often take
this form: the patient states one side of the conflict (resistance), and
not the other (unconscious will to health). Thus, the therapist mirrors
the resistance and mentions the unstated fact.

The therapist remains calm because she hears the unconscious will
to health and speaks to it whenever it appears. She does not fear denial
because she hears the denied: the unconscious will to health. She does
not fear projection because she hears the projected: the will to health

the patient rejects. She knows the patient would not have to deny or project the will to health were it not rising up for his acceptance.

The patient's unconscious will to health presents projections in the order in which he can accept them and with the dosage of language he can work with. In chapter 3, we saw how the underlined words reveal the order of projections and dosage the patient can bear. Projections, the apparent obstacles, are the portals to the unconscious will to health. As we deactivate the projections of his will to health, his projections decrease and his conscious alliance increases. The will to health that was unconscious—because it was split off, denied, or projected—becomes conscious.

Whispers from the Unconscious: Verbal Forms of the Unconscious Will to Health

As the patient shifts into the resistance system of isolation of affect, the unconscious will to health takes other forms, whispers from the unconscious (Abbass 2015; H. Davanloo, supervision 2000–2004). The unconscious will to health appears in the form of negation, vivid dreams, and, finally, imagery arising when the patient experiences a breakthrough to unconscious mixed feelings. The more mixed feelings you mobilize toward you, the more the unconscious will to health rises to the surface. Verbally, the unconscious will to health communicates through new words, metaphors, and defenses. The patient, when describing an experience, reveals a new word. Perhaps instead of saying she is "upset" with her abusive boyfriend, she says "irritated," revealing her increased affect tolerance. We can use the new word, the affect dosage she can now tolerate.

After mentioning to a patient how she had to give up her sanity to keep her mother, she said, "I remember feeling as if my soul slid out of me." Now we could call defenses the ways her soul slid out of her. Metaphor provides a royal road to her depths.

The following sequence of defenses illustrates a rise in awareness of feelings, illustrating the shift of the will to health from unconscious to consciousness:

1. *Denial:* "I don't have a feeling." [*Unconscious will to health: I have a feeling.*]

2. *Splitting:* "Maybe I have a feeling. No, I don't." [*Unconscious will to health: I have a feeling.*]

3. *Projection:* "You look like you are feeling something." [*Unconscious will to health: I am feeling something.*]

4. *Projection:* "You look like you are angry." [*Unconscious will to health: I am angry. Anger is now conscious but within the projection.*]

5. *Negation:* "I'm not angry." [*Unconscious will to health: I am angry.*]

In isolation of affect, the defense of *negation* allows the feeling word to enter awareness while the link to the patient is denied. Negation simultaneously conceals and reveals the feeling (Freud 1925/1957g). The word has arrived, but the patient denies that it applies to her. When this word arrives in awareness while negated, the patient's affect tolerance has risen a great deal.

6. *Feeling:* Within a few minutes, the patient can directly state, "I'm angry."

The feeling is finally conscious. As the therapist continues to mobilize the patient's mixed feelings, the unconscious will to health reveals itself in new ways. For instance, the patient may spontaneously offer links between feelings she has with the therapist and experiences with people in her past. Mobilizing feelings opens the memory systems so that insights arise from her. At higher levels of mixed feelings toward the therapist, the patient may spontaneously report images of other people. As the therapist invites the patient to elaborate on an image, memories and feelings arise based on the patient's past.

Each of these examples, illustrated below, of denial, splitting, projection, negation, verbal links, images, and then conscious memories illustrate the progressive power of the patient's unconscious will to health as it overwhelms the unconscious resistance.

- Whispers from the unconscious at a low rise of transference feelings:
  - Within denial
  - Within splitting
  - Within projection
- Overt unconscious will to health at a midrise of transference feelings:
  - Within negation

- Verbal links to the past
- Links to images

Having seen how the unconscious will to health is revealed verbally, we can examine its nonverbal forms.

Nonverbal Forms of the Unconscious Will to Health: Anxiety

The unconscious will to health also communicates to us nonverbally through bodily signs of anxiety. Unconscious bodily anxiety points to the unconscious will to health. Although we regulate anxiety in the smooth muscles or cognitive/perceptual disruption, we always come back to the unconscious will to health that triggered it. All anxiety points to the next element of the unconscious will to health that the patient is struggling to embrace.

Nonverbal Forms of the Unconscious Will to Health: Affect Activation in the Body

As the patient's affect tolerance rises, we will see a sequence of corresponding bodily shifts. This sequence illustrates the spectrum of affect tolerance as revealed in physical symptoms in the body:

1. Flatness in the body due to low affect tolerance, often accompanied by splitting and projection
2. Cognitive/perceptual disruption due to the patient's emerging capacity to tolerate mixed feelings
3. Teariness, indicating a shift into repression
4. Teariness starts to disappear
5. Scratchy voice (the vocal cords are smooth muscles which, when activated, cause the patient's voice to become scratchy)
6. Tension in the body, indicating a rise of anxiety in the striated muscles
7. Small sighs that become larger as affect tolerance increases
8. Sitting up due to increased tension in the chest and torso
9. Clenching of hands
10. Arm gestures start to appear
11. Flashes of heat in the body after the patient declares a feeling
12. Impulses start to rise in the hands and arms, and then fall due to defense

13. Impulses rise in the hands and stay, now that repression of the impulse has disappeared and the unconscious is further mobilized

14. An image appears in the mind related to the impulse

This sequence illustrates the spectrum of affect tolerance as revealed in physical symptoms in the body.

Building the Unconscious Therapeutic Alliance

The unconscious therapeutic alliance relies on communication between the therapist and the patient's unconscious will to health. When the therapist invites the patient to share his problem, will, positive goal, or feelings, he invites the patient's will to health to rise. Inviting relatedness mobilizes the patient's unconscious longings for a secure attachment. No wonder she becomes anxious. By feeling, she breaks the rules of an insecure attachment. The therapist builds the unconscious therapeutic alliance each time he explores feelings, explores what triggered anxiety, regulates anxiety, uses new words from the patient's unconscious, speaks in metaphors, and invites the unconscious will to health. We tend to think that the patient "tells" us what to do through words. Yet the body also speaks through unconscious feelings, unconscious anxiety, and unconscious defenses, giving voice to the unconscious will to health. By inviting feelings, regulating anxiety, and reaching through the defenses, we find the person under the words, the one who learned to hide to be loved but wanted to be loved without hiding.

SUMMARY

Any effective therapy requires that the therapist and patient form a conscious therapeutic alliance based on an agreed sense of the patient's problem, will to work on the problem, and a positive goal to work toward. To help the patient face reality and the feelings it triggers, the therapist can regulate the patient's anxiety and deactivate her projections so she feels safe. And the therapist can help the patient see the defenses that hurt her so she can face her feelings instead.

Fragile patients may appear to have no motivation because they relocate it onto other people. Thus, look for the projections where the patient has placed his motivation. Deactivating projections helps the patient recognize his motivation. We listen to the unconscious will to health and speak to it since it is the healing force of therapy. With that force made conscious, we can face and bear the patient's feelings, the subject of the next chapters.

PART TWO

Strengthening the Patient

CHAPTER SIX

Systems of Self-Protection
The Hierarchy of Affect Thresholds

The stark nakedness and simplicity of the conflict with which humanity is oppressed—that of getting angry with and wishing to hurt the very person who is most loved.

—JOHN BOWLBY, *THE MAKING AND BREAKING
OF AFFECTIONAL BONDS*

When a child cannot depend on parents for affect regulation, she learns to rely on their defenses for affect dissociation (Schore 2002). These defenses limit the amount of feelings she can tolerate and become aware of so she cannot put her feelings into words or adaptive actions (Freeman, Cameron, and McGhie 1966, 31; Rapaport 1953). We call this hierarchy of limits her affect thresholds (Rapaport 1953).

She learns the feelings her parents can tolerate and the defenses they prefer. Put simply, she learns what to hide, when to hide it, and how. She conceals feelings and wishes when their force is too great for her caretakers. Defenses protect her when she cannot find a protector.

We can use over a hundred different defenses (Blackman 2004). But they fit into three patterns we refer to as *systems of resistance*. Each system correlates or occurs clinically with an anxiety pathway, set of defenses, and a strategy for avoiding feelings. See table 6.1 for examples.

Table 6.1   The systems of resistance

Systems of Resistance	Splitting and Projection	Repression	Isolation of Affect
Strategy	Split-off mixed feelings as "not-me" relocate internal feelings onto an external person: "I put my feelings in you and fear them there."	"I feel love toward you and turn rage on me to avoid mixed feelings toward you."	Moderate resistance: detach from the internal mixed feelings. High resistance: "I detach from you to detach from my mixed feelings."
Defenses	Splitting and projection: projective identification. Secondary defenses: devaluation, idealization, acting out, discharge, yelling. Denial	Self-attack, weepiness, depression, tiredness, conversion, somatization, character defenses	Moderate resistance: intellectualization, rationalization, tactical defenses. High resistance: defenses operate together to form a transference resistance.
Result	Angry at or scared of the projection. Scared of an "angry" therapist. Scared of the desire projected onto the therapist. Or scared of merger with or envy of a therapist upon whom the patient has projected everything good within himself.	Depressed, sick, or anxious	Moderate resistance: detached from self but engaged with you. High resistance: detached from self and you.
Anxiety pathway	Cognitive/perceptual disruption	Smooth muscles	Striated muscles

Patients use three strategies for avoiding feelings: (1) detaching from mixed feelings, (2) turning anger onto the self while feeling love for the other, and (3) splitting mixed feelings apart and projecting them onto others. Isolation of affect and repression prevent us from being aware of our feelings so we don't express them. In splitting and projection, we are aware of our feelings but in other people. Thus, we can discern a spectrum of awareness and expression of feelings.

The terms *repression* or *repressive defenses* have traditionally referred to any defenses that keep feelings out of awareness (Freud 1913/1957b). Here, we differentiate two systems of resistance that accomplish this aim: isolation of affect (detaching from feelings) and repression (turning anger on the self). Thus, the term *repression* here is more limited in scope. (See table 6.2.)

Table 6.2   Resistance systems and the awareness and expression
of feelings

Resistance System	Awareness of Feelings	Expression of Feelings
Isolation of affect III	The patient is aware of his feelings and experiences them.	He expresses himself emotionally and thoughtfully.
Isolation of affect II	The patient is aware of his feelings but does not experience them.	He expresses his emotions in a detached, uninvolved way.
Isolation of affect I	The patient does not know what he feels.	He expresses thoughts instead of feelings.
Repression	The patient is aware of anger toward himself, not toward others.	He expresses love toward others but rage toward himself.
Splitting and projection	The patient is unaware of feelings in himself. He is "aware" of them in other people where he has projected them.	He expresses anger, rage, fear, or grief toward projections. Through splitting, he feels pure rage without the love that would inhibit acting out. Or he feels pure love without the mixed feelings inherent in human relations.

The systems of resistance correlate with the pathways of anxiety. Patients who use isolation of affect experience their anxiety in the striated muscles. Those using repression suffer from anxiety in the smooth muscles with motor conversion and weakness. And people who split and project experience symptoms of cognitive/perceptual disruption. Now we can turn to the concept of affect thresholds (Rapaport 1953).

Imagine a patient who intellectualizes while experiencing 10 percent of her feelings. You might think her resistance system is isolation of affect. However, when her feelings rise to 15 percent, she crosses an affect threshold. Her anxiety shifts into the smooth muscles, the defense of self-attack emerges, and she becomes depressed. Above 15 percent of feelings she uses the resistance system of repression. The patient does not consciously or intentionally choose to use a resistance system. When the amount of feelings exceeds her capacity to isolate affect, the resistance system of repression automatically appears. And if repression is too weak at a higher intensity of feelings, splitting and projection emerge. Thus, emergent forms of organization arise in response to the amount of affect mobilized in therapy (Palombo 1999).

These unconscious systems for warding off feelings emerge at specific thresholds of unconscious affect intensity. These thresholds of intensity (Rapaport 1953) vary between patients based on how much their parents regulated them in childhood (Schore 2002). Recognizing these thresholds tells us when to regulate anxiety, how to invite feelings, and how to address defenses according to the patient's affect tolerance. Table 6.3 illustrates the thresholds of affect tolerance, anxiety, and resistance systems.

Table 6.3 Thresholds of affect and anxiety tolerance and systems of resistance

Thresholds of Affect Tolerance	Systems of Resistance	Thresholds of Anxiety Tolerance
High	Isolation of affect	Striated muscles
Moderate	Repression	Smooth muscles
Low	Splitting and projection	Cognitive/perceptual disruption

A patient who tolerates all her feelings while using isolation of affect has high affect tolerance. But if she shifts into splitting and projection at 10 percent of her feelings, her affect tolerance is low. Recognizing these thresholds, anxiety pathways, and resistance systems allows us to tailor our work to the patient's capacity. Let's review the systems of resistance.

ISOLATION OF AFFECT

In isolation of affect, we intellectualize, ruminate, and remain vague. These defenses allow us to detach from feelings and the people who trigger them (Freud 1923/1961c; A. Freud 1936; Blackman 2004). Detaching isolates a feeling word from the experience of the feeling. A patient might say that she feels sad, but she doesn't look or sound sad. She looks and sounds detached. The feeling word *sad* is isolated from her experience of sadness. Intellectualizing, rationalizing, and ruminating help her distance from her feelings and people. Thus, she feels unconnected to her life, career, and relationships. That is why she is anxious, lonely, and depressed.

Patients who use isolation of affect have anxiety in the striated muscles. We need not regulate it. We can explore high levels of feelings when anxiety is in the striated muscles.

REPRESSION

As fragile patients' mixed feelings rise, their resistance can shift from isolation of affect to repression. When they feel angry toward people they love, they turn anger back on themselves to protect their loved ones and to preserve the bond. They use defenses such as self-attack, weepiness, conversion, and somatization. People who use isolation of affect look detached. But patients using repression appear depressed and tired and suffer limpness and weakness due to motor conversion.

Patients who use repression have anxiety in the smooth muscles. If it is severe, we regulate it. Then we ask about feelings coming up toward the therapist. If anxiety in the smooth muscles is accompanied by intellectualization, we can ask about feelings coming up toward the therapist. Why? The patient becomes depressed in session because her unconscious defenses protect the therapist from mixed feelings. She protects the people she loves by turning anger onto herself. It happens unconsciously, automatically, and unintentionally. To block that unconscious resistance system, the therapist invites feelings toward him so they don't go back on the patient to make her depressed. In a secure attachment, we accept all the patient's feelings. She does not have to protect the therapist from her anger to preserve an insecure attachment. Self-attack was her learned language of love: "If I protect you from my anger by turning it on myself, can you love me?"

PROJECTION AND SPLITTING

As mixed feelings rise more, isolation of affect and repression may collapse. When they do, the boundary between conscious and unconscious feelings disappears. Higher-level defenses fail, and forbidden feelings and impulses break through into awareness. They trigger massive anxiety, which no longer serves as a signal that a feeling is about to come into awareness (Freeman 1973). Overwhelming panic signals that feelings have broken into awareness. Now anxiety shifts further into the parasympathetic branch of the autonomic nervous system, creating cognitive/perceptual disruption (Abbass 2015; H. Davanloo, supervision 2002–2004; Frederickson 2013).

To end the cognitive/perceptual disruption caused by mixed feelings, the patient's mind splits those feelings apart. Then they cannot come together to trigger anxiety in the form of cognitive/perceptual disruption. Next, projection relocates one of the feelings onto other people, often anger because it triggers the most guilt. And once relocated, the anger can be judged there. Or projection can relocate the inner judge (Freeman, Cameron, and McGhie 1966). Then the patient might hate or fear the therapist as that supposed judge. Once projection has located feelings and urges in others, the patient sees those qualities there, and then she may try to control the impulses she perceives in other people. While the therapist can see that the patient projects, the patient may perceive her projection as reality.

Splitting can be mobilized by guilt over mixed feelings rising (Freud 1938/1963b; Kernberg 1975; M. Klein 1975b; Reller 2005), triggered by fear of losing a relationship. In a disorganized attachment (Liotti 1992; Main and Solomon 1990), the child discerns what the parent needs her to split off to decrease parental anxiety. The frightening parent, projecting, stares at his child and yells, "What are you looking at?" The child learns that she must not look. So she splits off and projects the urge to look elsewhere. Perhaps she projects that her father looks at her or people look at her or she may project that eyes in the trees are looking at her. The more dangerous the wish, the more distantly it is split off and projected. In such a case, fear triggers the splitting since the relationship's end equals death. The less affect the parent could bear, the more of the child's being had to be relocated onto others or, at worst, onto the animate and then inanimate world (Searles 1960). Splitting and projection was her learned language of love: "If I empty myself of what you cannot love, can you accept the rest?"

Once the patient splits off her feelings, she regards them as "not-me" (Havens 1962; Sullivan 1953b). Then she projects them onto other people. Next, she may interact with these split-off and projected feelings she imagines live in others. Once she interacts with those projections, the risk of acting out increases because now she sees an angry, all-bad person. Interacting with her projections rather than her loved ones, her relationships become stormy and unstable.

The following statements illustrate this pattern.

> Pt: I can't do anything right. You constantly criticize me! [*Projection of the patient's self-criticism onto the therapist.*]

Pt: You expect too much from me. You are so demanding. [*Projection of the patient's tendency to demand too much from herself.*]

Pt: You are always trying to find something out about me. [*Projection of the patient's wish to find something out about the therapist.*]

Pt: I don't feel comfortable. You look at me funny, like you are sexually interested in me. [*Projection of the patient's sexual wishes.*]

Pt: I sense there is something you are holding back from me. [*Projection of the patient's wish to hold back information from the therapist.*]

How could patients who act out, yell, and scream have low affect tolerance? Affect tolerance refers to our ability to bear anger toward people we love and to love people with whom we are angry. Patients suffered because they felt angry toward people they loved who rejected their mixed feelings. "You must reject your anger, or I will reject you!" To preserve their insecure attachments, patients detached from their feelings, turned rage on themselves, or split apart the feelings of love and rage—expelling the rejected feelings to live in others. Their defenses protected their loved ones from anger. We never focus only on rage in therapy. We explore the mixed feelings of love *and* rage that inevitably rise when we connect. To feel pure rage toward someone and express it through acting out or yelling requires no tolerance of mixed feelings, just splitting and denial. To feel only pure love requires no capacity to bear the feelings reality triggers. But to feel angry toward someone we love, to love while being angry, and to bear the guilt, anxiety, and grief these mixed feelings trigger—that is affect tolerance, the test of our love and compassion.

The fragile patient often developed defenses to adapt to parents with low affect tolerance. Her defenses enact how she protected parents to preserve an insecure attachment. Every time she uses a defense in therapy, she unconsciously asks, "If I remove what you cannot love, can you care for the remains?" With every defense, she protects you from her feelings so she can protect herself from the loss of a relationship and the threat of death: "What you reject in me I will project out of me so you can accept what is left."

LEVELS OF AFFECT TOLERANCE

Now we can examine the levels of affect intensity where resistance systems emerge. Moderately and highly resistant patients use isolation of affect and can tolerate most of their feelings. Their anxiety is in the striated muscles. We don't need to build their affect tolerance, nor do we have to regulate their anxiety. We help them let go of defenses so they can access their feelings. With more emotionally intimate relationships, they no longer feel isolated, lonely, or depressed. (See table 6.4.)

Table 6.4   High affect tolerance, resistance, and anxiety

High Level of Affect Tolerance	System of Resistance	Pathway of Anxiety Discharge
0–100 percent of feelings	Isolation of affect	Striated muscles

Patients who use repression tolerate a lower level of mixed feelings. Their anxiety is in the smooth muscles. A person using repression might have affect thresholds like those shown in table 6.5.

Table 6.5   Moderate affect tolerance, systems of resistance, and anxiety

Moderate Level of Affect Tolerance	System of Resistance	Pathway of Anxiety Discharge
Over 30 percent of feelings	Repression	Smooth muscles, somatization, and motor conversion
0–30 percent of feelings	Isolation of affect	Striated muscles, such as tension in the chest, arms, and hands, and sighing

At a very low rise of feelings, the fragile patient may be able to intellectualize. As feelings rise, her anxiety shifts into the smooth muscles and her resistance into repression. Now she becomes weepy and depressed while attacking herself. As feelings rise more, her anxiety shifts into cognitive/perceptual disruption, and she splits and projects. Table 6.6 illustrates the quality of awareness within the different resistance systems.

Table 6.6   Systems of resistance and quality of consciousness

Intervention	System of Resistance	Response to Intervention	Quality of Consciousness
Th: What feelings do you have toward him?	Isolation of affect	*Pt:* I think it has to do with his issues with the boss.	Intellectualization keeps feelings out of awareness
Th: What feelings do you have toward him?	Repression	*Pt:* Maybe it was my fault.	Self-attack keeps mixed feelings out of awareness
Th: What feelings do you have toward him?	Splitting and projection	*Pt:* He is angry with me.	Higher-level defenses collapse. She is aware of a feeling but in another person.

Fragile patients may bear about 10 percent of feeling intensity while still isolating affect. Over that threshold of 10 percent, anxiety shifts out of the striated and into the smooth muscles. And resistance shifts into repression. At 25 percent of feelings, anxiety may go into cognitive/perceptual disruption. If 5 percent more of their feelings are triggered, they *have to* relocate the excess 5 percent. The more feelings you trigger over the threshold, the more they *have to* project. This automatic, unconscious reaction results from low affect tolerance. Thus, the more mixed feelings they can bear, the less they have to rely on splitting and projection. Table 6.7 illustrates how these thresholds might appear in a fragile patient.

Table 6.7   Thresholds of affect tolerance in a sample fragile patient

Low Level of Affect Tolerance in a Fragile Patient	System of Resistance	Pathway of Anxiety Discharge
Over 25 percent of feelings	Splitting and projection	Cognitive/perceptual disruption
10–25 percent of feelings	Repression	Smooth muscles
0–10 percent of feelings	Isolation of affect	Striated muscles

Levels of affect tolerance correlate with resistance systems. If you recognize the new symptoms, anxiety pathway, or defenses when the patient crosses a threshold, you can intervene quickly to prevent a regression. (See table 6.8.)

Table 6.8   Thresholds of anxiety tolerance in a moderately fragile patient

Levels of Affect in a Moderately Fragile Patient	Thresholds of Anxiety Tolerance
Over 25 percent of feelings	*Loss of reality testing:* The patient, unable to compare his projection to reality, believes his projection is the same as reality.
20–25 percent of feelings	*Projection:* Dizziness stops because the patient, no longer able to repress feelings out of awareness, must split them apart and project them onto others.
15–20 percent of feelings	*Dizziness:* This sign of anxiety indicates that the patient is still able to bear and repress feelings out of awareness.
10–15 percent of feelings	Smooth muscles
0–10 percent of feelings	Striated muscles

Once the fragile patient experiences cognitive/perceptual disruption, regulate anxiety before she projects. If she projects, deactivate and restructure the projection. If she loses reality testing, intervene to prevent a regression. If we do not see the thresholds, and feelings keep rising, we will see the following sequence in a regression:

1. Rising feelings being explored in the therapy
2. A shift into repression
3. A shift into cognitive/perceptual disruption
4. A shift into projection
5. A loss of reality testing

Intervene early in this sequence to stop the regression and restore self-reflective functioning.

In the spectrum of fragility, a mildly fragile patient might isolate affect until experiencing 70 percent of her feelings. Then, she may experience cognitive/perceptual disruption, but she will not project. She needs only a little anxiety regulation before exploring feelings again. A moderately fragile patient could isolate affect until experiencing 25 percent of her feelings until she disrupts and projects. A severely fragile patient might experience cognitive/perceptual disruption, projection, and loss of reality testing even before the session. If we cannot regulate anxiety, we try to deactivate projections to prevent a further loss of reality testing.

THE TASK: RESTRUCTURING THE SYSTEM OF RESISTANCE

If eradicating defenses is neither possible nor necessary, why do we work with them? We try to change the system of resistance from splitting and projection to isolation of affect. With isolation of affect, the patient can feel and deal rather than feel and flood with anxiety.

Changing Character Structure in the Fragile Patient

To change the fragile patient's character structure, we help him bear his feelings without anxiety leaving the striated muscles and while using isolating affect as his resistance system.

1. *Restructure the pathway of unconscious anxiety discharge:* Help fragile patients tolerate 100 percent of their feelings while anxiety is discharged into the striated muscles.

2. *Restructure the unconscious system of resistance:* Help fragile patients tolerate 100 percent of their feelings while using the resistance system of isolation of affect.

Therapeutic Task for the Resistance System of Splitting and Projection

Each resistance system requires a specific therapeutic task. In splitting and projection, the patient splits off a feeling as "not-me." Next he projects that feeling onto another person, denying that it is in him. You can help the patient do the following:

- *Task for splitting:* Bear mixed feelings inside without splitting them apart
- *Task for projection:* Bear a feeling inside without projecting it outside
- *Task for denial:* Recognize his feelings and the reality triggering them without denial

Therapeutic Task for the Resistance System of Repression

In repression, the patient cannot bear feeling anger toward the person she loves, so she protects him by turning the rage onto herself. You can help her do the following:

- *Task for repression:* Help the patient feel mixed feelings toward people without protecting them by turning the anger on herself

Therapeutic Task for the Resistance System of Isolation of Affect

In isolation of affect, the patient detaches from mixed feelings and from the person who evokes them. You can help the patient do the following:

- *Task for isolation of affect:* Experience his feelings rather than detach from them
- *Task for isolation of affect:* Experience emotional closeness with people rather than detach from them

Address the specific strategy each resistance system uses for dealing with feelings. Each strategy represents a specific problem in affect tolerance.

THE PURPOSE OF INVITING FEELINGS WITHIN EACH RESISTANCE SYSTEM

Since affect tolerance and resistance systems differ, the purpose of inviting feelings differs as well.

Inviting Feelings within the Resistance System of Splitting and Projection

The fragile patient avoids mixed feelings by splitting them apart. Then he projects one feeling onto another person and denies having it. The following are examples of inviting feelings to build affect tolerance when dealing with splitting and projection:

- *Invite consciousness of denial:* "You say everything is fine. And your son just said he wants to kill himself."
- *Invite the patient to recognize inside what he projected outside:* "I have no right to explore something if you don't want to. [*Deactivate the projection.*] That's why we have to find out what *you want* to explore for your benefit that *you think* would *help you.*" [*Invite him to declare his desire. The italicized intervention words invite the patient to recognize his will inside himself.*]
- *Invite consciousness of splitting:* "You say you have a problem, *and* you say maybe you don't." [*The italicized word brings together what was split apart.*]

- *Invite the experience of feelings inside while blocking projection:* "If you let that feeling be *inside* you, how do you experience that feeling *inside* you?" [*The italicized words invite the patient to bear mixed feelings inside rather than project one outside.*]
- *Invite the experience of feelings inside while blocking splitting:* "*As you let those two feelings be inside you at the same time,* how do you experience those feelings inside you?" [*The italicized words block splitting.*]
- *Invite the experience of feelings inside while blocking denial:* "What feelings come up inside *as we face the fact that your son wants to kill himself?* What feelings are coming up inside you?" [*The italicized words block denial.*]

Inviting Feelings within the Resistance System of Repression

In repression, the patient avoids mixed feelings by feeling love for a person and turning rage on herself. We invite her to feel mixed feelings toward that person without turning the rage on herself.

- "*If you're nice to yourself and you don't protect me,* what feelings are coming up here toward me?" [*The italicized words block repression.*]
- "*If you're nice to yourself and you don't protect me,* how do you experience that anger here toward me?" [*The italicized words block repression.*]
- "Notice how the anger is toward me, and then it goes on to your neck? [*Somatization.*] *If you are nice to your neck and let the anger come this way,* how do you experience that anger here toward me?" [*The italicized words block somatization. Somatic symptoms can result from the discharge of anxiety in the somatic and autonomic nervous systems, as illustrated in chapter 1. However, in somatization, the patient feels rage and identifies with the body of the person she wants to attack. For instance, if she wants to choke an ex-boyfriend, she may experience choking sensations in her throat. If she has an urge to stab her father, she may experience a "stabbing" pain in her chest. Rather than feel rage toward a loved one, she identifies with his body and suffers the symptoms herself.*]

The self-hatred that has strangled the patient must be unmasked and transformed into anger outward. And the first person the anger can be redirected toward is often the therapist. Help her feel her feelings toward you without choking herself so her feelings can rise and her depression can drop. By feeling this rage toward a therapist she cares for, she becomes able to face the rage toward people she loves. Teach the patient "to feel like killing you, to tell you about it, and *not* to do it" (Semrad 1966, 170). Then she will not have to kill herself by turning rage onto herself.

Inviting Feelings within the Resistance System of Isolation of Affect

In isolation of affect, the patient avoids experiencing mixed feelings by detaching. We invite him to feel mixed feelings toward another person without detaching from those feelings or that person:

- "What feelings are coming up here toward me?"
- "How do you experience that anger here toward me physically in your body?"

THE FUNCTION OF DEFENSES ACCORDING TO THE RESISTANCE SYSTEM

Each resistance system relies on different strategies for warding off mixed feelings. While a few defenses occur in all resistance systems, their function changes within each system (e.g., detaching, repressing, or splitting and projection). Thus, we have to address the defense differently. To illustrate that, let's look at how projection functions differently in the three resistance systems.

Projection within the Resistance System of Isolation of Affect

In isolation of affect, projection serves the specific function of the resistance: to distance from the therapist and remain detached and uninvolved.

Th: What's the problem you would like me to help you with?

Pt: [*Sighs.*] I don't know. You should ask my wife. She's the one who thinks I should be here.

Th: Since your wife isn't here, I can't help her. So what is the problem you would like me to help you with?

The patient's anxiety is in the striated muscles (the sigh). He uses the defenses of intellectualization, rationalization, and vagueness. Reality testing is intact. He projects his awareness of a problem onto his wife. In isolation of affect, projection functions as a tactic to distance from the therapist.

Projection within the Resistance System of Repression

Within repression, projection serves the function of the resistance to protect the other and turn anger on oneself.

Th: What's the problem you would like me to help you with?

Pt: [Becomes teary.] You will think I'm a fool. And you probably think I'm fat too, and ugly. [She cries.]

Th: I'm not aware of thinking that. Is there any evidence you see that I am having those thoughts? [Identify the projection and invite her to compare her projection with reality.]

Pt: No. It just feels that way. [Reality testing returns quickly.]

Th: Although it feels that way, you don't see any evidence that I'm having those thoughts.

Pt: No.

Th: Sometimes when people have these thoughts about me, they suffer from too much self-criticism. Is that something you suffer from? [Identify the defense.]

Pt: Oh, gosh, yes!

Th: Could we look under those critical thoughts and see what feelings are coming up here toward me? [Invite feelings toward the therapist to block the turning of anger onto herself.]

The patient protects people from her mixed feelings by loving them and turning rage on herself. She suffers from self-attack, weepiness, and cramping in the gut. Within repression, projection functions as a form of self-attack.

Projection within the Resistance System of Splitting and Projection

Within splitting and projection, projection serves the function of the resistance to split off a feeling and relocate it in another person to avoid the experience of mixed feelings.

Th: What's the problem you would like me to help you with?

Pt: I'm not comfortable answering that question yet.

Th: You certainly don't have to. It's just that if we don't learn what your problem is, I wouldn't be able to help you with it. [*Point out reality in a kind, matter-of-fact voice. Like a docent at a museum, be friendly. Use the same tone of voice to say "It's a cloudy day today" as when you say "If we don't have a problem, we won't be able to help you with one." There is no confrontation, judgment, sarcasm, or emotional reaction. We have no right to judge anyone. But we have an obligation to mention facts so the patient can make a more informed choice about how to proceed. Like a tour guide, you introduce the patient to an inner world he has never seen and defenses he never detected. Gently and kindly point things out.*]

Pt: See, that's what therapists always do—trying to control the patient. [*Projection.*]

Th: I have no right to ask you to talk about your problem if you don't want to. [*Deactivate the projection.*] I just wouldn't be able to help you with it. That's why we have to find out if you have a problem you want help with so you could feel more in control. [*Invite him to recognize his awareness of his problem rather than project it onto the therapist.*]

Pt: I'm confused. [*Possible sign of cognitive/perceptual disruption.*]

Th: What do you notice feeling in your head right now? [*Assess for anxiety.*]

Pt: I'm a little dizzy. [*Sign of cognitive/perceptual disruption.*]

This patient uses only one defense: projection. Anxiety is in cognitive/perceptual disruption. Reality testing has not been restored. Here, projection relocates a desire onto the therapist because the patient cannot bear it inside himself.

Each system of resistance uses a specific strategy for handling emotions. Defenses that occur across resistance systems have different functions, requiring different interventions. In isolation of affect, we block projection and maintain our focus. In repression, we restructure the projection and invite feelings toward the therapist. In splitting and projection, we deactivate the projection. Then we invite the patient to bear inside what he projected outside. And we continue until the patient regains his reality testing. Here, projection results from the inability to bear mixed feelings inside.

LEVELS OF CHARACTER ORGANIZATION

Fragile patients can have a neurotic, borderline, or psychotic level of character structure. People in the borderline and psychotic groups can have psychotic symptoms, so we have to assess their level of character structure to plan treatment.

When we address splitting, projection, and denial in the patient with a borderline level of character structure, reality testing improves. He begins to isolate affect, and anxiety moves into the striated muscles. The loss of reality testing was temporary.

In contrast, reality testing does not improve in the patient with a psychotic level of character structure because the loss is permanent (Freeman 1973; Kleiger and Khadivi 2015; E. Marcus 2017). Instead, primitive splitting and projection continue. Anxiety remains in cognitive/perceptual disruption, and the patient regresses and becomes more disorganized (Kernberg 1977a, 1977b; Rosenfeld 1987). (See chapter 12 on severe fragility for the assessment and differentiation of borderline and psychotic levels of character structure.)

If the therapist reminds the borderline patient of the difference between reality and his perception, he can perceive the difference. He empathizes with the therapist's confusion about the contradictions, and he becomes more realistic. The psychotic patient may not understand the difference. Or he may interpret the therapist's comment as an attack. Reality testing becomes worse.

Patients at a borderline level of character structure may form a *transference psychosis*. A delusional thought about the therapist is accompanied by intense feelings. These patients may temporarily lose the sense of a separate identity from the therapist. However, their functioning outside of therapy remains intact. The borderline patient's transference psychosis responds to structuring the therapy, and interpreting reality improves reality testing.

In contrast, the psychotic patient's transference reflects the loss of reality testing throughout his life, and it does not respond to intervention (Kernberg 1977a, 1977b). When people present with delusions and hallucinations, assess their level of character pathology to choose the right treatment. We base our assessment and treatment planning on their responses to intervention, not their symptoms. (See chapters 11 and 12.) Otherwise, assumptions rather than careful assessment will determine the treatment.

SUMMARY

Three patterns of unconscious resistance correlate with three pathways of unconscious anxiety discharge. The systems of resistance and the pathways of anxiety discharge create the patient's symptoms and presenting problems. To build the alliance, we assess the pathway of anxiety discharge and resistance system. And we assess the levels of affect intensity where these resistance systems emerge. Then we know where the thresholds occur and which capacities to build. Although relatively simple with persons whose anxiety is in the striated muscles, assessing these thresholds is complex with fragile patients. Some can isolate affect up to a low level of mixed feelings intensity, then shift into repression. Then they use splitting and projection at a higher level of mixed feelings. Recognizing these thresholds and the intensity of affect that triggers them is essential to block regressions and build capacity. Building these capacities is the focus of the next two chapters.

CHAPTER SEVEN

Declaring One's Feelings
Is It Safe to Share Feelings?

Love is simply the name for the desire and pursuit of
the whole.

—PLATO, *THE SYMPOSIUM*

We have learned how to identify and regulate anxiety in fragile
patients for whom depending was dangerous. And we can now
help people who hide their wish to depend. Then we learned how to
invite them to declare their will rather than conceal it.

At this stage, we help patients share feelings they were taught to
bury. The more traumatic their past, the more forbidden it has been
to feel, express, or even know their emotions. As a result, they never
developed much affect tolerance. To build that capacity, we explore
feelings until anxiety goes out of the striated muscles. Then we keep
feelings at this level while regulating anxiety until it returns to the striated muscles, establishing a new threshold of affect tolerance.

Invitations to a secure attachment mobilize feelings because they
generate memories of the fragile patient's relational pain. In the school
of life, known as insecure attachments, fragile patients have learned
the following:

- *Problem:* "If I show my need, you will abandon me."
- *Will:* "If I show my will, you will withdraw from me."
- *Feelings:* "If I share my feelings, you will leave me."

To counter this, follow these three steps in building a secure attachment:

- *Problem:* Offer a relationship where the patient can declare a problem and depend so she can get the help she needs.
- *Will:* Offer a relationship where the patient can declare her will, thoughts, and desires. Build a therapy based on her desire to achieve her goals.
- *Feelings:* Offer a relationship where the patient can feel her feelings. Then she can have emotionally close relationships and channel her feelings into effective action.

These steps develop a secure attachment. However, each step triggers feelings and anxiety based on earlier experiences. We explore gradually so anxiety rises gradually. And when it goes too high, we can regulate it quickly. Our first goal is not to have a breakthrough into unconscious feelings. Rather, we build the capacity to bear those feelings inside without unregulated anxiety, splitting, or projection. By recognizing inside what she imagined she could place outside, the patient experiences her wholeness.

Fragile patients have different levels of affect tolerance, requiring a range of approaches for building capacity. First, we will describe the basic principles for building anxiety and affect tolerance. Then we will show how to apply these principles across the spectrum of fragility.

BASIC INTERVENTIONS IN THE GRADED FORMAT

To build anxiety and affect tolerance, we rely on four interventions: inviting a healing relationship, recapitulation to regulate anxiety, bracing to build affect tolerance, and consolidation to build understanding. See table 7.1 for a description of these interventions and their purpose.

Table 7.1   Primary interventions for fragile patients

Interventions for Fragile Patients	Purpose
Invitation: The therapist invites the patient to co-create a healing relationship—a secure attachment.	Mobilizes mixed feelings Builds the conscious alliance Mobilizes the unconscious will to health Raises the threshold of affect tolerance Changes the attachment pattern

Table 7.1 (continued)

Recapitulation: Both the therapist and patient reflect on and summarize what just occurred in the relationship if anxiety becomes too high.	Regulates anxiety if it goes so far above the threshold of affect tolerance that bracing is not possible (e.g., the patient experiences severe cognitive/perceptual disruption and cannot intellectualize) Offers an anxiety-regulating secure attachment
Bracing (Abbass 2015): The therapist reminds the patient of his feelings while regulating anxiety.	Builds affect tolerance at a higher threshold Stabilizes the patient and builds capacity when used at the moment the patient starts to experience cognitive/perceptual disruption Builds the patient's experience of a secure attachment at a higher level of feelings
Consolidation: The therapist summarizes the process after the patient's threshold of anxiety or affect tolerance has increased. And then the patient does as well.	Builds a consensual understanding of the process that just unfolded Helps the patient engage in metacognition (thinking about thinking) Makes her aware of and solidifies the progress she just made Builds her awareness of a shift from an insecure attachment to a more secure one

When we invite a secure attachment, the patient may experience the following:

- Feelings (*Intervention:* explore feelings)
- Anxiety over the threshold (*Intervention:* regulate anxiety)
- Anxiety at the threshold, slight cognitive/perceptual disruption (*Intervention:* bracing)
- Defenses (*Interventions:* invite consciousness of split-apart feelings, mirror denial, deactivate projections)

We help patients increase the amount of mixed feelings they can bear without anxiety going into cognitive/perceptual disruption and without having to use the defenses of splitting, projection, or denial. Implicitly, we constantly help the patient experience a secure attachment where these feelings can be held and felt together, rather than rejected through defenses. Eventually, the patient can bear 100 percent of his feelings while intellectualizing rather than using splitting or projection. The closer patients get to this goal, the more their symptoms diminish, and their risk of relapse drops.

RESPONSES TO INTERVENTION AND HOW TO INTERVENE

All invitations to form a healing relationship will trigger feelings, anxiety, and defenses based on the history of insecure attachments. In fact, feelings, anxiety, and defenses are how the unconscious tells us that implicit, nonverbal history. The emerging warded off feelings, anxiety in the body, and the defenses by which the patient had to hide her inner life—all of these are songs of the unborn, how the past talks to the future.

Response: Feelings

To help the patient learn about, bear, and channel his feelings into adaptive action, we invite him to share those feelings.

Intervention: Invitation to feelings

Pt: I didn't like it when my mother told me to shut up when I said I had been hospitalized for being suicidal. [*The patient has reported a stimulus to feelings. Hence, we explore feelings.*]

Th: When you say that you didn't like it, what are the feelings toward your mother?

We explore feelings to build affect tolerance and to find the threshold of affect tolerance. Then we know where patients need our help to build capacity.

Response: Anxiety above the Threshold: Cognitive/Perceptual Disruption

Inviting feelings may trigger anxiety in the form of severe cognitive/perceptual disruption and a loss of the ability to intellectualize.

Intervention: Regulate anxiety through a recapitulation

Pt: I'm dizzy. [*She shakes.*]

Th: Notice how you are a little dizzy and shaking all over? That's a sign of anxiety. When these feelings toward your mother come up, your body gets anxious, and then some dizziness happens. Do you notice that too? What's that like to notice that? [*The therapist describes the sequence of events: feelings trigger anxiety. Invite self-reflection to help the patient use a higher-level defense instead of splitting or projection. Regulate anxiety until it returns to the striated muscles. If it does not within five minutes, assess defenses that are perpetuating anxiety (e.g., projection).*]

Response: Anxiety at the Threshold

Inviting feelings may trigger slight cognitive/perceptual disruption while the patient can still reflect.

Intervention: Bracing (Abbass 2015)

Hold feelings at the threshold while regulating anxiety to raise affect tolerance.

Pt: I'm starting to get dizzy. [*The patient intellectualizes about her dizziness: a sign that she is at the threshold of anxiety tolerance but not flooded with anxiety.*]

Th: Notice how you get a little dizzy after we talk about these mixed feelings? These mixed feelings trigger anxiety, leading to dizziness. Do you notice how those mixed feelings do that? [*Remind the patient of feelings to keep them at the threshold of affect tolerance. Regulate anxiety at the same time by cognizing. Continue bracing until she sighs or intellectualizes, signs of a new threshold of affect tolerance (isolation of affect at a higher level of mixed feelings).*]

Response: Increase in Capacity

Once the patient sighs and intellectualizes again at this higher level of feeling, we can talk about the process we just witnessed.

Intervention: Consolidation to summarize what has happened and to solidify progress

Pt: It's weird to see how my anger travels like that, but I see that happens at work too. [*The patient can reflect about a projection rather than project, a higher level of affect tolerance.*]

Th: When these feelings came up here, you got anxious and became dizzy. Then you had the idea I was angry with you. And we discovered that when you felt irritated with me, the irritation traveled over here, and you became afraid of me. Now we see that it felt scary to let that irritation be inside you. Then you realized that this happens with your wife too. When you feel irritated with her, you think she feels irritated with you. What's that like to notice how your irritation can travel to other people when it makes you anxious? [*Describe the triangle of conflict (feeling, anxiety, defense) that occurs in therapy and the patient's marriage. Then invite the patient to offer his understanding.*]

Fragile patients have three different levels of defense structure and three patterns of anxiety, requiring three strategies for building affect tolerance. As shown in figure 7.1, inviting a secure attachment triggers the same pattern in all fragile patients: (1) rising mixed feelings, (2) anxiety in cognitive/perceptual disruption, and (3) defenses of splitting, denial, and projection.

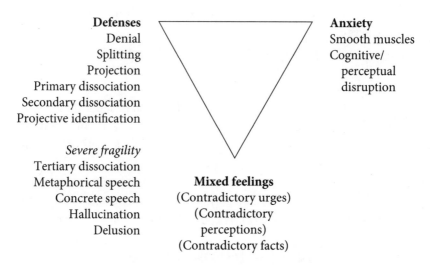

Defenses
Denial
Splitting
Projection
Primary dissociation
Secondary dissociation
Projective identification

Severe fragility
Tertiary dissociation
Metaphorical speech
Concrete speech
Hallucination
Delusion

Anxiety
Smooth muscles
Cognitive/
    perceptual
    disruption

Mixed feelings
(Contradictory urges)
(Contradictory
    perceptions)
(Contradictory facts)

Figure 7.1   The triangle of conflict for all fragile patients

In the fragile spectrum, we always invite the patient to face mixed feelings. These mixed feelings will trigger anxiety over the threshold of tolerance in the smooth muscles or cognitive/perceptual disruption. To end the cognitive/perceptual disruption, the patient will rely on splitting to separate mixed feelings so they cannot trigger anxiety. Then projection is used to relocate one of the mixed feelings. Splitting and projection occur on a spectrum from mild to severe forms. Mildly fragile patients may experience cognitive/perceptual disruption without splitting or projection. Moderately fragile patients will split apart contradictory facts, urges, thoughts, or feelings to avoid cognitive/perceptual disruption. Severely fragile patients rely on primitive forms of splitting and projection such as hallucinations, delusions, and tertiary dissociation. As patients tolerate those contradictory elements, they will become aware of the mixed feelings those elements trigger.

The same principles guide all our work: inviting a healing relationship, assessing the response to relating (the triangle of conflict), and increasing relatedness (blocking barriers to secure attachment and building affect tolerance so patients can tolerate greater emotional closeness). (See table 7.2.) But the interventions that apply those principles will vary according to patient capacity.

Table 7.2 Responses to inviting the relationship and interventions for them

Responses to Inviting the Relationship	Intervention
Feelings	*Invitation:* Invite feelings
Anxiety far over the threshold	*Recapitulation:* Summarize the triangle of conflict to regulate anxiety
Anxiety at the threshold	*Bracing (Abbass 2015):* Hold feelings at the threshold while regulating anxiety to build capacity
Progress	*Consolidation:* Summarize the process that led to progress

Before we describe the clinical approach to fragile patients, let's clarify what we mean by a *healing* relationship. Fragile patients have suffered, and no therapy can unring that bell. What was lost is lost and cannot be replaced. The fragile patient may wish to be healed by being given what no one can give—the past he did not receive. Bearing this loss and pain was unbearable. And therapists, to avoid that pain, may wish they could undo the harm of past hatreds through empathy and love. Both therapists and patients face a terrible abyss, this horrible—even if universal—gap between what we want and what is possible.

What healing we find occurs through surrendering our defenses against reality, primarily the beliefs that reality should not have happened and that our fantasy should have. Through facing the love, rage, grief, and guilt that are triggered in the therapy relationship—echoes of her early life—the patient finds a way to bear the unbearable together with a therapist rather than avoiding it alone through her defenses. By facing the feelings reality elicits, the patient finds a way to live into life. By letting go of impossible expectations based on fantasy, she discovers what is possible in reality. These can be great possibilities or modest. But whatever their range, always unknowable in advance, they offer the prospect of a better life.

By healing, we return to the original meaning of the word: to make whole. We become ill by rejecting our inner life. We become well by becoming at one with the rejected emotional truths of our lives (Bion 1970). But this emotional truth washes away what we thought was real: our fantasies. Each wave of grief—another reunion with the truth. One illusion after another dissolve until what is left is *what is*—unspeakable, unknowable. And through this knowing-seeing, there is a recognition.

The patient comes to know that she is not any of the thoughts or ideas she had. She recognizes that toward which words can only point: the wholeness in which those thoughts and feelings arise. By accepting the rejected fragments of her being, she recognizes the wholeness we are but that she pretended not to be through the imaginary expulsion of her inner life into her projections.

As we become more integrated, we realize that what was "not-me" is now me. What I thought was "you" is also me. What I hated is what I am. We help each other accept what we rejected through splitting and projection, learning to embrace rather than hate our humanity.

BUILDING CAPACITY IN THE SEVERELY FRAGILE PATIENT: EXPLORING FEELINGS WITHIN THE DEFENSE

The spectrum of people who suffer from fragile character structure ranges from the graduate student recovering from a psychotic break (E. Marcus 2017) to the patient suffering from a borderline personality disorder (Kernberg 1975) to the client who experiences cognitive/perceptual disruption briefly at higher levels of mixed feelings (Abbass 2015; Coughlin 1996; Frederickson 2013). Thus, we tailor our work to the level of affect the patient can bear. Let's look at how to help severely fragile patients who use primitive defenses.

These patients *must* use splitting and projection to avoid being overwhelmed with unconscious feelings, flooding anxiety, and psychotic reactions. Thus, we explore feelings *within the defense* to build their affect tolerance. As affect tolerance rises, the patient can talk about feelings more directly, or she may shift to less primitive forms of splitting and projection, as we will see for moderately fragile patients. (See pp. 230–258.)

In the following four vignettes, a patient is working with a therapist who will soon leave the clinic. Overwhelmed with rage toward a therapist she cares for and who has helped her, she relies on primitive defenses.

Inviting Feelings within Splitting

When severely fragile patients use the defense of splitting, we can invite feelings within the defense.

Pt: [*Stands up and yells at her empty chair.*] I hate her!

Th: Why do you hate her? [*The therapist explores feelings toward the split-off self to explore feelings indirectly toward himself.*]

Pt: She is bad.

Th: What is bad about her? [*Invite feelings within the defense of splitting.*]

Pt: She wants to do something bad.

Th: What feelings do you have toward her? [*Invite the patient to explore feelings toward the therapist within the defense of the split-off personality. With increased affect tolerance, she will be able to talk more directly about anger toward the therapist.*]

Inviting Feelings within a Delusion

When severely fragile patients present a delusion, we can sometimes explore feelings within the defense.

Pt: The president has fired me. [*Refers to the president of the country: a defense against anger toward the therapist who is "firing" her by leaving the clinic.*]

Th: What feelings do you have toward him for doing that? [*Invite feelings within a delusion.*]

Pt: I'm angry. He betrayed me! [*Patient can describe anger within the displacement of a delusion.*]

Inviting Feelings within a Hallucination

When severely fragile patients have a hallucination, we can sometimes explore feelings within the defense.

Pt: I'm hearing a voice.

Th: What is the voice saying?

Pt: It is saying I am a bad person. [*Defense against facing rage toward the therapist.*]

Th: Why does it think you are bad? [*Explore feelings within the hallucination.*]

Pt: Because I have bad feelings.

Th: What feelings does it think are bad? [*Explore feelings within the hallucination.*]

Pt: Anger.

Th: Why does it think anger is bad? [*Explore feelings within the hallucination.*]

Pt: Anger means I am bad.

Th: Could I ask the voice a question?

Pt: [*Looks up at the therapist.*] Sure!

Th: I'm sure you wouldn't judge Jane for being angry if you didn't think you were protecting her. So I'm wondering, what do you think is dangerous about the emotion of anger? What are you afraid would happen if Jane had an emotion? [*Explore conflict within the hallucination.*]

Pt: It says that anger can destroy relationships. [*The patient's fears that her anger toward the therapist would destroy their relationship.*]

Th: But anger could destroy a relationship only if Jane and the other person forgot that she also loves. Do you have trouble remembering that Jane is loving when she is angry? [*Interpretation of splitting within the defense.*]

Pt: I'm getting dizzy. [*Cognitive/perceptual disruption with a rise of mixed feelings. A boost in affect tolerance.*]

Exploring Feelings within Projection

When patients project onto other people, we can sometimes explore feelings within the defense of projection.

Pt: The homeless people are having a protest march today at city hall. [*Defense against rage toward the therapist who, by leaving the clinic, takes away her therapy "home."*]

Th: I wonder what feelings they have toward the government. [*Invite feelings toward the therapist within the defense of projection.*]

Pt: They're really angry.

Th: I bet they are. What are they angry about? [*The therapist invites the patient to intellectualize about her anger within the displacement. He builds the patient's affect tolerance until she can talk about things she doesn't like about the therapist.*]

Pt: They were promised some housing, but the government has reneged on that promise. [*In the metaphor, the patient describes her anger toward the therapist for taking away her therapeutic home.*]

In each of these examples, the therapist symbolically explores the patient's rage toward the therapist but within the patient's primitive defenses. As her affect tolerance increases, she can eventually describe conflictual feelings toward the therapist. For instance, she might start a later session by saying she is anxious, and she is not sure she wants to be there.

Th: Coming here and not wanting to be here. Being here and not wanting to be here. And something about being here and not wanting to be here makes you anxious. What is it like to notice this complexity as we sit here today? [*Invite consciousness of splitting.*]

Pt: I'm getting dizzy. [*Cognitive/perceptual disruption.*]

Th: Something about coming here and not wanting to be here, something about this complexity triggers some anxiety and dizziness. What's it like to see that?

Pt: Weird. I know I'm here. And, yet, I'm not sure I want to be here. [*The patient can intellectualize about her conflict without cognitive/perceptual disruption: an increase in affect tolerance. She tolerates her inner conflict: to depend or not to depend without having to split it off and project it onto a delusion or a split-off personality.*]

Rather than relate to a split-off personality, she splits apart her motivations in therapy. Her shift to a milder form of splitting represents progress in affect tolerance. Thus, the therapist no longer invites feelings within the defense of primitive splitting: dissociation. Instead, he encourages the patient to observe and reflect on split-apart feelings in herself to build affect tolerance, the strategy for moderately fragile patients.

Differences within the Spectrum of Fragility

In treatment, severely fragile patients gradually become able to bear mixed feelings toward a split-off personality. Moderately fragile patients, with a higher level of affect tolerance, no longer split themselves into multiple personalities. Instead, they split apart feelings and urges within themselves. Thus, we build the capacity to bear those split apart feelings and urges until they start to experience cognitive/perceptual disruption. And very mildly fragile patients tolerate cognitive/perceptual disruption without using splitting or projection at all.

The projections of severely fragile patients take concrete forms such as delusions or hallucinations. (See table 7.3.) In moderate fragility, the patient no longer has delusions. He projects onto people. When we invite him to reflect on projections, initially he will project again. But as his affect tolerance rises, he will experience slight cognitive/perceptual disruption when we invite him to reflect on his projections. And, eventually, he can reflect on his projections and regain his ability to test the difference between his projections and reality. In mild fragility, he can eventually tolerate some cognitive/perceptual disruption without projecting. He increasingly sees that what he projects onto people is equally true of himself. And he can tolerate feelings at low levels without disrupting or projecting.

Table 7.3   Patterns of anxiety and defense structure in severe fragility

Degree of Fragility	Anxiety	Defense Structure	Intervention
Severe	Absence of cognitive/ perceptual disruption because of splitting and projection Projective anxiety due to projections	Primitive forms of splitting (tertiary dissociation) and splitting of the self Primitive forms of projection such as hallucination and delusion	Inviting feelings within the defenses of dissociation, hallucination, and delusion

We help the severely fragile patient bear mixed feelings within the primitive defenses of dissociation, delusion, and hallucination. In moderate fragility, we help him bear split-apart feelings together until he can tolerate some cognitive/perceptual disruption and eventually sigh. We also help him recognize inside himself what he projects outside until he disrupts and then sighs. In mild fragility, he can bear mixed feelings toward people before disrupting or projecting. We raise his capacity to bear these feelings inside until he disrupts and then build another threshold until he can bear 100 percent of his mixed feelings without experiencing cognitive/perceptual disruption. We co-create a relationship in which we meet his feelings with interest and care.

The severely fragile patient struggles with the need for help and the fear that help may cause pain—the need-fear dilemma (Burnham, Gladstone, and Gibson 1969). Whatever primitive defense he uses is his best possible expression of his feelings, so we meet him there. Therapy unmasks this fear of connection. The patient learns how feelings and fears in the present link to pain in the past. Naturally, traumatized patients ward off intimate relationships and feelings to avoid pain, which formerly they had to face alone. In therapy, we offer a relationship where together we can bear the patient's pain in small steps. We build his capacity to face his feelings gradually. Then he does not have to avoid the people mobilizing his emotions. And he discovers how current fears may be based on former dangers. (See table 7.4.)

Table 7.4 Examples of primitive defenses in severe fragility

Defensive Structure in Severe Fragility	Examples	Invitations to Mixed Feelings
Primitive splitting: **tertiary dissociation (multiple personalities)**	A woman fears that one of her personalities might abandon her.	Explore feelings within the defense of primitive splitting.
Primitive projection: **delusion**	A man is angry toward a woman in his delusion who dumped him.	Explore feelings within a delusional projection.
Primitive splitting and projection: **hallucination**	A woman suffers from a voice that attacks her.	Explore feelings within a hallucination.

Severely fragile patients ward off feelings by using defenses such as projection, delusions, hallucinations, or concrete speech. Since these defenses represent the emergent structure warding off psychosis, we work within them during the initial phases of treatment (Rosenbaum et al. 2012). For instance, following a psychotic break, the first higher-level defense that appears may be *concrete speech*. Rather than interpret through the concrete speech, we might explore within the defense, a structure that wards off a psychotic regression. Or the first higher-level defense might be metaphorical speech. Rather than interpret through the metaphor, we can explore and interpret within it. When the patient's affect tolerance rises enough, he will refer directly to feelings and reactions toward the therapist. Or the patient might use primitive splitting, such as multiple personalities. Here, the therapist can explore feelings within the defense of splitting/dissociation. As affect tolerance builds, the patient can describe feelings directly toward the therapist that were previously split off and attributed to "personalities." The following examples illustrate how to explore feelings and conflict within primitive defenses.

Graded Invitation to Feelings with Concrete Speech

A depressed woman, following a psychotic break, was discharged to an outpatient drug rehabilitation facility. She contended that medications had damaged her brain. Yet there was no evidence, nor was it a common side effect from the medications she was taking. However, she had deteriorated while enduring her husband's verbal and emotional abuse. Her belief that medications had damaged her brain, *concrete speech*, functioned as a defense (Anderson 2012; Bass 2000; Freedman and Lavender 1997; A. Frosch 2012; J. Frosch 1983; Segal 1981) to ward off the painful feelings toward her husband whose unfaithfulness and emotional abuse had damaged her. She directed her rage toward medications, not the husband she loved. Thus, the delusion reflected not only her rage, but the displacement onto medication revealed her love. And the massive feelings of love and rage this rupture caused precipitated her psychotic break.

Before her hospitalization, her husband had been sleeping over with his longtime lover. Once she dumped him, however, he came home. The anger he felt toward his former lover he took out on his wife, berating her daily. Thus, her concrete language warded off her rage toward her husband. The "so-called concreteness of . . . thinking is frequently nothing more than attempts to establish communication by using precise meanings at a very simple level of abstraction" (Donnelly 1966, 151). That's why we say there is a kernel of truth in every delusion (Searles 1965/1986a).

When feelings overwhelm the severely fragile patient, her ability to symbolize her feelings in language collapses. When intense affects exceed what a metaphor can contain, it collapses into a more primitive defense: concrete speech. Concrete speech is a compromise formation between expressing and the inability to express unbearable psychic pain (A. Frosch 2012; Searles 1962/1986b).

We work within the primitive defense of concrete speech since it may be the only means the patient has to ward off feelings and anxiety.

I encouraged the therapist in the following vignette to mirror the patient's concrete speech.

Pt: The medication has damaged my brain.

Th: I agree. Something has damaged your brain. [*Mirroring does not contradict the patient's formulation. But it leaves an opening for her speech to symbolize something more.*]

The therapist mirrored the concrete speech for thirty minutes. Then the patient said, "I don't know what damaged my brain." The ability to tolerate not-knowing leaves space open for her to face her recent struggles more directly.

> Th: You don't know what damaged your brain, but you know that something damaged it. [*Reflect the patient's new statement while inviting her to face what happened and her feelings about it.*]

Later, in that same session, the patient began to sigh, her anxiety returning to the striated muscles, a change in unconscious anxiety discharge at this level of feelings. This revealed an increase in affect tolerance even though she was still unaware of her anger. In the next few sessions, she began to talk about her "upset" feelings with her husband. And later, she described her anger. What had been concrete ("Drugs damaged my brain") became symbolic ("His abuse made me angry"). A material problem (medication) turned into a psychological problem (anger and love). And a damaged brain was experienced as a broken heart. During a crisis three months later, she suffered from suicidal ideation. But she did not need a delusion or concrete speech to deal with her excess anger. Thus, even in a crisis, her functioning had increased. She could use a high-level system of resistance—repression (self-attack)—rather than regress into another psychotic episode.

We can celebrate small changes in the pathways of anxiety discharge, systems of defense, and symbolic use of language, not observable to the layman. In her case, anxiety returned to the striated muscles. Her resistance shifted from splitting and projection to repression at this low level of feelings. Her speech shifted from concrete to symbolic speech. And the feeling of anger had become conscious. Recognizing these incremental changes can give you and the patient the faith and patience needed when developing capacities gradually.

Graded Invitation to Feelings within Dissociation

In another supervised case, a patient was experiencing feelings because her therapist was going to leave the clinic in several months.

> Pt: I'm afraid Geraldine will abandon me. [*Refers to a split-off self. It also symbolizes her feelings toward the therapist.*]

> Th: What feelings do you have toward Geraldine for possibly abandoning you? [*Invite feelings within the defense of dissociation.*]

Pt: I'm getting dizzy. [*Cognitive/perceptual disruption.*]

Th: Something about feelings toward Geraldine makes you anxious and then you get dizzy. Do you see that too? [*Describe the triangle of conflict: feelings toward a split-off self, anxiety, resulting in dizziness. She disrupted when exploring feelings within the defense of dissociation. Thus, she cannot bear mixed feelings directly toward the therapist yet.*]

Pt: Yes. That happens a lot.

Th: Shall we take a look at these feelings toward Geraldine so you won't have to suffer from this dizziness? [*Invite the patient to work toward a positive goal.*]

Pt: Okay.

Th: What feelings do you notice having toward Geraldine for possibly abandoning you?

Pt: It's irritating. [*The patient declares a feeling toward the split-off self. The therapist explores feelings within the defense of splitting/ dissociation until the patient talks directly about feelings toward the therapist. Then the defense will no longer be necessary.*]

Th: How do you experience this irritation toward her? [*Build the patient's affect tolerance within the defense of dissociation.*]

Dissociation is a primitive form of splitting. The earlier and more severe the threat to the attachment, the more severe the degree of splitting necessary for the child to ward off the fear of death, to separate the killing one from the mothering one (Freyd and Birell 2013; DePrince and Freyd 2014). The spectrum of splitting ranges from dissociation involving personalities (severe fragility) to milder forms of splitting that separate mixed feelings, contradictory facts, or memories and awareness (moderate fragility) (Kernberg 1975).

Graded Invitation to Feelings within Metaphor

As the fragile patient's capacity to bear mixed feelings increases, he shifts from concrete thinking (Bass 2000) to *metaphorical speech* (Searles 1962/1986b). For instance, a patient might describe how medications damaged her brain (*concrete speech*). Several sessions later, she talks about a movie she saw where a man damaged a woman's car (*metaphor*). A month later, she says she feels angry with her husband (*symbolic speech*: words directly symbolize her experience).

Thus, metaphor is an achievement for the patient following a psychotic break. It represents an increase of affect tolerance, and, thus, we must not weaken it as an emerging higher-level defense following a psychotic break. If we weaken the defense of metaphor by interpreting before the patient can isolate affect, the interpretation may lead to regression.

Therefore, explore and interpret within the metaphor, not through it when the patient has had a recent psychotic break. For instance, do not mention that the metaphor refers to him. The following example illustrates this principle. As a new therapist, I worked with a client several weeks after he had a psychotic break. He spoke about break-ins, collapsing buildings, and thieves stealing his belongings. I heard the unconscious fears he had about therapy: his fear I could break into his mind; his fear that his mind was collapsing; and his fear that I would be a thief, stealing thoughts from him. Unfortunately, I interpreted through his metaphor. I described the unconscious fears his metaphors portrayed. My comment triggered unconscious feelings and enormous anxiety. As a result, his capacity to use metaphor collapsed. Without the only high-level defense he had, he became psychotic in the session and was hospitalized that night. My mistake caused his regression.

We should not interpret through his defense to the unconscious meaning the metaphor is warding off. He uses metaphor because he lacks the affect tolerance to talk about his fears more directly. Instead, we should explore and interpret within the metaphor (Aleksandrowicz 1962; Cain and Maupin 1961; Caruth and Ekstein 1966; Lindner 1999; Winnicott 1971, 1977). The metaphor tells us what to explore. And it tells us the dosage of language and displacement the patient needs for exploration.

For instance, I could have explored within his metaphor by asking him to talk about how to improve security in homes and buildings. *Metaphorical interpretation*: "How can we help you feel more secure?" I could have asked him what precautions people could take to protect their homes from thieves. *Metaphorical interpretation*: "How could we help you feel more secure with me?" I could have interpreted within his metaphor by saying, "Sometimes buildings [*you*] collapse when building inspectors [*therapists*] fail to identify and install the kinds of support a building [*patient*] needs. That's why it's important not to stress a building [*patient*] but to install the supports it needs and go through a period of rebuilding and renovation [*therapy*] before letting guests [*therapists*] into the building [*your inner life*]. That's why it's important to have a home inspector [*therapist*]. They can assess a building [*patient*] to see what needs to be fixed and how to fix it. And then they can work with you to help you repair the building [*patient*]."

For instance, a paranoid patient expounded on the topic of space invaders. If I had said that he feared I would invade him, his anxiety would have spiked. He would have feared me as an invader and bolted out of the therapy. I never talked directly about his fear that I would invade his space. Instead, I explored his fear of boundary loss within his metaphor.

We explored the possibility of building space stations where earthlings could meet space invaders. Since they were aliens, we could not figure out in advance if they were friends or foes. Within the defense of metaphor, we could put his fears into words.

> *Th:* I imagine that those space invaders could misinterpret our actions as hostile and then go on the attack. It would be important how we approach them. [*Interpret his paranoia within the metaphor.*]

> *Th:* I wonder what the space invaders might be afraid of since they are entering an alien world? [*Explore his fears within the metaphor.*]

In the *counterprojective technique* (Havens 1976, 1986; Sullivan 1953b), the therapist explores the patient's inner life within the projection (Wolberg 1973). Conscious fears about others represent unconscious fears about the therapist. Thus, the therapist counters the projection by exploring these fears within the displacement.

We can also interpret within the metaphor (Sledge 1977). A student was recovering after a psychotic break. But his parents wanted him to return to college when he didn't feel ready. And he feared I did too. Since his hospitalization happened in San Francisco where he had attended college, I offered a metaphor about that city to interpret his conflict.

> *Th:* You know, it's like driving on those streets in San Francisco. Remember how steep they are? You get to the top of a hill, driving your car. And then the light turns red. So you put on the brakes. Then the light turns green. Now it's tricky. If you let go

of the brakes, your car could go into reverse and just end up in the ocean. [*His fear of regression into psychosis.*] If you try to go forward, you have to take your foot off the brake, put it on the gas, and then your left foot has to put you in gear to go forward. It's an awful lot to coordinate. [*His fear of handling the complexities of going back to school.*] Or you could let the car go backward with the brakes on so you can park on the side of the street and have a sandwich until you are ready to go forward. [*His wish to take more time before he returned to school.*]

He calmed down. My interpretation within the metaphor countered his projection that I wanted him to go back before he felt ready. As the patient's affect tolerance increases, his metaphorical speech will become direct communication (Searles 1962/1986b). Then you can address feelings and conflicts explicitly.

Cues of higher-level affect tolerance let us know when we can interpret directly through the defense of metaphor. A patient was rushed into the clinic by her mother during a sudden manic episode. Her mother was perplexed because the patient kept babbling on about seemingly nonsensical material. As she and her mother sat in the office with me, the patient began to cry, "I sat on an oven and got burned by the flames." "Quit talking about that," her mother snapped. "You know that didn't happen!" The patient had mentioned in the previous session that she was going to see her boyfriend. I asked, "What happened with Jim?" "He left me," she said. Her ability to talk directly about her plight indicated that it might be safe for me to interpret her metaphor directly, "I see. You got burned." Her defense of mania cleared up, and she spoke normally again after a passage of grief. In this case, a direct interpretation, where we could bear her grief together, illustrates a higher level of affect tolerance than the previous cases we described. And the clue to her increased affect tolerance was her ability to refer to the loss of her boyfriend directly rather than only indirectly through metaphor or concrete speech.

Graded Invitation to Feelings within Projection

A man diagnosed with schizophrenia came in one day and said, "Jon, I've figured out your diagnosis."

Th: Oh, really? What's that?

Pt: Satyriasis: uncontrollable sexual appetite for women. [*Said while giggling.*]

Th: Oh, my God, how did you figure that out? Even my analyst didn't catch that.

Pt: Oh, it's obvious.

Th: Wow! That's embarrassing. I thought I had it pretty well hidden. Do you think there's any hope for my condition?

Pt: Yes, but it will take a lot of therapy.

Through projection, he invited himself to be the therapist for "my" problem. In this way, we could explore his problems about women as long as I agreed to be the location of his problem. I then invited him to be the therapist of "my" problem.

Th: What do you think is the cause?

Pt: You probably didn't get enough breastfeeding as a baby.

Th: Do you think that's why I'm obsessed with breasts?

Pt: Yes.

He continued to analyze my "problem" for twenty minutes. As we analyzed "my" problem, I could ask, "What feelings do I have when I'm with women?" "Why do these feelings make me anxious?" and "Why am I afraid of women?" We could explore these conflicts as if they were mine. After twenty minutes of analyzing me, he said, "Well, enough about you. I want to talk about something else."

Th: Alright, if you insist. What's that?

Pt: I have trouble talking to women.

He didn't need me to interpret that satyriasis was *his* problem. He needed me to be the place where we explored his problem until he could examine it within himself. Play therapy, *transitional relatedness*, can be used with psychotic and borderline patients (Feinsilver 1983, 1986, 1999; Frederickson 1991; Winnicott 1971). The therapist agrees to be the play space where exploration occurs (Feinsilver 1983, 1986; Winnicott 1971, 1977). I could explore his conflict as long as I agreed that it was in me. After exploring conflicts within the therapist, the patient can explore them within himself. This playful containment of the patient's projection builds his capacity to explore feelings within the defense of projection (Wolberg 1973).

The fact that he could project directly onto me instead of onto a delusion and his ability to play with the projection rather than believe it concretely speaks to a higher capacity.

Here's a look at a spectrum of projection within fragile patients:

Delusions, hallucinations, and concrete speech: Primitive projection onto ideas or objects. These are subject to the von Domarus principle: two similar things are regarded as the same (Arieti 1974). (Also, see chapter 12 on severe fragility.)

Metaphor: Unconscious, latent projection onto the therapist, displaced onto others. (See chapters 3 on will and 11 on projection.)

Projective identification: Conscious projection onto the therapist and attempting to control the location of projection. (See chapter 13 on projective identification.)

Projection onto the therapist: Conscious projection without trying to control the location and without inducing the projection in the therapist, as in projective identification.

Projection onto the therapist: Conscious projection with the capacity for playful containment.

Projection onto the therapist: Conscious projection with the ability to reflect on the projection and consider the difference between the therapist and the projection.

Graded Invitation to Feelings Based on Countertransference

We can also explore feelings in the patient based on what he induces in us. Severely disturbed patients may act out to induce feelings in us that they cannot bear in themselves or put into words. Louis Linn presented a vivid example. "Once, when Dr. Linn was on duty at the emergency ward of Bellevue Psychiatric Hospital, a schizophrenic man, very belligerent and paranoid, drew a gun on Dr. Linn during an interview. Dr. Linn, with a coolness and clinical savvy not all could summon at such a moment, quietly asked, 'What are you afraid of?'— whereupon the gunman relaxed and put his weapon on the table" (Stone et al. 1983, 28).

When working with threatening patients, the therapist can feel anxious. If we take the patient's threat literally, we may fail to see that he is afraid of us, due to projection. Here, the patient threatened the therapist because he felt threatened. He acted in a frightening way because he felt frightened. When we react only to the patient's aggression, we may fail to hear his communication. Translate his deed into meaning through words. Perhaps you feel with him what he feels with you. You don't have to calm your anxiety necessarily. Recognize your bodily resonance with him, so, speaking from your depths, you will speak to his. When working with a suicidal patient, the therapist may be afraid the patient will kill herself. If the therapist takes this literally, he may fail to see that the patient is afraid her defense of self-hatred may kill her. The therapist's anxiety might point to the patient's fear of her suicidality, even when she professes to be completely comfortable.

Likewise, patients in hospitals, halfway houses, or rehab centers often feel helpless, with no real power or control over their lives. Having projected their agency onto other people, they feel vulnerable. Hence, their violent behavior denies their feelings of helplessness and vulnerability. Fearful of his violent urges, the patient may act in a threatening manner to provoke staff to be his self-control (Hinshelwood 2004).

Sometimes patients regress to more primitive forms of communication when verbal communication fails. A patient in an internet therapy session cut her fingers and smeared messages in blood on paper to show her therapist that read "I want to marry you" and "I love you." The therapist interpreted her aggression, but since he failed to mention her love, his comments made her feel as if he had cut her. The messages felt cutting to the patient. Unable to communicate this in words, she cut herself and wrote again in blood, drawing a heart on her chest. The countertransference feeling in me as the supervisor was overwhelming pain, helplessness, and an inability to stop this visual violence. I suggested several interventions to the therapist.

Supervisor: Overwhelming pain, unable to stop it, helpless in the face of this pain. No wonder thoughts of wanting to die come up, just anything to stop the pain.

I suggested a direct use of countertransference so the patient would know her pain was felt and heard. Omitting the distancing use of any pronouns might give her the empathy she needed within a symbiotic transference (Searles 1965/1986a) during a temporary regression.

The therapist was afraid of her wish to marry him. I pointed out that this was concrete speech: she needed him to feel her pain, to co-suffer, the original meaning of the word compassion. When she cut herself, I suggested that she was offering supervision about his hurtful comment. Any time he saw her reaching for the knife, I suggested the following:

Supervisor: I'm sorry. I must have just hurt you. You wouldn't be cutting yourself if I hadn't just hurt you. I don't know what I said that just hurt you, but I'm sorry.

This would allow her to see the function of her cutting, interrupt her action language, and allow her to feel understood at the moment she felt the bond had been cut.

When she drew a heart on her chest, I suggested he interpret that he saw her love since she was afraid, due to splitting, that he saw only her hate, not her mixed feelings. If he did not see her love, she would feel as if he was killing her.

Supervisor: Of course, you want me to see your heart, your love. That in spite of all the feelings and all the pain, your heart, your love is still here.

Later, when the therapist referred to the patient's loving feelings, her cutting stopped immediately. And she began to communicate through words rather than blood.

Later, in the displacement she revealed an issue driving this need to be seen.

Pt: Gupta says you don't care about me. He says you forget about me as soon as our meetings end. I think of you all the time. But he says you never think about me.

Supervisor: I remember you very well. Perhaps Gupta has trouble believing that I remember you and your love between sessions. For some reason, he imagines I would have trouble holding onto you in my mind between sessions. Why do you suppose Gupta would have trouble seeing that? [*Within her projection, I invite her to analyze her problem of evocative memory: due to splitting, she forgets her loving feelings, so she imagines the therapist does as well.*]

In summary, we work within the primitive defenses of severely fragile patients to build affect tolerance. As their affect tolerance increases, their ability to isolate affect emerges, and their defenses of splitting and projection take less primitive forms. Eventually, the patient's defenses will shift, indicating the capacity to explore feelings at a higher level of affect intensity. For instance, exploring within the defense of dissociation can build the patient's capacity to refer to feelings about the therapy rather than toward a split-off personality. Exploring within the defense of concrete speech can build the capacity to reference feelings through metaphorical speech. Exploring within the metaphor can build the capacity to talk directly about feelings with the therapist. Exploring within the defense of projection can build the patient's capacity to talk directly about problems in himself rather than in other people. This may take many sessions to unfold, depending on the severity of fragility.

Principle for Severe Fragility:

Explore feelings within primitive defenses to build affect tolerance gradually. As capacity builds, the patient can express her feelings and conflicts more directly. Each new step becomes your next level of exploration.

BUILDING CAPACITY IN THE MODERATELY FRAGILE PATIENT: INTEGRATING SPLIT-OFF AND PROJECTED FEELINGS

When fragile patients' higher-level defenses collapse, they resort to splitting and projection. Rather than recognize that they have mixed feelings toward a person (love and rage), they split the feelings apart. They claim that they feel only rage or love toward another person, viewing him as only bad or only good.

To avoid mixed feelings, conflicts, and anxiety, they can split off aspects of themselves. I supervised a case once where the patient reported on her "other therapy" for "trauma." I wondered how many therapies she had. The therapist asked. "Seven," the patient replied. She had one therapist for trauma, another for childhood issues, and so on. I suggested that the therapist hold a treatment meeting with all the clinicians at the patient's halfway house. The seven therapists were shocked to learn about the concurrent therapies. But they agreed: there should be only one therapy to integrate the feelings she had split off into separate treatments.

We help the patient integrate each feeling she has split off and projected elsewhere. Once she can integrate those split-off feelings, we have collected a person at a given level of affect tolerance. As her feelings rise, anxiety will shift into cognitive/perceptual disruption again. Each time she uses splitting and projection, the therapist can help her bear her mixed feelings at increasing levels of affect intensity.

Inviting Consciousness of Split-Apart Feelings

In the following example, a woman with a borderline level of character pathology (Kernberg 1975) enters the office for her first session.

Th: What is the problem you would like me to help you with?

Pt: You didn't have anyone in your office. And there I was waiting for you! [*Anger rapidly rises toward the therapist based on a belief that is not yet clear.*]

Th: We agreed to meet at 4 p.m., and we met at 4 p.m. Was there some confusion about that? [*Remind her of reality to counter the projection.*]

Pt: You didn't have anyone in here. And I was waiting out there. I am suffering! [*Implicit projection: "You don't care about my suffering."*]

Th: Of course. You are suffering. That is what brought you here. [*Empathize with her suffering to deactivate the projection.*] And it sounds like there was a reaction when we met at the time we agreed upon. [*Remind her of reality and her reaction.*]

Pt: You made me wait! [*Projection.*]

Th: Really? We agreed to meet at 4 p.m. Right? [*Remind her of reality.*]

Pt: Yes.

Th: And we met at the time we agreed on. Right? [*Remind her of reality.*]

Pt: Yes. But I had to wait.

Th: Yes. We both waited until 4, the time we agreed to meet. And it sounds like when we waited for that time, your mind made that mean something. What did your mind make 4 p.m. mean? [*Invite her to see how the problem was not waiting but the meaning her mind assigned to waiting.*]

Pt: You don't care. [*She treats her assumption as a fact.*]

Th: A thought came up that 4 p.m. meant your therapist didn't care, even though we both agreed on 4 p.m. What is it like to see that thought? [*Invite her to reflect on her projection.*]

Pt: But I really wanted to see you.

Th: Of course! You wanted to see me. There were some positive feelings. And, in addition, some negative feelings came up about an image of a person who wouldn't care about your suffering. Something about mixed feelings gets triggered here even before we met today. [*Invite her to notice how depending triggered mixed feelings, which she split apart.*]

Pt: [*Sighs.*] Yes, because I don't know you. [*Anxiety returns to the striated muscles.*]

Th: That's right. You wanted to see me. And, at the same time, an image of an uncaring person comes in here. Then you saw that uncaring image and had a hard time seeing me. [*Price of projection.*] What's it like to see that?

Pt: I just get anxious when I come here. [*She sees that she gets anxious but not why.*]

Th: Sure. You want to see me, so there are positive feelings. Then there's some image from some other time and place that triggers negative feelings. So positive and negative feelings come up as we begin here together. [*Invite her to observe her mixed feelings.*]

Pt: [*Sighs.*] Yes.

Th: And when these mixed feelings come up, an image comes up of an uncaring person. Is that one of the problems you would like us to help you with?

Pt: I hadn't thought of that. But it's true. I do that.

Th: I don't know if we would say you do it. You didn't want that thought to get in your way. But could we agree that that thought happens? [*Help the patient see how unconscious defenses happen without her intent or awareness. Differentiate her from her defenses so we can look at mechanisms hurting her.*]

Now she can bear her mixed feelings toward the therapist. And she can think about them while her anxiety is in the striated muscles (sighing), without splitting them apart or projecting onto the therapist. Each time her feelings become more intense, however, she will split again. We can use the same intervention to help her tolerate mixed feelings at higher thresholds, building her affect tolerance. (For more on splitting, see chapter 10.)

Before exploring further, however, we will assess and regulate her anxiety to make her feel physically safer in her body. Her mixed feelings rose rapidly because her higher-level defenses failed, and she went into cognitive/perceptual disruption. That's not her fault. Since she doesn't have brakes to slow down a rise of feelings, we have to provide them. We need to teach her how to identify and regulate her anxiety. To do so, we invite her to help us.

> *Th:* Any time you experience any anxiety symptoms, let me know right away because I don't want this to be an unpleasant experience for you. And if your anxiety gets too high, it will be too uncomfortable. Let me know whenever you have any anxiety symptoms so we can help you regulate it before it gets too high.

Then, from a position of calm and an agreement to work while regulated, we can explore feelings gradually. (See table 7.5.) We do not want to cross her threshold of affect tolerance quickly. Only with these conditions is it possible to explore feelings in therapy with a moderately fragile patient. If you don't provide the brakes, she will be flooded. Later sections will illustrate how to offer the patient higher-level defenses to help her experience feelings without being overwhelmed by them.

Table 7.5   Patterns of anxiety and defense in moderate fragility

Level of Fragility	Amount of Anxiety the Patient Can Tolerate	Structure of the Defense	Intervention
Moderate I	Splitting and projection occur before cognitive/perceptual disruption can occur. The patient cannot tolerate cognitive/perceptual disruption. Projective anxiety.	Splitting apart not of the self but of contradictory ideas, feelings, or urges. Projections onto people rather than onto delusions or hallucinations.	Invite consciousness of split-apart feelings. Invite the patient to bear inside what he projected outside.
Moderate II	Cognitive/perceptual disruption appears briefly before splitting and projection. An increase in anxiety tolerance. The longer the patient can tolerate the cognitive/perceptual disruption before splitting, the greater the affect tolerance.	Splitting apart not of the self but of contradictory ideas, feelings, or urges. Projections onto people rather than onto delusions or hallucinations.	Invite consciousness of split apart feelings. Invite the patient to bear inside what he projected outside.

Inviting Consciousness of Split-Apart Feelings

The following vignette illustrates how feelings and anxiety rise when we invite the patient to form a healing relationship. The patient had many failed therapies. He suffered from splitting, projection, and dissociation. This excerpt comes from the second session.

Pt: I feel anxious today. I didn't want to come. [*Splitting and denial.*]

Th: You came, and you didn't want to come. You're here, and you didn't want to be here. As we let both urges be here, what's that like to notice this complexity? [*Invite him to be conscious of his split-apart urges.*]

Pt: I get dizzy. [*Cognitive/perceptual disruption occurs because he is aware of two urges he previously split apart. When splitting stops, anxiety starts. His anxiety means he is tolerating mixed feelings instead of splitting them apart. That is progress.*]

Th: Isn't that interesting! Something about being here and not wanting to be here makes you anxious. Being here and not wanting to be here triggers this dizziness. What's it like to notice how this complexity triggers anxiety? [*Bracing (Abbass 2015): remind him of the mixed urges and feelings while regulating his anxiety by pointing out the triangle of conflict—his mixed feelings trigger anxiety and dizziness.*]

Pt: Strange.

Th: It is strange, isn't it! Wanting to be here, not wanting to be here. Both true. Both here. And something about these mixed urges in your mind triggers anxiety. [*Bracing: remind him of the mixed urges while regulating his anxiety.*]

Pt: [*Sighs.*] I did want to come. [*He can acknowledge the previously split-off desire while anxiety is in the striated muscles. His affect tolerance has risen.*]

Th: Right. You wanted to come and didn't want to come. And we're just noticing this complexity, these mixed urges within yourself. And when they arise, your body gets anxious and dizzy. [*Invite him to observe his mixed desires at a higher threshold.*] What do you notice as you let these two contradictory urges be inside you without having to do anything about them? [*This consolidation builds the patient's capacity to tolerate and reflect on his inner conflict.*]

Principle:	When a patient splits apart contradictory thoughts, feelings, or perceptions, invite him to experience his inner conflicts. Don't ask him to take one side in his conflict. That would be splitting. Help him tolerate both sides without cognitive/perceptual disruption or splitting.

Inviting Consciousness of Projected Feelings

To avoid cognitive/perceptual disruption triggered by mixed feelings, fragile patients may split off a feeling and deny it. Or they can mention contradictory feelings and thoughts without noticing the contradiction. Or they can split off and project a feeling onto another person.

The therapist helps the patient become conscious of feelings inside, which she projects outside. (See table 7.6.) For instance, a patient, anxious about her anger, may ask, "Are you angry with me?" Rather than notice a feeling inside herself, she relocates it onto the therapist. She needs help to bear inside what she projects outside.

Pt: Are you angry?

Th: No. [*Block the projection.*] But since this question comes up after my last comment, I wonder what reaction you might be having to it. [*Invite her to notice her "reaction" inside herself. If the therapist asked about her anger, the patient would project again because she cannot yet tolerate the feeling inside herself. The therapist invites the patient to use the defense of intellectualization by using the word "reaction." By exploring within the defense of intellectualization, the therapist supports the patient so she can explore her feelings toward the therapist more gradually.*]

Pt: I'm feeling dizzy right now. [*Cognitive/perceptual disruption, a sign that anxiety rose when the therapist invited her to notice a reaction inside rather than project it outside. She became dizzy rather than project: progress. She tolerates a "reaction" inside without projecting.*]

Th: Something about having a reaction to my comment seems to trigger this anxiety, which makes you dizzy. [*Cognize about causality.*] This anxiety rises as soon as we explore your reaction to my comment. [*Causality.*] Do you notice that too?

Pt: Yes.

Th: Something about a reaction, this dizziness, and then you wondered if I had a reaction. [*Cognize about her conflict. Help her observe the process her projection creates.*]

Pt: I wondered if you were angry. [*She cognizes about her projection: a sign that anxiety is dropping.*]

Th: I wonder what that reaction was to my comment? [*Invite her feelings by asking about her "reaction." Graded format: if a stated feeling leads to projection, use a lower-dosage word to build her capacity to bear mixed feelings.*]

Pt: I didn't like it. [*Intellectualization: a thought about the feeling. She can intellectualize about her feeling rather than project it onto the therapist: progress.*]

Th: Sure. You didn't like it. That's the thought. [*Identify her defense.*] If we look under that thought, what feelings did that comment trigger? [*Invite her feelings.*]

Pt: I was a little angry with you. [*She can face the anger within herself. There is no sigh. She intellectualizes, a defense within the system of isolation of affect. Since isolation of affect is correlated with anxiety in the striated muscles, we view an emergent defense in isolation of affect as the equivalent of a sigh. She may need many interventions before she sighs.*]

Th: Sure. You were a little angry with me. Then you got anxious and dizzy. And then the anger left you and went in a little helicopter over here. And then the feeling was located over here on me. Do you see that too? [*Describe the triangle of conflict. The fragile patient cannot see an invisible defense like projection. The metaphor of the helicopter transporting her feeling helps her represent or picture in her imagination how the defense works. I don't say that she projected. Projection happened without her knowledge or conscious desire. Do not accuse her of doing something she did not consciously do.*]

Pt: Yes, though it sounds funny when you put it that way. [*Her ability to see some humor reveals a higher capacity for self-reflection: progress.*]

(For more on projection, see chapter 11.)

Table 7.6   Defenses and interventions in moderate fragility

Defensive Structure in Moderate Fragility	Examples	Interventions
Splitting intervention: bring together split-apart feelings, urges, or thoughts to build the capacity to bear mixed feelings.	*Pt:* The doctors say I should give up drugs, but I don't want to.	Invitation to consciousness of splitting: *Th:* Not wanting to give up drugs and finding yourself in a therapist's office. What's it like to notice that complexity inside you?
Projection intervention: accept a projected feeling, urge, or thought to build the capacity to bear mixed feelings.	*Pt:* I'm afraid of what we are going to get into here.	Invitation to consciousness of projection: *Th:* I have no right to get into anything you don't want to get into. That's why we have to find out what you want to get into that you think would be helpful for you.

Deactivating Projection, Regulating Anxiety, and Inviting Feelings

The following vignette illustrates how to invite feelings with a woman who has suffered from hallucinations and delusions. The context is that I will be out of the office for six weeks. Her English reflects that she is a nonnative speaker. I asked about her feelings toward me, and her anxiety shifted into cognitive/perceptual disruption. She has just mentioned that my listening to her scares her.

Th: Can we notice that? How do you experience that in your body?

Pt: Itching everywhere. Eyes less blurry but blurry. [*Cognitive/perceptual disruption.*]

For a review on the relationship between anxiety and itching, see Sanders and Akiyama (2018).

Th: Notice that.

Pt: Itching everywhere.

Th: Can we just slow down and notice? [*Build observing capacity to lower anxiety.*]

Pt: Uncomfortable.

Th: You are uncomfortable when I listen to you. [*Causality.*]

Pt: I was good to listen to others. Never found anyone. Friend says, "I can't believe you don't have anyone."

Th: You are noticing that you do a beautiful job of listening to others.

Pt: Not to me. [*She does not listen to herself. She projects that I want to listen to her. Then she fears me. I deactivate her projection and ask if she wants to listen to herself.*]

Th: It feels scary to listen to you.

Pt: Yeah.

Th: Notice that discomfort in your body now to listen to you.

Pt: Bubbling. Waking up the lion. The lion is getting ready to defend itself.

Th: Can we notice that sensation?

Pt: Just to know we are going to do that. I felt uncomfortable in the waiting room. Not going down easily. [*Her difficulty with swallowing is a sign of nausea. Bearing her wish to listen to herself triggers anxiety, so we build her capacity to want to listen to herself.*]

Th: That's why we need to check: do you want to listen to you? [*Invite her will to listen to herself. Otherwise, if she projects her will onto me, she will fear me.*]

Pt: I'm getting a turtle neck. [*Rise of anxiety.*]

Th: Can you describe that? How would you describe that turtle neck reaction?

Pt: I came. I am scared.

Th: Exactly.

Pt: I don't know how to bring.

Th: You shouldn't bring anything out until you're sure that you want to listen to yourself. [*Invite her to hold things in (reinforcing the defense) to deactivate her projection that the therapist wants her to bring things out. Mirroring her defense mobilizes her will.*]

Pt: I want to. [*She declares her will, but there is no sigh.*]

Th: What tells you that you want to listen to what is inside you? [*Invite her will.*]

Pt: Scared because—[*sigh*] more than half a century without me going to this territory. [*Her sigh tells us that anxiety has shifted into the striated muscles. Her will is online.*] Even if I listen to myself, will I be a disappointment to myself? To avoid I'm not a disappointment, I won't go there. [*Defense: self-attack.*]

Th: "I don't want to listen to myself because I might disappoint myself." How do you experience: "I don't want to listen to myself?" [*Invite her to experience her conflict: wanting and not wanting to listen to herself.*]

Pt: Not good. Devastated if I tell this to myself.

Th: It is true: you want to listen to yourself.

Pt: But I don't.

Th: Both are true. [*Invite consciousness of splitting.*]

Pt: I want help, might be a disappointment. Angel and devil fight. [*New metaphor to describe her inner conflict: wanting and not wanting to listen to herself. The metaphor, a higher level of symbolic speech, indicates higher affect tolerance.*]

Th: What happens if you let the angel and devil be here? [*Invite consciousness of splitting by using the higher dosage words in her metaphor. Do not ask her to take a side in her conflict. That would encourage splitting. Instead, invite her to tolerate her conflict.*]

Pt: A big fight. I'm going to finish vomiting. Growing sensation of not digesting well. [*Experiencing mixed feelings triggers anxiety in the smooth muscles. When she uses the word "vomit," she is not vomiting. But she does feel food moving up into her throat.*]

Th: Noticing wanting to listen, not wanting to listen, and letting both of those urges be in you without having to listen yet. [*Invite consciousness of splitting.*]

Pt: I already feel.

Th: Something is happening. Before we listen to you, you have a wish to listen to yourself and not to listen. Without listening, without not listening—there are two urges inside you at the same time. What happens in your body as we notice this urge to listen and urge not to listen? As you let them both be there without having to do anything. [*Invite consciousness of splitting.*]

Pt: Just to hear, stomach goes nuts. [*Rise of anxiety into the smooth muscles.*]

Th: Just by listening, your stomach goes nuts. [*Causality: listening to her desire triggers anxiety.*]

Pt: Water is right here. Going down again.

Th: Noticing, just to notice any desire. [*Point out causality: listening to her desire triggers anxiety.*]

Pt: [*Sighs. Anxiety is in striated muscles for the moment.*]

Th: Makes your anxiety go up.

Pt: Yeah.

Th: Desire not to listen and to listen. [*Invite consciousness of splitting.*]

Pt: Water coming up. [*Rise of anxiety in the smooth muscles again. We cross over and under the threshold of affect tolerance.*]

Th: Notice what triggered that. [*Invite her to observe the relationship between her desire and her anxiety.*]

Pt: Desire to speak or not speak.

Th: Isn't that interesting. As if it is against the law to state any desire. And just notice what happens in your body right now. There's a new reaction.

Pt: Itching. In my head. Ball in my stomach. [*As she sees the link, her anxiety rises again into the smooth muscles.*]

Build the capacity to tolerate internal conflict: This patient had difficulty accepting her wish to listen to herself. This cognitive summary of her conflict triggers anxiety in the smooth muscles. We gradually build her capacity to bear this conflict until she can see it while anxiety goes into the striated muscles.

Together, we explore her wish to listen to herself and her reluctance to do so.

Th: Can we let the hesitancy be here since it's here? [*Invite her to bear her conflict.*] What do you notice?

Pt: Croissant came up. [*Rise of anxiety in the smooth muscles.*]

Th: Notice what triggered it?

Pt: What you said.

Th: Whether we could give your hesitancy permission to be here. [*Why does such a gentle invitation trigger so much anxiety? Her hesitation expresses her counterwill (Rank 1930/1936), her will against me—thus, a bit of unconscious anger.*]

Pt: Oh, my God! [*Another rise of anxiety in the smooth muscles.*]

Th: Isn't that interesting? As if it is against the law to let hesitancy be here when it is here.

Pt: It's here.

Th: How do you experience this hesitancy in your body? [*Graded invitation to experience her anger toward me.*]

Pt: I am confused about the word. [*Intellectualization: a sign her anxiety is moving into the striated muscles at this level of feeling.*]

Th: Hesitant means you're a little reluctant to move forward.

Pt: Yes. I want, but something pulls me back. [*She can intellectualize about her conflict without being overwhelmed with anxiety: another rise in affect tolerance.*]

Th: How do you experience the pullback? [*Graded invitation to experience her anger toward me.*]

Pt: Pullback makes me feel sad and stuck.

Th: That's your reaction to the pullback. How do you experience the pullback physically? [*Graded invitation to experience her anger toward me.*]

Pt: Like growing something here.

Th: Can you describe the sensation in your neck?

Pt: Hold on.

Th: What's happening now?

Pt: Food is going up and down. [*Rise of anxiety in the smooth muscles.*]

Th: Can you describe that sensation in your body? [*Invite her to observe the anxiety symptoms so they will come down.*]

Pt: Croissant going up and down.

Th: What other sensations of anxiety do you notice? [*Invite her to observe the anxiety symptoms.*]

Pt: Trying to go into a shell.

Th: Can you let your body go like that and hold it tight? Hold yourself like that. [*Reinforce the defense to help bring anxiety down.*]

Pt: I sleep like that.

Th: Let yourself hold like that. What do you notice feeling as you do that?

Pt: A comfortable zone, a shell is protecting me.

Th: As you let yourself protect yourself with the shell.

Pt: The food is coming up. Oh, my God! That's why I drank water. [*Rise of anxiety into the smooth muscles.*]

Th: Let's pay attention to that anxiety. [*Invite attention to bring anxiety down.*]

Pt: It's right here. Was here. [*Points to her throat.*] Now it's here. [*Points to her chest.*]

Th: Can you form your hands into two fists and hold them tight for a moment? [*Invite her to tense up to bring anxiety into the striated muscles.*]

Pt: [*She holds her fists.*] Oh, God!

Th: Keep holding those fists.

Pt: [*Sighs.*] It went down. [*Anxiety returns to the striated muscles.*]

Th: Keep holding the fists. Now push your hands together like this. Just push together. [*Invite her to tense up to bring anxiety into the striated muscles.*]

Pt: [*She pushes her hands together. Sighs. Anxiety is in the striated muscles.*]

Th: What do you notice feeling now?

Pt: It calmed down the craziness in my stomach. Why? Put attention somewhere else?

Th: What do you notice feeling now?

Pt: Much calmer. Cramps is almost, almost, almost gone. No food, no water. [*No anxiety in the smooth muscles.*]

Build the capacity to bear rising mixed feelings toward the therapist: Every fragile patient experiences the conflict between relating (love) and distancing (rage). When she becomes aware of her wish to pull back, reinforce her defense to bring her anxiety down. Reinforcing her defense also allows her to enact her urge to distance—her unconscious rage toward me. This builds her capacity. Since anxiety floods her again, I offer her an anxiety regulation technique.

A few minutes later, we continue.

Pt: I could never imagine this would make the food go down. ·

Th: Is this better now in your stomach?

Pt: My brain is now. "How this work? Why this work?" Like a scientist. What makes this come down? [*She can intellectualize again, so we can explore again.*]

Th: As we look at what we've learned here, what's the sequence we've seen? What makes your body anxious?

Pt: This is crazy. Stomach. Oh, my God! [*Another rise of anxiety.*]

Th: Notice.

Pt: Immediately. You don't even finish the question. [*Since the previous question triggers a sudden rise of anxiety, I invite her will to bring anxiety down by deactivating a projection.*]

Th: I'll ask you a silly question for a therapist: do you want to talk? [*Invite her will.*]

Pt: Yes. [*No sigh. Thus, her will is not online.*]

Th: What tells you that you know you want to talk? [*Invite her will.*]

Pt: If I give up on that, I wouldn't be here. [*No sigh.*]

Th: How do you feel that inside that you want to talk? [*Invite her will.*]

Pt: I know because anxiety goes up. If not go up, no fight. [*She sees causality.*]

Th: How do you experience this anxiety now? You want to talk, and then there is anxiety. [*Invite her to observe causality.*]

Pt: Like an electrical shock.

Th: [*I play as if I was a policeman tasering her and calling her a devil.*] Tazing. "No! Little devil." And how do you experience that anxiety?

Pt: [*Sighs.*] Just because we played a little bit, I relaxed. [*Anxiety returns to the striated muscles.*]

Th: What's that like to see? "I want to talk" and anxiety. To see and notice? [*Invite her to see her mixed feelings and motivations.*]

Pt: It's good because it shows that we are on the right path, but if you want me to talk, I don't know what I have to talk. [*Projection: "If you want me to talk."*]

Th: Oh, no! Not whether I want you to talk. [*Block the projection of will.*]

Pt: I don't know what to say.

Th: Don't worry about that. First, how do you experience inside yourself that you know that you want to talk? [*Invite her to recognize her will to talk to deactivate the projection.*]

Pt: Oh, my God! [*Rise of anxiety. Accepting her will triggered high anxiety.*]

Th: Isn't that fascinating? Press your hands together. [*Invite her to bring her anxiety back into the striated muscles.*]

Pt: Oh, God. Like three hours like that?

Th: If that's what we have to do.

Pt: Sorry about that.

Th: I'm sorry you have to suffer like that. All you want to do is talk.

Pt: Silly.

Th: But it happens.

Pt: So fast.

Th: Amazing.

Pt: Blood coming.

Th: Do you want to talk? [*Invite her will.*]

Pt: [*Nods.*]

Th: How do you experience that, that you want to talk? [*Invite her will.*]

Pt: Anxiety.

Th: What's it like to notice, to see that here together?

Pt: [*Presses hands together.*] It's good that this helps. [*The patient soothes her anxiety without being prompted by the therapist: increased therapeutic alliance.*]

Th: Yeah.

Pt: Next time I come, no food, no water.

Th: What's it like to notice, to pay attention to desire in you? Anxiety happens.

Pt: I'm going to finish vomiting. Oh, come on. [*Sighs. Anxiety in the striated muscles.*]

Th: What happens when you look here?

Pt: I feel calm because I trust. But as soon as I say that, the little devil brought up food.

Th: Wonderful you can see that. Looking at this microscopically, right?

Pt: Vomit. [*Sighs.*] Food is here. Tube of croissant. But I'm here.

Th: You're here.

Build the capacity to recognize her wish to talk: She becomes more aware of her wish to talk and her hesitancy to do so. Help her observe the relationship between her wish and the anxiety. This mobilizes her wish to be here with me, which accounts for her next projection.

Pt: I'll be here, if you allow me. [*Projection: "If you allow me."*]

Th: Are you willing to allow yourself to be here? [*Invite her to recognize her will.*]

Pt: Yes. [*No sigh.*]

Th: What do you notice feeling?

Pt: What do you think? [*She has had another rise of anxiety.*]

Th: Isn't that interesting? [*A statement to help her step back and observe her anxiety.*]

Pt: Food is here again. [*Rise of anxiety in the smooth muscles.*]

Th: Let's notice that. Just to allow yourself to be here, giving yourself permission to be here triggers anxiety.

Pt: [*Sigh. Summarizing causality brings her anxiety back into the striated muscles.*]

Th: Fascinating. [*A statement to help her step back and observe her anxiety.*]

Pt: Yes.

Th: Interesting. Amazing. [*A statement to help her step back and observe her anxiety.*]

Pt: It is.

Th: What do you notice feeling? [*Check on her anxiety.*]

Pt: At the same time, so annoying because if this wouldn't be there, I would be developing much faster. [*Repeated invitations to step back and observe her anxiety have brought it down. Now she can intellectualize and see the cost of the defense.*]

Th: That's why it's important to pay close attention to this in detail.

Pt: Vomit. [*Anxiety is in the smooth muscles. The invitation to pay attention in detail likely triggers the rise in anxiety.*]

Th: What word did I say that triggered the anxiety?

Pt: This room is my world, and I can be myself, feel myself, speak myself, but this little devil comes cutting me down. [*Improved ability to reflect: progress.*]

Th: What's that like to see that and observe this reaction that happens? [*Invite her to cognize about her reactions. Thinking about her thinking solidifies a gain, so it persists.*]

Pt: It's good. If intention was to sabotage.

Th: You don't have a wish to sabotage, but this anxiety comes up. We don't have to fight the anxiety; just let ourselves notice. [*Remind her of the task: paying attention to anxiety to regulate it.*] Isn't that interesting? With your higher mind, you are with Jon. [*Form an alliance with the nonpsychotic part of her mind (Bion 1957; Katan 1954; Lotterman 2015).*] But your lower mind is anxious. Old information comes up in your body as we pay attention to you and your anxiety. And do you want to pay attention to this anxiety? [*Invite her will.*]

Pt: Yes.

For several minutes, we help her see how paying attention to herself triggers anxiety in the smooth muscles and cognitive/perceptual disruption.

Pt: [*Sigh. Anxiety is in the striated muscles.*]

Th: What do you notice feeling now?

Pt: Disappointment. [*Defense: self-attack.*]

Th: Is that a thought about you?

Pt: Yeah.

Th: Could that be a critical thought? Could it get you depressed? [*Identify the defense and clarify its price.*]

Pt: Yeah.

Th: What feelings are coming up here toward me? [*Since self-criticism turns anger on her, I invite her to notice the feelings toward me. Feeling her anger toward me blocks her self-criticism and the resulting depression.*]

Pt: The positive me wants this to continue because we are fighting these things. But the little devil says, "See, he makes you depressed." [*Now she intellectualizes: a positive change.*]

Th: What feelings are coming up here toward me? [*Invite feelings toward me.*]

Pt: The little devil would say negative things, and the little angel would say good things. Always.

Th: Devil reactions, angel reactions, both in you. [*Invite her to face mixed feelings toward me to block splitting. Invite her to face mixed feelings inside herself to block projection.*]

Pt: Vomit. [*Anxiety is moving into the smooth muscles.*]

Th: Feeling now? [*Invite feelings toward me.*]

Pt: Is this going to work? [*Defense: self-doubt.*]

Th: Would that be a critical thought? What feelings are coming up here toward me? [*Invite feelings toward the therapist.*]

Pt: I already said.

Build her capacity to bear mixed feelings toward me: We see progress. She shifts from projection to repression: the self-attack and self-doubt. I invite feelings toward me so that her anger does not go back on her through self-attack. She can intellectualize about her conflict by using the metaphors "little devil" and "little angel." This reveals increased affect tolerance even though her feelings toward me are not yet conscious.

Th: Angel reactions, devil reactions, but what feelings coming toward me? [*Invite mixed feelings toward me.*]

Pt: Two feelings: one feeling is a desperate "Don't give up. Shut up! This is not working," and the food keeps coming up! This one says, "No, it is working." Then the devil says, "So what! You're going to be here all day, up and down." [*Instead of self-attack, now she can intellectualize about her mixed feelings: a sign of progress.*]

Th: What's that devilish feeling? [*Invite feelings toward me.*]

Pt: [*Sighs. Anxiety is in the striated muscles.*]

Th: What's that devilish feeling coming up here toward me? [*Invite feelings toward me.*]

Pt: I already said.

Th: And what else could you say about that devilish feeling? [*Invite feelings toward me.*]

Pt: You keep repeating the same thing.

Th: What feelings are coming up toward me for being repetitious? [*Invite feelings toward me.*]

Pt: No. Devil saying the same thing. Are you the devil? [*Laughs. Previously, she hallucinated the devil onto photos. Now she can play with the metaphor as a step in accepting her anger.*]

Th: Wondering if I'm the devil. What's the feeling toward me? Is Jon the devil? What's the feeling toward me? [*Playing with her metaphor to invite feelings toward me.*]

Pt: [*Sighs. Anxiety is in the striated muscles.*] Feelings, I have problems with this word. I need to look in dictionary. I got used to being frozen. Vomit. [*When she says the word "vomit," she is not vomiting. But she feels it come up in her throat: rise of anxiety in smooth muscles.*] It's gross just because I said the word "feeling" or "frozen." Next time I will come with empty stomach.

Th: You are letting me know you kept these feelings frozen. [*Describe her defense.*]

Pt: Feelings of a life. Feelings of being alive, everything related to life, I'm frozen. I killed everything I liked to do. [*She can intellectualize about feelings without anxiety going into the smooth muscles at this level of feeling: a big increase in affect tolerance.*]

Th: Feelings that have been frozen. What are these feelings coming up here toward me? [*Invite feelings toward me.*]

Pt: Feelings.

Th: What feelings? [*Invite feelings toward me.*]

Signs of Greater Affect Tolerance

In this section, she sighed: her anxiety is moving into the striated muscles. She begins to intellectualize more. Her playful question about whether I am the devil reveals that her anxiety has dropped and her symbolic thinking has improved. This higher access to feelings will mobilize memories.

Pt: When you ask about feelings since the beginning of therapy, every time you ask, I have an image in my head. This comparison is based in real life because in my elementary school . . . those four years of my school. Vomit. Wow! I should go to the bathroom. [*Describing a childhood incident triggers anxiety in the smooth muscles at a higher level of feelings.*]

Th: Just take a moment. Don't say anything for a moment. You had a big feeling. Give yourself a moment. You have a big feeling. Give yourself a moment before saying anything more. [*I provide a defense ("Don't say anything for a moment") to help her anxiety come down.*]

Pt: In elementary school, we are not allowed to speak.

She felt anger toward a teacher with whom she was supposed to be silent, answering questions only on demand. Anger in the displacement (the teacher) triggers a wave of anxiety.

Pt: Vomit. [*Anxiety is in the smooth muscles.*]

Th: You had a big feeling there.

Pt: Madness. [*Flooded with anxiety. Now her anger is conscious. Exploring feelings toward the former teacher builds her capacity to face mixed feelings toward me later in the session.*]

Th: Just hang on a second. Just hang on a second. No more words for a moment. No more words. Just give yourself a moment. [*Reinforce her defense to bring anxiety down.*]

Pt: Wow!

Th: No more words; just give yourself a chance. You had a big feeling there. We have to go slowly. You had a big feeling. Take your time. You just had a big feeling there. Right?

Pt: Oh.

Th: You just had a big feeling there.

Pt: Yeah.

Th: We see the feeling you had and the anxiety it provokes. [*Cognize about causality in the moment.*]

Pt: The feeling of anger. [*Now she can feel this level of anger without flooding with anxiety. However, each higher rise of anger will trigger anxiety again.*]

Build her capacity to bear her feelings and the resulting memories: As her feelings rose, memories rose, which triggered more feelings and anxiety. I introduced high-level defenses to slow her down so anxiety would not overwhelm her. As I remind her of her feeling and anxiety, she finally identified the feeling: anger.

She describes a professor who was interested in what she thought and another who discussed the dictatorship in her country. These symbolize her experience of the therapist, an interested person who discusses the dictatorial defenses controlling her. Feelings rise toward her parents, which trigger a defense: a self-critical thought.

Let's review her progress.

Step one—Invite her will to listen to herself: Help her face her conflict, her wish to listen to herself and not listen to herself. Then help her regulate her anxiety by holding both sides of the conflict inside, and deactivate her projection of will until she can accept her will to listen to herself while anxiety is in the striated muscles.

Step two—Invite feelings toward the therapist: This triggers the metaphor of the devil.

Step three—Rage emerges in the displacement: A memory of rage toward a past teacher rises. Regulate her anxiety over the feeling of anger, which is now conscious.

Step four—Rage emerges toward her parents.

Step five—Shift into repression: She relies on self-attack rather than projection as her defense. Her reliance on the resistance system of repression rather than splitting and projection represents increased affect tolerance.

Th: Would that be a critical thought? [*Defense identification.*]

Pt: Yes.

Th: Could it make you depressed? [*The price of the defense.*]

Pt: Yes.

Th: What feelings are coming up toward me underneath the critical thoughts? [*Invite the feelings the defense covers up.*]

Pt: Toward you? My mother comes to mind. They told me, "Don't think." You ask me to do the opposite. Why should I be mad at you? [*Her reality testing is good: she can see that I invite her to think. This triggers positive feelings and a memory of her mother with negative feelings—thus, mixed feelings toward the therapist.*]

You may ask, "Why is he asking for feelings toward him? She was talking about her mother." It's true, *and* she is relating to me. When she shares feelings, she becomes emotionally closer to me. Then she attacks herself in our relationship. She turns anger onto herself to protect me from her anger. Thus, I invite her to direct feelings toward me so she doesn't turn them onto herself and get depressed. If I were to be more explicit, I might say, "Notice how these thoughts are attacking and hurting you? They are attacking you in our relationship and getting you depressed. So naturally, I'm concerned about anything that could hurt you in our relationship. Could we look under those critical thoughts and see what feelings are coming up here toward me?" Our implicit message is "You don't have to protect me from your feelings by hurting yourself. I can accept any feelings you have toward me." When a patient shares feelings, she forms a closer bond with you that evokes feelings based on her history of intimacy.

Increasing Access to Isolation of Affect

In the following section, my invitations to mixed feelings build the patient's affect tolerance. As a result, she uses more intellectualization, a defense within isolation of affect.

Th: What feelings come up here toward me? [*Invite feelings toward me.*]

Pt: Thankful. Without you, I would be completely mad. [*Fragile patients always have mixed feelings: positive feelings based on their hope for a secure attachment and negative ones based on past insecure attachments.*]

Th: How do you experience the thankfulness? [*Invite her positive feelings.*]

Pt: Speaking. Letting me calm down.

Th: How else do you experience these positive feelings? [*Invite her positive feelings.*]

Pt: Vomit. [*Anxiety moves into the smooth muscles: a sign of mixed feelings rising. She has positive feelings because she sees that I want to know what she thinks and feels. These feelings are linked to negative feelings toward her mother, who did not want her to think. Thus, if I ask about her anger, positive feelings will arise. If I ask about her positive feelings, her negative feelings will arise. These mixed feelings, together, trigger her anxiety.*]

Th: A big feeling came up. Take your time. [*Reinforce her defense to bring anxiety down.*]

Pt: Feeling, live it. My boyfriend called me life. That's why I liked him so much. He gave me the comfort you give me.

Th: How do you experience the gratefulness? [*Invite positive feelings.*]

Pt: [*Sighs.*] Good and scary. I have to practice. [*Anxiety is now in the striated muscles.*]

Th: Gratefulness should make you feel good.

Pt: I'm going to feel it: anxiety.

Th: What other feelings are coming up that would trigger anxiety? [*Invite mixed feelings toward me. If she felt only positive feelings, no anxiety would rise. Anxiety rises because she is, outside of her awareness, feeling anger toward someone she likes.*] What other feelings are coming up that provoke the anxiety? Are you prepared to live, to step out of the shell?

Pt: [*Sighs. Anxiety in the striated muscles signals that unconscious feelings are rising. Whenever she sighs, I speak to her unconscious by inviting those feelings to build an alliance between the therapist and the patient's unconscious will to health.*]

Th: Are you prepared to disconnect from the past? What feelings are coming up toward me? [*Invite mixed feelings toward me.*]

Pt: Difficult when you ask. Two things you ask: "How are you feeling?" and "What are the feelings?" I don't know how to see these things. [*Defense: intellectualizing, a sign that anxiety is in the striated muscles.*]

Build the capacity to bear mixed feelings toward the therapist: Since she attacked herself to protect me from her anger, I invite her to look at feelings toward me. In response, her anxiety is shifting into the striated muscles. She intellectualizes instead of engaging in self-attack. These changes in unconscious anxiety and defense reflect greater capacity at this level of mixed feelings.

Th: Let's see. What feelings are coming up here toward me? [*Invite mixed feelings toward me.*]

Pt: So you are saying I shouldn't ask, "Are you ready to feel?"

Th: You're saying that some self-doubting thoughts come up. If we look under those thoughts, what feelings are coming up here toward me? [*Invite her to look under the defense at the mixed feelings toward me.*]

Pt: Now I don't see you but my adorable literature teacher. Stranded on an island with lots of sharks around. [*Defense: she tries to have only positive feelings to avoid her mixed feelings. In her metaphor, she projects her anger onto the sharks.*]

Th: What feelings come up here toward me? [*Invite mixed feelings toward me.*]

Pt: I am a mummy, and you are unwrapping me. I feel exposed and scared. [*Defense: intellectualization. She offers a thought, not a feeling. Plus, she projects "You unwrap my defenses." Only she can do that.*]

Th: What feelings are coming up toward this therapist who exposes you? [*Invite feelings.*]

Pt: Scared.

Th: What feelings are you scared of? [*Invite mixed feelings toward me.*]

Pt: Scared that you are going to expose me to danger. [*Projection.*]

Th: The good news is that I can't expose you to danger. [*Remind her of reality to block the projection.*]

Pt: I have to do it.

Th: You're the only one who can. Do you want to unwrap yourself? [*Invite her to engage in the therapeutic task.*]

Pt: Before I die.

Th: How do you know that you want to unwrap yourself? [*Invite her will.*]

Pt: Itching me. [*Sighs.*] Shaking. Tremble inside me. If it is me that has to do it, I literally don't know how. [*She sees that her will to unwrap herself triggers anxiety.*]

Th: I have no right to unwrap you. If you want to be wrapped, I must respect your wish. [*Remind her of reality to deactivate the projection.*] You wrap yourself up. Do you want to unwrap your-self? [*Invite her will.*]

Pt: I want to. [*No sigh.*]

Th: How do you experience that this is what you want for yourself? [*Invite her will.*]

Pt: Feel my heart beating fast. A little dizzy. [*Cognitive/perceptual disruption. She sees that her will to unwrap herself triggers anxiety.*]

Th: Wanting to know yourself triggers anxiety. [*Point out causality.*]

Pt: Stomach is growing a big ball. [*Rise of anxiety, perhaps in the smooth muscles.*]

Th: That you want to know yourself? [*Invite her will.*]

Pt: Yes. [*No sigh.*]

Th: What's that like to notice that? You want to know yourself. [*Invite her will.*]

Pt: It's a battle. Oh, my gosh. If it depends on me.

Th: It depends on us.

Pt: You said I have to unwrap. [*Projection of will: she wants to unwrap her feelings.*]

Th: I'll help you, but first we have to make sure that is what you want. How do you experience that this is what you want for yourself? [*Invite her will to deactivate her projection of will.*]

Pt: I want to be alive. The life that I have is not the life I wish to have. [*Increased conscious will.*]

Th: Do you want a life where you know who you are? [*Invite her will.*]

Pt: I want a life where I am where I want to be. So different.

Th: Do you want a different life where you come out from the wrappings of the mummy? [*Invite her will.*]

Pt: It is in my throat. [*Accepting her wish to unwrap herself triggers anxiety in the smooth muscles but not cognitive/perceptual disruption. An increase in affect tolerance.*]

Th: Isn't that interesting. What feelings are coming up here toward me? [*Since her anxiety is going into the smooth muscles, I invite feelings toward me so they will not go back on her.*]

Pt: You, devil. Unwrapping me and wrapping me back up. [*Intellectualizing suggests that her anxiety is moving into the striated muscles again.*]

Th: What are the feelings toward me: wrap, unwrap? [*Invite feelings.*]

Pt: Blank. Feelings in the middle of the question. It's a blank thing. [*A mind going blank can be a sign of cognitive/perceptual disruption. But she intellectualizes about the blankness. Her higher-level defense means we can safely explore feelings.*]

Th: If we look under the blankness, can we find out who you really are? [*Invite her to look at the feelings under the defense.*]

Pt: A woman with a mind stuck in childhood. [*Defense: intellectualization. The word "stuck" is new, a possible cue from her unconscious. Thus, I use this word.*]

Th: If you let your mind get unstuck, what feelings are coming up toward me? [*Invite her to look at the feelings under the defense.*]

Pt: You ask about feelings. [*Defense: intellectualization.*]

Th: If you let yourself get unstuck, what are the emotions toward me? [*Invite her to look at the feelings under the defense.*]

Pt: Feelings, emotions, the same. I don't know what to do or to say. [*Defense: intellectualization.*]

Th: What feelings are coming up here toward me?

Pt: I don't know. [*Defense: intellectualization.*]

Th: Wouldn't it be nice to know?

Pt: Nothing comes to mind. If there is something, I don't know what it is. [*Defense: negation. "I do know what it is." Negation allows her knowing to be conscious as long as it is denied. We call this intermediate level of awareness, preconscious.*]

The reader might find our exchange puzzling. "Maybe she doesn't know! Why do you keep asking?" Most fragile patients have been punished for telling the emotional truth. They learned to conceal their feelings to keep a relationship. When she consciously says, "I don't know," she unconsciously says, "I cannot know my feelings if I want to keep your love." This is her implicit relational knowledge (Lyons-Ruth 1998) of how insecure attachments work. When I ask for a feeling, I invite her to a secure attachment where she can reveal her feelings. These interventions are not cognitive questions with correct answers, they are invitations to a secure attachment, which she answers with insecure attachment behaviors. Let's see what happens as I keep offering this invitation.

Th: What emotions do you notice having here toward me?

Pt: [*Laughs.*] I don't know. [*Defense. The laughter, a sign of anxiety, indicates that feelings are nearing consciousness.*]

Th: Wouldn't it be nice to know?

Pt: I am open minded.

Th: If you open your mind, what feelings are coming up here toward me? [*Invite her to look at the feelings under the defense.*]

Pt: Zero. Strange. I feel like a kid the teacher is asking. [*Defense: intellectualization.*]

Th: If we look under the zero, what feelings are coming up toward me? [*Invite her to look at the feelings under the defense.*]

Pt: I don't know. [*Defense: intellectualization.*]

Th: What reactions are you having?

Pt: Blank. [*Defense.*]

Th: What reactions are you having to me? [*Grade the invitation.*]

Pt: Here. [*Defense.*]

Th: What thoughts are you having about me? [*Grade the invitation further.*]

Pt: Blank. [*Defense.*]

Th: Under the blank?

Pt: Nothing comes. If I knew, my brain would not blank. [*Defense: Intellectualization.*]

Th: When you have feelings, you get anxious.

Pt: Vomit. [*As feelings rise, her anxiety moves again into the smooth muscles.*]

Th: Take your time. This is why you try to go blank. You try to blank out the feeling so the anxiety doesn't do this. [*Cognize about the triangle of conflict—feelings, anxiety, and the defense of blanking— to bring anxiety down. Her anxiety returns to the striated muscles more quickly—a sign of increased affect tolerance.*]

Pt: [*Laughs.*] Well put. [*Intellectualization: anxiety is in the striated muscles.*]

Th: You try to blank out feelings so the anxiety won't come up with this.

Pt: So what? I am pure of heart. [*She engages in playful denial as if she is an angel. I play with her. Play therapy with adults, transitional*

> relatedness (Feinsilver 1983; Frederickson 1991; Winnicott 1971),
> is a useful way to invite feelings gradually.]

Th: An angel.

Pt: I'm an empty angel.

Th: You empty yourself of feelings to be an empty angel to avoid anxiety.

Pt: I'm confused. Feelings is what? The feeling is anger. Now some-one is asking me. It's too late. Is that what you mean, I'm trying to cover? [She understands her defense.]

Th: Let's find out. How do you experience this anger? [Invite feelings.]

Pt: My stomach.

Th: What does that tell you?

Pt: I'm anxious.

Th: Right. The anger makes you anxious.

Pt: When you say feelings toward you, it doesn't make sense. [Denial.]

Th: You're such an angel. [Playful enactment of her denial.]

Pt: [Laughs.]

Th: You're such an angel. [Playful enactment of her denial.]

Pt: [Laughs.] Stop.

Th: You're so empty of these devilish feelings. [Playful enactment of her denial.]

Pt: I have a lot of anger. That I know. That I know I have. [Play allows her to reveal her anger.]

Th: When you have this devilish feeling of anger, and when you empty yourself of anger, anxiety goes away. Anger makes you anxious. You empty yourself of anger to empty yourself of anxiety. [The triangle of conflict: anger toward me, anxiety, and the defense of emptying herself.]

Pt: Frozen.

Th: If you empty yourself of anger, there is no anxiety. If you freeze the anger, no anxiety.

Pt: If I am an angel, there are no devilish feelings that make me anx-ious. [She can acknowledge her mixed feelings toward me.] One thing I can't understand is why you ask for feelings toward you because when I came to you, I wouldn't have come if I had anger. I want to be here. [She does not see why she would have mixed feelings toward me.]

Th: You have mixed feelings. Your past is filled with a mixture of feelings, an Amazon jungle of feelings. With me, the whole Amazon jungle comes up. [*She is from South America.*]

Pt: I get angry because you bring all these memories up. So you think I feel angry with you because you make me bring memories up? I want to be here and speak of this, but I don't want to feel any emotion? [*She interprets why mixed feelings rise with me.*]

Th: Yeah.

Pt: Oh. [*Laughs.*] That's crazy.

Th: What's that like to see?

Pt: Crazy.

Th: What's that like to notice that?

Pt: Yeah. Sure, I do have it. Welcome to my anger group!

Th: Wonderful. I've been waiting to meet the anger group.

Pt: Okay. Now I understand. I was lost. "What does he mean by that?" Just for bringing the memories and feelings, I feel anger toward you. You are an angel to be here and a devil for bringing feelings up. So for sure, every time you come, I feel feelings toward you. That's a fact. [*Intellectualization in a fragile patient is the equivalent of a sigh, so her anxiety is regulated.*]

This vignette illustrates how mixed feelings in fragile patients trigger anxiety in the form of cognitive/perceptual disruption and the defenses of splitting and projection. As I regulate her anxiety and help her accept what she projected, her anxiety moves into the smooth muscles. As her affect tolerance increases, she starts to intellectualize—a sign that her anxiety is going into the striated muscles. As her affect tolerance increases, she shifts to negation to deny her feelings. We playfully enact her denial until she sees her mixed feelings toward me and understands why she has them. Careful, repeated invitations of feelings, regulation of anxiety, and deactivation of projection build affect tolerance in fragile patients. And we see the patterns of anxiety and defense shift as affect tolerance increases. The more patients can bear feelings inside, the less they have to project outside.

Negation is an important signal of increased affect tolerance and increased alliance. To illustrate this spectrum of affect tolerance, see table 7.7.

Table 7.7   The spectra of defense and affect tolerance

Spectrum of Defense	Spectrum of Affect Tolerance
No defense: The patient can describe how she experiences feelings in the body.	"I feel angry now. There's heat coming up through my body."
Isolation of affect: The patient can describe her feeling but not how she experiences it.	"I feel angry." [*Said in a detached manner.*]
Negation: Feeling is revealed and concealed.	"I am not angry." The word is conscious but the feeling is preconscious.
Splitting and denial: Feeling is denied	"I feel fine."
Projection: Feeling is projected	"You are angry and can't admit it."
Primitive splitting	"Adriana [*split-off personality*] is really angry."
Primitive projection (delusion)	"The government is trying to kill me."

As we help patients tolerate their mixed feelings, they shift from primitive forms of splitting and projection to less primitive forms. Then they shift to negation. Once they shift to negation, they have moved from the resistance system of splitting and projection to isolation of affect. They can bear mixed feelings inside themselves toward other people without splitting and projection. This is a major accomplishment. Now patients become more aware of feelings inside and begin to tolerate the physical experience of those feelings in the body.

As this patient uses less projection, we see more repression: anxiety in the smooth muscles and self-attack. This is progress. She shifted from projection and splitting to repression. Then she shifted from repression into isolation of affect at this level of feeling.

Principle: *Our goal is not to eliminate defenses but to change the system of resistance from splitting and projection to isolation of affect.*

BUILDING CAPACITY IN THE MILDLY FRAGILE PATIENT: EXPLORING FEELINGS DIRECTLY

Table 7.8 illustrates the spectrum of mild fragility, ranging from those who suffer from cognitive/perceptual disruption, to those who disrupt but use repression at lower levels of feeling, to those who start to intellectualize before they disrupt, to those whose ability to isolate affect is much stronger so that cognitive/perceptual disruption does not occur until higher levels of mixed feelings.

Table 7.8   Levels of capacity within mildly fragile patients

Level of Fragility	Anxiety	Resistance System	Intervention
Mild Fragility I	Anxiety primarily in the striated muscles Brief cognitive/perceptual disruption at higher levels of feelings	Isolation of affect is the predominant resistance system. But it weakens at higher levels of mixed feelings, such as when the patient resists emotional closeness or when guilt is about to break through	Brace (Abbass 2015) Invite the patient's feelings toward the therapist
Mild Fragility II	Cognitive/perceptual disruption without splitting or projection	Beginning capacity for isolation of affect Patient starts to intellectualize	Brace Invite the patient's feelings toward the therapist
Mild Fragility III	Cognitive/perceptual disruption with mild splitting or projection Little loss of reality testing	Repression Self-attack Somatization Conversion Splitting Projection	Brace Invite the patient's feelings toward the therapist

When we invite feelings with fragile patients, we grade the dosage of affect words we use according to the patient's anxiety tolerance. Some mistakenly think it is dangerous to explore feelings with fragile patients. It is dangerous not to! If we do not, we cannot assess the patient's capacity and build it. However, like in a fitness center, we adjust the weights according to what the patient can lift.

We tailor our invitations to feeling to the patient's affect tolerance. When inviting feelings, use the words the patient uses. For instance, if the moderately fragile patient says she is "upset," that word is a defense. It is a compromise between her feeling (rage) and the prohibition against expressing it. Thus, you can use the fragile patient's word "upset" to explore within the defense and work within her threshold of anxiety tolerance or *window of tolerance* (Siegel 1999). If you don't know the patient's threshold of affect tolerance, use low dose words to explore. Then increase the intensity until the patient crosses her threshold of affect tolerance and begins to self-attack, suffers cognitive/perceptual disruption, or splits and projects. Then you have found the optimal level of feeling intensity for building the patient's capacity.

The interventions below illustrate increasing levels of affect intensity:

1. What thoughts and ideas are you having about the therapy?
2. What thoughts and ideas are you having about the questions?
3. What thoughts and ideas are you having about the therapist?

The previous interventions allow you to find out what projections the patient is placing on the therapist. The following interventions explore feelings toward the therapist through the defense of displacement at increasingly higher doses:

4. What reactions are you having to the therapy?
5. What reactions are you having to the questions?
6. What reactions are you having to the therapist?
7. What thoughts and ideas are you having about me?
8. What reactions are you having to me?
9. What feelings are you having about the therapy?
10. What feelings are you having in response to the questions?

The following questions explore feelings directly toward the therapist:

11. What feelings are coming up here with me?
12. What feelings are coming up here toward me?
13. What feelings are you having here toward me?
14. How do you experience that feeling here toward me inside your body?

The patient's affect language tells you the dose of words to use for exploring feelings. Increase the dosage of your words as long as anxiety remains in the striated muscles until anxiety shifts into cognitive/perceptual disruption. Now you know which words to use without shooting over the threshold.

Inviting Feelings with a Mildly Fragile Patient

At the beginning of her initial session, this young woman experienced cognitive/perceptual disruption. After some anxiety regulation, she projected that I would criticize her. Unable to bear mixed feelings toward me, she split off her anger and placed it on me as a potential critic. After I deactivated that projection, I asked her about feelings toward me. Exploring feelings allows us to assess whether she can bear feelings inside rather than project them outside. Deactivate projections first. We want to explore the mixed feelings in our relationship. We do not want to explore split-off rage when the patient equates the therapist with an all-bad projection.

Th: Given that you had this idea that I would be critical, I wonder what feelings might be coming up here toward me? [*Now her projection is a thought we can question and reflect on, not a belief equated with reality. Thus, we can treat her projection as a defense within isolation of affect. I can ask for the feelings toward me underneath this intellectualization.*]

Pt: Mm-hmm. I'm aware of very loving feelings, probably sexual feelings. [*Since positive feelings alone would not make her anxious, we explore additional feelings that trigger the anxiety.*]

Th: There are some loving feelings. What other feelings are coming up in addition, if we get a sense of the whole complex of feelings? [*Invite mixed feelings: "The whole complex of feelings."*]

Pt: I just had a shot of anger. [*But no sigh.*]

Th: How do you experience that anger? [*Invite the experience of mixed feelings.*]

Pt: It just zipped through. Very mild. I wouldn't call it anger. [*Denial.*]

Th: But you did. [*Block denial.*] A shot of anger. If you give it attention, how do you experience this anger here toward me? [*Invite the experience of mixed feelings.*]

Pt: Because you're not reciprocating. [*Rationalization: she explains the reason for the feeling, not how she experiences it.*]

Th: That's an explanation for the feeling, but how do you experience this anger here toward me? [*Block the defense and invite the experience of mixed feelings.*]

Pt: Like it was in the air here. [*She gestures with her hand outside of her body.*] A wisp.

Th: If you pay attention to that wisp of anger, how do you experience it in your body? [*Invite the experience of mixed feelings.*]

Pt: I think I—How do I experience it?

Th: Yes. How do you experience this anger physically in your body? [*Invite the experience of mixed feelings.*]

Pt: It's outside me. It felt outside of me. [*Defense: projection. Thus, she didn't sigh. If the feeling is outside her, it can't trigger anxiety inside her. She projects a feeling outside of her before giving it a location.*]

Th: There's a feeling inside, and it has to go outside. [*Identify the defense of projection.*]

Pt: Yeah. I don't know if I felt it inside. [*The sooner projection occurs, the less time she has to become aware of her feeling.*]

Th: You felt the anger inside, and then it went out of you. [*Identify the process of projection.*]

Pt: Yeah.

Th: If you let the anger be inside you, how do you experience this anger inside your body? [*To help patients who project, we ask, "If you let the feeling be* inside *you, how do you experience that anger* inside *your body?" My invitation blocks the projection and invites her to bear a feeling inside without projecting it outside—the precondition to experiencing feelings internally.*]

Pt: I don't feel it. I haven't felt it since the wisp. I have never felt my anger, like—I don't think I feel it much. [*Once she projects a feeling outside, she won't feel it inside.*] There's a lack of reciprocation here, and so there's anger.

Th: Let's notice how you experience this anger inside you. How do you experience this anger inside you? [*Invite mixed feelings toward me.*]

Pt: My head is expanding.

Th: How do you experience this anger inside you? [*Invite mixed feelings toward me.*]

Pt: I want to hit you. [*An impulse does not describe how she experiences the anger inside of her. Fragile patients may act out an impulse to avoid the internal experience of feelings.*]

Th: How do you experience the anger that goes with that? [*Invite mixed feelings toward me.*]

Pt: I'm not. I can't think the anger. I feel my head. In rage, it feels like my head is going to pop off. Seems good that I can feel it in my head.

As we explored how she experienced the anger in her body, she reported feeling dead. Just before my next intervention, she reported feeling a pain in her heart, a bodily symptom due to somatization. We pick up a few minutes later.

Th: You felt this anger toward me. Then it went back onto you, and you went dead. Then it turned around onto you, and now it's your heart in pain. If you don't hurt yourself, if you let the anger come this way, let's see—wouldn't it be nice to feel anger and not be in pain? If you let it come this way, how do you experience this anger here toward me? [*Remind her of the triangle of conflict: anger toward me, anxiety, and the defense of somatization that turns the anger back onto her: her heart that is in pain. This is progress. Earlier, she used the resistance system of splitting and projection. Now she uses the resistance system of repression. Her affect tolerance is higher. In repression, we help the patient see how she felt anger toward me, but it went back upon her, causing her heart pain. Clarifying the defense of somatization helps patients recover from the symptoms that result.*]

Pt: [*Sighs. Anxiety returns to the striated muscles.*]

Th: If you let yourself experience this anger and let it come this way. How do you experience this anger here toward me? [*Invite mixed feelings toward me. Since she turns the anger onto herself, I say, "If you let yourself experience this anger and let it come this way." In repression, the patient turns anger onto herself to protect the people she loves. Thus, we invite her to let feelings come toward the therapist to reverse self-attack and its effects on the patient. This builds her capacity to tolerate mixed feelings of love and rage toward the therapist and others without having to hurt herself.*]

Pt: Physically in my body. I'm having an anxiety reaction. Weakness. I feel constantly like hitting you. There's an impulse, but then the arm goes weak. [*Defense: conversion.*]

Th: You notice how your arms are going weak on you. [*Identify the defense.*]

Pt: I felt like hitting you all along. Now this moment, I started to feel weak. [*Defense: conversion.*]

Th: You feel anger toward me. And you dealt with the anger by going dead, by getting pain in your heart, and now your arms go weak. These are all protective mechanisms, protecting me from your anger. [*Cognize about her triangle of conflict: anger, anxiety, and the defenses that protect me from her anger.*]

In response, she suddenly remembers an incident when she was a tiny child. She expressed mild irritation toward her mother who then collapsed onto the floor. This echoes the therapy. I invited feelings toward me. Then, the patient identifies with the mother in the present, by becoming weak in her limbs. This memory triggered a breakthrough of guilt and grief.

In the session's opening, her mixed feelings triggered cognitive/perceptual disruption and projection. She was initially aware of her loving and sexual feelings, but not her anger. She saw anger in me: projection. As we helped her recognize and experience her anger inside rather than project it outside, the mixed feelings of love and rage triggered anxiety and a new set of defenses: somatization and conversion. As she became able to bear these feelings at a higher level and let go of the defenses, a breakthrough of painful emotions occurred. Now we could see how somatization and conversion resulted from her identification with the mother, who physically collapsed. And we could also understand her implicit relational knowledge: "If I say what I feel, my mother may die." No wonder she emptied herself of feelings! The patient unconsciously protects the relationship with her therapist in the present through the use of conversion and somatization. We return to a later vignette in the session.

Th: Shall we find out about your power now? [*Invite mixed feelings toward me.*]

Pt: [*Sighs. Anxiety is in the striated muscles.*]

Th: Can we find out how you experience this power? [*Invite mixed feelings toward me.*] You've been protecting people.

Pt: No.

Th: You've been protecting people. How do you experience this anger toward me? Can we let the power come out? [*Invite mixed feelings toward me.*]

Pt: It's very sad. My novel would have been a real powerhouse. [*Sees the price of her defense.*]

Th: A real price to hold your power back.

Pt: Just as bad as not having children.

Th: It really hurt you a lot.

Pt: Massively.

Th: Is that something you would like to turn around today? [*Invite her to work toward a positive goal.*] How do you experience this anger toward me? [*Invite mixed feelings toward me.*]

Pt: Weakness. I'm getting weak. [*Defense: conversion.*]

Th: We're seeing this pattern now: power, then weakness. But this weakness hides your power. [*Identify the defense and clarify its price.*]

Pt: Yeah.

Th: It hides your rage. [*Identify the defense and clarify its price.*]

Pt: Hmm.

Th: It's a way to identify with Mom and her collapse. [*Identify the defense and clarify its function.*]

Pt: Oh. Rather than I created her collapse. [*The insight occurs: she thought her anger made her mother collapse.*]

Th: You become the collapsing mother. [*Defense: identification. To punish herself for "making" her mother collapse, she became the collapsing mother.*]

Pt: Oh. Right.

Th: Instead of the powerful child, you become the collapsing mother. [*Show the function of the defense: to hide the powerful child.*]

Pt: [*She sobs.*] I loved her so much.

In this case of mild fragility, there was cognitive/perceptual disruption in the opening and some projection. But she could bear mixed feelings inside quickly. And she shifted from projection to the defense of somatization within the resistance system of repression. At this rise of feelings, she tolerated two breakthroughs to guilt and grief within the first hour without experiencing cognitive/perceptual disruption or projection. At higher levels of feeling, cognitive/perceptual disruption and projection would occur. But the process is much faster because her affect tolerance is stronger than in the more fragile cases we looked at previously.

We have addressed how to grade our invitations of feelings according to structural indications of affect tolerance (symbolic language, anxiety, and defense). We can also grade the invitation of feelings through (1) dosage of affect language through defenses in isolation of affect, (2) tempo of speech, and (3) cues from the unconscious will to health.

Dosing the Intensity of Affect through the Defense of Displacement

The following interventions illustrate a spectrum of increasing language dosage through the defense of displacement.

Th: It sounds like you have some thoughts about what I said. What thoughts are coming up?

Th: It sounds like you have some reactions about what I said. What reactions are coming up?

Th: It sounds like you have some thoughts about what I said. What thoughts are coming up? [Not "What do you think?" but "What thoughts come up?" We invite the patient to observe thoughts that arise, differentiating him as an observer from the thoughts he observes.]

Th: It sounds like some reactions came up about what I said. What reactions do you notice?

Th: It sounds like there are some feelings about what I said. What feelings are coming up?

Th: It sounds like there are some feelings about what I said. What feelings are coming up here with me?

Th: What feelings do you have toward me?

Dosing the Intensity of Affect through the Defense of Vagueness

Fragile patients may offer vague feeling words that represent their level of affect tolerance. We do not treat the vague word as a defense as we would with a high capacity patient. Instead, we accept her vagueness as a compromise formation: what she can express given her affect tolerance. We can explore feelings within that defense to build her affect tolerance until a higher dose word emerges. Then we can use the new word she has provided.

The following invitations to feeling illustrate a spectrum of language dosage. The therapist will be gone for a month. Each of these interventions followed changes in her words as her affect tolerance rose. When the patient's intensity of affect language increases, the therapist shifts to the next higher dose. Thus, the therapist works within her capacity for affect tolerance.

Th: You're having some feelings about time. What feelings are coming up?

Th: You want more time. What feelings are coming up about the time?

Th: You find the lack of time frustrating. How do you experience that frustration?

Th: You are upset over the lack of time. How do you experience that upset feeling?

Th: You are feeling irritated with me. How do you experience that feeling of irritation toward me?

Th: There is an angry feeling you say. How do you experience that angry feeling?

Th: There is an angry feeling with me. How do you experience that angry feeling with me?

Th: How do you experience that angry feeling here toward me?

Th: How do you experience that anger here toward me?

Introducing Higher-Level Defenses to Explore Feelings

Suppose the patient uses the word "anger" and floods with anxiety and becomes cognitively confused. If you use the word "anger" again, she will flood with anxiety and become cognitively confused. Instead, invite feelings with a lower dose word.

Th: You are a bit dizzy as soon as we touch on this feeling. As we look at that feeling, how do you experience that frustration right now?

With a lower dose word, she can focus on her feeling. Then, the disruption should stop. Exploring "frustration" will improve her affect tolerance over the following minute or two. Then we can use the word "anger" again when she has more capacity.

Here are some examples of how to introduce higher-level defenses to explore feelings when the word "anger" makes the patient flood with anxiety.

Th: It sounds like you were less than delighted. [*Introduce the defense of minimization.*]

Th: Some people would not be happy about that. [*Introduce the defenses of displacement and minimization.*]

Th: Sounds like you have some thoughts about that situation. [*Invite him to intellectualize before exploring the anger again.*]

Principle: *Pay close attention to any feeling word that makes the patient go over the threshold of affect tolerance.*

A severely fragile woman suffering from PTSD and hallucinations became flooded with anxiety in the session and could barely talk after something I had said.

> *Th:* I have something that may be a bit difficult for you to hear. Do I have your permission to ask? [*Prepare the patient for a stressor.*]
>
> *Pt:* Yes.
>
> *Th:* I wonder if you felt a little miffed with what I said. [*I offer the defense of minimization so she can explore the feeling within a higher-level defense.*]
>
> *Pt:* Miffed? I—I was . . . uh, angry! [*When I provide a higher-level defense, she can explore the feeling word at a higher level.*]

Principle: *When a word takes the patient over the threshold of affect tolerance, use a lower dose feeling word to work just under the threshold. Build capacity there until she introduces a higher dose word.*

Principle: *When a word takes the patient over the threshold of affect tolerance, introduce a higher-level defense to help her work just under the threshold.*

When a patient lacks brakes, provide them. When she is emotionally bleeding to death, put on a tourniquet (personal communication, E. Harper).

Grading the Invitation of Feelings through Tempo of Speech

We can also grade the rise of feeling through the tempo of our speech. If you ask quickly, "What feelings are coming up here toward me?" feelings and anxiety might spike in a second. If you speak slowly, feelings and anxiety might rise gradually over a longer time, building the patient's affect tolerance. While we don't have omnipotent control over how quickly patients' feelings rise, we can adjust our speech tempo to try to avoid provoking more than what the patient can bear.

> *Th:* [*Speaking very slowly.*] If we take a moment, how do you experience this anger in your body physically? As you let yourself notice

it, how do you experience this anger physically in your body here toward me?

Speak with an unhurried, gentle voice to allow feelings to rise slowly. If the patient goes over the threshold of affect tolerance, she does so slowly and becomes dizzy. As soon as she gets dizzy, we can intervene before she projects and loses reality testing. If feelings rise rapidly, she becomes dizzy, projects, and loses reality testing in a matter of seconds. Slowing the tempo of your speech can also block defenses while you speak so she can pay attention to feelings for a longer time, giving her the chance to observe and feel them. Then her answers will be clearer. Grade invitations for a slow rise of feelings to prevent regressions.

We invite the experience of mixed feelings to achieve two goals: (1) restructure the pathway of anxiety discharge until it remains in the striated muscles at high levels of mixed feelings, and (2) restructure the system of resistance so it remains in isolation of affect. In chapter 1, we addressed how to assess anxiety and restructure the pathway of anxiety. Below are the steps in restructuring the system of resistance:

1. Gently invite a secure attachment.
2. Identify defenses, such as denial, splitting, and projection.
3. Help the patient bear inside what he splits off, denies, and projects outside.
4. Once he tolerates his feelings inside without projecting them outside (he sighs or intellectualizes), invite him to experience these feelings to build his affect tolerance further.
5. Repeat this sequence at higher levels of feeling until he can bear all of his mixed feelings inside while using the resistance system of isolation of affect.

To build affect tolerance, follow these treatment principles:

- Restructure weaknesses in affect tolerance and anxiety regulation, such as losses in mental boundaries, splitting, projection, and cognitive/perceptual disruption. (See chapters 1, 8, 10, and 11.)
- Strengthen the patient by reinforcing higher-level defenses. (See this chapter as well as chapters 1 and 8.)
- Improve self-observation. (See chapter 1.)

Here is what you should not do when building affect tolerance:

- Do not explore anything that weakens his use of isolation of affect or makes mental boundaries inactive. For instance, do not emphasize emotional closeness if it threatens him with fears of merger. (See chapter 8.)
- Do not encourage any pathological regression or psychosis.

Grading the Invitation according to Unconscious Signaling

Mixed feelings and motivations mobilize anxiety. When the patient splits them apart, no anxiety will rise. For instance, a patient, sitting comfortably in his chair, says he wants to kill himself. Since he splits apart the wish to live and the wish to die, no unconscious anxiety rises in his body. The absence of unconscious anxiety in fragile patients often signals that they are splitting or projecting. Invite the avoided mixed feelings and wishes. As they bear mixed feelings and motivations, anxiety will return to the striated muscles (sighing), and defenses within isolation of affect will appear, such as intellectualization.

Defense Work with the Fragile Patient

We do not interpret patients' unconscious defenses initially because they do not know they are using them. If we interpret something they do not see, they can only take our word for it. We would rely on our authority to convince them, thus reinforcing projections that we want to control them.

Instead, we first use noninterpretive interventions for graded defense work. For splitting, we can mirror back what she sees and has split off and denied. (See chapters 9 and 10.) We remind her of two split-apart realities of her inner life or two split-apart realities of another person. Invite her to observe her mixed feelings. For projection, we attempt to deactivate the projection and invite her to bear inside herself what she attributed to another person. (See chapters 3 and 11.) For denial, we can mention her denial and a fact she denies. We help her face the reality she denies and the feelings reality triggers. (See chapter 9.) We build the capacity to bear internal experience patients avoid through splitting, projection, and denial.

Also, we do not address the fragile patient's agency in defense work initially. Since self-attack is an unconscious defense, we cannot talk about what the patient "does." She does not wake up in the morning and say to herself, "Remember to attack myself when I see my therapist today." Defenses happen outside of her awareness and without her intent. Rather than talk about what the patient "does," we point out what the defense does.

Pt: I hate myself. [*Self-attack.*]

Th: Could that be a critical thought? [*Identify the defense.*] Could that critical thought be hurting you? [*Clarify the price of the defense.*] Could it be making you depressed? [*Clarify the relationship between the defense and her symptoms.*] If we look under that critical thought, could we see what feelings are underneath? [*Invitation to the therapeutic task.*] If we look under that critical thought, what feelings are coming up here toward me? [*Invite her to feel feelings toward another person rather than turn them on herself. Use two invitations to feelings toward the therapist to block the repressive system and mobilize feelings in the body.*]

"Could that be a critical thought?" The therapist invites the patient to observe a thought so she can think about it. If the therapist said, "Notice how you attack yourself?" the fragile patient would experience this as a criticism, triggering a rise of feelings and self-attack or cognitive/perceptual disruption. The patient replies, "It's another thing I'm doing wrong!" and then she sobs, feeling like she failed. In fragile patients, avoid addressing agency since it will trigger guilt too quickly, causing her to go over the threshold.

Principle: *With fragile patients, do not comment on their agency regarding self-attack.*

We do not say, "Do you see how you attack yourself?" Instead, we wonder aloud, "Could that critical thought be attacking you?"

Th: Could that critical thought be hurting you? [*Price of the defense.*]

Th: Could we join forces so that we could help you defend yourself from that critical mechanism? [*Invite collaboration.*]

Th: If I see a thought that is unfair to you, do I have your permission to interrupt that thought so it can't hurt you? [*Build consensus on the therapeutic task.*]

Whenever we interrupt a self-attack, we invite her to collaborate, observe, and engage in a task. We say, in effect, "Shall we see if we can help you do something good for yourself?"

In graded defense work, always end a comment on a defense by inviting feelings. If we comment only on defenses, the fragile patient will experience you as a critic (A. Freud 1936). And in response to that criticism, he may become more self-critical or even go into cognitive/perceptual disruption. Always end a defense intervention by mobilizing the patient toward health by inviting the problem, his will, or his feelings.

> Th: I can't know what your problem is because I'm not you. That's why I have to ask you what the problem is you want to work on that you think would be good for you? [*Deactivate a projection. Then invite the patient to declare a problem.*]

> Th: Wanting to be here and not wanting to be here. What's it like to notice this complexity inside you? [*Point out splitting. Then invite the patient to be aware of his mixed feelings and motivations.*]

> Th: If we look under those critical thoughts, what feelings are coming up here toward me? [*Identify self-attack. Then invite feelings toward the therapist.*]

The only reason to point out a defense is to help the patient face what he avoids. So always end your interventions by inviting a secure attachment.

Likewise, we do not usually challenge defenses in fragile patients by asking something like, "What do you want to do about that?" This heavier intervention can cause a sharp rise in feelings. That rise can push him over the threshold of anxiety tolerance into projection, loss of reality testing, and a misalliance. Do not challenge defenses until anxiety goes into the striated muscles and the patient uses isolation of affect. Instead, identify defenses and invite the experience of mixed feelings. Rather than challenge, encourage the patient to face what he avoids.

Our encouragement is informed by what the patient can do. When extremely anxious, a fragile patient's abilities to understand, think, and reflect become impaired. Unable to understand your longer comments, the patient may need very brief statements and simpler interventions. At those moments, in graded defense work, we might not comment on defenses. Instead, we can block defenses by encouraging secure attachment behaviors. Here's an example of using invitations to block defenses to help stabilize a patient who is extremely anxious.

Pt: [*Experiencing cognitive/perceptual disruption.*] It's no big deal. [*Defense: self-dismissal.*]

Th: Could we pay attention to this anxiety so we could help you regulate it? [*Block the defense by encouraging mutual regulation.*]

Pt: I don't usually look at my anxiety. [*Defense: self-dismissal.*]

Th: Shall we look at it so we can help you regulate it so you could feel more comfortable? [*Block the defense by encouraging mutual regulation.*]

Before commenting on a fragile patient's defenses, we can block defenses and encourage the opposite behavior. Once the patient becomes more regulated, and his thinking and self-reflection return, then we can comment on defenses. First, we might focus on anxiety. As he becomes calmer, we can comment on two corners of the triangle of conflict: "Wanting to share a problem makes you anxious." As he becomes calmer still and his thinking improves, we can comment on all three corners of the triangle of conflict: "Something about sharing a problem makes you anxious, and then one way you deal with the anxiety is to hide a problem. Does that make sense to you?" In the face of high anxiety, the patient's ability to think and reflect collapses. Pare down the complexity of your intervention to match the patient's capacity in the moment.

As you invite patients to face their mixed feelings, help them see their defenses and bear the mixed feelings those defenses ward off. As the capacity to bear those feelings increases, primitive defenses will no longer be necessary. The chapters on restoring capacity, splitting, denial, projection, and severe fragility will show how to work with these defenses.

Breakthroughs

As the patient gains the capacity to bear feelings inside without splitting them apart or projecting them onto others, breakthroughs to unconscious feelings occur. This occurs only when she gains the capacity to bear the conflict between opposing feelings and motivations inside herself. As long as she uses projection to avoid the experience of mixed feelings, she will not be angry at you but at a projection and unable to distinguish you from a projection. Furthermore, she is angry with a projection, feeling split-off rage toward an all-bad figure. Portraying a feeling under these conditions reinforces the defenses of splitting and projection, leading to worsening symptoms, deteriorating relationships, and a misalliance.

If we encourage a premature breakthrough of mixed feelings, while anxiety and defenses have not been restructured, the fragile patient will suffer from cognitive/perceptual disruption, projection, a possible loss of reality testing, and stronger anxiety and guilt, resulting in increased self-punishment. First, build affect tolerance so that anxiety is in the striated muscles and the resistance is in isolation of affect.

As you build affect tolerance, small breakthroughs will open up feelings for a second. Every small rise in affect tolerance is progress. But since these rises of feelings will be small, the initial emotional breakthroughs may be nearly invisible, such as a new insight, a flash of sadness in the face or a tear in the eye. While insignificant to the observer, they can be very intense and transformative for the patient. Always value any small emotional breakthroughs since they reveal increasing affect tolerance.

When affect tolerance is low, expect the initial affect expressions to be low. The patient can experience only a tiny bit of his primitive murderous rage initially without experiencing cognitive/perceptual disruption. Thus, respect the brief partial breakthroughs and do not push them to be more powerful than they are. A series of multiple small, unremarkable breakthroughs will build affect tolerance gradually. Careful anxiety regulation and defense work co-create a frame for the patient's internal house, brick by brick. Although this methodical work may seem unglamorous, it will pay off dividends later, when your patients can experience feelings more deeply without cognitive/perceptual disruption. Dramatic, premature breakthroughs will only disrupt the process and lead to cognitive/perceptual disruption, increased somatic complaints, projection, and acting out.

With each successive exploration of mixed feelings, try to raise the threshold of feeling and anxiety tolerance. By exploring feelings, you show the patient that you are not afraid of her emotions and impulses. The deeper you go, the more primitive the feelings and impulses will be.

Due to low affect tolerance, the patient may not experience any impulses, but images of impulses may appear in his mind. Visualizing these impulses can help him bear the feelings associated with angry and violent thoughts so that thinking or fantasizing about rage becomes desensitized, leading to a new freedom of thinking and feeling. As the ability to think and fantasize about rage increases, he experiences impulses and can imagine enacting them in a fantasy without acting them out in reality. This builds affect tolerance and impulse control.

When the fragile patient visualizes a fantasy of expressing his rage, guilt will rise since he is expressing in his fantasy rage toward a person he loves. These mixed feelings trigger guilt. Help the patient experience that guilt and describe the triangle of conflict to build his ability to bear conflict and guilt.

> Th: You mention feeling guilt. Since you are feeling rage toward your mother, whom you love, naturally guilt comes up. It's a sign of your love. We see that when you feel rage toward the mother you love, guilt comes in, and, to deal with the guilt, these thoughts come in to punish you. Do you see that too?

Portrayals Illustrating a Spectrum of Affect Tolerance in Fragile Patients

As you build the patient's affect tolerance, unconscious feelings rise to the surface, triggering the fantasies linked with them. Finally, a previously unconscious fantasy becomes conscious. For instance, a dissociative man said with surprise, "For some reason I want to put my hands around my father's neck!" We do not pull for this fantasy. Rather, we build the patient's capacity and mobilize feelings until such an image spontaneously appears.

When an unconscious fantasy emerges into awareness, we encourage the patient to portray it in his imagination in thoughts, ideas, and words. By doing so, we help him face his complex mixed feelings and the fantasies that arise. Then he can experience deeper feelings of guilt that unlock the memories his feelings kept at bay. This process differs, depending on patients' affect tolerance. To illustrate those differences, let's review different portrayals with fragile patients.

A fragile woman feared that kidnappers would attack her when she landed at the airport in Rio de Janeiro. Kidnappers had attacked and kidnapped her in the past. She lost reality testing in the session, froze with fear, and panicked.

Th: If you had a gun and saw one of the kidnappers, what would you do?

Pt: I would shoot him in the middle of his forehead right above his eyes. [*She calmed down and then panicked again.*]

Th: And if you had the same gun and saw another kidnapper, what would you do?

Pt: I would shoot him in the middle of his forehead right above his eyes. [*She calmed down and then panicked again.*]

Th: And if you had the same gun and saw another kidnapper, what would you do?

Pt: I would shoot him in the middle of his forehead right above his eyes.

She calmed down. And then she cried as the memories of the kidnapping came out. Her portrayal here gave her rage an outward channel so we could accept her impulse in our relationship where it became less scary.

I worked with a severely fragile man on his splitting, helping him bear the complex and contradictory feelings and motivations inside himself. Each time his splitting decreased, he experienced a second of cognitive/perceptual disruption. But his ability to recognize and bear his conflicts increased.

Pt: This is a big insight. I can accept these urges without having to do anything. I don't have to judge them. I have been unfair to myself. [*Pause.*] But if I accept myself, I also have to accept my mother. [*A wave of pain appeared in his face. Accepting mixed feelings toward his mother triggers guilt.*]

Th: A painful feeling comes up about accepting your mother. [*Support him in feeling his guilt without splitting or projection.*]

Pt: [*He nodded and continued to feel pain while remaining quiet.*]

Th: Just notice this painful feeling. Something important here. [*Support him in feeling his guilt without splitting or projection.*]

Accepting the mother with whom he felt rage triggered his guilt. His breakthrough to guilt unlocked a painful memory of her beating him and his wish to run away. Although there was no outburst of feelings, this increase in affect tolerance gave him great relief.

When you help fragile patients bear feelings inside without projecting them outside, they bear increasing amounts of feelings inside. As a result, a fantasy, image, or memory may emerge.

Fantasy: For some reason, my hands want to go around my father's neck.

Th: And how do you picture that in your imagination? [*Invite a portrayal within the fantasy.*]

Image: I see a truck running over my mother.

Th: What does that look like in your imagination? [*Invite a portrayal of the image.*]

Memory: There's a memory coming up now when my dad hit me.

Th: If there was some big guy who could protect you, how do you picture that big guy going after your dad? [*Invite a portrayal of rage to rewrite the trauma. Instead of the memory of his father beating him, in the portrayal, a man protects him from the father. Introducing another figure uses the defense of displacement. The patient is not beating the father; someone else does it. This fantasy exposes him to his rage at a bearable level at an early stage of treatment.*]

Patients who use primitive defenses such as delusions, hallucinations, and tertiary dissociation can portray feelings within their defenses. For instance, a woman might portray her rage toward a personality that threatens to abandon her. With moderate fragile patients, our invitations to consciousness of splitting and bearing projections inside mobilize mixed feelings. These feelings trigger images, fantasies, or memories. And we can invite portrayals within those images. Mildly fragile patients no longer use primitive forms of splitting or projection. And they tolerate mixed feelings toward people without splitting or projection. However, since mixed feelings can trigger cognitive/perceptual disruption, we may grade their portrayals by introducing the defense of displacement: "If your rage was an animal, what might the animal do?"

The portrayal of rage may seem puzzling. Why do patients have these fantasies? Why explore them? Most fragile patients suffered traumas. When violence was done to them, they felt an urge to fight back, to do violence to the violator. When hit, they wanted to hit back—the law of the talion. The more violence they suffered, the more violent their retaliatory rage. And what is rage but "the radical tip of a grief that time will never root out" (Powers 2018, 332).

Often, the perpetrator was a parent they loved. This combination of love and rage triggers guilt. And, to protect the relationship, the child protected the violator from her violent urges. As an adult, she may turn the rage upon herself and cut her arms. She may pick a partner who rages at her. She may split off her rage, project it onto the world around her, and live in fear. And some patients do to others in adulthood what was done to them in the past, the transgenerational transmission of trauma.

In therapy, we help the traumatized patient face this enormous rage toward the people she loved and loves. And when she becomes aware of the depth of her rage through a violent image arising in her thoughts, we help her explore that image and her feelings. The deeper she can feel this rage toward a loved one, and bear the guilt, the less she will have to turn that violence onto herself or others. The tragedy of trauma is not only the violence done to the child but the violence she felt toward the violator, a violence that had to be silenced. Perhaps the silenced violence is voiced in self-criticism, suicidality, or a hallucinated voice screaming at her. In therapy, we help her feel this rage outward so it does not go inward onto her. We help her feel the rage where it belongs, on an abuser, so the rage no long abuses her through self-hatred. Then she can own the inevitable rage she felt inside so she no longer fears it outside. And by bearing her mixed feelings and the guilt they trigger, she no longer has to use self-punishment as a defense to avoid the guilt.

In the following vignette, a drug addict who heard a voice telling her to use drugs has explored a rageful fantasy toward her former boyfriend, who sexually abused her daughter. She had been using drugs and asked her former boyfriend to take care of her kids until she got clean at rehab. After imagining tearing his body to pieces, she imagines talking to his dead body.

Pt: You should not have done that all the [*rise in emotion*] in the world, why, really, it doesn't make sense. I don't want to ask him because there is no explanation.

Th: No explanation.

Pt: I want to ask him how? Why? There is no reason. Doesn't he think that is sick?

Th: What else do you want to say to him about what he did and how it was wrong?

Pt: I wouldn't know what I would say. Never thought about what I would say. [*Sighs.*]

Th: With his body parts scattered, and he's dead. If his spirit could speak to you, what would it say to answer your question? What would his spirit say to you? [*The therapist helps her face her guilt over her rage toward a man she loved and to let go of the defenses of self-blame and self-torture.*]

Pt: Probably say it was my fault because he doesn't take the blame for anything. Never thinks he's wrong. [*Sighs.*] [*He and his family blamed her for what he did.*]

Th: I see. So what do you say to his spirit?

Pt: It's his fault. [*Previously, she took all the blame.*]

Th: "This is your fault." Tell him that. Tell him that, and he should feel guilty.

Pt: I guess this is your fault. For eighteen years, you've been blaming me for your crime. [*This molester blamed her for his crime.*] No shit, you knew I was on drugs, and you knew it when I called, and I was messing up, and I can't keep these kids like this, and I needed his help. [*Sighs.*] I told him I didn't want child protection services taking these kids, and I'm not living right. I was scared [*rise of emotion*], and I didn't want them to see me doing drugs. You are doing good, and you can take them [*rise in emotion*].

Th: You didn't want the kids seeing you doing drugs because you love them. You didn't want them to see you like this.

Pt: Please take them. Please take them [*Wipes eyes.*]. I just needed time to get together. I was homeless, running from the cops. I was shoplifting to eat. I can't. I'm hurting these kids like this. I can't hide anymore, and he said, "Okay. I want my daughters back anyway." [*Wipes eyes, sniffs.*] He said, "Okay, I will give you a year to get yourself together." I was going to treatment. I was really going to try, give myself a chance. I was going to get the kids settled. [*Tearful.*] It was about two weeks later [*wipes eyes*] that I sent the kids to him that he did that. [*Deep sigh.*] I had a nervous breakdown when I learned it.

Th: You had a nervous breakdown when you learned that he did that? [*She had a psychotic break after learning he had abused her daughter.*]

Pt: Oh, yeah. [*Wipes eyes.*]

Th: Can we take a look at that? What did you feel toward him when you learned?

Pt: Just shock. [*Sighs. Anxiety in the striated muscles.*]

Th: What is that feeling toward him when you learned he did it? [*Invite feelings.*]

Pt: I don't remember, just started screaming,

Th: What is that emotion when we start screaming? [*Invite feelings.*]

Pt: I don't know. I just started screaming.

Th: What is that emotion when we start screaming? [*Invite feelings.*]

Pt: Mad.

Th: Yeah. And we see that when you felt tremendously mad, a rageful feeling toward him, right?

Pt: [*Nods.*]

Th: You got anxious and turned it on yourself and had the nervous breakdown. [*The triangle of conflict: rage toward a man she once loved, anxiety, and a nervous breakdown to erase the complex mixed feelings.*]

Pt: I was in the hospital for fourteen days.

Th: Yeah, but now do you see the pattern here that when you felt the rage that you turned it onto yourself? You turned it into anxiety, kind of went crazy rather than face the depth of your rage toward him. [*Function of the defense.*] I can understand that this would have been an overwhelming rage toward him and that you felt the rage toward him and turned it into anxiety, covered the rage with craziness, and went to the hospital. Then when you were in the courtroom, you felt the rage. You tried to kill him because you wanted him dead. [*In the courtroom trial, her daughter testified about the abuse. The patient lost control of herself, jumped over two rows of chairs, and tried to strangle her ex-boyfriend.*] Then we see that you felt this rage ever since for eighteen years and turned it on yourself and then punished yourself for really wanting to torture this man and tear him to shreds. What you are also seeing is that it is bad enough that he did what he did, but he also blames you for his crime. He had not taken responsibility.

Pt: He still blames me.

Th: He blames you for his crime. Asking you to bear his guilt when his guilt is his to bear for his crime. It is bad enough that he molested your daughters but then psychologically trying to molest you by inserting his guilt into your head. Do you see what I mean?

Pt: Yeah.

Th: Isn't that despicable? [*Turn her against the defense: she accepted the molester's projection to ward off her mixed feelings toward him.*]

Pt: Yes, it is.

Th: Isn't that despicable?

Pt: That is like him.

Th: It may be like him, but can we agree that is despicable?

Pt: Yes, it is.

Th: Can we agree that that is despicable? You have your guilt and you've been carrying that. I don't have a problem here, but let's understand what I'm talking about. You've been carrying your guilt plus his guilt. Do you see what I'm talking about?

Pt: Okay, so how do I not? [*She lets go of the defense of accepting his projection.*]

Th: By facing the rage where it belongs. When his spirit tries to do one more molestation and his spirit says, "It is your fault I molested our daughter," what do you tell his spirit?

Pt: It's crazy. It is not my fault. I really thought I was doing the right thing. I honestly did when I called him.

Th: He betrayed your trust. He betrayed your trust. When he tries to ask you to bear his guilt, what do you say to him?

Pt: Fuck no, excuse me but no. It really wasn't my fault it happened. It really wasn't. [*For the first time, she places the blame for his crime where it belongs.*]

Th: Uh-huh.

Pt: No, it really wasn't my fault.

Th: What do you say to him about his attempt to get you to carry his guilt to blame you?

Pt: No, it doesn't belong to me. It's not my fault. It is yours to carry; it's not fair.

Th: "I already have my guilt, and it's heavy, and you need to carry your guilt." What do you say to him?

Pt: It is his fault, and he should feel guilt. But he doesn't feel guilt at all.

Th: What do you say when he asks you to carry his guilt?

Pt: I can't carry it. I can't bear the weight of your guilt on top of mine. Mine is heavy enough, and on top of that, the rest belongs with you. It is not my fault and not my guilt. Mine is heavy enough because I was out there doing drugs, and I put them with you. And at that time, I didn't think it was the wrong thing. I thought it was the right thing. I feel guilty because I should have never been out there with the drugs. [*She is now bearing her guilt over what she did without accepting guilt over what he did.*]

This was her first portrayal of complex mixed feelings. She accepted her guilt for putting her children at risk through drug abuse. She faced the mixed feelings toward her former boyfriend, a man she loved who molested their daughter. And she let go of the defense of self-punishment by which she avoided these mixed feelings. By accepting the ex-boyfriend's projections, she punished herself for having failed her kids. In the following month, she had only two migraine headaches instead of twelve, the usual amount, and her depression dropped by one-third. This represented a large shift from anxiety in the smooth muscles to the striated muscles. And a year later, she was still sober, working in a full-time job in a day-care center for children.

Premature Breakthroughs

In order for the patient to have a rageful image come to mind about a person she loves, she must be able to tolerate a rise of mixed feelings without cognitive/perceptual disruption, splitting, or projection. Otherwise, if she projects, she will feel split-off rage toward an all-bad projection. Portraying split-off rage reinforces splitting and projection leading to worsening symptoms and a misalliance.

For instance, if you mobilize too much feeling in a depressed or suicidal patient, he may turn even more rage on himself, resulting in severe somatic complaints, increased depression, lost work days, or more suicidal ideation. Unable to bear the guilt triggered by rage, he will have to punish himself after the session. Thus, build affect tolerance gradually and invite the patient to explore images only when they appear—the signal that his affect tolerance is sufficient. As his capacity increases more, he can experience impulses and can imagine enacting them in fantasy without doing so in reality. This builds impulse control.

SUMMARY

Fragile patients fall on a spectrum of anxiety tolerance. As a result, we use a graded approach tailored to their capacities. The following list illustrates the levels of affect tolerance and how they correlate with symbolic language in the fragile spectrum.

Phase One: Invite feelings within primitive defenses:

- Within the delusion, hallucination, or split-off personality
- Within concrete speech
- Within metaphorical speech
- *Rationale:* Following a psychotic break, the capacity for isolation of affect has not yet become established. Thus, we invite feelings within primitive defenses to increase affect tolerance until higher-level defenses become emergent.

Phase Two: Build the capacity to bear mixed feelings to integrate the patient:

- Invite the experience of split-apart feelings. (See chapters 10 and 12.)
- Invite the patient to bear feelings inside without projecting them outside. (See chapter 11.)
- Invite the patient to bear his capacity to see reality and bear the feelings it triggers. (See chapter 9.)
- *Rationale:* Patients split apart feelings and project them to avoid cognitive/perceptual disruption. Build the patient's capacity to tolerate mixed feelings inside without splitting and projecting

and tolerate anxiety in the form of cognitive/perceptual disruption without splitting or projecting.

Phase Three: Invite mixed feelings directly:

- Invite mixed feelings within the defense of displacement: toward other people.
- Invite mixed feelings within the defense of intellectualization: thoughts and reactions.
- Invite mixed feelings with feeling words at their full dose (e.g., anger, sadness).
- Invite the bodily experience of mixed feelings.
- *Rationale:* Build the patient's capacity to bear mixed feelings so that anxiety moves into the striated muscles and the resistance system moves into isolation of affect.

As we build affect tolerance with fragile patients, certain patterns of response (feelings, anxiety, and defense) indicate the optimal interventions for each phase of treatment. Table 7.9 summarizes those patterns within the spectrum of fragile patients.

Table 7.9   Responses to inviting a relationship across the spectrum of fragility

Levels of Fragility	Responses to Interventions Addressing Splitting and Projection
Psychotic level of character structure	Patient becomes more psychotic and disorganized, losing reality testing.
Severe Fragility	Patient exhibits primitive forms of splitting and projection: tertiary dissociation, hallucination, and delusion. Reality testing improves, thus a higher capacity for affect tolerance occurs.
Moderate Fragility II	Splitting of thoughts, ideas, and feelings occurs *before* cognitive/perceptual disruption could occur. Patient projects onto people and experiences projective anxiety. Less primitive defenses indicate a higher level of affect tolerance.
Moderate Fragility I	Splitting and projection occur *after* cognitive/perceptual disruption occurs. Tolerating a few seconds of cognitive/perceptual disruption represents an increase in anxiety tolerance.
Mild Fragility II	Cognitive/perceptual disruption occurs without splitting or projection. This represents an increase in affect tolerance.
Mild Fragility I	The patient sighs and intellectualizes during a rise of feelings before cognitive/perceptual disruption occurs. This represents a higher level of affect tolerance.

We build the fragile patient's capacity to bear mixed feelings without anxiety shifting into cognitive/perceptual disruption and without resistance shifting into splitting and projection. We offer graded exploration of feelings, anxiety regulation, bracing to bear feelings at the threshold until anxiety returns to the striated muscles, and restructuring of the defenses of splitting, denial, and projection. The next chapter will show how to restore capacities when they are lost.

CHAPTER EIGHT

Restoring Lost Capacities

Things fall apart; the centre cannot hold.

—W. B. YEATS, "THE SECOND COMING"

We have described how anxiety can cause a loss of reality testing. However, that capacity is only one of many that can vanish with a rise of anxiety. And those capacities must be restored to create a therapeutic alliance.

Each of us has capacities that enable us to perceive and adapt to reality (Hartmann 1939/1958, 1964; Hinsie and Campbell 1970). However, when anxiety becomes too high, fragile patients can lose those abilities. They develop problems perceiving reality accurately. Their ability to think abstractly and to use words to understand and manage their felt experience can abandon them, leaving them at the mercy of intense, inchoate experiences that feel unbearable (Garfield 1995). Affects become too intense when they trigger traumatic memories. Anxiety shifts into cognitive/perceptual disruption (Abbass 2015; Coughlin 1996; Frederickson 2013). Severe projections and loss of reality testing trigger unmanageable affects that seem inescapable (Frederickson 2013; E. Marcus 2017). And neurodevelopmental deficits can exacerbate these difficulties (Blatt and Wild 1976; DeGangi 2017; Greenspan 1992; Marcus 1992/2017; Weiner 1996).

How does this happen? When the fragile patient's anxiety crosses the threshold of affect tolerance, higher-level defenses collapse. Isolation of affect and repression create the boundary between conscious awareness and unconscious feelings. When isolation of affect and repression collapse, the boundary between unconscious feelings and consciousness dissolves. Unconscious feelings rush into awareness (Freeman, Cameron, and McGhie 1966). The patient floods with anxiety, which leads to cognitive/perceptual disruption. Then he loses mental boundaries between emotional and logical thinking, affect and perception, affect and behavior, awareness and thoughts, emotional experience and reality experience, word presentation and thing presentation, impulse and reality, inside and outside, and reality and fantasy. As a result, fragile patients may misperceive reality, other people, and themselves. Due to these misperceptions, the way they create meaning becomes distorted. And those distortions lead to severe internal and interpersonal problems.

A mental boundary refers to a person's ability to separate one experience from another. For instance, can he separate feelings from perception? Or do feelings determine what he perceives? We need certain mental boundaries for exploratory therapy. Higher functioning patients have these capacities. Since fragile patients may lose them under stress or lack them altogether, we restore those capacities before we can explore other issues in psychotherapy. The rest of this chapter explores the mental boundaries patients need and the ways to restore them.

THE BOUNDARY BETWEEN UNCONSCIOUS AND CONSCIOUS EXPERIENCE

In therapy, we bear and face feelings that we avoided. But we do not usually see these feelings due to defenses. To become aware of those feelings, the boundary between our conscious awareness and our unconscious feelings needs to be slightly porous. Then we can access an amount of previously unconscious feelings that does not disrupt our conscious functioning. But when feelings rise in the fragile patient, higher-level defenses collapse. A flood of feelings rises into awareness. And mental boundaries begin to dissolve.

For example, a woman, describing how her father sexually abused her, suddenly feared that the therapist would rape her. The boundary between her unconscious feelings and consciousness collapsed. The resulting surge of feelings and anxiety erased her ability to separate a past memory from present reality. As a result, she began to fear the therapist.

By contrast, a woman with a similar history but with the capacity to isolate affect would look very different. She might present in an avoidant manner and dismiss the therapist's comments, complaining that his questions are intrusive. She would unconsciously enact the rape memory—viewing him as trying to put foreign thoughts in her—yet remain unaware of the memory itself. Only after facing her feelings toward the therapist might the memory of her molestation become conscious.

Restoring the Boundary between Unconscious and Conscious Experience

We help the patient use isolation of affect by intellectualizing to create a boundary between unconscious feelings and conscious awareness. When intellectualization is working, she can observe, think about, and feel her feelings without anxiety flooding her.

THE BOUNDARY BETWEEN EMOTIONAL THINKING AND LOGICAL THINKING

We also need the ability to differentiate thoughts from feelings. Fragile patients can lose the boundary between logical and emotional thinking. Logical thinking requires us to gather our perceptions of reality. We assemble those perceptions into patterns to engage in inductive and deductive reasoning (Freud 1911/1958d). To think logically, we differentiate causes from effects. We differentiate the part from the whole and one part from other parts, and we differentiate the steps of causation in time (E. Marcus 2017). Concepts organize realistic perceptions into logical thinking. Therefore, we must be able to differentiate concepts from perceptions and affects. For instance, a father claims his child "never listens to me." He hears his child say no, and eternalizes that moment. He does not perceive it as a temporary, discrete self-state. Instead, he equates that momentary perception with his concept: "He *never* listens to me." Anger determines what he perceives and guides how he acts with his child. He is thinking emotionally, not logically. It's as if anger erased all his memories of the listening son.

Logical thinking is conscious and slow (Kahneman 2011). But emotional thinking can be irrational, fast, and unconscious. Reality no longer directs our thoughts. Instead, the content, quality, and flow of feelings (Freud 1913/1957b) direct our thoughts. The quality and quantity of affect determine how we collect information, sort it, and process it. Emotional thinking shrinks the kinds of meaning we create by distorting causality, plot, content, and narrative. The fragile patient does not imagine being terrified; he *is* terrified (Eissler 1954). What he feels, he believes is reality. What he feels strongly becomes a cosmic truth. As a result, his view of a relationship may become bizarre or even incoherent.

Logical and emotional thinking work together to help us make sense of the world. What happens when emotional experience determines thinking? There is reality and the picture emotions paint. If the patient cannot differentiate the two, emotions can take her experience of reality hostage. She no longer thinks; her *feelings* do the thinking.

How does that happen? Mixed feelings in fragile patients trigger cognitive/perceptual disruption. To stop the cognitive/perceptual disruption, splitting and projection separate those mixed feelings. These defenses generate powerful split-off rage toward a projection. And projection and the split-off rage drive the resulting thoughts. On the surface, the power of the emotions is obvious. But underneath the surface are the secret drivers: early memories, unconscious mixed feelings, unconscious anxiety, and unconscious splitting and projection. Together, they create the so-called emotional thinking. One might say that the nonconscious and unconscious products of her conditioning do the thinking.

Restoring the Boundary between Emotional Thinking and Logical Thinking

In the following vignette, a woman, waiting in the parking lot to pick up her husband from work, saw a woman talk to her husband and pat his shoulder before leaving. Flooded with anger, she bolted out of her car, slammed the door, raced up to them, and screamed, "I know you are having an affair!" Later, she convinced her husband to quit his job so he would have no further contact with the presumed mistress.

Pt: And I told her I knew what she was doing, trying to steal my husband from me—[*Anger is in her voice, and her speech is picking up speed, driven by her affect.*]

Th: [*Therapist interrupts before the level of affect becomes higher. Otherwise, affect would drive her thinking even more. And he speaks slowly to slow her down.*] Thanks so much for letting me know. Could you help me out here so I can understand this? [*Help her stand outside of her experience. Then she can observe it.*] If we walk back through this, where was your car parked? [*Ask for details to get her out of global thinking. Invite her to observe rather than relive the experience. Then her feelings will not escalate.*]

Pt: In the parking lot at Costco.

Th: And was this in the back of the parking lot or the front? [*The therapist slows her down and encourages her to observe details. He introduces intellectualization as a defense.*]

Pt: The back.

Th: And what time was this?

Pt: Six o'clock because he was getting off work.

Th: At six o'clock he walked out of the building. And when he walked out of the building, was he walking alone, or were other people with him?

Pt: There were a bunch of people coming out because it was quitting time, but she touched him! [*Since the memory will trigger feelings, which will overwhelm her logical thinking, the therapist interrupts to put on the brakes.*]

Th: [*Interrupts.*] Thanks for reminding me. I wanted to get to that. Now, did she touch him, or did she touch his jacket?

Pt: His jacket, but she—[*The memory will trigger feelings, which will overwhelm her logical thinking. The therapist interrupts to put on the brakes.*]

Th: [*Interrupts.*] And did she stroke his elbow, or did she touch it?

Pt: She touched it. [*Now she can observe the memory without escalating emotionally.*]

Th: And did she hold onto his elbow, or did she just touch it?

Pt: She touched it, but she's trying to take him away from me! [*Emotions determine how she thinks and makes meaning.*]

Th: That's what the anger thinks. That's because anger always thinks angry thoughts. [*Help her see how anger does her thinking right now. Differentiate her as a thinker from the anger she could think about.*] Now that we know what the anger thinks, could we look at this with your higher mind too? What other reasons could there be for a person to touch your husband's jacket? [*Invite her to consider other possibilities. Then she can think about her emotions rather than her emotions controlling what she thinks.*]

Pt: She wants to have an affair with him. [*Emotions overwhelm and limit her logical thinking.*]

Th: That's what the anger thinks. [*Differentiate her as a thinker from the anger.*] What are other possibilities if we think about this with your higher mind? [*Invite her to consider other possibilities so she can reflect rather than react.*]

Pt: I don't know.

Th: That makes sense. Because anger knows only one thought. Notice that when anger thinks, it has only angry thoughts?

Pt: But it's real! [*Loss of the ability to think about her thinking. The stronger her feelings, the more real her thought feels. Feeling, not reality, is how she measures the accuracy of her thoughts.*]

Th: You're right. Anger is real. And when anger is so strong, its thoughts feel real. Is it possible when your anger is powerful that it keeps you from having anything but angry thoughts? [*Validate how strong feelings make thoughts seem more real.*]

Pt: That is all I can think right now. [*Increase in self-observation.*]

Th: Exactly. I think you're right. When you feel angry, all you can think are angry thoughts. Could we work on this together so you could be in control instead of the anger being in control of you? [*Get consensus on the therapeutic task.*]

If the therapist explores thinking based on split-off rage, the patient will project more. And her reality testing will worsen. Instead, slow her down and help her focus on details to reduce the affective intensity. Then facts, rather than flooding feelings, can drive her thinking.

THE BOUNDARY BETWEEN AFFECT AND PERCEPTION

To think about reality, we must perceive it. However, when flooded by emotions, we perceive reality through them. Think of a child who looks at his mother through rage-colored glasses. A depressed woman sees the world through her mood of depression. She has lost the boundary between affect and perception. What she feels determines what she perceives.

Restoring the Boundary between Affect and Perception

In the following vignette, we continue with the same patient, illustrating how to restore the boundary between how she feels and what she perceives.

Pt: I just know she wants to steal him from me. I could see it! [*Her affect of anger determines what she perceives.*]

Th: Your eyes saw a woman touch your husband's jacket. But your anger saw a woman trying to steal your husband. [*Help her see how anger does the perceiving, not her. Differentiate visual perception from emotional perception.*]

Pt: But I saw her! [*Her affect still determines what she perceives. She sees a woman touching her husband's arm. But she perceives a woman trying to steal her husband. She cannot differentiate between what she sees and what she makes that mean.*]

Th: Right. You saw her touch his jacket. That's what your eyes saw. But your anger saw a woman trying to steal your husband. [*Differentiate visual perception from emotional perception.*] The problem is that if your anger does the seeing, your anger will be in charge instead of your eyes being in charge of what you see. [*Point out the price when she perceives her husband through the lens of emotions.*] Shall we look at this situation, so we can help you be in charge of what you see instead of the anger being in charge of what you see? [*Get consensus on the therapeutic task by appealing to her fundamental goal: to be in control.*]

Perhaps perceiving another woman touching her husband triggers a terrible history with unbearable feelings. But as long as those feelings determine what she perceives, she cannot think about reality. She can react only to the fantasy her feelings create. Differentiating her feelings from her perception can help her relate to reality. Then she and the therapist can examine where those feelings belong—in the past—and help her work through them there.

THE BOUNDARY BETWEEN AFFECT AND BEHAVIOR

Obstacles trigger feelings. They mobilize us to think so we can test out different trial actions in our imagination (Freud 1911/1958d) and channel our behavior into effective action. When the fragile patient projects, the boundary between affect and behavior becomes strained (E. Marcus 2017). Affects he cannot bear inside he projects onto others. And those projected affects determine how he experiences reality. He thinks about acting out against these imaginary enemies, but he doesn't.

In the behavioral borderline group, the boundary between affect and behavior breaks. Patients act out before their feelings become conscious and put into words. As soon as a man felt enraged, his hands encircled his girlfriend's neck. He felt terrible guilt. He lacked a boundary between feeling and behavior. His impulse went to his hands before he could become aware of it, think about it, and consider the consequences.

At a lower level of affect tolerance, the patient cannot tolerate the mixed feelings of love and rage inside, so he splits off and denies his love for that person. Instead, he feels pure rage. Viewing that person as all-bad justifies his attacks and pleasure in attacking.

The severely fragile patient may equate a person with his projection and act out to gain omnipotent control over that person. For instance, a therapist set a limit in a drug rehab unit. As a result, mixed feelings rose in the patient. Due to guilt over the rage, he split off and projected his rage and his wish to control onto the therapist. Then he interacted with his projection: an "angry, controlling" therapist. He began to act dominating and threatening to control the therapist so he wouldn't have to bear the feelings the limit triggered. The addict saw reality. But he acted out to make the therapist change reality (E. Marcus 2017, 104). Psychotic patients who lack the affect tolerance to bear reality remain blind to it.

Restoring the Boundary between Affect and Behavior

The following example illustrates how to restore the boundary between affect and behavior.

Pt: [*Rises out of the chair and walks toward the door. With the rise of affect, the patient acts.*]

Th: Notice how your legs want to walk out of the room? [*Differentiate him from the behavior. Now instead of being the walker, he is the observer of his legs.*]

Pt: I just have to leave. [*As soon as feelings rise, he acts to get away from them.*]

Th: Right. It's as if your legs want to walk away from your feelings. [*Describe the unconscious fantasy: "I can place a feeling outside of me."*] But no matter where you go, your feelings follow you like a shadow. [*Remind him of reality.*] Shall we see if we can help you face these feelings so you don't have to live this life on the run? [*Remind him of the price of denial. We cannot run away from a feeling inside us.*] Wouldn't it be nice to be able to hold on to your power so you could be in charge instead of your legs being in charge of you? [*Mobilize him to a positive goal: greater inner control.*]

The impulsive person acts before he observes, acts before he thinks. Thus, help him observe the impulse without having to do anything. Once he can observe the impulse without acting on it, he can think about it and reflect (Wishnie 1977).

Often, the impulsive patient acts out due to fear of a projection. He might act in a threatening manner if he feels threatened by you. He may frighten you if he feels frightened of you. He may want to attack you if he feels attacked. Thus, deactivating projections can prevent the loss of reality testing that leads to acting out. (See chapters 3 on will and 11 on projection.)

Patients give clues of impending acting out. They describe anger toward people whom they want to attack. That symbolizes a potential urge to attack the therapist. When the impulsive patient splits and views people as all-bad, the risk of acting out increases. As feelings rise, the impulsive patient's legs become jumpy as if they are preparing to run. Impulses may appear in his arms and hands, and anxiety will disappear because he no longer has mixed feelings. He feels split-off rage toward the therapist. In these situations, do not explore split-off rage. Instead, help the patient bear mixed feelings. (See chapter on 10 on splitting.)

Certain therapist behaviors can trigger acting out: criticizing the patient, focusing too much on defenses so the patient feels attacked, exploring split-off rage while ignoring the mixed feelings, encouraging the patient to view the therapist as all-good while others are all-bad, and actions that abandon the patient, such as unannounced vacations and cancellations. Listen to the symbolic meaning of his descriptions of other people. Those descriptions symbolize his unconscious experience with you in this moment. If you systematically deactivate his latent projections, you can sometimes avoid a psychotic transference that will lead to acting out. (For more on deactivating latent projections, see chapters 3 on will, 11 on projection, and 12 on severe fragility.)

THE BOUNDARY BETWEEN AWARENESS AND THOUGHTS

Fragile patients often have suffered from verbal abuse. When they call themselves names, they show us how caretakers equated them with a label or thought.

Pt: I'm just a piece of crap. [*The patient cannot differentiate his thought from the awareness in which it appears.*]

Restoring the Boundary between Awareness and Thoughts

The patient distrusts the therapist and has lost reality testing.

Pt: I don't trust you.

Th: And would that be an idea you are aware of? [*Differentiate the patient as an aware person from the contents of his awareness.*]

Pt: Yes.

Th: And would that be an idea your brain produces? [*Differentiate him from the ideas he is aware of.*]

Pt: Yes.

Th: Would that be one of the brain products you observe? [*Restore the mental boundary between awareness and the contents of his awareness.*]

Pt: Yes.

Th: As we step back for a minute and observe those thoughts your brain produces, what other thoughts does your brain produce? [*Therapist points toward the wall at his side. Now they can look at the thoughts metaphorically on the wall. Then the patient can think about ideas rather than equate the therapist with them.*]

In another case, a patient on several antipsychotic medications is suffering from hypomania.

Pt: [*Racing speech.*] I am worried that I will crash into a horrible depression. I felt depressed and despondent yesterday afternoon. But today, I am feeling kind of "up" again. I am also worried because I have read that as people age, they often develop a more severe pattern of episodes, with fewer interepisode periods of remission. I already tend to have very little symptom-free time. I usually tend toward depression rather than mania. I have read that bipolar illness is primarily a depressive condition. Prior to this manic phase, I was depressed for two years. During that time, I had "double depression" where I would sink into a severe episode for several months, then come out of that into a mild/moderate depression. It was awful. I hope that does not happen now.

Th: What is aware of the mania? [*Differentiate awareness from the contents of her awareness.*]

Pt: What do you mean?

Th: Well, you know there are all these manic thoughts going through, right?

Pt: Yes.

Th: So, what is aware of those manic thoughts? [*Differentiate awareness from the contents of her awareness.*]

Pt: I feel like those thoughts are me. [*Symbolic equation: she equates a symbol (a thought) with the symbolized (herself).*]

Th: Are you a thought? [*Differentiating awareness from the contents of her awareness helps restore her symbolic thinking. She is not a thought. A thought symbolizes her. But the symbol is not what it symbolizes. She is not a symbol. The map is not the territory (Korzybski 1994).*]

Pt: No.

Th: What is aware of those thoughts? [*Differentiate her as awareness from the thoughts of which she is aware.*]

Pt: Me?

Th: Are you the mania, or are you the awareness in which the mania appears and disappears? [*Differentiate awareness from the contents of her awareness, the centerless clearing in which the apparent centers appear.*]

Pt: For some reason, I feel calmer now. There's a silence.

Differentiate awareness from the contents that appear and disappear in awareness. Grounded in awareness, she is no longer destabilized by shifting contents. As her affect tolerance increases, eventually she will no longer lose this mental boundary.

THE BOUNDARY BETWEEN REALITY EXPERIENCE AND EMOTIONAL EXPERIENCE

When we tolerate intense mixed feelings toward people we love, we view them as a whole. We remember the entire relationship, not just the parts agreeing with one feeling. When we cross the threshold of affect tolerance, this capacity collapses. Then, patients lose the boundary between reality experience and their emotional experience. They equate the reality of the other person with their emotional experience. A man, frustrated with his wife, became filled with fury. The memory of his mother's past withholding blinded him to his wife's current generosity. An emotional memory of his mother washed away the reality of his wife in the present. Powerful emotions make misperceptions appear real. For instance, one woman, flooded with anger, said her father had a "heart of concrete." [*Splitting.*] Yet, when he died, she sobbed, recalling his love.

E. Marcus (2017) has described a spectrum of reality testing in relationships. The near-psychotic patient can differentiate his emotional experience from reality, but he doesn't care. He may agree that his emotional experience and reality are not the same. But he still equates his emotional experience with reality. For example, he may say that he thinks his psychiatrist doesn't care about him so he wants to quit therapy. The very ill neurotic person can tell the difference between his emotional experience and reality, and he cares. But he wants to change the therapist today to alter a memory of a person in his past. Healthier neurotic patients can tell the difference between the therapist and their emotional experience. But they feel no strong urge to change the therapist.

Restoring the Boundary between Reality Experience and Emotional Experience

A woman felt rage when her boyfriend did not pick her up on time. "He's worthless," she said and dumped him. Her negative emotion erased her positive memories.

Th: That must be puzzling.

Pt: Why? He's no good.

Th: You say he's no good, and yet he's the same guy who sat by your bed in the hospital after you overdosed. [*Remind her of reality experience that contradicts her emotional experience that results from splitting.*]

Pt: That doesn't mean anything. [*Denial and splitting.*]

Th: Really? It doesn't mean anything that he found you on the floor, called 9-1-1, and followed the ambulance to the emergency room? It doesn't mean anything that he saved your life? Is that true? Or is it just hard to put together that the guy who saved your life is the same person who showed up late for a date? That can be confusing. [*Remind her of the reality she splits off and erases.*]

Pt: I—uh—I don't know. [*Difficulty speaking due to a rise of anxiety in cognitive/perceptual disruption. This is progress: she tolerates anxiety for a second without splitting.*]

Th: It can be confusing that the same guy who was late for a date is the person who saved your life, something about this complexity. [*Pressure to consciousness of her splitting to increase affect tolerance.*]

Pt: He really pissed me off.

Th: Yes. He pissed you off when he was late and made you feel grateful when he saved your life. Something about this complexity is hard to bear. [*Pressure to consciousness of her splitting to increase affect tolerance.*]

Pt: He should not have been late.

Th: But he was. And you felt angry with the same guy who saved your life. And when the anger came up toward the late boyfriend, you forgot the boyfriend who saved your life. And yet both are true.

In this case, reminding the patient of the reality experience and positive feelings she split off helped restore the boundary between reality and her emotional experience, the split-off rage that temporarily erased the boundary between her reality experience and emotional experience.

THE BOUNDARY BETWEEN THE WORD PRESENTATION AND THE THING PRESENTATION

Some people do not use language to represent their experience; they use words to enact it. For instance, they enact both sides of an argument as if it is happening now. They cannot stand back from a feeling experience and reflect on it. For them, an emotional experience is not a perspective; it is a fact to enact. When the therapist tries to interrupt, the patient keeps talking. While describing the event, she may even yell at a person in her vignette. Rather than describe the episode through words, she enacts it as if she is presenting you with the thing itself, the situation (Bass 2000; Loewald 1989; E. Marcus 2017). Inquire about the triggering event to slow her down so we can reflect together.

The way some patients use language reveals a drop in symbolic functioning. For instance, if I say, "You sound angry," you might agree that you feel angry. But you would not explode into a rage when you heard the word "angry." However, for some people, the feeling word triggers the feeling (Ekstein 1966). The therapist might say, "You sound angry." And the previously calm person might yell, "You're goddamned right!" The feeling word no longer symbolizes the feeling; it triggers the feeling experience. Here, avoid words that take the patient over the threshold of affect tolerance. Do not say, "You sound angry." Say instead, "It sounds like you had some thoughts about what he said. What thoughts do you have about what he said?" Help him intellectualize about what stimulated his feelings so he can bear more intense emotions while putting them into words. Since the feeling word can trigger the feeling, such a patient may flood with anxiety when you use the word "anxiety." Say instead, "It sounds like you are feeling uncomfortable. Shall we work together to help you feel more calm?" Avoid trigger words that lead the patient to lose the capacity for symbolic thought. Use lower dosage, intellectualized words to build the capacity to isolate affect. For instance, if the word "anger" triggers too much anxiety, you can use the word "upset." If the word "anxiety" triggers too much anxiety, you can use the word "nervous." If the word "feelings" triggers too much anxiety, you can use the word "reactions." You can build the patient's affect tolerance by offering higher-level defenses when he doesn't have them.

Restoring the Boundary between the Word Presentation and the Thing Presentation

In the following example, the patient acts as if she were talking to her partner while speaking to the therapist. She uses speech to enact an event rather than to describe it. Unable to describe her feelings in words, she discharges them through actions, yelling, cursing, and rapid speech. We might consider her discharge a projectile vomiting of emotions. She tries to expel emotional experience that is too much to bear and think about (Bion 1959; Meltzer 1992; Rosenfeld 1987). She attempts to get rid of experience through speech while communicating it through enactment (Bion 1959; T. Ogden 1982; Spotnitz 1986). She relives her experience rather than observes it in the past. The boundary between herself as an observer and the experience she observes has been lost.

Pt: And then he said, "You're a bitch." And so, I told him [*she raises her voice*], "Get out of my fucking house, you asshole!" And then he came at me, and so I said, "Come on. Come on. Do it, and I'll haul your ass to jail!" [*She cannot describe the event in the past in verbal/representational speech. She enacts the event as if it is occurring now.*]

Th: [*The therapist interrupts the enactment. Then he slows her down through his quiet, slow speech.*] As we step back for a moment to observe what happened, could you remind me where this took place? [*Provide a boundary between here and there.*]

Pt: This was at my apartment.

Th: Right. And when did you say this took place? [*Providing a boundary between past and present.*]

Pt: It was, uh, Thursday night. [*She needs a moment to step out of reliving the past to remember that event.*]

Th: And can you remind me of what happened before he called you a name? What was he reacting to? [*The therapist does not use the* term "bitch," *which would trigger more feelings and deepen the regression. The question helps her stand back, observe, and think about causality.]*

Pt: I said I didn't want to go out. [*Now she describes what happened without acting it out: verbal representational speech.*]

The following hypothetical vignette uses the same situation to illustrate verbal representational speech.

Th: And then he called me a bitch. I got angry with him and told him he had to leave the house. I won't tolerate that kind of treatment anymore. But then he walked toward me. So I told him that although I can't stop him from hitting me again, I can report him to the police. Then he backed off and left.

This woman represents the event in words. The previous patient used *action language* (Ekstein 1966) instead of *verbal representational speech* (Loewald 1989). She did not describe a memory. She presented an emotion. The thing presentation quality is revealed when she presents her emotion as the thing, the event itself, not a feeling about the event.

THE BOUNDARY BETWEEN IMPULSE AND REALITY

For some patients, a rising impulse—based on a projection—erases the awareness of reality and the consequences that would occur after acting out. It's as if the experience of acting out an impulse wipes out reality. "I took action. Therefore, my view of reality must be true" (Marcus 1992/2017, 94).

Restoring the Boundary between Impulse and Reality

In the following vignette, a patient proudly describes an instance when he acted out. He sees no problem because for him, acting out justifies the action.

Pt: I beat the crap out of him, so now he knows I'm right. [*He believes that his ability to beat a body equals the capacity to convince a person.*]

Th: Well, he knows you can beat him up. But the problem is while you can beat up a person, you can't beat up an attitude. You can make people shut up, but you can't stop them thinking what they think.

Think of all the wars we have had, and people still think what they think. [*Remind him of reality: an impulse cannot change reality.*]

Pt: Yeah. Well, maybe we just need to kill enough of them. [*He believes that if he eliminates people who have a thought, the thought will disappear. An unconscious fantasy drives his impulsivity: "If I kill reality, I won't have feelings about it."*]

Th: It's just that while we can kill a man, we can't kill an attitude. [*Remind him of reality. Impulses do not make reality go away.*]

Pt: Hmm.

Remind him of reality: acts cannot make facts go away. Then invite him to pay attention to reality and the feelings it triggers. When he can bear those feelings, he can face facts and learn from them. Then he can relate to reality and act accordingly.

LOSS OF THE BOUNDARY BETWEEN INSIDE AND OUTSIDE

Patients need a boundary to differentiate inside from outside (Anzieu 1985/2016; Freud 1920/1961d). Without a boundary, they feel like a kernel without a shell, a person without skin, a sieve (Anzieu 1985/2016). They feel as if their inner life leaks out and the feelings of others seep in. "You can see through me," "You know what I am thinking," and "You are putting words into my mouth."

To perceive reality and other people accurately, we need a boundary between inside and outside. For instance, an angry woman believes that the therapist wants to make her angry. She sees no boundary between what she feels and what another person feels. A psychotic man hearing the therapist's stomach rumble may complain about his own upset stomach. He recognizes no boundary between his experience and the therapist's.

Restoring the Boundary between Inside and Outside

In the following vignette, a patient reveals that he has lost the boundary between inside and outside: he believes the therapist can read his mind.

Pt: The room is getting leaky. I feel like you can read my mind. [*The patient has lost the boundary between inside and outside. He believes that, without a boundary, the therapist can read his thoughts.*]

Th: I can't read your mind. Only you can do that. I know only what you decide to reveal to me. [*Remind him of reality.*]

Pt: But it feels like you are looking through me. [*He still does not feel like he has a boundary between inside and outside. His belief that I am looking through him is a projection: he wants to look into himself. We deactivate that projection so he will not fear me. Then we can find out if he wants to look into himself in therapy.*]

Th: I can see only your eyes. I can't see what's in you. Only you can see what's inside you. [*Remind him of reality.*] That's why we have to find out if you would like to look at what is inside you so you have better information about yourself, so you can make better decisions for yourself. [*Invite him to recognize his wish to look inside himself. The more he can accept it, the less he needs to project it on the therapist.*]

THE BOUNDARY BETWEEN REALITY AND FANTASY

When the patient equates his fantasy with reality (Segal 1981), he believes his fantasy is a fact: "You are trying to control me." He operates according to the belief: "If I think it, that makes it so." A patient learns that her therapist will soon take a vacation. The sudden rise of anger may alter her experience of reality (her therapist): "I thought you cared, but now I know you don't!" She equates the therapist with her fantasy. Logical thought no longer organizes the relationship between reality and her emotional experience. (See chapters 9 on denial, 10 on splitting, 11 on projection, and 12 on severe fragility.)

SUMMARY

When feelings and anxiety become too high, the fragile patient's higher-level defenses break down. Anxiety goes into cognitive/perceptual disruption, and mental boundaries dissolve. Therapy can restore these mental boundaries to form a realistic therapeutic alliance.

Regression occurs in therapy when too much pain rises in the relationship. Immediately evaluate your role in the regression. Perhaps the patient feels you do not accept him as he is. Did he pick up your impatience, frustration, or anger with his demands? Did he perceive your dissatisfaction with his progress? Or did he experience you as abandoning him when you sided with his relatives? (Semrad 1966, 164).

When regression occurs, did you invite too much feeling, fail to regulate anxiety, criticize the patient, or confront his defenses? The sharp rise of feelings can cause him to go over the threshold of anxiety tolerance, leading to a regression.

"When stress goes beyond the sum total of supports, especially from the therapist, the interactions and relationships take on a more disruptive, primitive, or disorganized character, often referred to as *transference psychosis* (Semrad 1966, 168). Thus, examine any drops in support coming from the therapist before a regression. Did the therapist cancel a session, come late, or announce an upcoming vacation or termination? Did the patient experience an empathic lapse from the therapist? For instance, a patient might threaten the therapist after feeling threatened by the therapist's comments. Did the therapist comment on the destructiveness of the patient's defenses without clarifying how they were the best solution the patient had and were, in fact, an attempt at adaptation and self-cure?

When regression occurs outside the session, what did he lose or who did he lose? Did he lose his connection to you? What was the relational stressor that triggered a sharp spike of feelings that would have overwhelmed his capacities? Careful inquiry can uncover the trigger, although the patient may not be aware of it when you first ask. Discovering that emotional trigger allows you and the patient to make sense of the regression and repair the rupture (Muran and Safran 2003).

He suffers interpersonal problems like everyone, but he lacks the capacities to deal with them. The following chapters will show how to build affect tolerance. As the patient gains the ability to experience his mixed feelings, he will be able to bear the relationships that trigger them.

PART THREE

Integrating the Patient

CHAPTER NINE

Denial

Learning to Face Reality

The conflict between the will to deny horrible events and the will to proclaim them aloud is the central dialectic of psychological trauma.

—JUDITH HERMAN, *TRAUMA AND RECOVERY: THE AFTERMATH OF VIOLENCE—FROM DOMESTIC ABUSE TO POLITICAL TERROR*

D enial refers to the things we do unconsciously that interfere with our perception of reality (Basch 1983; Wurmser 1989). We deny reality to avoid the feelings it triggers. We can also deny the meanings of reality. Or we deny facts to avoid the feelings linked with them (Basch 1983; Fenichel 1945; Freud 1915/1958e; Wurmser 1989). These could be aspects of our inner world, such as impulses, feelings, thoughts, wishes, or memories. Or these could be facts about the external world. When the patient does not have the reality he wants, he may try to create the fantasy he desires (Rank 1929/1978, 195). Then he lives in his fantasy world as if it is reality in the external world. Or he can try to make other people change so he won't have to face the realities of difference and otherness.

THE IMPACT OF DENIAL

Denial erases reality. Thus, the patient who is "in denial" lives in an altered world. He cannot think about, adapt to, or work with any part of reality he has unconsciously denied (Dorpat 1985). But it's even worse.

Whatever denial erases, fantasy replaces (Green 1977). Fantasies stand in for facts, people utter "alternative facts" from the alternate "reality" known as denial, and act as if the laws of life have been deleted by the demands of fantasy (A. Freud 1936, 95). Denial creates a map in which the parts of reality not denied are depicted. But the rest of the map is filled in with fantasy.

Once the false replaces the real, people engage in destructive actions. And we wonder, "What was that person thinking?" He thought about his fantasies, not reality. To help him, we assess the substitute fantasy and what it denies. Then we can help him think about the world of reality that lives outside his illusion. We always live in reality. Denial is a fantasy that we can make reality vanish. We can learn about reality only by overcoming our tendency to deny everything we do not want to see, hear, or perceive (Rank 1929/1978, 39).

Denial creates a picture of the world as did the medieval mapmakers who filled in the areas beyond the horizon of the known world with mythical continents, beasts, and peoples. The resulting map is part real and part fantasy, but the patient doesn't know which is which. When such fantastical maps guide thinking, behaviors become irrational and maladaptive.

Let's examine how denial precludes us from thinking about reality. When the brain first appraises a painful situation, feelings rise. If we bear them, we can pay attention to painful facts. We unconsciously register information about reality. However, denial turns our attention away before we become aware of that information (Brown 1972; Erdelyi 1974; G. Klein 1959; Werner 1948). Unconscious denial prevents us from consciously seeing an aspect of reality. Thus, we cannot think about it (Dorpat 1985).

Unable to pay attention to a part of reality, the patient focuses on the fantasy that replaces it. Unable to see reality, he cannot compare it with his fantasy. If he equates his thought with reality, the result will be a delusion. Immersed in his fantasy world, he doesn't know what he avoids in the real world. Therapists may imagine that a patient knows what he denies and pretends not to know. That may not true. Denial occurs unconsciously, warding off what is not yet conscious (Wurmser 1989). Denial differs from repression. Repression blocks our awareness after we thought about reality in words. Denial blocks our awareness of reality before we can think about it. The result is pseudothinking about pseudorealities.

If we deny that we have certain thoughts, feelings, and deeds, we surrender ownership of what we have denied. We do not reflect on reality because we deny that there is a reality to reflect upon. Instead, we fantasize about illusions that lead to "obvious" conclusions and justify acting out. That is why impulsivity results from denial. A simplistic fantasy demanding action erases a complex reality requiring thought.

DENIAL AND ENACTMENT

Whatever has been denied, we cannot remember consciously in verbal representational memory because it never became conscious and translated into words. The denied is registered unconsciously in the form of nonverbal enactive memories (Dorpat 1985, 103; Loewald 1989). Thus, the patient, unable to describe her past in words, may portray it unconsciously through her relational behaviors.

Our ability to deny reality evolves developmentally. First, the infant uses sensorimotor behaviors. By spitting out, turning the head, or arching the back, the baby tries to avoid reality physically. Next, she can close her eyes to avoid reality perceptually. Finally, the child can use verbal defenses. Now she can avoid thinking about reality (Dorpat 1985, 118)—reality being our relationships and the feelings we have in them.

A past relationship is registered unconsciously as an *enactive memory*, and the patient unconsciously enacts that memory in therapy. A memory contains a picture of the other person and ourselves, and the feelings between us. In this sense, feelings are memories of relationships (Kernberg 1975). If I fear that you will dominate me, I might try to dominate you. However, I might not realize that I am acting like my dominating father.

The denied appears in the form of an enacted relationship. For instance, in chapter 10 on splitting, a man denies that he suffered any traumas. As the session unfolded, we learned that his mother wished him dead and wanted him to burn alive. His father beat and kicked the mother repeatedly. Then he remembered a phone call where his parents wondered, "There was nothing traumatic. Why don't you call?" His denial with me enacted the denial he suffered from them (Loewald 1989).

What we have seen, faced, and felt consciously, we can remember and put into words. What was denied, we put into action (Loewald 1989). When we put our memory into words, we can differentiate the past from the present. When we enact our past, we unconsciously relive through actions and feelings rather than consciously remember through thoughts. The patient may enact a past relationship in therapy (Ferenczi 1933/1994; Freud 1917/1961a; M. Klein 1975b). Or his memories may be enacted in other forms: bodily sensations (Howell 2005; Nijenhuis 2004), pseudohallucinations, or pseudodelusions (E. Marcus 2017).

DENIAL AND ACTING OUT

When fragile patients believe fantasies based on denial, they enact them. Thus, we set limits on acting out to protect the therapy. For instance, if people destroy property in the session, they will feel guilty. Then they will be at more risk of trying to provoke someone to punish them. If they yell or scream, we may become too anxious to listen effectively.

Th: I realize you may feel you have to yell right now. But there is a problem. I can't think while you yell. And if I can't think, I can't understand you or help you. I wonder if you would be willing to lower your voice so we can try to understand you together.

Pt: No. I have to yell. It's how I get my feelings out. [*Denial that yelling would prevent others from wanting to listen.*]

Th: That may be. But if that's your need, then we'll need to find you another therapist who can think while you yell. That is not something I'm able to do. [*The therapist admits his limitations without judging the patient.*]

Fragile patients do not yell at the therapist. They yell at the projection they place on the therapist. For instance, they may project that you will not listen. Thus, they have to yell to be heard. Or they may fear you as a judge, so they yell over your feared judgments. Anytime a patient tries to control you, find out the projection he is trying to control.

Pt: [*Yelling.*] And I don't want anyone telling me what to do! [*Projection: you want to control me. Denial: the patient denies that he told himself to come to therapy.*]

Th: Good! Because I have no right to tell you what to do. Would you like us to explore this situation so you could feel in control instead of the anger being in control of you? [*Deactivate the projection onto the therapist by reminding the patient of reality. Then invite him to recognize his wish to be in control of himself. Then remind him that rage, not the therapist, is controlling him.*]

We have to set limits when defenses destroy the therapy. Treatment is not possible when the patient is intoxicated. Making continual suicidal threats at all hours will sabotage the therapy relationship. Sabotaging behavior at work will make it impossible to pay for therapy. Acting out with parents might provoke them to stop paying for therapy.

A patient enters his session at a rehabilitation facility while high. [*Denial that being high would make a therapy session impossible.*]

Th: Since you're high, we won't be able to work together today in therapy. Let's set up an appointment tomorrow so we can find out what happened that led you to deal with your feelings this way. [*Set a limit and offer another appointment.*]

Pt: But I need to see you. [*Splitting and denial: he sees his need for therapy but splits off his awareness that certain conditions are necessary to do therapy and denies that fact.*]

Th: I agree. You need to see me sober, but you came high instead. We need to meet again when you are sober. Until I see you tomorrow, try to figure out what triggered you to hurt yourself this way. [*Set a clear limit about the conditions under which therapy is possible.*]

A suicidal patient calls at all hours of the day and night talking about how she is feeling suicidal.

Pt: Why didn't you call me back? [*Denial of the previous conditions under which they agreed to do therapy.*]

Th: When we started, I told you I am a therapist, but I cannot be a hospital. If you are at risk of killing yourself, you should go immediately to the hospital. [*Set a limit by reminding the patient of reality.*]

Pt: But I need someone to talk to. [*Denial: the patient remembers her need but denies the limit to which they agreed.*]

Th: If that's the case, then you can call a suicide hotline because I cannot be available around the clock. [*Set a limit.*]

Pt: But I want to talk to you. [*Denial: the patient remembers her need but denies the limit to which they agreed.*]

Th: Yes. We learned that you want to talk to me at any time of day. But, unfortunately, that is not possible. [*Set a limit by reminding the patient of reality.*]

Pt: Jane's therapist takes calls from her at any time of the night and day. [*Denial: the patient remembers a fact about her friend but denies the limit to which they agreed.*]

Th: I'm not able to do that. If you feel that you can't work this way, I understand. This is a limit I have. It may not be a limit you can work with. [*Avoid a battle of will.*]

Pt: I just want to kill myself. [*Defense: the patient threatens to kill herself to ward off feelings toward the therapist.*]

Th: Given that you want to kill yourself while you are sitting here with me and that you want to hurt yourself in our relationship, what feelings are coming up here toward me? [*Explore feelings toward the therapist so she will not have to turn rage against herself. Suicide is the defense against homicidal rage. The less you explore anger toward the therapist, the more the patient will become suicidal.*]

A patient on probation blew up at his boss at work.

Th: I can appreciate how angry you were with your boss. But I'm wondering if blowing up at him is a way you invite him to punish you at the very moment you are angry with him. [*Remind the patient of his denial: to act out, he had to deny the effect it would have on his boss and his job.*] And when you blow up, he'll hear your yelling but not your justified concerns. The anger is happy because the anger gets what it wants, but then you're the one who gets punished. Would it make sense for us to look at these feelings so you could assert yourself in a powerful way instead of inviting your boss to fire you? Otherwise, you risk losing your job, and then we would lose the chance to help you when you really need it.

When under the pressure of impossible demands, we might forget that the patient may be enacting her history: someone placed her under impossible demands, always the case during a trauma.

NEUROTIC DENIAL

In neurotic denial, we acknowledge that reality exists. But we deny the meanings of what happened, the impact, or the feelings aroused by reality (Basch 1983). For instance, when I say I feel nothing, I disavow the meanings of my feelings, which would arouse anxiety (Wurmser 1989).

In one form of denial, disavowal, we repudiate the feelings and meanings of what we perceive. A patient in therapy has recounted that her husband is having an affair.

Pt: But it didn't mean anything. It was just a one-night stand. [*Denial.*]

She separates reality (her husband's affair) from the anxiety-provoking personal meaning ("Our marriage is in trouble"). She sees reality but not the feelings and meanings it provokes.

Anna Freud (1936) proposed the following four ways to deny the existence of reality:

Denial per se: Saying that a fact does not exist

Denial through fantasy: Paying attention to fantasy rather than reality

Denial by words: Paying attention to false words rather than real deeds

Denial in deed: Behaving as if a fact does not exist

To assess denial, we ask whether it is due to an inability to test reality, a sign of psychotic illness. Or does he see reality but deny it to avoid internal emotional conflict? That is a sign of neurotic illness (Blackman 2004). The neurotic denies the meanings of reality (Freud 1924/1957f, 185). The psychotic person denies part of reality itself.

We can enlist many defenses to ignore reality, including any of the following:

Withdrawal of attention: The patient sees neither the stimulus nor her feeling because she does not look at them.

Ignoring: In this less extreme form of denial, we can bring reality back into focus. When the patient ignores the stimulus to feeling or his feelings, he does not see essential aspects of reality and misperceives the meaning of events.

Negation: The patient perceives her feeling but negates its meaning. For example, a woman who has been cruelly rejected by her ex-fiancé says, "I don't feel angry." Negation simultaneously reveals and conceals what is denied (Freud 1925/1957g). In response, the therapist might say, "You say you don't feel angry, but what do you feel toward him?" Negation is a signal from the unconscious. The previously unconscious feeling (anger) is conscious. Thus, we would say that her anger is *preconscious*—the word is conscious but the link to the patient is unconscious.

Minimization: The patient perceives the stimulus (the rejection). But she minimizes her emotional reaction to it. "Maybe I feel a little bothered."

Overexaggeration: The patient denies reality and exaggerates the opposite feeling. "I am even more in love with him than ever. I can hardly wait to make love to him again."

Reversal: The patient changes her experience of anger into its opposite. "I feel happy."

Ridicule: The patient perceives the stimulus (the rejection). But she denies its importance and, thus, any feeling response. "Oh, that? That was nothing. I've had many men before. I'll have many men in the future."

Fantasy: The patient acknowledges her perception of reality. But she changes it into a less threatening fantasy and relates only to those portions of reality consistent with her fantasy. Her fantasy takes precedence over her perception of reality. (See Cramer 2006, 44–46.) Reality does not threaten her because she does not perceive it. "I know he'll get over it. He really loves me. It's just a phase he is going through."

Negative hallucination: The patient fails to see what is present: "He is not going to leave me."

Positive hallucination: The patient sees what is not present: "He loves me."

DENIAL PER SE

With denial per se, the patient denies reality despite overwhelming evidence to the contrary. Remind him of his denial and the reality he denies. Do not argue with him. Show him how denial argues with reality.

A middle-aged man was mourning the recent death of his wife from cancer. He planned to visit a woman who enjoyed bondage and discipline, a form of sadomasochism.

Pt: I know when I go to see her that either I'll feel guilty for going, or she'll make me feel shitty.

Th: I want to visit a woman who makes me feel guilty and shitty. [*Mirror the contradiction.*]

Pt: I find her very interesting. [*Defense: denial of who he is meeting and why.*]

Th: I am very interested in a woman who makes me feel guilty and shitty. [*Mirror the contradiction.*]

Pt: I know I'll feel worse about myself.

Th: I want to meet a woman who will make me feel worse about myself. [*Mirror the contradiction.*]

Pt: [*Laughs.*] I know it sounds crazy. I know she will either reject me or run away from me.

Th: I want a woman to reject me or run away from me. [*Mirror the contradiction.*]

Pt: Hmm. It is a distraction from all this sadness over Anne's death.

Th: I want a woman to reject me so I don't have to face the sadness over Anne's leaving me through death. [*Point out the function of the denial: to avoid the mixed feelings over his wife's death.*]

Pt: It's so painful. [*His face contorts in pain as he cries.*]

DENIAL IN FANTASY

With denial in fantasy, the patient denies reality by paying attention to a fantasy. Help her see the contrast between reality and her fantasy.

A patient's son, with a history of lying to her, was recently arrested.

Pt: He said he was not drinking anymore, so I was shocked to learn that he was drinking again. [*Defense: denial through fantasy.*]

Th: I expect my son who lies to tell me the truth. [*Point out the defense: she pays attention to the fantasy son she wishes she had rather than her real son.*]

Pt: But I was shocked! [*Defense: denial through fantasy.*]

Th: Of course, you were. If you see the truth—that he lies—and then deny it, you will be shocked when the truth shows up again. You pay attention to his words in the present and ignore his lies in the past. [*"Shocked" is the result when she denies reality, and reality shows up anyway.*]

Pt: I see. If I deny the truth, then I am surprised when he lies again. [*Improved reality testing.*]

Th: You see the truth. You deny it. Then you are shocked. The denial hurts you. When you deny it again, you set up the whole cycle of self-harm.

Pt: But he really hurts me. [*Projection: she hurts herself when she uses denial.*]

Th: May I offer another perspective?

Pt: Yes.

Th: The first time, he hurt you by lying to you. But if you had faced the truth that first time, he could never have hurt you again because you would have been prepared to deal with a liar. Instead, each time you denied the reality that he lies, you set yourself up to be shocked and hurt. I would propose that he hurt you once, but your denial has hurt you hundreds of times. [*Point out the externalization: she punishes herself by denying his lying. But she blames him for hurting her when her denial hurts her.*]

Denial keeps her enslaved to his lies. Facing the truth is the proof that she has found freedom.

DENIAL IN WORDS

With denial in words, the patient pays attention to a person's words, not his deeds. Reminding her of the difference between what someone says and does may not help. Point out that she listens to what the other person says and ignores what he does. Selective inattention is the key (Sullivan 1953a).

A patient in an abusive marriage says her husband hit her.

Th: What do you feel toward him for hitting you in the face this week?

Pt: We talked about it, and he said he's sorry, and he won't do it again. [*Defense: denial by words.*]

Th: You pay attention to his words rather than his deeds. [*Point out the denial.*]

Pt: But he said he wouldn't do it again. [*Defense: denial by words.*]

Th: That is what he said. Do you notice you pay attention to what he said but not what he did? [*Point out the denial by words.*]

Pt: But he said he was sorry. [*Defense: denial by words.*]

Th: But do you notice that you pay attention to what he says and ignore what he does?

Pt: My mom says that too. [*Defense: projection. "That's not what I think; that's what my mom thinks."*]

Th: What's your opinion? Do you notice you believe his words and try not to believe his fists? [*Point out the denial.*]

Pt: Hmm. I hadn't thought of it that way.

DENIAL IN DEED

With denial in deed, the patient denies reality by acting on the basis of his fantasy. Remind him of the difference between reality and the fantasy, which drives his actions.

Pt: I talked to Jennifer on the phone and told her I thought we could still work things out between us. I asked her if I could come over to her place and talk things out, but she said, "Don't even think of it. I don't ever want to see you again." But I figured, "Hey if we don't talk this through, we can't ever work this out." So I drove over to her place and went up to the door and pushed the doorbell. She comes to the front door, opens it, curses at me, throws a glass of water on me, and then tells me to get the hell out of her life. Can you believe that? [*Defense: denial in deed. Rather than face reality, he acts as if reality does not exist.*]

Th: You went to see a woman who said she didn't want to see you again. [*Point out the denial through fantasy.*]

Pt: But how are we going to work this out? [*Denial per se.*]

Th: I want to work things out with a woman who doesn't want to work things out with me. [*Point out the denial in fantasy.*]

Pt: But shouldn't we be able to work things out? [*Defense: denial in fantasy.*]

Th: Shouldn't reality be different from what reality is? [*Mirror his denial in fantasy.*]

Pt: Shouldn't it? [*Defense: denial in fantasy.*]

Th: No. Reality is what it is, but you act as if Jennifer should want to work things out when she doesn't want to. And when you act as if you can ignore reality, you get hurt and set yourself up for more punishment. Don't get me wrong. You can keep on acting as if reality doesn't exist, but we shouldn't be surprised when reality shows up.

Pt: [*Chuckles.*] That's true.

DENIAL IN THE THERAPIST

Since all people use denial occasionally, that includes therapists. Here are common forms of denial in therapists:

- "Maybe this person doesn't have any feelings." [*Therapists deny that a patient has feelings to avoid the mixed feelings toward the therapist.*]
- "Maybe his wife is horrible." [*Therapists may unwittingly agree when patients split and devalue their spouses. Always question all-bad images of other people.*]
- "I think this patient is a monster without empathy." [*Therapists can engage in splitting, calling a patient a psychopath or a narcissist. When we deny the humanity of the person, viewing him as all-bad, we deny our own humanity.*]
- "This patient has a severe superego and needs to install the therapist's healthy superego." [*The therapist denies the patient's wish to become well when he should mobilize it. Instead, the therapist believes the patient should take in the therapist's health: "therapy" through projection and splitting.*]

Any time we view a person as all-good or all-bad, we should question ourselves. How are we colluding with denial and splitting? What are we trying to split off and deny? Whatever we pathologize in others, we need to accept in ourselves.

PRIMITIVE DENIAL

The neurotic patient sees reality, but he denies the feelings and meanings that reality triggers. The neurotic may also deny reality. But a simple reminder may help him see it. In contrast, the fragile patient denies *her* factual experience of reality. "If I deny that reality exists, I don't have to have feelings about it." A woman saw a puddle of water in the driveway and said to her mother, "Mom, it rained last night." Her mother replied, "There's no water in the driveway." The water in the driveway was a fact in reality. The mother denied it. Further, she asked her daughter to deny her experience of reality. A relationship based on the denial of reality set off a lifetime of crippling self-doubt.

Primitive denial can suspend reality testing temporarily in near-psychotic patients. When we address their denial, we can help them see reality and the feelings it triggers. *Primitive*, or *psychotic*, *denial* can lead to a permanent loss of reality testing in people with a psychotic level of character structure. (Psychotic denial is beyond the scope of this book. See Berney et al. [2014]; Jacobson [1967]; Kleiger and Khadivi [2015]; and E. Marcus [2017].)

The more of reality we perceive, the more we feel. The less affect tolerance we have, the more reality we have to deny. Thus, fragile patients have to deny any aspect of reality that can trigger overwhelming affects. The degree of denial correlates with affect tolerance. (See table 9.1.)

Table 9.1 The correlation between affect tolerance and type of denial

Level of Affect Tolerance	Type of Denial	What Is Denied
Highest affect tolerance	No denial	Nothing.
High affect tolerance	Neurotic denial	Patients do not deny reality, just the feelings and meanings triggered by reality.
Low affect tolerance	Primitive denial	Perception of factual reality is denied, but reality testing can be restored.
Very low affect tolerance	Psychotic denial	Perception of factual reality is denied. Reality testing cannot be restored.
No affect tolerance	Manic denial	The opposite of reality is claimed to be reality. Chronic anticipation of the best or worst both attempt to avoid pain. (See Jacobson 1971; Lewin 1950.)

Patients can use the following forms of denial:

Negative hallucination: I do not see what is here.

Positive hallucination: I see what is not here—what I prefer.

Conversion symptom of anesthesia: I do not feel a part of my body that exists.

Depersonalization: What is happening to me is not happening to me.

Derealization: What is real is not real.

Delusion: Whatever I deny leaves a hole in reality, which I fill in with my delusion and believe. A woman whose psychotic break led her to drop out of college had a delusion that she was God. The delusion in fantasy restored a loss in reality.

All defenses used by fragile patients include an element of denial: *Psychotic denial:* An addict nearly died from a drug overdose the day before. In the session, he claims, "I am not addicted." [*He denies internal and external reality.*]

Projection: I attribute a quality to you and deny that it exists in me. "You are angry; not me."

Splitting: I split apart my mixed feelings and deny they are connected: "I don't have a problem, but you shouldn't listen to me." Splitting and dissociation always involve denial (Dorpat 1985). Thus, whenever dealing with defenses, we address denial.

When the fragile patient's higher-level defenses collapse, he can rely on only more primitive defenses. "But the more he denies, the more he isolates himself; the more he projects, the more he isolates himself; the more he distorts, the more he isolates himself. Ultimately, he can win his own peace of mind only at the price of giving up reality" (Post and Semrad 1965, 84).

PSYCHOTIC DENIAL

In psychotic denial, the patient refuses to acknowledge aspects of internal or external reality. He is blind to what he denies. Frequently, the denial is found in what he does not mention (Berner et al. 2014). In the following example, a father reveals his denial regarding his three-year-old son, whom he has ignored following a divorce.

Th: What's the problem you are having with your daughter?

Pt: She is always wanting more, but I can't do more because I have so many things to do. With my son, things are easier because he doesn't need me. [*Psychotic denial: he not only denies his internal feelings about failing his son, he denies external reality: his son needs him.*]

Th: Your three-year-old son doesn't need you. [*Mirror the patient's denial to assess whether his split-off reality testing will arise within him.*]

Pt: No. [*The absence of a sigh (absence of inner conflict) and denial of reality suggest that this may be psychotic denial.*]

BLOCKING DENIAL IN A NEAR-PSYCHOTIC PATIENT

A woman entered treatment following a six-month hospitalization. She had been hospitalized over thirty times and had not worked in years. Since she could not live independently, she lived in a halfway house for the mentally ill. She missed the session before I left for vacation and the one when I returned. Unable to put her anger into words, she acted it out. The following vignette comes from our first meeting after the two missed sessions.

Pt: I don't know what happened.

Th: That's very surprising because you've been very consistent.

Pt: I can tell you what happened the night before. I get so nerveracking, nerveracked over something at [her halfway house], that's all I can think about. Like, when I was sick, I was sick for a week. I wore the same thing every day because I was sick. I didn't feel like getting up or washing or anything like that. I mean, I wasn't dirty dirty. I had on this red top and these like, um, running pants. And sweats. And this guy says to me, his name is Ike, he says to me, "You shouldn't wear those three things three days in a row." I get all excited. I get all upset about these corrections, and it's all I can think of. [*Her thoughts do not form a logical sequence: a sign of thought disorder due to excessive anxiety. No signs of striated tension in her body.*]

Th: Did this happen last night?

Pt: No. What's happened is, because of my room situation, and I didn't keep it up. And now they're checking on me all the time. And so now my room has to be perfect. And it's been pretty good. But I overworry it.

Th: Last night, something happened?

Pt: No, nothing happened. I asked Ike if he would help fix the edges of my bed so it would go over the bed. And I had a fit. One would think, "What's the big deal?"

Th: You find yourself getting really angry.

Pt: Not angry but really anxious.

Th: Really anxious over this detail.

Pt: Over the detail. What if they find the bed's not made right?

Th: And you had this thought, "What if the bed's not made right?" And you got really anxious.

Pt: And I can't think of anything else.

Th: And all you could think of this morning was "What if they find out?"

Pt: So I went down to the clinic instead because I knew I needed help.

Th: What were you afraid would happen if they saw that your bed wasn't perfectly neat?

Pt: They would throw me out. [*Projection: she often equated people with her projections. Then she acted out in response to her projections. Deactivate her projection to restore reality testing.*] They made me write a contract that said—they make me do these stupid things. They made me write a contract that said I will obey the rules. I will keep order in my room. I will keep clothes hung up.

Th: But was there any evidence that if your bed wasn't made right that they would kick you out? [*To address denial, remind the patient of reality.*]

Pt: No. [*No sigh means no rise of anxiety. Thus, she still denies reality. Address the denial until her anxiety returns to the striated muscles. Once her affect tolerance rises, she will spontaneously reveal something about reality that contradicts her denial.*]

Th: We see that there was an idea you had in your head [*her back tenses up and she pushes back against the chair: a sign of striated tension*] that actually didn't fit the facts. [*Contrast reality and fantasy.*]

Pt: It didn't fit the facts. [*Again, her back tenses up and she pushes back on the chair.*] And, so, what happened was—I just—I get—so overwhelmed by the whole jell of it [*slight cognitive confusion*], and then you were out. And then, you know, I hadn't thought of that. And I thought all week of you coming back.

Th: Right.

Pt: I recognized every minute that I wished you were here.

Th: And then last night and this morning you had this fantasy that they would kick you out if your bed wasn't perfect. And then you thought that fantasy was the same thing as reality. [*Contrast reality and fantasy.*]

Pt: Right. [*No sigh, so she still denies reality.*]

Th: And then you were even more terrified.

Pt: And they had someone come up and check it for me.

Th: Right. Because you couldn't make this distinction between your fantasy—[*She interrupts me to stop the rise of feelings. They rise when I contrast reality and fantasy. The intervention worked. Otherwise, no anxiety would rise, and no defense would be necessary to stop that rise.*]

Pt: Right. [*No sigh.*]

Th: —and reality. Reality being that even if your bed isn't perfect, they'll still let you stay.

Pt: Right. And so, I just didn't think of where I was supposed to go this morning. [*Defense: shifting topics. Rather than elaborate on the difference between reality and her fantasy, she resumes her story.*] I knew I was anxious. And I went to the clinic. And when I was at the clinic, I realized, holy cow! That's where I should have been. To see Jon. Which is what I really wanted to do all week.

Th: We see that you had this fantasy that they would abandon you, but—[*I begin to contrast reality and fantasy. She interrupts me: a sign that contrasting reality and her fantasy triggers anxiety.*]

Pt: I get a lot of fantasies.

Th: But you had a fantasy that they would abandon you if your bed wasn't right. But the fact is that they would never abandon you just because your bed wasn't right. Right? [*Contrast reality and fantasy.*]

Pt: No. But they have cited me for not hanging my clothes up. [*Instead of changing the topic, she begins to argue with me: a sign of increased affect tolerance.*]

Th: Sure. They've gotten on you when your room is messy. But the fact is that even if your bed isn't perfectly neat, you still get to live there. They're not going to abandon you just because of that. [*Contrast reality and fantasy.*]

Pt: Right. But then they said you can't wear the same clothes three days in a row, so I went out and bought some clothes. [*Again, she argues.*]

Th: Right. But you see, again, you thought that if you didn't have different clothes every day that they would abandon you. But that's also not true because you wore the same clothes three days in a row and all they said was you need to change your clothes. [*Contrast reality and fantasy. Keep reminding her of the elements of reality she denies.*]

Pt: Right.

Th: They didn't say you're out of here. [*Contrasting reality and fantasy.*]

Pt: No. They didn't say "you're out of here." [*Her back tenses up, and she rises in her chair. Anxiety in the striated muscles indicates that her denial is decreasing.*]

Th: You had this fantasy that they were going to abandon you, but the fact is they didn't. [*Contrast reality and fantasy.*]

Pt: No, they didn't.

Th: There's something about abandonment that came up, but it has nothing to do with [the halfway house], right? [*Contrast reality and fantasy.*]

Pt: No. It didn't. The abandonment felt overwhelming. I thought, where am I going to go?

Th: But the fact is, it had nothing to do with [the halfway house]. [The halfway house] never said, "We're going to abandon you." When you wore clothes three days in a row, they didn't say, "You're out of here." They said, "Change your clothes." [*Contrast fantasy and reality.*]

Pt: In fact, they said, we want you to budget your money better because we don't want you to buy any more clothes. [*For the first time, she reveals an aspect of reality that contradicts her projection and denial. Reality testing is improving. She reaches for a cup of coffee: a sign of dry mouth. That means the sympathetic nervous system is getting activated, sending more blood to the brain. It should function better very soon.*]

Th: Right. They were saying you don't need to do that. Right?

Pt: Right.

Th: We can see that you had a fantasy that they were going to abandon you. But they are glad to have you stay there as long as you need to. [*Contrasting her fantasy with reality.*]

Pt: Right.

Th: We know there was some feeling about abandonment, but it had nothing to do with the halfway house. Right?

Pt: And the feeling of abandonment felt—I felt you were abandoning me a little bit. [*Now the projection returns home.*]

Th: Of course you did. So maybe this is where we need to look because this is where the feeling of abandonment belongs. Because I did abandon you for a week, right? [*Referring to my vacation.*]

Pt: And I abandoned you this morning. [*Smiles.*] [*Referring to the missed session.*]

Th: That's right, and I think you abandoned me the morning before I left.

Pt: I think I did.

Th: There's a lot here about abandonment.

Pt: I feel like if the one guy abandons you, it's better to abandon him first.

Th: So you abandoned me because I had abandoned you.

Pt: I didn't think of it; it wasn't conscious.

The patient had been diagnosed as psychotic. But her responses to intervention revealed a borderline level of character pathology. Blocking her denial and projection triggered anxiety in the striated muscles. Her resistance shifted from splitting and projection to intellectualization. Her reality testing improved. And she could accept feelings inside rather than project them outside. She no longer believed that the half-way house was angry with her and wanted to abandon her. She could face her anger toward me for going on vacation. This session did not end her use of projection and denial. But her responses to interventions suggested that she would have an excellent outcome. And she did.

In near psychosis, defenses avoid reality. Otherwise, reality would be in conflict with how the patient perceives it. Even tiny reality stimuli can trigger high levels of affect. Thus, denial of reality must be everpresent. Otherwise, a sudden encounter with reality will trigger anxiety and a loss of mental boundaries.

WORKING WITH DENIAL, PROJECTION, AND SPLITTING IN A RECOVERING DRUG ADDICT

In the previous case, the therapist reminded the patient of reality when she used denial. This built her capacity to tolerate reality and her feelings about it. In the following case, a young man denies his awareness of problems. He argues with others, hoping they will try to convince him that he has problems that he denies having. Since he does not admit having a problem, I cannot remind him of a problem he has not admitted. Instead, I mirror his denial and block his projections to build his capacity to tolerate the feelings triggered by having a problem and asking for help.

> *Th:* What is the problem you'd like me to help you with?
>
> *Pt:* Uh, I don't know. [*Denial.*] I'm in a substance abuse program, and they suggested that I see a therapist. [*Projection: he doesn't think he needs to be there; the program thought he should.*]
>
> *Th:* Mm-hmm.
>
> *Pt:* Mm-hmm. I don't think there are any obvious reasons. [*Denial.*]
>
> *Th:* Mm-hmm.
>
> *Pt:* You know, like, there's been no like acting out or anything weird, no instability, but—
>
> *Th:* Mm-hmm.
>
> *Pt:* But, like, a lot of people see therapists so . . . [*Denial of a problem.*]
>
> *Th:* Yeah.
>
> *Pt:* And they suggested . . . [*Projection.*]
>
> *Th:* Yeah.
>
> *Pt:* So here I am! [*He invites me to do therapy when he sees no need for it.*]
>
> *Th:* Yeah. Well, they seemed to think it was a great idea for you to see a therapist, but, um, still kind of wondering why *you* came. [*Block the projection.*]
>
> *Pt:* Oh, I—I guess I'm interested too. Um, a lot of people, like I said, a lot of people see a therapist, so I'm like, "Why not?"
>
> *Th:* Mm-hmm.
>
> *Pt:* Ya know.
>
> *Th:* Yeah.
>
> *Pt:* They're paying for it.
>
> *Th:* Yeah. So what's the problem you'd like me to help you with? [*Block the projection and denial.*]
>
> *Pt:* I don't—I don't think that I have a problem. [*Denial.*]
>
> *Th:* You're a lucky man. [*Mirror denial. It might seem peculiar to mirror his denial. However, if I insist that he has a problem, he could deny*

*having one. And the conflict would be between me and his denial. If
I mirror his denial, only one person can be in conflict with it: him.*]

When I mirror this patient, I do so with a friendly, matter-of-fact
voice. I never forget that behind his denial is a man who longs for a
better life and hopes for help in therapy. That is the person we speak
to. There should be no judgment, sarcasm, or anger. After all, *if* he has
no problem, that *is* a wonderful position to be in. *If* is the key. When
angry with such a patient, you cannot mirror his denial because you
judge rather than identify with him. Therapists can struggle with this
intervention. They want to identify with sanity. But then they refuse to
identify with the patient's wish to deny reality. Empathy requires us to
identify with the patient's entire conflict.

Each of us has used denial to avoid painful facts in our lives. Thus,
when we meet a patient who uses denial, we meet ourselves. If we can
relate as one defense user to another, we can listen without judgment
or desire. Completely accept the patient's denial. We can be tempted to
accept one aspect of the patient and reject his denial. But whatever we
reject in the patient, we reject in ourselves. If you reject the patient's
denial, your mirroring will reflect your inability to accept him as he is.
Instead, your radical acceptance of him allows him to accept himself,
and in that mutual acceptance change occurs.

We do not mirror him to make him change. We mirror him as an
act of identification, accepting him as he is since we don't need him to
change. And since we don't need him to change, the wish for change
can arise within him.

Therapy requires our faith that the patient is something more than
his denial, his defenses, or even our understandings. Radical acceptance. Mirroring can express this implicitly through your manner,
feelings, and words. With your acceptance and faith in his potential,
much is possible. Without it, nothing is.

Pt: Well, I don't think that it's a problem that I don't already know
the answer to. [*Denial: omniscience—"I don't need answers since I
have them."*]

Th: That's wonderful. [*Mirror denial.*]

Pt: That sounds—that sounds some kind of weird, doesn't it? But no,
but . . . [*Splitting and denial: he sees that his denial sounds weird,
then he denies it.*]

Th: No, but if you have a problem, and you know the answer to it, that's a fantastic situation to be in, isn't it? [*Mirror denial.*]

Pt: Yeah.

Th: Yeah.

Pt: But I guess adhering—adhering to the solution is . . .

Th: It may be that you don't have a problem—don't get me wrong. That would be fantastic for you. But, obviously, if you don't have a problem, there'd be no reason to see a therapist. Right? [*Mirror denial and splitting: "I don't need therapy, and I am in a therapist's office." Mirror the contradiction between what he says and does.*]

Pt: I don't, maybe. I mean, I have a drug—I have a—I have a . . . okay. I've been in treatment for four months and . . . [*Mirroring his splitting causes a rise in anxiety, which makes it difficult for him to speak for a moment. As I mirror his denial and block his projections, the wish for therapy rises in him. This causes a brief rise of anxiety, manifested by laughter and sudden movements.*]

We continue two minutes later in the session.

Pt: You know, most people there have—[*Projection.*]

Th: Well, if we don't go to "most people"—[*Block the projection.*]

Pt: We don't want to . . . okay. I'll—I'll say it this way.

Th: Mm-hmm.

Pt: Some of the reasons they give for using, the counselors— [*Projection.*]

Th: Well, if we don't go to the counselors' solutions and their explanations, I'm really just interested in your own opinion. [*Block the projection.*] You know if you have a problem that you need my help with, and it may be that you don't. Don't get me wrong; some people don't have a problem. [*Mirror his denial.*]

Two minutes later, I check in again.

Th: I just have to check with you if there's a problem that you need my help with here.

Pt: Yeah. I don't know. [*Denial.*]

Th: Mm-hmm.

Pt: I don't think so. [*Denial.*] Which doesn't mean that I'm right. [*Splitting: "I don't think I have a problem; I may not be right." He makes two contradictory statements without noticing the contradiction.*]

Th: Uh-huh.

Pt: You know, ummm.

Th: You don't think you have a problem, and, at the same time, you may not be right. [*Mirror splitting.*]

Pt: What does that mean? Does it mean something? [*Projection: rather than explore what his contradiction means, he asks me whether it means something.*]

Th: No. I'm just reflecting. [*Block the projection.*] I don't know if it means anything at all. [*Block the projection.*] It's just, you're reflecting. On the one hand, you say you don't have a problem. At the same time, you're saying you may not be right. We're noticing, okay, there's two statements. They're side by side. And we're just noticing that. [*Mirror splitting.*]

Pt: Okay.

Th: On the one hand, you think you don't have a problem. On the other hand, you think, "Maybe I'm not right." [*Mirror splitting.*]

Pt: Yeah. I think I'm a pretty well-rounded, umm, individual, uh. [*Denial. His life was in ruins after dropping out of college and a decade of drug use and unemployment.*]

Th: Mm-hmm.

Pt: Uh, uh.

Th: Fantastic! [*Mirror denial.*]

Pt: Uh, am I perfect? No. Of course not!

One minute later, he continues.

Pt: But there's a drug addiction. So that's why I'm here today because the folks, the powers that be, and—and—and I'm open. I'm not—it's not that I'm here to satisfy any kind of . . . [*Denial and projection.*]

Th: Yeah, well, that's why we're just trying to figure out, you know. I mean, the drug addiction, I gather, is being dealt with there. And so we're just trying to find out—[*His drug rehabilitation center helps him with his addiction, it is a nonproblem for therapy. I asked about his psychological problem. As a defense, he invites me not to focus on it.*]

Pt: Yeah.

Th: —is there an internal emotional problem, psychological problem—

Pt: Right!

Th: —for us to work on. You know, and there may not be. [*Mirror denial, block projection.*] And that's why I'm just having to check in.

Pt: I'm interested in that. What do we—how do we start exploring that? [*Projection: he asks me to tell him how to explore his problem rather than explore it himself.*]

Th: Well, we first have to find out if you have some kind of problem that you'd like me to help you with. And you're not sure just yet. [*Block the projection. If I answered his question, I would reinforce his projection that I should explore his problems and tell him how to do it. Then we would have a battle of will between us.*]

Pt: No.

Th: And we're just having to notice that although you're here in a psychologist's office, you're not sure that you have a psychological problem. [*Mirror splitting.*]

Pt: Yes.

Th: Yeah.

Pt: Duly noted. [*Anxiety.*]

Th: Yeah. Isn't that fascinating?

Pt: Yeah.

Th: So a man without a psychological problem finds himself in a psychologist's office. [*Mirror splitting.*] Isn't that the wildest thing?

Pt: Maybe.

Th: Yeah.

Pt: I don't know what to say. [*Projection: he acts as if I know what he should say.*]

Th: Yeah, I don't either. [*Block the projection of knowing. If I state that he has a problem, he can deny knowing this and argue with me.*] That's why I'm asking because I'm here to help people with psychological problems. And so naturally I'm asking you if there's some kind of emotional/psychological problem you need my help with and—Yeah! There may not be. [*Mirror denial.*] We're just kind of checking in to find out if there is.

Pt: Hmm! I don't know. I can't think of anything. [*Denial.*]

Th: Yeah. Yeah.

Pt: I don't know what to do. [*Denial and projection. He takes a passive stance, inviting me to tell him what to do, and then he could either comply or defy. The conflict would be between us. Hence, my next intervention.*]

Th: Yeah, well, take your time. No rush. [*Block the projection.*]

Pt: Are you waiting for me to say, like, "Oh yeah! There's that thing!" Is that what—[*Projection. And he raises his voice, becoming more anxious. He expects me to say what his problem is. Expressing his projection ("you waiting for me" when he is waiting for me) verbally, rather than through action (passivity), is progress.*]

Th: I'm not waiting for anything. [*Block the projection.*] I'm just noticing that a guy without a psychological problem finds himself in a psychologist's office. And I'm just thinking, "Oh, yeah! Very interesting." [*Mirror splitting: he wants my help (he came to my office) and denies that he needs help. To avoid this conflict, he splits off his desire for help and attributes it to me.*]

Pt: Ummm. [*Defense.*]

Th: Because I have no right to be digging around or exploring anything with you. I mean if you don't—[*Block the projection.*]

Pt: But I thought that's what the purpose—the purpose of coming to—[*Projection.*]

Th: Oh, no.

Pt: —to dig.

Th: Oh, no. I have—

Pt: —and search. [*He projects that I will dig in him. Then he would have to protect himself from an invader. Since he projects that I want to dig, he unconsciously wants to dig within himself and do the work of therapy. The wish is conscious but projected onto the therapist—an important move forward.*]

A few minutes later in the session, he says that everything is going well in his life.

Th: Your family's fine. Your career is fine. [*Mirror denial.*]

Pt: Yeah. Well, career's not "fine." [*Emergence of a problem.*]

Th: Oh.

Pt: It's not fine. But I'm fine with it not being fine. Because I know that it will—things will come together. [*Splitting: "It's not fine, but I'm fine with it not being fine." Denial: "Things will come together." His awareness of a problem lasts for a second before he denies it. Even so, it is progress.*]

One minute later, he continues.

Pt: I feel great! I don't feel discouraged or, um, troubled. [*Negation: he simultaneously denies and reveals his problem (feeling discouraged and troubled)—another sign of progress. He reveals his problems within the defense of negation ("I don't feel troubled" meaning "I do feel troubled").*]

Th: Mm-hmm.

Pt: I don't feel troubled in any way. [*Negation: he does feel troubled.*]

Th: That's wonderful. [*Mirror negation.*]

Pt: This was suggested. [*Projection.*]

Th: Yeah.

Pt: It wasn't like a recommendation. So that's why I kind of wish I had something. Because I do want someone who's studied, you know, to be able to say, "Look, maybe you should take a look at this." [*Emergence of a desire for therapy and for a realistic confrontation.*]

Th: Mm-hmm.

Pt: But I don't—I don't know. You know. Um. [*Denial: his desire for therapy emerges, followed a second later by denial—another sign of progress.*]

Th: But you're saying family life is good; emotionally, you're good; career now will be good. No kind of psychological problems you've been aware of. It's almost like there's nothing to explore, really. Seems like things are going great. [*Mirror denial.*]

Pt: But in your experience, isn't there always something to explore? [*Projection of his wish to explore himself—another sign of progress: the wish emerges within the defense of projection.*]

Th: I mean, it's not a matter of whether there's something I think should be explored. Because this is not my job to tell you what you should explore. [*Block the projection by reminding him of reality.*] It's really for me to find out if there's something you would like to explore for your benefit. I'm really here to serve you. So if there's something that you want to explore—that you think is a problem for you—then that's something I would help you with. [*If I had agreed that there was something to explore, I would have voiced his wish, which he could deny. When I avoid being the spokesperson for his wish, it can rise in him instead.*]

We resume a few minutes later in the session.

Th: Yeah. But in this case, it's not clear that you have anything that you need to talk about. Family's going well. . . . [*Mirror denial.*]

Pt: Well, there's always. Everybody has something to talk about. It's just that there is no problem. There's no emotional thing that's happening with me that's making me do things that are not appropriate. [*Denial.*]

Th: That's fantastic. [*Mirror denial.*]

Pt: You know.

Th: That's fantastic. [*Mirror denial.*] If only everyone were so lucky not to have psychological problems. I mean, in a way, you've reached a terrific position. [*Mirror denial.*]

Pt: Yeah.

Th: To be in a position where you don't have psychological problems— that's a wonderful position you've gotten to. [*Mirror denial.*]

Pt: Um.

Th: You seem to be having some reaction to my saying that. [*Point out feeling.*]

Pt: Ah, it almost sounds sarcastic, in a way. Like I'm the only one in the whole world who doesn't have psychological problems. [*Projection: when I mirror his irrationality, he can see it more objectively. This helps him to reflect on his thinking.*]

Th: No. [*Block the projection.*]

Pt: I'm not saying that I don't have psychological problems. I'm just saying that I don't have psychological problems that are so serious that they're making me act out. [*Denial.*]

Th: That's fantastic! [*Mirror denial.*]

Pt: Or behave in a way that, and a lot of people are like that. [*Denial.*]

Th: Exactly. [*Mirror denial.*]

Pt: It's not that rare. [*Denial: he uses one fact (many people do not need therapy) to deny another fact (he needs therapy).*]

Th: Exactly. Not everybody needs to go to therapy. Obviously. And it may be that although you have some psychological problems, they're not enough to make you act out. So not really requiring the help of a psychologist. [*Mirror denial.*]

Pt: Yeah! And that's really where I'm at. [*Denial.*] I don't think that it requires—but I came. [*Splitting: "I don't have a psychological problem, and I came to a psychologist's office." But he sees no contradiction between these two thoughts.*]

We resume a minute later.

Pt: Which doesn't mean that there might not be something deep-rooted—[*awareness of a problem*] I—I don't think there's any—[*Denial.*] But who knows? [*Splitting.*] I don't know. [*Denial.*] This is your area of expertise. This is what you studied for. [*Projection: he invites me to know for him—dissociation of his capacity to think.*]

Th: Yeah, but . . .

Pt: I don't know. [*Denial.*]

Th: But I have no right to go digging around in you. [*Block the projection.*]

Pt: Well, you said that three—three or four times. I don't know that you don't have a right because I'm here. And you're being paid to dig. [*Projection. I deactivate the projection so he can acknowledge his wish to explore his inner life. Otherwise, he will oppose my wish to explore or deny that there is anything to explore.*]

Th: But why should I dig if there's nothing to dig for? [*Block splitting: "You should dig, but there is nothing to dig for."*]

Pt: I don't know that. You can't take my word for it. You're the expert. [*Projection. Acknowledging that we can't take his word is a sign of progress.*]

Th: I absolutely have to take your word for it. [*Block the projection.*]

Pt: How can you take my word for it? I don't know. [*Denial.*] I mean, who's going to come in here and say, "Doc, I'm crazy." I mean, who? [*Projection: a huge sign of progress. He acknowledges through the projection that what he says sounds crazy.*]

When patients project, therapists may try to return projections back prematurely: for instance, "You really want to dig inside yourself, but you attribute this to me." Or "So you see that what you are saying here is crazy." In response, patients may experience a sharp rise of anxiety, project, and then act out or leave. Blocking projections non-interpretively allows for a gentle rise of feelings and anxiety. Then he can recognize what he projects gradually. The therapist must not give voice to the patient's dissociated capacity for thinking.

When patients do not see a defense, help them see it. This man's defenses were denial, splitting, projection, and projective identification. Since he had not declared a problem, I could not explore one. I could mirror his denial of a problem and block his projection that others saw his problem. As I mirrored his denial and blocked his projections, his longing for health and awareness of denial emerged.

As those feelings rise, some fragile patients flood with anxiety. Others project and then threaten to act out. Given his twelve-year history of drug abuse, we should not be surprised at his impulsivity. At this point, I explore the feelings coming up now that lead him to want to leave the session. If he can bear them, he will not have to run away from them or the session.

As I focused on the feelings toward me that were leading him to want to quit, he admitted his anger. But eventually, he denied ever feeling angry. At that moment, I felt a strong feeling rise within me. I took it as a sign that a high rise had also taken place in him. That meant I could address his denial more directly. The following section shows how I do so.

Now we shift to twenty minutes later in the session.

Pt: People have told me that I'm very straightforward. You know. I'm very in touch with my emotions. [*Denial.*]

Th: Oh, I don't think you're straightforward at all. [*Point out reality.*]

Pt: Hmm. That's weird.

Th: No, you should get that feedback. I don't think you're straightforward at all. [*Point out reality.*]

Pt: Why? Because of the little thing we just did there.

Th: No. Just the way you come across. You have a very friendly facade that you put on that people relate to. But no one actually gets to meet you. You're very practiced, and you're very smooth, and most people don't catch on to you. But you have a very smooth, friendly facade that people really like, and they really enjoy it. And they think they're in a relationship with you. But you know they are not anywhere near the inside of you. You've got a very practiced way, a very smooth way. It's very nice, and it's very polite. And it's very smooth. And there's a little bit of nervousness to it in the way that you present. So people get, "Hmm, he seems kind." They think, "Maybe he's energetic. But no, he's just kind of nervous, and he can't—he's kind of like this guy moving all over." It's like where you have the cups and the pea but you never find the pea. It's always missing. And they're looking for the pea, and no matter how many times they move that cup, they never find it. And you've got it down. And it's very, very good. But you're not straightforward. You are the master disappearer.

And for some reason, at some point in your life, you learned it was important not to be found. And it was important to be someone who could look like they're there but is never findable. And you've got it down in a very, very good way. Very good, and it's smooth and I imagine it works almost all the time. It does mean no one really gets to know you. And it does mean your close relationships don't get too close because no one really gets to know what's. You are kind of the eternal mystery for people. But you're the man who's the master of the disappearing act. And you're good. You're very, very smooth. And you're actually very, very smart too. I don't know if anyone's told you that. I don't know how well you did in school, but you've got a great deal of native intelligence, and you have learned, somehow, to be not findable. [*Point out his defenses against emotional closeness.*]

Pt: And you got all that from the fake argument we had?

Th: And the opening fifteen minutes. But you're good, and I bet it works almost all the time. Like 95 percent of the time, I bet it works. [*To deactivate any projection that I am critical of him, I compliment him on how easily he can keep people at a distance.*]

Pt: So, the 5 percent of the time it doesn't work, are those the people who are just not buying it? [*Alliance: his curiosity shows that he wants to understand himself more deeply.*]

Th: People don't buy it or people actually want to be close and it takes them a while to figure out this is not going to happen. [*Point out the price of his defenses: no emotional closeness.*]

Pt: Hmm. I'm speechless.

Th: But it's important for you to know that you are very smart. And you're very good at this. And that's why most people don't catch on. You're very good at this. I'm not sure what happened to you that made it so important to not be visible or findable. You would know best about that. But people don't usually do this unless somebody important to them, early in life, made them learn, "Wow, if I show up in some particular way emotionally, it's going to be big trouble." And you learned what it is they liked to see, what it is they don't want to see. And you just make sure they see whatever it is they like to see. And you're good. [*Accept his defense and compliment him on it to deactivate any projection that I am critical of him.*]

Pt: But everyone doesn't like me. I mean there are people who choose not to like me from the first moment. [*Rise in engagement: he reveals the projection that drives his behavior.*]

Th: Yeah.

Pt: For no reason.

Th: Well, no, they have a reason. They catch on to the facade, and they don't like it. There will always be some people who catch on to the facade, and they're just not going to like it. You're going to have some people who don't catch on. And that kind of works on them—they enjoy the friendliness. But some people catch on to the facade and the rapid patter that gives them the idea that there's some kind of facade you're putting up. There are going to be people who react to that. It's not that they don't like you. They don't like the facade. They never get to meet you. That's the deal to be really clear about: people aren't rejecting you. They're not reacting to you. They're reacting to the facade. They're meeting the facade. They never get to meet you. But that facade and that patter and all that, there are going to be some people that just can't stand it. They're just going to want to stay away. But even though they will have rejected your facade, they will have never met you. They will have no clue about who you really are. And they'll often equate that facade with you, not realizing they don't have a clue. They don't know who you are. And there's a part of you that knows that. [*Differentiate him from the facade so he will not feel criticized. Point out the price of the facade.*]

Pt: Hmm.

Th: A part of you knows you're actually being unfairly judged. Part of you knows they're judging a facade, but they haven't actually.

met you. And part of you really resents that they equate you with the facade and that they don't see who you really are underneath. [*Differentiate him from his facade.*]

Pt: So what do I do about that? [*Projection. On the one hand, his question is a sign of health. However, he also invites me to tell him what to do. Then he could oppose me.*]

Th: You don't have to do anything. [*Block the projection.*]

Pt: What do you mean?

Th: You don't have to do anything. [*Block the projection.*]

Pt: I'm living a lie. [*Alliance. For the first time, he speaks honestly about his facade and his denial—a huge movement forward.*]

Although my language is paradoxical, it worked because I had faith in the person behind the denial. I accepted him, his denial, and his lie unconditionally. Paradox is not a technique; it is the result when we embrace the entire person, his contradictory longings, anxiety, and conditioning. When we accept the entirety of his conflict, our comments embody this paradox. Relate to the whole patient as he is—the man we have met with all his defenses and the person whom we have not yet come to know.

Later, we learn that he doesn't let anyone get close to him. He believes 99 percent of people will slit him open if he shows his underbelly. No wonder he puts up the armor of invincibility: to keep an attacker at bay. Thus, we need to identify, clarify, and restructure his projection to establish a conscious therapeutic alliance.

A spectrum of affect tolerance requires a range of interventions for denial. The woman with psychotic symptoms needed reminders of reality that conflicted with her denial. The drug addict denied that he had a problem and projected that I thought he had one. In his case, I had to mirror his denial because he projected his awareness of reality. If I voiced his sanity, I would have reinforced the projection of his capacity to think. I would have described reality, and he would have denied it, arguing with me. And if I had challenged him, I would have enacted his fear that I wanted to slit open his belly.

When we remind the moderately or severely fragile patient of reality or mirror denial, feelings and anxiety rise, leading to cognitive/perceptual disruption and projection. As soon as denial breaks down, regulate his anxiety while he faces reality and the feelings it triggers. Or deactivate his projections to build his affect tolerance.

DENIAL AND DISSOCIATION OF THE PATIENT'S SANITY

Sometimes, fragile patients present with their psychotic beliefs and project their sanity onto the therapist (Bion 1959; Bychowski 1952; Kernberg 1975, 1977b; M. Klein 1975b; Rosenfeld 1987). They split off the nonpsychotic capacity to think from the part of the mind flooded by affect (E. Marcus 2017). A patient may hold a pseudodelusional idea or act out. But he wards off his capacity for reality testing. We have to elicit his disavowed sanity so he can join us as an ally. To do so, the therapist must bring out the patient's capacity for reality testing, which he has split off and denied (Kernberg 1977b). Then together, we can observe his psychotic beliefs (Brandt 1968; Katan 1954; Kernberg 1975, 1977b; Lotterman 2015; Marcus 1992/2017; Nelson 1962, 1968; Spotnitz 1986; Wexler 1952).

Ordinarily, the therapist will do the following:

1. Remind the patient of reality to improve reality testing
2. Address any defenses he uses to ward off awareness of his capacities for reality testing
3. Help him face the feelings that his denial wards off

As these feelings rise, anxiety will rise. If the therapist does not immediately regulate the anxiety, the patient may project again. This can lead to another regression to pseudodelusional thinking or acting out. Thus, regulate anxiety immediately to prevent another regression.

Reminding severely fragile patients of reality does not always work. They register and see reality. But they split off and project their awareness of reality onto the therapist. They act as if the therapist sees reality while they do not, and they may treat the therapist as if she is crazy when she describes reality. They dissociate their awareness of reality (which is still intact). Then they project it onto the therapist where they can argue with it, deny it, or ignore it.

Some advocate interpretation (Bion 1959; M. Klein 1975b; Rosenfeld 1987). But interpreting a projection may reinforce it. For instance, the therapist who interprets the projection of thinking is the one thinking about reality. That can reinforce the patient's projection of his sanity onto the therapist. Instead, the therapist can mirror the denial of reality testing. If the therapist does not give voice to the patient's sanity, there is only one place that awareness can rise: in the patient.

The following vignette illustrates how mirroring denial can increase reality testing. The patient asked for a consultation after having seen dozens of therapists for over thirty years. He still suffered from crippling depression and was not functioning. He had told me that therapy would not work. No therapy had worked. He wondered if he was a hopeless case. Since he asked for a consultation, he wanted to get well, yet he professed no hope for therapy, and he projected his hope onto the therapist.

> Th: Since nothing has worked, we must honestly approach this without any promises or expectations of benefit. Since all previous efforts have met with failure, most likely this effort will fail as well. We can agree to explore and assess responses in a joint effort to see if together we can find some way of working that is effective for you. Until then, it makes no sense to me that you would spend that much money for a long-term commitment that would probably be worthless. [*I do not voice his disavowed hope, which he would deny. Instead, I mirror his denial of hope, which he had described as "realistic."*]

> Pt: You don't sound very promising. If you already think this will fail, why bother to do it at all? [*He argues with this voice in me rather than submit to the voice within himself.*]

> Th: Given your past experience, there is a very high likelihood that we would fail. However, as long as both of us recognize that, and as long as we are willing to conduct several assessment sessions, I am willing to try for several times with you. [*Mirror his denial of hope.*] Only you can know if this would be worth doing for you. If you decide this is not worth the bother, I will understand.

> Pt: I'm willing to try, but your pessimism is not encouraging. [*Now he argues with "my" pessimism. This strengthens the realistic side of his personality.*]

> Th: I don't view it as pessimism. Just realism. Pessimism is an irrational attitude about the future. You have seen seventy-two different therapists at last count. Your past experience is not very encouraging. We just need to be realistic. [*I mirror his claim that*

pessimism is just realism. When others pointed out his irrationality, he maintained that he was being "realistic."]

Pt: What's the point of sessions with you if you think they'll fail? Seems like a waste of time and money. My case shouldn't be this difficult. I had a relatively healthy childhood. I don't suffer from an illness like schizophrenia. I have no substance addictions. I shouldn't be this mentally ill. Treatment for me should be pretty straightforward. I don't understand why nothing has worked. I just want to live a normal life. Instead, I have voices in my head all day that punish me. I'd like to get them to stop. How hard can that be? [*Now he voices his hope and speaks more realistically.*]

Th: Only you can know if it would be worth it. If you bring the voices to our session, we can find out what they have to say. And we can find out why they say it. You can listen to the voices or to yourself. Your call.

Pt: I'm willing to do some sessions with you. I just thought being more optimistic might be a better way to approach therapy. Saying it is likely to fail isn't encouraging. I'd rather take a more neutral attitude that it may or may not work. I have no idea if therapy with you will fail as I can't predict the future. [*Now he voices a realistic attitude without splitting off his hope.*]

The patient seeks out therapy while denying that it can help. Through his stance of splitting and denial, he expresses irrational despair. And he invites the therapist to express rational hope (his dissociated sanity). If the therapist voices the patient's split-off sanity, the patient can remain identified with his insane defenses. When I mirrored his hopeless attitude, I blocked the projection of his sanity. Eventually, he voiced the previously denied awareness of reality. When he expressed his belief that therapy was hopeless, he denied the existence of his sanity. He used denial to ward off his hope and his awareness of reality. He split off his awareness of reality while denying its existence (Kernberg 1975; Wurmser 1989). Then he encouraged the therapist to voice the split-off and denied awareness.

LYING AS A FORM OF DENIAL

In contrast to the forms of unconscious denial, lying is a form of conscious denial. The liar is the person most aware of the truth since he works so hard not to say it (Bion 1970). Lying is a unique form of denial because it involves projective identification. The liar not only denies reality. Through his lies, he often provokes others to be the location of his disavowed sanity. As a result, they feel compelled to argue with his lies, thereby voicing his dissociated sanity. And then he can dismiss them as deluded when he has a deluded view of the world.

The liar needs the other person to agree with his lie (Dorpat 1985). Through lying, the liar tries to have omnipotent control over what others think. Thus, he claims, "These are alternative facts," "There is no such thing as truth," and "All truths are just constructions." By insisting that you believe his lies, he invites you to a master-slave relationship where you are enslaved to his lies.

Assertions that deny the existence of truth are, in fact, truth claims. Through these strategies, the liar tries to control people's ability to perceive a lie. "If you tell a lie enough times, people will eventually believe it." Liars have no interest in reality, only in controlling how people perceive it.

Some liars are not content with their lie. They need others to share it, thus betraying the insecurity that comes with living the lie. The liar needs others to repeat his lies. Otherwise, his illusory world will disappear. Thus, he has to tell his lies repeatedly to compensate for their lack of reality. But no lie became truer when shouted more loudly.

While all of us avoid the truth at times, the lie strips the listener from access to the truth. A lie tries to infect the other person with falsehood. If other people believe the lie, the liar is not threatened. But the truth keeps bumping into the lie, threatening the liar's fantasy—which to him seems to be his very being. That's why truth threatens the liar so much.

The lie threatens the very basis of therapy: being honest with each other about the truth. Thus, if the patient continues to lie, therapy cannot succeed. We have to find out why he lies. Often, he lies to have omnipotent control over a projection he has placed on you. What is he afraid you will see or think? (Kernberg 1984; Kernberg et al. 1989).

People may lie to avoid being judged if they told the truth. Or a liar may lie in order to cheat. Or he might lie because he imagines you would attack him. A drug addict may lie to avoid seeing how he is killing himself through drugs. And he may hope the therapist buys the lie and colludes with his suicidal quest. Lying is a treatment-destructive defense. Thus, we identify lies as well as their function.

Address lies in a factual, nonjudgmental voice. Otherwise, the patient will experience you as a judge to avoid his own internal judgment. We do not judge the liar's behaviors. We describe them. A sharp rise of judging thoughts in you may signal a rise of guilt in him (Racker 1968). Observe the urge to judge without acting on it so his unspoken guilt can rise.

SUMMARY

The less affect tolerance the patient has, the more of reality he must deny. When patients deny the meanings and feelings triggered by reality, we can remind them of contradictory facts. When they deny responsibility, we can remind them of how their defenses cause their suffering. When they deny their perception of reality, the therapist can mirror their "blindness." Then they can begin to experience their perceptions and thoughts about reality. When they deny reality, we can remind them of reality.

When denial breaks down, the patient perceives reality. And he experiences the feelings he avoided. The sudden awareness triggers massive anxiety. At that moment, regulate anxiety immediately. Then help him face reality and the feelings it triggers to build his affect tolerance. Doing so makes it possible for him to experience reality and think about it.

RECOMMENDED MATERIALS

For a DVD illustrating how to work with an addict who denied having a problem, visit the ISTDP Institute at https://istdpinstitute.com/dvds/treatment-resistance-addict-no-problem/.

CHAPTER TEN

Splitting

Learning to Tolerate Complex *Feelings and Realities*

And if spirit has fallen away from me why does a skeleton
follow me?

—PABLO NERUDA, *LATE AND POSTHUMOUS*
POEMS 1968–1974

When someone we love frustrates us, we face two contradictory
feelings—love and anger. Bearing these contradictory facts
and feelings triggers anxiety. Why? Feeling rage toward the person we
loved endangered an early relationship. Thus, we may split apart mixed
feelings to avoid the anxiety and guilt they trigger (Freud 1938/1963b;
Fairbairn 1952/1969; Grotstein 1985; Kernberg 1975; M. Klein 1975b).
For instance, we may split apart contradictory experiences to avoid
mixed feelings.

> *Pt:* Doug overdosed yesterday. But he didn't use today. [*The patient*
> *splits apart two contradictory facts. Denial: pay attention to the*
> *pleasant fact and ignore the unpleasant one.*]

We may split those feelings apart so we experience only one feeling
toward that person. The patient ignores the overdose because feeling
anger toward the boyfriend she loves makes her too anxious. She has
difficulty bearing both her love and anger.

> *Pt:* I hate Doug. He lied to me. [*Splitting: she feels anger toward some-*
> *one she loves. But she splits off the love and claims to feel only hatred.*]

We may split two aspects of the person apart so we see him as all-good or all-bad. By splitting off her loving feelings, she avoids the anxiety she would feel if she faced the fact that she loves this man with whom she is enraged.

Pt: Doug is a piece of shit; I always knew he was just a druggie. [*Splitting: rather than see Doug as a whole person who has good and bad traits, she views him as all-bad.*]

We can split two feelings apart, so we see ourselves as all-good or all-bad. By splitting off what is good, she avoids the anxiety that would be triggered by feeling rage toward a good man whom she loves.

Pt: What a screw-up! I told him what would happen. But did he listen? No. Good riddance to bad rubbish. I'm better off without him. He doesn't deserve someone like me. [*Splitting: rather than accept her good and bad traits, she views herself as all-good and him as all-bad.*]

By splitting off her anger, guilt, and regret, she avoids the anxiety that would be caused by facing her love for him and her guilt and regret over her choices.

Pt: It's my fault. He wouldn't have used if I hadn't kicked him out. It's just another piece of evidence of what a piece of crap I am. [*Splitting: rather than see her good and bad traits, she views herself as all-bad.*]

By splitting off what is good in herself and placing it on her boyfriend, she can preserve him as all-good while viewing herself as all-bad. While this preserves an idealized image of him, the self-devaluation destroys her.

Splitting can separate contradictory facts in the external world or the mixed feelings they trigger. For instance, a patient says, "I'm anxious. I don't want to be here." He splits apart two facts: he does not want to be here, and he came here. Or a woman says, "I hate this therapy. When is our next appointment?" She splits apart her hatred of therapy and her desire for it.

We can also split apart our contradictory experiences of our loved ones. Every person we love pleases us and displeases us. If we cannot bear the complexity of others, we can split and view them as all-good or all-bad. If we cannot bear our complexity, we can split and view ourselves as all-good or all-bad. Or we might claim to feel only pure love or rage. In each case, we deny the complexity of others, ourselves, and our feelings. Splitting separates what belongs together: rage toward the person we love. When we split, we view people in all-or-nothing terms, not as complex beings with contradictory desires.

A fiancée whose boyfriend hit her might say, "I love him, and I know he loves me." She separates the hitting boyfriend from the loving boyfriend. Otherwise, she would have mixed feelings. As a fragile patient, if she experiences those mixed feelings at the same time, she will flood with anxiety and experience cognitive/perceptual disruption. To avoid the cognitive/perceptual disruption those mixed feelings trigger, she splits off and denies the beating and the anger it triggers. She remembers the split-off image of the all-good boyfriend who loves her. We might believe the boyfriend doesn't love her because he hit her. But that would be our splitting: viewing him as all-bad. If you see him as all-bad, she may defend him as all-good, and your outer conflict will prevent her from experiencing her inner conflict.

Splitting and primitive denial ward off not only contradictory feelings, thoughts, and desires but also the awareness of external reality (Freud 1911/1958f). Splitting allows us to perceive part of reality and ignore the rest. If the patient sees only her boyfriend's love, she will not see the beating, nor her feelings in response to it. Blind to the problem, she can have no desire to deal with it.

In the following vignette, the therapist helps her to link contradictory perceptions she split apart.

Th: The boyfriend who beat you also loves you. That can be confusing. [*Invite the patient to see his contradictory actions and her contradictory feelings.*]

Pt: But he gave me flowers. [*Splitting and denial: she focuses on the flowers, not the beating.*]

Th: Yes. The boyfriend who gave you bruises also gave you flowers. [*Invite her to notice his contradictory actions and her contradictory feelings.*]

Pt: This is making me anxious. [*Unable to see her mixed feelings, she feels the anxiety those feelings trigger.*]

Th: Something about seeing that the same boyfriend who gives you bruises also gives you flowers makes you anxious. [*Seeing both facts triggers mixed feelings and anxiety. This helps her tolerate contradictory feelings without splitting.*]

If she denies the beating and sees only his love, she could view her boyfriend as all-good (Fairbairn 1952/1969). But then she sees herself as all-bad, which would justify further beatings. The therapist helps her link contradictory facts that she split apart.

In another vignette, a drug addict at an outpatient rehabilitation clinic claimed he wasn't using drugs. His urine screen revealed that he was.

Pt: I'm telling you: I wasn't high. [*Splitting: separating what he says from another fact—the urine screen.*]

Th: Your lips tell me you weren't high, and your bladder says you were on cocaine. [*Invite him to see the contradiction between what he says and reality.*]

Pt: But I need to be here.

Th: Your lips say you need to be here, and your bladder says you need to be in inpatient treatment. [*Invite him to notice how he tries to split what he says apart from what he does.*]

Pt: Why do you keep mentioning my bladder?

Th: You wonder why I listen to your lips and your bladder. [*Invite him to notice his splitting.*]

Pt: Okay. It wasn't my urine. [*Denial.*]

Th: Okay. We can take another urine screen right now. [*Block denial of reality.*]

Pt: This isn't a good time for that. [*Conscious lying.*]

Th: This isn't a good time for your bladder to talk at the same time as your lips? [*Invite him to notice his splitting and denial.*]

Pt: Look. I've got to go. [*His feelings are triggering anxiety so he wants to walk away from his feelings and leave them in the office.*]

Th: Something about listening to your bladder makes you anxious now.

Pt: Are you calling me a liar? [*Progress: he admits that he is lying, albeit within the defense of projection.*]

Th: Not at all. Your bladder has been very honest. It has always been telling the truth. [*Deactivate the projection.*] It's just that you seem to get anxious when we listen to your bladder. [*Point out causality: facing his self-destructive addiction triggers anxiety.*]

Pt: [*He looks at the floor.*] So if my bladder says I've been using, are you going to kick me out? [*Projection: he already kicked himself out of treatment through using.*]

Th: If your bladder tells us you've been using, it will tell us you need some inpatient treatment. [*Remind him of facts to deactivate the projection.*] But then you and I will have to find out what your crime is that makes you treat yourself like you don't deserve to get well.

Pt: Jane died of an overdose when I gave her the fentanyl.

Th: I see. It's sort of like since you gave her the murder weapon, you killed her. And you've been trying to kill yourself ever since. Shall we see if we can turn that around?

Splitting prevents the patient from bearing love and anger toward the same person. For instance, a woman loved one man. And she had an affair with another man whom she hated and devalued. Unable to integrate love and hate within one relationship, she split them between two relationships.

The fragile patient may split apart mixed feelings toward the therapist. She may idealize the therapist as all-good and then view herself as all-bad. Or she may view the therapist as all-bad and herself as the all-good victim (M. Klein 1975b). Splitting prevents her from learning to bear mixed feelings toward the therapist. Like all people, her therapist gratifies and frustrates. And she feels mixed feelings—a sign of our humanity.

Accepting our contradictory feelings and impulses allows us to become integrated. Splitting says, "This feeling is not-me. I hate it." Integration says, "I am what I hate" (Schneider 2009). When the therapist invites the patient to recognize what she has split off, he encourages her to accept her inner life, excluding nothing. "The hateful act generates madness, and the act of acceptance creates sanity" (Symington 2002, 24). Each of us has an unconscious longing within ourselves to love everything we hated and tried to eliminate. In that embrace we become free.

THE ORIGINS OF SPLITTING

Ideally, caretakers respond to the child's frustrations with compassion. They accept his anger when reality does not match his fantasy, and they do not ask him to be happy when he is not. When parents accept his feelings, the child learns to accept himself and reality too. But with too little compassion and too much frustration, rage floods the child.

His immature brain cannot grasp how the same person who gratifies also frustrates. The parent he loves makes him angry. Unable to tolerate these contradictory feelings, the child uses denial and splitting. He thinks there is a good baby who elicits a good mother and a bad baby who elicits a bad mother (L. Hill 1955; M. Klein 1975b). He interprets the world through the lens of splitting: "What is good is me; what is bad is not-me" (Sullivan 1953a).

The child splits off what leads to despair so he can maintain hope in a hopeless home. If frustration increases, splitting takes other forms. With the paranoid view, "What is good is me; what is bad is you." The patient splits off his rage, places it in the other person and judges it there. He escapes the torments of his inner judge by becoming the judge. With the depressive view, "What is good is you; what is bad is me" (Guntrip 1968/1993). If the child believes he is the source of badness, he can make himself good and loveable again. Then he need not face the despair of being unable to make his parents love him as he is. These examples illustrate how splitting arises from massive anger when depending leads to pain (Sullivan 1953a, 1953b).

We can split off awareness of an aspect of reality (Freud 1938/1963b). We can split apart mixed feelings triggered by reality. Or we can split apart opposing qualities in oneself or others (Fairbairn 1952/1969; M. Klein 1975b). "The outcome always lies in two contradictory attitudes" (Freud 1938/1963b, 204).

Some view splitting as the universal basis for defenses in children (Fairbairn 1952/1969; M. Klein 1975b). But others (Ferenczi 1933/1994) note how childhood trauma triggers splitting. Ferenczi likened the violence of trauma to a psychic rape. The perpetrator must split off and deny the child's thoughts and feelings to abuse the child. Then the abuser tells the abused child to split off and deny his painful experiences: "You like this, don't you?" A mother, beating her son, says, "This hurts me more than it hurts you." Without splitting off and denying the feelings of the child, the abuser could not abuse children. To survive, the child identifies with the aggressor's defenses of splitting and denial. A patient who suffered under a tyrannical, verbally abusive father said, "If I ever write an autobiography, it will be entitled 'Pardon My Existence.'" Years later, she committed suicide.

When the abused child grows into an adult, we meet a seemingly capable person. But behind his facade, we find a "murdered ego" who wants nothing further to do with "the remains of the actual person" (Ferenczi 1932/1988, 10). And these remains appear as a mass of affect. These "two personalities . . . do not want to know about each other. . . . [They] are grouped around different impulses, [to avoid] subjective conflict. The task of the analyst is to remove this split" (Ferenczi 1932/1988, 38–39).

Through splitting, the patient hopes for an all-good person who never frustrates him. Or he fears an all-bad person whom he believes *wants* to frustrate him. The rage he feels erases his loving memories. As a result, he relates to an image of an all-bad person whom he thinks wants to deprive him, abandon him, or hurt him. He views others through the lens of splitting: "I was stupid to believe her. I should have known she was a liar all along." The person who splits may personalize this experience and believe he is bad: "I'm unlovable."

Children may learn the defense of splitting from parents. A recovering drug addict told me, "In the morning, my mother would ask, 'Who are you today? The good Jane? Or the bad Jane?'" The child learns to split off part of herself to be loved: "Do I lose a feeling to keep my mother? Or do I keep my feeling and lose my mother?" To avoid the pain of loss, the child splits off the feelings her mother cannot tolerate. Later, in adulthood, pain triggers cognitive/perceptual disruption in fragile patients. And to avoid the cognitive/perceptual disruption, they split apart the mixed feelings.

Suppose the therapist cannot offer the patient a different appointment time she wants. She will feel frustrated. However, unable to tolerate her frustration, she may split off her rage and project it onto the therapist. Now she believes the therapist is angry and wants to punish her. Unless the therapist can help her recognize this pattern, she might leave therapy. She won't be leaving the therapist. She will leave a distorted, all-bad image that she equates with the therapist.

When addressing splitting and denial, the key factor is hatred. Hating hides the hated. Whatever others hated in us, we hate in ourselves, split off, and deny. And what remains is the absence of our split-off being. The more we hate ourselves, the more we hide, make invisible, and try to eradicate: "The function of madness is the strangling of sanity" (Symington 2002, 82). In therapy, we embrace the rejected. If we do not accept what is within us, what we reject will destroy us.

WHAT DO WE SPLIT?

The patient splits off the core of her trauma, a feeling, desire, thought, or impulse. For instance, a woman splits off and projects her will onto the therapist. Perhaps years of verbal abuse crushed her will. In a coherent split, she splits off and projects her will. Then she opposes it, as perceived in the therapist. Her stance is coherent as well as the therapist's: he supposedly wants something from her.

If she was more severely traumatized by physical and sexual abuse in childhood, we might see fragmented splitting where she splits off many aspects of herself. One man split off his capacity to observe himself by fearing people who could see him. He split off his capacity to listen to himself by fearing people who were listening to him. And he split off his judgments of himself, hearing four voices who yelled at him. His fragmentation resulted from massive splitting and projection. The degree of splitting reflected the traumas he suffered, the early age when he suffered them, and the number of years they continued.

When considering splitting, we should remember that there is no resistance (Bion 1965) unless "there is also a contrary feeling that becoming conscious of something alien in oneself is the most useful approach" (Symington and Symington 1966, 123). The question becomes, what is this split-off alien aspect of the patient? The patient would not need to deny, split, or project if feelings and urges were not coming up to awareness to be embraced and accepted. In the following vignettes, the therapist tries to find the split-off alien element longing to be reunited with the patient.

INVITING CONSCIOUSNESS OF SPLITTING

To help these patients, we invite them to experience mixed feelings inside without splitting. We can invite the consciousness of split-apart feelings, perceptions, thoughts, and urges in the following ways.

Remind the Patient of the Denied Split-Off Reality

A patient may present one aspect of a person while splitting off and denying a contradictory fact about that person. To help the patient experience mixed feelings, the therapist can remind the patient of elements of reality she has split off and denied. The therapist reminds the patient of a fact she mentioned earlier but has forgotten in this moment.

Pt: My dad is a narcissistic psychopath.

Th: And at the same time, you mentioned that he sat by your hospital bed until you became conscious after your overdose. This must be confusing, how the same father who infuriates you also loved you, took you to the hospital, and sat by your bed while you were on the verge of death. [*Remind her of both sides of her father. Build her capacity to tolerate the mixed feelings she has toward her father.*]

Mirror the Split-Apart Realities

A recovering drug addict in the initial session shares her split-apart realities.

Pt: I don't think I have a problem, but you shouldn't listen to me.

Th: You don't think you have a problem, and, at the same time, you say I shouldn't listen to you. [*Mirror the contradiction/splitting.*]

Mirror Splitting and Denial

When the patient offers a fact and a contradictory fantasy (denial) without awareness of the contradiction (splitting), the therapist can mirror the denial and splitting to build her affect tolerance.

Pt: My husband is having an affair. But, really, he loves me.

Th: The husband who is making love to another woman loves you too. [*Mirror the contradiction/splitting.*]

Mirroring the patient's splitting triggers mixed feelings, which evoke anxiety. Regulate her anxiety (see chapter 1) while reminding her of the mixed feelings. Continue until she sighs and can intellectualize about her mixed feelings. You may need to invite the consciousness of splitting many times to build her affect tolerance.

Table 10.1 illustrates how splitting occurs within the spectrum of fragility as the patient's affect tolerance improves. Initially, at 10 percent of feelings the patient may have a delusion. As affect tolerance increases, at 10 percent of feelings, the patient engages in a less primitive form of splitting rather than use delusions or hallucinations. Later, at 10 percent of feelings, the patient starts to experience cognitive/perceptual disruption instead of using splitting right away. This represents an important boost in anxiety tolerance. The patient can tolerate some anxiety without immediately splitting or projecting. With further increases in affect tolerance, at 10 percent of feelings the patient will start to sigh and intellectualize. Having now established a threshold of anxiety tolerance in the striated muscles, we build the amount of feeling the patient can bear while anxiety remains in the striated muscles.

Table 10.1   Levels of fragility and forms of splitting

Level of Fragility	Form of Splitting	Intervention
Severe	The patient uses primitive forms of splitting before experiencing cognitive/perceptual disruption. The patient can split the personality, or split off of a feeling, thought, or impulse and project it into a delusion or hallucination.	Inviting the consciousness of split-apart feelings, thoughts, and impulses within the defense until the patient experiences cognitive/perceptual disruption. Then cognize about the process to solidify the increase in affect tolerance.
Moderate	The patient uses splitting before experiencing cognitive/perceptual disruption. Splitting of contradictory feelings, ideas, or impulses can occur.	Invite the consciousness of split-apart feelings, thoughts, and impulses until the patient starts to experience cognitive/perceptual disruption. Then cognize about the process to solidify the increase in affect tolerance.
Mild	The patient tolerates some cognitive/perceptual disruption before splitting.	Brace to build affect tolerance as soon as cognitive/perceptual disruption occurs and before splitting occurs.

During splitting, no signs of anxiety in the striated muscles, such as sighing, will rise. Why? When patients split feelings apart, love and rage cannot combine to trigger anxiety. Mirroring splitting and denial builds the capacity to bear mixed feelings until anxiety rises in the striated muscles.

When fragile patients feel pure rage toward an all-bad figure, they feel no hesitation about punching that person because they have split off the love that would trigger guilt and self-restraint. If you are a beginning therapist, do not mobilize a split-off feeling of pure rage. That may encourage the patient to split, project, and act out. Instead, build his capacity to bear *mixed* feelings. He has feelings that want to kill a person he loves. When feelings rise too high, he splits them apart. At that moment, we cannot necessarily appeal to reason because reason cannot be found. It is split off too. Regulate anxiety to restore the capacity to think and reflect. Then explore mixed feelings gradually to help the patient think while feeling.

More advanced therapists can explore the patient's split-off rage toward another person. Once the patient has experienced this rage, remind him of his split-off love. This triggers his guilt and builds his capacity for bearing mixed feelings without splitting.

Pt: I just imagine beating the crap out of him until he is battered on the ground. Stuff coming out of his head after smashing it to bits. [*The patient has imagined expressing his murderous rage toward his father. But no anxiety or defenses arose because the pure rage resulted from a defense: splitting off his loving feelings.*]

Th: Tremendous rage toward your father. Imagining beating him to death, stuff coming out of his head. And at the same, positive feelings toward your dad, who paid for your rehab and visited you in the hospital. [*Remind the patient of the positive, loving memories he had split off. Bring his hatred and love together to build affect tolerance.*]

Pt: He didn't mean anything by that. [*Denial to avoid the mixed feelings.*]

Th: That's how you try to erase his love, just like you try to erase your loving heart. Just like you wanted to beat the crap out of him, you have tried to beat the crap out of your heart. But we see there are these mixed feelings coming up.

Pt: [*Sighs.*] [*Reminding the patient of his mixed feelings and guilt triggers a sigh. His anxiety has moved into the striated muscles.*]

Never encourage split-off rage. Help patients tolerate their mixed feelings.

Mirror Split-Apart Feelings That Trigger Dissociation

A fragile patient who experienced cognitive/perceptual disruption dissociated in the session. He experienced himself as if he was outside his body. What triggered this defense? He had just described a conversation with his uncle who told him that his father once yanked the patient out of his highchair and threw him against the wall.

Pt: I just went away. [*He dissociated.*]

Th: Sure. Wonderful you see that. Something about this memory about your dad triggered some feelings. You got anxious. And you went away. [*Cognize about the triangle of conflict.*] Do you see that too?

Pt: I didn't see that.

Th: Right. Okay. Something about this memory about your dad triggered some feelings. You got anxious. And you went away. Are you present now? [*Cognize about the triangle of conflict: mixed feelings, anxiety, and dissociation.*]

Pt: Yes.

Th: I wonder, from the perspective of the adult man you are now, what feelings do you have as you look back at that father? What feelings do you notice toward him?

Pt: [*Fists form.*] I feel angry.

Th: Right. You feel anger toward him. So we notice when you get angry at your dad, you get anxious, and you go away. Shall we take a look at this anger toward your father? [*Cognize about the triangle of conflict so he sees his feeling and the defensive function of dissociation.*]

Mirror Secondary Dissociation to Promote the Experience of Mixed Feelings

A fragile patient experienced cognitive/perceptual disruption in the session. The therapist regulated the patient's anxiety. Then the patient wanted to run away.

Th: Right. Although you obviously wanted to come here today so I could help you, another urge comes up that wants to run away. What do you notice feeling as you notice these two urges inside you: wanting to come and wanting to run away? [*Invite him to notice his two contradictory urges.*]

Pt: I'm dizzy again. I feel like I am behind a shield now. [*Anxiety is in cognitive/perceptual disruption followed by dissociation.*]

Th: As soon as you get anxious, notice how you go behind a shield.

Pt: Like I'm over there. [*Dissociation.*]

Th: Right. You want to be here so I can help you. This triggers anxiety. Then you go out of your body. You notice that too? [*Point out the triangle of conflict: connecting, anxiety, and dissociation. The function of dissociation becomes clear.*]

Pt: I know I shouldn't. But this feels safe. [*Projection of will, as if he should comply with my desire.*]

Th: Obviously, you should go as far away from me as you think you need to do to feel safe. What happens as you let yourself go out of your body, as far from me as you think would be helpful to be safe? [*Encourage him to dissociate to deactivate his projection that I want him to be close. As a result, he can experience his wish to be close. And he can observe what he feels while he dissociates.*]

Pt: But now I feel like telling you to ask me about my feelings. [*He becomes aware of his desire inside himself rather than project it onto me. Then he doesn't have to distance from the desire he attributed to me.*]

Th: Are you sure you want me to ask about your feelings?

Pt: Yes. Otherwise, we'll just talk about how I go out of my body.

Th: How do you know that this is really what you want for yourself? [*Make sure his will is online.*]

Pt: [*Small sigh.*] Because when you ask for my feelings, something different happens in me. [*The sigh indicates that his will is online. Minutes later he shared a memory of running away from his mother when she beat him.*]

SPECTRUM OF AFFECT TOLERANCE AND THE FORMS OF SPLITTING

Patients split apart contradictory feelings, perceptions, thoughts, and behaviors to avoid anxiety. So we invite them to bear these contradictory experiences. Their affect tolerance yields a range of responses. Table 10.2 illustrates that spectrum.

Table 10.2 Splitting across the spectrum of character structure

Inviting Consciousness of Splitting	Assessment of Character Structure
Th: You mention that you don't need therapy, and, at the same time, you say that you might. *Pt:* [*Sigh.*] I know that sounds contradictory. I guess it's just that I don't like coming here. [*Awareness of splitting.*]	A neurotic patient has anxiety in the striated muscles.
Th: You mention that you don't need therapy, and, at the same time, you say that you might. *Pt:* [*Patient becomes dizzy.*] I'm sorry, what did you say? [*Anxiety is due to awareness of splitting. The anxiety temporarily prevents the patient from thinking clearly.*]	A mildly fragile patient experiences cognitive/perceptual disruption but does not project. He can tolerate cognitive/perceptual disruption temporarily without projecting.
Th: You mention that you don't need therapy, and, at the same time, you say that you might. *Pt:* Yeah. I don't think I need therapy. Maybe I do, but, no, I don't think so. [*Denial and splitting.*]	A moderately fragile patient does not experience cognitive/perceptual disruption because he engages in splitting and denial to keep mixed feelings apart.
Th: You mention that you don't need therapy, and, at the same time, you say that you might. *Pt:* Yeah, that's what I said. So what? Does that mean something? [*No awareness of the splitting. Splitting off of the capacity for self-observation, followed by projection.*]	A severely fragile patient does not experience cognitive/perceptual disruption because he uses splitting and denial to keep mixed feelings apart. He acknowledges what he said. He just denies that it meant anything. In addition, he splits off, denies, and projects the ability to think about reality onto the therapist.
Th: You mention that you don't need therapy, and, at the same time, you say that you might. *Pt:* I didn't say I might need therapy. That's what you said. [*Primitive denial of what he said and projection.*]	There is perhaps a psychotic level of character structure due to the primitive denial of reality. He splits off and projects the awareness of reality onto the therapist. Work on primitive denial to assess his reality testing to determine if he is at a psychotic or borderline level of character pathology.

ALL-OR-NOTHING THINKING AS THE RESULT OF SPLITTING

When patients cannot tolerate mixed feelings, they cannot tolerate the complexity of life. If someone discerns a flaw in the patient, he may hate himself and believe he is all-bad. Or the patient pursuing a doctoral degree may believe that his dissertation is useless unless he achieves a grandiose goal. The patient who cannot wait may insist, "It's now or never!" The person who cannot tolerate indecision during a period of ambiguity may try to convince others to tell him what to do. The enraged patient may fear that he will explode, a reasonable fear if he splits off the awareness of his loving feelings. Table 10.3 illustrates common forms of all-or-nothing thinking and the alternative integrative thinking we hope to promote.

Table 10.3   All-or-nothing thinking due to splitting

All-or-Nothing Thinking Due to Splitting	Integration
Others are "good" or "bad"	Others have mixed qualities
Attack entire problem or avoid it	Approach a problem part by part
"It's now or never!"	Ability to tolerate delay
Murderous rage or denial of anger	Adaptive partial expression of anger
My way or your way	Shared responsibility and cooperation
This way or not at all!	Ability to consider a variety of options
Irrational optimism or irrational despair	Realistic appraisal of what is possible
Ideal expectations or despair	Stable realistic goals
Instant recovery or no progress	Improvement by increments over time
Either I'm special or nothing	I am special and nothing special (Schulz 1980)

> **Principle:**   *All-or-nothing thinking results from splitting. Thus, assess what is being split off by all-or-nothing thinking to help the patient with the task of integration.*

WORKING WITH SPLITTING AND VOICES: THE NEAR-PSYCHOTIC SUPEREGO

Near-psychotic patients suffer from a severely harsh superego. Unable to bear it inside, they often project it outside onto a voice. Next the critical voice attacks them and encourages them to kill themselves. If the patient is projecting his wish to live, the therapist can mirror the patient's superego to induce conflict within the patient.

Pt: I just want to kill myself. [*Patient implicitly projects the wish to live onto the therapist: "Convince me not to kill myself."*]

Th: Why live if you don't want to? [*Mirroring the superego blocks the patient's attempt to project his wish to live onto the therapist. As the wish to live rises in the patient, anxiety rises.*]

Pt: [*Sighs.*] Aren't you supposed to convince me to live? [*Projection of the wish to live. Moving from implicit to explicit projection is progress.*]

If the patient is splitting and not projecting, mirroring one side of the split (the superego) will make the patient more suicidal. He will split again and think you want him to die. Here, we can explore the wish to die within the defense of splitting.

> Th: May I talk to this part of you that wants to die? [*This allows the therapist to imply that part of the patient does not want to die. If he said this explicitly, this patient would deny it.*]

The therapist can attack the voice the way the voice attacks the patient. The therapist joins the patient against the voice to differentiate him from the voice and to restore reality testing (Levin 2018).

The following woman had received various psychotic diagnoses and was on four antipsychotic medications. She had suffered many traumas in childhood. Previous therapists told her she had multiple personalities as the result of growing up in a satanic cult, an experience for which the patient had no memory. As a result, she became much worse. She heard a voice for years, named Myra, which constantly criticized her, telling her she deserved to die. Many therapies had ended in failure. The following vignettes come from the beginning phase of her therapy.

> Pt: I feel unsettled about what I just said regarding my progress. I realized Myra was saying to me, "You think you are a safe person? Ha! You think you are decent at all? You think you deserve anything other than suffering for what you have done? For who you are?" I tell her, "Leave me alone. You are not helping me." Now I feel tears. I think they are my tears of truth rather than my tears of despair. But, who knows. This recovery thing is likely to be anything but linear.

> Th: If I were to talk to her, I would say, [*I look to the side now, not directly at the patient*] "Myra, you fucking bitch! How dare you fuck with her mind like that. You know as well as I do Myra that she is the one who is safe and *you* are unsafe. She is decent, and *you* are indecent. Just look at this indecent way you treat her. You're just feeding her lies like always. And all because you are jealous, seeing that she is beginning to relate to reality instead of you. And you can't stand it. You know you are losing control over her. She's not believing your lies so easily."
>
> [*Since the voice is a defense, I talk to it to differentiate the patient from her defense. My yelling at the voice makes the patient experience me as defending her against that defense/voice. It also gives*

her a vision of a day when she could defend herself against this punitive voice. I interpret within the hallucination by saying that the defense is unsafe and indecent. By saying these things about "Myra," I can clarify the price of the defense to the patient. The defense also functions as a transference, an object relation. The voice acts like an abusive controlling, lying parent with an abused, terrified child. I interpret the transference within the defense of hallucination: "And . . . you are jealous, seeing that she is beginning to relate to reality instead of you. And you can't stand it. You know you are losing control over her. She's not believing your lies so easily."

Later we learned that her father had been an abusive, controlling liar. By yelling at the hallucination, I defended the patient in a way her mother never had. Since the voice yelled at the patient, I yelled at the voice. We meet hatred with strength (Winnicott 1960/1965a). The transference had a verbal form within the hallucination. And, by being yelled, it also took the form of enactment. Thus, the counterenactment offers an interpretation within the language of enactment (Havens 1976; Loewald 1989). Later, we learned that this hostile, hallucinated voice also represented the rage she felt toward her mother.]

Pt: [*Giggles.*] I love to hear you say that. Especially when you called her by name. Then I know you are speaking to her. You can believe me when I say that I will think about that over and over. I will most likely print that out on a small index card. I will take it everywhere with me. I would say you have no idea what having you say that means to me, but I don't have to. I know you know. And I really do love you for caring.

Th: Let me know what happens when you talk back to Myra. These voices always blame us for what they are doing.

Pt: I will. She was saying to me a little while ago, "Everyone will leave you if you get well. You know this. You are not strong enough without me." I didn't even realize she was speaking to me at first. It was this awful sinking feeling that made me stop and listen. I didn't say anything this time. I believed her, I think.

Th: I would say to her, "Myra, you bitch! No one is going to leave her when she gets well. You're just afraid because you know she is going to leave *you* when she gets well. You know this. She has already started leaving you, and you are scared shitless, Myra. And, Myra, you know that *you* are not strong enough to survive without her. *You* are the one who is scared."

Pt: I can hear that she wants to fight with you. I don't want to fight with you. I feel a great tension inside. Like she can't decide who she wants to hurt. And I am not sure that she is wrong. I want to believe what you just said. I think I need to pay a lot of attention to the differences between her and me. She says we are identical psychic twins, but she loves people who hurt me and hates people who love me. She tried to run every good person away from me. She says I don't know what is good for me. But she threatens to kill me all the time.

Th: I would say to her, "There you go again, Myra, telling the same old lies. You are not her psychic twin. Myra, you are a parasite, and she is the host. You love people who hurt her because *you* want to hurt her. You hate people who love her because you realize that once she lets them love her, she will drop you in a second. You try to get her to run away from people because once she lets them love her, she will run away from you. You're actually afraid, Myra. And then you lie again, Myra. You say she doesn't know what is good for her. The only reason she is still alive is because she does know what is good for her. Myra, *you* are the one who doesn't know what is good for Marie. You threaten to kill her because the truth is starting to kill you. After all, she exists. You don't, Myra. You, Myra, are just a thought in her awareness."

Pt: Thank you. I notice that my chest constriction is less, and the familiar urge to cry is there. The truth type of tears. I am aware of that thought. And, yes. It went away. And yes, I am still here.

Between sessions, I encouraged her to talk back to her voice any time it tried to abuse her. After several sessions, she no longer reported hearing voices. Several months later, she stopped taking her antipsychotic medications. Now she struggled with internal self-criticism instead of hearing a critical voice. Later, she was able to feel angry with me without criticizing herself.

Patients need our support when the psychotic part of the mind dominates the nonpsychotic part (M. Evans 2016). If the psychotic part tries to kill the patient, we hospitalize her. The psychotic part of her mind argues with us, but the sane part feels relief. In this case, I could support the nonpsychotic part of her mind by yelling at the psychotic voice. In a less severe case, we could talk to the sane part of her mind about the difficulties she has managing the psychotic part of her mind.

A CASE EXAMPLE OF SPLITTING OFF THE CAPACITY FOR REALITY TESTING

Isolation of affect and repression keep feelings from the patient's awareness. In contrast, splitting can remove the capacity for awareness. The patient, faced with a frustrating reality, unconsciously denies reality. Part of him sees reality while denying that he sees it. The first attitude takes reality into account. The second attitude disavows reality and replaces it with a fantasy. "The two attitudes persist side by side without influencing each other. Here is what might be called splitting of the ego" (Freud 1913/1957b, 115; 1938/1963b, 203). The patient maintains double bookkeeping. "[O]ne part of [him] maintains a correct view of reality while another part freely distorts it" (Bychowski 1956, 11). It's as if there is a nonparticipating observer in the patient, looking at the patient's denial (Hartke 2009). And he hides his capacity from the therapist.

The patient splits off the capacities for observing, experiencing, and thinking about reality. He may project the capacity for seeing reality onto the therapist. Now, he equates the therapist with his split-off ability (Willick 1983). He acts as if the therapist sees reality and thinks about it while he doesn't (Bion 1959, 1962). If the therapist talks about reality, the therapist enacts the patient's disavowed sanity. Then the patient enacts the insane part of the mind: "I don't know what you are talking about." "I don't' see that; you do." "I didn't say that; you are putting words into my mouth." He acts as if he doesn't see reality. Only the therapist does (Kernberg 1975; M. Klein 1975b; Rosenfeld 1987; Spotnitz 1986). He may act as if the therapist is crazy for talking about reality. The patient cannot destroy himself and know he is doing it at the same time (Symington 2002). Either he must split off and deny his awareness of the act. Or he must split off and deny the pain the act causes.

The following patient emailed me following seventy-two treatment failures. We had met for an assessment earlier, which he had not found useful. After seeing more therapists, a year later, he emailed me to have a consultation. What follows is our first interview.

> *Th:* How can I help you?
>
> *Pt:* [*Laughs dismissively.*] I think I've been pretty thorough. I've been suffering from depression and anxiety. And therapy has not helped. [*Splitting: he comes to therapy for help but believes therapy will not help.*]
>
> *Th:* Right. And given that right now, you have contacted me. What is it you want to work on today?
>
> *Pt:* Well. The same things I've been struggling with. Depression and anxiety. They don't seem to get better.
>
> *Th:* Yeah.
>
> *Pt:* Therapy doesn't seem to have helped in that regard. [*Splitting: he comes to therapy for help yet believes therapy won't help.*]
>
> *Th:* Right. And yet, you contacted me. [*Pointing out the contradiction: a man who believes therapy won't help comes to a therapist for help.*]
>
> *Pt:* Well, you know the whole story. I don't have to go over all the background because I've been pretty thorough. You have the reputation of being a very good therapist, and other therapists have failed me. [*Splitting: he says I have the reputation of being a very good therapist. Yet, he sent several emails questioning why he should see me since seventy-one therapists had failed.*]
>
> *Th:* And I failed before, too, from what you said. Of course, in our beginning, we knew that this could quite likely fail too. We're entering into this with the possibility or likelihood that this will fail too. We just have to take a look at whatever you want to work on here today with the recognition that whatever we do today may fail too. Sure. And I totally understand that. And yet, with that understanding, you contacted me. [*Invite him to be aware of his splitting. He wants my help, but he thought I would fail.*] So I wonder if there is anything you want to work on today, even though it may not work.
>
> *Pt:* Well, I would like to get a handle on this depression and anxiety.
>
> *Th:* Are you feeling depressed right now?
>
> *Pt:* [*Detached voice.*] I've felt depressed for probably thirty years. [*Defense: he doesn't answer the question.*]

Th: And right now?

Pt: [*Detached voice.*] Sure. [*Defense: detachment and noninvolvement.*]

Th: And how do you experience the depression right now?

Pt: I'm depressed. I do things. I force myself to do things, but I don't get joy out of it.

Th: That you don't get joy out of things.

Pt: Not really. When I went to the DBT clinic here for two years, they had me do lots of exercises where they had me do busy work basically, lots of things. Of course, they had me do a lot of CBT with that, and I didn't feel any better. [*Splitting: a man who doesn't believe therapy can help comes to a therapist for help.*]

Th: And I remember from the other work with therapists you've done, the therapy hasn't made you feel better either. Right?

Pt: No.

Th: And from the previous meeting we had, that our work also did not make you feel better.

Pt: Correct.

Th: Right. But for some reason, you contacted me even though our previous work did not help you get better. [*These interventions remind him of the splitting: a man who believes therapy won't help comes to therapy for help.*]

Pt: Well, I keep holding out hope that something else might work. [*Splitting.*]

Th: You are hoping that a therapist who didn't help you last time will help you this time. [*Invite him to be aware of his splitting.*]

Pt: [*Laughs.*] Well, as you know, I have had a lot of therapists and a lot of types of therapies, so I feel, without therapy, I'm not going to get better. I know that's true because I've gone long periods without therapy. And I didn't get better on my own. So, I need the help of a professional. [*Splitting: he states one fact while forgetting or not mentioning a contradictory fact.*]

Th: Right. And asking a professional who didn't help you to help you. [*Invitation to become aware of splitting.*]

Pt: Well, I'm hoping that whatever professional I seek out will help me with some answers to help me. [*Splitting.*]

Th: Right. And hoping that a professional who didn't help you will help you. Uh-huh. [*Invitation to become aware of splitting.*]

Pt: Well, you've seen lots of clients. I'm sure you've seen lots of people with lots of different problems. I would hope that you have some expertise to bring to the session that might bring help. [*Splitting.*]

Th: Right. And hoping that this therapist with expertise who failed you last time would not fail you this time. [*Invitation to become aware of splitting.*]

Pt: Correct.

Th: Right. There's something about hoping that a process that continually fails you will finally help you. [*Invitation to become aware of splitting.*]

Pt: Well, the alternative is that I do nothing. I don't seek help, and then I don't get better. [*Splitting.*]

Th: Right. Either you don't see a therapist and don't get better, or you see a therapist and don't get better. [*Invitation to become aware of splitting.*]

Pt: Well, it's like having an injury. Say you hurt your ankle snow-boarding or whatever. If you don't go to a doctor, it may not get better. It may even be a lifetime injury. If you go to a doctor, it's possible it will not heal quickly, it's possible you will have problems in the future. I've injured a shoulder. It's plagued me for years. But at least there's hope that treatment will at least alleviate some of the pain. Doing nothing could make it worse. [*Splitting.*]

Th: Right. You're saying that not going to therapy could make it worse, and going to therapy has actually not made it better. [*Invitation to become aware of splitting.*]

Pt: Correct.

Th: Right. That there's something about entering a process here that hasn't made you any better. Sometimes, in fact, it has made you worse. [*Invitation to become aware of splitting.*]

Pt: Correct.

Th: It's either doing nothing and getting worse or seeing a therapist who doesn't help or makes you worse. [*Invitation to become aware of splitting.*]

Pt: Well. There's always the possibility that therapy could be beneficial. I don't know. [*Splitting.*]

Th: Yeah. Yeah. It's just with the seventy-two therapists you said you had seen and—

Pt: [*Interrupts.*] It's over sixty. I can't remember exactly. I know it's over sixty.

His interruption indicates that anxiety is rising when I invite him to become aware of his splitting. We resume a few minutes later in the session. He has admitted having a chaotic childhood but denies it has had any impact, so I mirror his denial and splitting.

Pt: Yeah. Lots of people have chaotic childhoods. I don't find it to be. [*Splitting and denial.*]

Th: You're saying that the fact it was a chaotic childhood doesn't mean it was a traumatic childhood. And even if it's a chaotic childhood, it wouldn't explain any of these difficulties. It's a pretty simple case. A lot of people have chaotic childhoods. [*Mirroring splitting and denial.*]

Pt: Yeah. I mean, my brother grew up in the same household, and he's never seen a therapist in his life. [*Fact enlisted in the service of denial.*]

Th: And I assume totally normal. [*Mirror denial.*]

Pt: Yeah. I mean, he was a judge in the US navy for years. He has a stellar record. He's never seen a therapist, never had a mental health issue. [*Facts enlisted in the service of denial.*]

Th: So you're wondering, if he is doing so well, why am I having so much trouble? [*Mirror his denial.*]

Pt: Yeah, it doesn't make any sense to me. I don't understand why, for example, I don't talk to my parents. I haven't talked to them in years. People don't understand why, and it's hard to explain why because I don't really have much of a reason. I mean, yeah, they yell. [*Splitting and denial: he admits they yell yet sees no contradiction in that he doesn't want to talk to them.*]

Th: And just because they yell, that wouldn't be a reason not to talk to them. [*Mirror denial.*]

Pt: Well, I would think that, yeah. [*Denial.*]

Th: Just because they yell, that wouldn't be a reason not to talk to them. Not really sure why you don't talk to them. [*Mirror splitting and denial.*]

Pt: Yeah. I don't feel I have any traumas that explain all these troubles I struggle with. [*Denial.*]

Th: It's just a chaotic childhood. And if it's just a chaotic childhood and your brother turned out totally fine, you're wondering why am I having these kinds of difficulties? Same childhood. [*Mirror denial.*]

Pt: Yeah. And then I have these thoughts and fantasies that disturb me. I mean, I'm a person who has great empathy because if I didn't have great empathy, I would be a very dangerous person. I know it. Because I have these thoughts and fantasies that are very disturbing. I would never act on them. I'd never hurt anybody. But they're very dark and disturbing. [*After mirroring his denial and splitting, his denial weakens, and thoughts and fantasies rise to the surface.*]

Th: And you're thinking, if my brother is so normal, and all we had was a chaotic childhood, why am I having these disturbing images and he isn't? [*Mirror denial.*]

Pt: Correct. I can't explain why I seem to be so disturbed. [*Denial.*]

Th: It's just a chaotic childhood, and all they did was yell, why am I having all this disturbing imagery? [*Mirror splitting and denial.*]

Pt: Right.

Th: Why is this disturbing imagery coming up in my mind. [*Mirror denial.*]

Pt: Yes.

Th: That it doesn't make any sense that you would have this disturbing imagery coming up. [*Mirror denial.*]

Pt: No. And what does that say about me as a person that I would have that kind of grim, violent thoughts, especially toward women? I don't really understand that either.

Th: If I have this disturbing imagery coming up about women in my mind, it must mean something really bad about me. [*Mirror his self-judgment, a defense against rage toward others.*]

Pt: Well [*laughs*], I don't think most people have the kinds of thoughts I have. I honestly think that. [*Reality enlisted in the service of denial. "I am bad," not that "my parents did bad things." His laughter reflects a rise of anxiety.*]

As I keep mirroring his splitting and denial, new details rise into consciousness. We return a few minutes later in the session. He revealed that he has troubling violent fantasies about women and doesn't know why.

Pt: And I have read a lot about people who are violent, like serial killers. And they, the thing they have in common is head injury.

Th: Right. Mm-hmm.

Pt: And bedwetting. Both of which, like, I wet the bed until I was fifteen, which I think is highly unusual. [*Emergence of new memory.*]

Th: Right, so thinking if it's just a chaotic family, why would I have had bedwetting? [*Mirror his splitting. Since he splits feelings apart and denies them, we cannot ask about mixed feelings he does not feel. When he engages in splitting, I invite the consciousness of contradictory experiences. When he engages in denial, I mirror the denial so that thinking occurs in him. Confrontation would be inappropriate because he cannot bear conflict internally. Thus, he cannot see a defense or its price and reflect upon it. All those capacities need to be built before confrontation would be appropriate.*]

Pt: I don't know. [*More anxious. Smiles.*] I don't know. [*Raises voice.*]

Th: It just doesn't make sense. [*Mirror his splitting and denial.*]

Pt: I was just too afraid to get up at night. [*Emergence of new memory.*]

Th: Uh-huh. It was just a chaotic family, so why would I have been afraid to get up at night? [*Mirror his splitting and denial.*]

Pt: I don't know. [*Laughs.*] That's the thing. There's something wrong with my brain.

Th: Uh-huh. Always a possibility. [*Mirror his denial.*]

Pt: Well, that's what I'm thinking, but how does one fix that if there's physical damage?

Th: Right.

Pt: That's what I can't figure out what to do. But I do think it's unusual from everything I've read for someone to wet the bed for that long. I don't know. I can't explain it other than I was terrified of the dark.

Th: And wondering, it was just a chaotic family, so why would I have been terrified of the dark? [*Mirror his splitting.*]

Pt: I don't know. That's why I'm wondering, did something happen?

Th: Why would I have been terrified of the dark until I'm fifteen? [*Mirror his splitting.*]

Pt: I don't know. [*Denial.*]

Th: These are good questions. [*Block the projection that I will think for him.*]

When we mirror, we mirror a fellow defense user. To speak to the patient's depths, we must speak from our own. If we speak from judgment, we teach the patient to hate his inner life. If we speak from acceptance and identification, we teach the patient to accept his internal life. The tone of voice must embody our radical, complete, unconditional acceptance of his feelings, his anxiety, and his defenses. We have used every defense our patients have used, so we are in no position to judge. As a mirror, we accept his inner life and defenses without needing him to modify, alter, or change himself in any way. We can mirror this way because we *are* the mirror image. We, too, use defenses to avoid the pain in our lives.

We resume a few minutes later.

Pt: Well, I've been rageful for my entire life. I've just never expressed myself because I fear I would be dangerous.

Th: Yeah. And it was just a chaotic home, so why would you be feeling this rage your whole life? [*Mirror his splitting and denial.*]

Pt: I don't know. That's why I'm saying that maybe something happened. That maybe this EMDR uncovered something that was quite traumatic. I just have—I did strange things when I was younger. Like when I was seven, I waited at the bottom of the stairs for my parents with a shotgun. I would have killed them. You hear these stories about little kids that kill their parents. I would have been one of those kids. And that's not normal. That's not normal behavior. Do you think that was normal? [*Emergence of new memory.*]

Th: So you're thinking, geez, it's just a chaotic home, so why would you have felt the urge to have a shotgun on them? Yeah. [*Mirror his splitting.*]

Pt: Maybe it was misdirected rage because something happened when I was four for which I don't have a recollection.

Th: Uh-huh.

Pt: That's the only thing I can think of. But you would agree: that's not normal for a seven-year-old.

Th: Yeah. And it's just a chaotic home, so why would you be having a shotgun on them? Yeah. [*Mirror his splitting and denial.*]

Pt: I don't know. [*Splitting and denial.*]

Th: It's a good question. These are good questions.

Pt: [*Laughs.*] But you're the professional. I'm not. I don't have an answer, other than that. [*He projects his disavowed sanity: only I should know.*]

Th: I hear that. I'm not going to waste your time by guessing. I hear you. [*Block the projection that I can answer questions only he can answer.*]

I mirror his denial and splitting for a few minutes, then more memories surface.

Pt: I think a lot of people with problems of impulse control, men who beat their wives, my father used to beat my mother all the time. [*Emergence of a new memory.*] I would never hit someone. I would never punch someone or kick them downstairs. I've never done any of that because I realize the fallout from that would be significant. You can't have a healthy significant relationship if you are beating all the time. [*I had mirrored his conflict: a wish to hurt people and take pleasure in it countered by taking a stand against it. Now a memory emerges of a father who hurt the mother. His treatment of himself enacted a trauma he observed.*]

Th: Right. You can't have a healthy relationship if you're being beaten all the time or seeing beatings all the time. Uh-huh. [*Mirror his rational thinking.*]

Pt: Yeah. So when I start to feel that kind of rage, which I do, I'm able to take a step back and logically say this would be a step too far, even if I were to say something. It doesn't have to be physical. [*A whisper from his unconscious. He can intellectualize about rage inside himself. However, there is no tension or sighing. Since the mirroring of his denial is building his capacity, and his unconscious cues continue to rise, I keep mirroring his denial.*]

Th: You remember times when your father was beating your mother, and he couldn't stop himself. And you're aware you have big impulses to hurt women, too, but the difference is you're able to stop yourself. [*Mirror his splitting. He makes no connection between his treatment of himself and his father's treatment of his mother. Mirroring of the splitting and denial has enabled the memory to become conscious. But the connection between the memory and his self-treatment remains unconscious.*]

Pt: Correct. Or not just physical. Like my mother would tell me she wanted me to burn alive in a car accident when I was a child. I wouldn't say that to someone because I know that's hurtful. I may think that.

Th: Yeah.

Pt: Actually, I've never really thought that. But I wouldn't say that to somebody if I did think that. I certainly wouldn't say that to a child because a child doesn't have the capacity to think that.

Th: Your mom would say that she wanted you to burn alive. And now you've got voices that are yelling at you in kind of a similar way it sounds like.

Pt: Well. They're critical for sure. Look, my brother didn't seem to be very affected by those things. Yeah, my mother would say cruel things like she wished I was dead or never born. When I wet the bed, she would put my sheets out for the neighbors to see. I didn't like that. And I wouldn't do that to someone. [*Emergence of a new memory.*]

Th: Your mom said she wished you were dead. And then there's these voices that are trying to get you dead, too, trying to get you to do something where you would end up dead. Something about harsh voices in your head. And something about your mom wishing you would burn to death, wishing you were dead. [*Mirror split-apart facts.*]

Pt: Yeah. And to this day, I don't talk to them now, but they'll send me emails, "What did we ever do? Why do you treat us this badly? Why don't you visit?" [*Emergence of new memory. He reveals how his parents engage in splitting and denial about the past.*] Quite frankly, I don't like spending time with them. I don't. I don't like being in confined spaces with my dad. So if I have to get on an elevator, I get really freaked out. Or if I get in the cab of his truck or whatever. I try to explain that to them, and they don't understand.

Th: You explained to them, and they don't understand. You explained that your mom wished you burned alive. Your mom wanted you dead. And you're not sure why you don't want to talk to them. [*Mirror his splitting and denial.*]

Pt: Well, my brother talks to them. He's close to them. Parents make mistakes. It's not like—no parent is perfect. They'll say things to their kids that are not the best. [*Denial.*]

Th: And even though she wished you were dead and wanted you to burn alive, it's just a mistake. So it's not clear why you wouldn't want to talk to them. [*Mirror his splitting and denial.*]

Pt: Well, again, I think there are degrees of cruelty or being unkind to one another. And if I were rating this on a scale of one to ten, maybe this is a two or whatever. [*Denial.*]

Th: Since it's just a two, wondering—since it's just a two, wanting you to burn alive—since it's just a two, why wouldn't I want to talk to them? [*Mirror his splitting and denial.*]

Pt: Well, yeah, and that makes me feel worse about myself. My parents and my brother will say I'm not a good son. Or when I've tried to have conversations with my parents about what happened, my father and brother will say, "Well, your mother needed to be disciplined. She had to be controlled. When she started screaming, she had to be disciplined." [*After I mirror his denial, he reveals his parents' denial in the past.*]

Th: That your mother needed a beating because she needed to be disciplined? Is that right? [*Mirror the family's denial.*]

Pt: Right. Because she was too out of control. They wouldn't say it was a beating. They would just say she needed to be disciplined. There were times my parents would fight. So my mother would ask me to call 9-1-1. Then my father would say, "Don't. Don't you dare call 9-1-1." I'm five or six years old. I don't know what to do. Do I call 9-1-1, or do I not call 9-1-1? There were times I had to break down the door with my brother because my mother was threatening to commit suicide. [*Emergence of new memory.*]

Th: It wasn't a beating; it was just a disciplining she was getting then. [*Mirror the family's denial.*]

Pt: Well, that's what they would say. That she was out of control. [*Now it's no longer his denial. He remembers their denial.*] Because she would often go out into the yard and scream. And neighbors would hear, and that would be a problem for the family. So my father would have to take steps, he said, to discipline her to keep her quiet. [*Emergence of new memory.*]

Th: To keep her from screaming out in the yard. Uh-huh.

Pt: I don't think that kicking her in the stomach and calling her a fat cunt is very necessary. [*Negation: emergence of a defense within isolation of affect—a whisper from the unconscious.*] I've never done that. But they would beat each other down the hall. [*Emergence of new memories.*]

Th: Your thought is that kicking her in the stomach and calling her a cunt probably wasn't necessary for your dad then. [*Mirror his minimization.*]

Pt: I wouldn't say, probably. I'd say it's not necessary. I would never do that. I have been angry before, but I've never done anything.

Th: For some reason, we don't know, you have a lot of violent feelings toward women. And at the same time, you witnessed a lot of violence toward your mother. Not sure why those two would be connected. [*Mirror his splitting and denial.*]

Pt: Not, really, no.

Th: Not clear why they're connected.

Mirroring splitting and denial gradually builds his affect tolerance. As his affect tolerance builds, memories become conscious. Later, we addressed the splitting between the memories and their meanings. The therapist must avoid becoming the one who thinks. Instead, mirror the patient's denial to help him think about himself, his past, and his experience.

The patient who splits may avoid conflict by projecting one aspect onto the therapist. Or he may voice one side of conflict while denying the other. Or he can voice two sides without noticing the contradiction. When he projects one side of his conflict, he expects the therapist to voice the other side. Therefore, the therapist mirrors the projection. As a result, the other side of the conflict, not voiced by the therapist, rises in the patient instead, inducing conflict in him.

When the patient splits without engaging in projection, the therapist mirrors both sides of the split. If the therapist mistakenly mirrors one side of the split, the patient will believe the therapist incarnates that split-off part. Thus, we mirror both split-apart elements so he can experience conflict. For instance, if he splits without projecting and I mirror his suicidal wishes, he may believe that I want him to kill himself. This will be a sign that he was splitting without projecting, thus we need to mirror both sides of the split. (See table 10.4.)

Table 10.4   Interventions for splitting, splitting and projection, and splitting and denial

Defense	Strategy	Intervention
Splitting	Mirror splitting by inviting consciousness of splitting.	*Pt:* Therapy hasn't worked, but I keep hoping it will be different this time. *Th:* You keep hoping that something that hasn't worked will work this time.
Splitting and projection	Mirror splitting and projection by inviting consciousness of splitting, and blocking projection.	*Pt:* I waited at the bottom of the stairs with a shotgun. Is that normal? *Th:* You waited at the bottom of the stairs with a shotgun, and you wonder if that's normal. That's a good question. I think you are asking yourself the right question.
Splitting and denial	Mirror splitting and denial by inviting consciousness of splitting and blocking projection of his disavowed sanity.	*Pt:* My brother grew up in the same household, and he doesn't have any problems. *Th:* So, naturally, you're wondering, if he doesn't have problems, why do I?

Principle: *When the patient engages in denial, the therapist mirrors the denial. Mirroring blocks his implicit projection that you will voice what he denies.*

If you do not express what the patient denies, the denied rises in him instead of the therapist. This builds his capacity for affect tolerance. Gradually, he gains the ability to be aware of two feelings at once without denying one of them.

SPLITTING IN THE THERAPIST

Just as fragile patients use the defense of splitting, therapists can too. Patients may describe a parent as all-bad, as a "psychopath:" "He never loved me" or "He's just a worthless piece of shit." They are splitting. If the therapist agrees, she looks at the parent through the lens of splitting and supports the patient's splitting. No one is all-bad without a single good quality.

Therapists may refer to the patient's parents as "perpetrators" or "collaborators." They take a piece of the truth and mistake it for the whole. The therapist's splitting reinforces the patient's splitting, viewing parents as all-bad. And the therapist "becomes" the all-good savior. In reality, every person gratifies us and frustrates us. Splitting supports the fantasy that all-good and all-bad people exist.

The delights of demonization should never be underestimated. How convenient to reject parts of ourselves, relocate them in other people, and condemn them from afar. However, demonization exacts the price of living in a delusional world filled with demons. The price for the therapist is treating demonized patients, who, by definition, cannot be healed. And, at worst, the therapist treats demons she placed in the patient. (See the literature on satanic ritual abuse, a form of pseudotherapy based on therapist projection, e.g., Frankfurter 2008.)

Therapists also split when they jump to the conclusion that the patient is incurable: "She only wants to suffer" or "She is filled with destructiveness" or "She wants to destroy the therapy." No statement contains the entire truth of a patient. The therapist who sees only pathology becomes blind to the patient's longing for health. A distorted perspective masquerades as a "deep" insight into her pathology. The therapist equates the patient with her problem. He becomes blind to the person behind the defenses. If the patient believes the therapist's "insight," she loses faith that she can find herself.

We can understand this response as a concordant identification with the patient. A therapist views her as all-bad, just as she sees herself. We can also understand this response as a complementary identification. A therapist sees her as all-bad, as perhaps the patient's parents occasionally did. Splitting can also result from the therapist's difficulties.

We should not accept the therapist's splitting as a fact to believe. We should accept it as a countertransference response to examine. If the therapist splits, so will the patient. The therapy will be doomed. Everyone wishes life was simple, full of all-good people. The challenge is to accept that nothing human is alien to us. But splitting denies the complexity of our humanity. As Joyce McDougall said, "The child first sees itself in the eyes of the mother" (personal communication). If patients see our splitting, they will see our soul blindness.

SUMMARY

For splitting, we help the patient bear mixed feelings. For splitting and projection, we help him bear inside what he projected outside. For splitting and denial, we mirror the splitting and denial. Then he can bear mixed feelings together without splitting them apart. As affects rise, anxiety will rise, triggering cognitive/perceptual disruption. Regulate anxiety while keeping affect intensity at the same level. Through this bracing, the patient gains the ability to tolerate this level of mixed feelings. His anxiety shifts into the striated muscles, and his resistance shifts into isolation of affect. Now able to experience the mixed feelings inherent in life, he integrates inside what he relocated outside. Then he can embrace his inner life rather than split it off and project it out to live in other people.

CHAPTER ELEVEN

Projection

Learning to Feel Inside What We Placed Outside

We pack the physical outline of the creature we see with all the ideas we have already formed about him, and in the complete picture of him which we compose in our minds, those ideas have certainly the principal place. In the end, they come to fill out so completely the curve of his cheeks, to follow so exactly the line of his nose, they blend so harmoniously in the sound of his voice that these seem to be no more than a transparent envelope, so that each time we see the face or hear the voice it is our own ideas of him which we recognize and to which we listen.

—MARCEL PROUST, *SWANN'S WAY*

Although our wants are unlimited, our loved ones are limited, like us. To some degree, they will always frustrate us, and we will always frustrate them. Thus, we inevitably have mixed feelings toward anyone we need or desire: love and anger.

Yet, while we learned in school that two plus two equals four, we never heard that love plus anger occurs in every relationship. Instead, we often receive the message that we shouldn't feel angry with someone we love or we shouldn't love someone with whom we feel angry. Rather than learn to embrace our complex feelings and the complexity of those we love, we learn to hate and reject our forbidden feelings.

Patients can detach from their feelings and the people who trigger them. Others protect the ones they love by turning the rage against themselves. Fragile patients split love and rage apart and project one of them onto other people. What do we mean by the defense of projection?

Definition: A child feels rage and love toward the person causing her trauma. As the anger grows, demanding a solution, unbearable anxiety rises. But the potential provider of help is producing the pain: the abuser. The child cannot get rid of the external trigger (the person causing the trauma), so she tries to rid herself of her internal responses. She splits off the unbearable parts of her experience and attributes them to others. Thus, she projects the most painful parts of her trauma.

The dynamics of projection: Trauma triggers overwhelming feelings and anxiety. At the moment of trauma, the child splits off elements of her experience or her awareness of them and regards them as "not-me" (Freud 1911/1958f; Sullivan 1953a). Having split off a feeling, wish, or aspect of her awareness, she will deny and then project it onto another person. The child's experiences, now erased, can no longer trigger unbearable anxiety in her. And, if she has erased herself sufficiently, she no longer triggers rage within the abuser. Thus, projection wards off unbearable anxiety.

The content of projections: The child projects what she has to project, what she cannot bear inside. She may project the unbearable feelings the trauma triggers, or she may project experience that was dangerous (e.g., her will, thoughts, or awareness). Usually, she projects the area of trauma most contaminated by her rage (Bion 1959; Rosenfeld 1965, 1987). If she had to submit, she projects her will. If her life was threatened, she relocates her will to live: "My doctor hospitalized me because I wanted to commit suicide." If the parent she loved punished her, she may project her love onto others and punish them. A woman whose mother rejected her said, "My partner wants to get married, but I'm not into that. I keep him at arm's length. He's constantly trying to get too close." Her desire was split off and placed in him where she could reject it as her mother did. If the child had to be quiet during a rape, she might hallucinate the screams she silenced or the voice of her rapist. She will project the most salient trigger in the trauma to rid herself in fantasy what she could not bear in reality.

The more severe the traumas, the more primitive the splitting and projection. For instance, a patient may project her desires onto others, or she may appear to have no desires since she projects her will. At the most severe level, she may project her capacity to think, see, or listen. Patients may present with desires, the absence of desires, and, finally, the absence of a person who can see or think. The content of projections correlates with the severity of the traumas and the patient's affect tolerance.

For instance, she may split off and project her awareness of her need to be in therapy.

Pt: Why do you think I should be here? [*She splits off her awareness and projects it upon the therapist. She struggles with her conflict: being aware of her need or hiding it.*]

Th: Since I'm not you, I can't know the answer to that question. That's why I have to ask you.

She may split off and project her desire to be in therapy.

Pt: What do you want from me? [*Projection: she projects her desire for therapy.*]

Th: Nothing. The question is what you want from the therapy. [*Block the projection and invite the patient to notice her desire.*]

She may split apart her mixed feelings toward the therapist.

Pt: I hate this therapy. I don't feel comfortable with how close you want to get to me. [*She struggles with her mixed feelings of love and rage toward the therapist.*]

Th: I don't need to get close to you because this isn't my problem. [*Deactivate the projection.*] The question is, do you want to get close to your own inner feelings so you have better information and can make better decisions for you? [*Invite her to recognize her wish inside herself.*]

In each example, the patient disowns a feeling, thought, or impulse and then projects it onto the therapist.

The sequence of splitting and projection correlates with the stages in building the alliance, (1) projecting the awareness of a need, (2) projecting the desire for help, and (3) splitting apart love and hate and projecting one feeling. Thus, the content of a projection may reflect the relational need: dependency, will, or emotional closeness.

When the trauma remains unaddressed, it continues to be an unspoken, enduring threat. In an adult, current relationships trigger feelings related to earlier traumas. Overwhelmed by feelings that trigger cognitive/perceptual disruption, the fragile adult *has to* project again. Otherwise, her unbearable feelings can trigger cognitive/perceptual disruption and the loss of mental boundaries. First, we regulate anxiety. Then we help patients accept inside what they projected outside. Each feeling is a piece of the unbearable, a memory of the trauma that required projection. Projection by projection, feeling by feeling, we process the attachment traumas the defenses warded off.

PROJECTION IN THE FRAGILE PATIENT

Imagine a child as a pint jar. When traumatized, she must hold a gallon of emotion, but she cannot. The amount of frustration children can tolerate varies due to differences in genetics, temperament (Kagan 1994; Parens 1979), neurocognitive development (DeGangi 2017; Greenspan 1992; Piaget and Inhelder 1969), and neurocognitive deficits resulting from trauma (Almas et al. 2012; Bos et al. 2009). But no child can withstand the overwhelming feelings of love, anger, and anxiety that trauma triggers. The abuser does not help her process the trauma or put her feelings into words. Through physical violence and verbal threats, the abuser offers the defenses of splitting, dissociation, and projection for the child to use. Unable to depend upon her parents for affect regulation, the child *has to* rely upon defenses for self-erasure.

Thus, we need to build her affect tolerance so her pint-sized container can grow into a gallon jug. We help her bear her mixed feelings of love and rage rather than split them apart or place them outside herself. As she bears her experience, she gradually puts her past unfelt, and thus unformulated, experience into words (Freud 1911/1958f; Stern 2003).

First, the fragile patient splits off a feeling or urge, so it becomes "not-me" (Freud 1911/1958f; Sullivan 1953a, 1953b). The "not-me" represents everything within the fragile patient that provokes too much anxiety in her mothering ones, so she cannot consider it to be a part of herself (Sullivan 1949, 1953a). Next, she relocates that feeling or urge by projecting it onto another person. For instance, a woman having an affair with a married man who verbally abused her said, "I love him. [*Splitting and denial.*] I understand him. He doesn't mean what he says to me. [*Denial.*] But his wife! She's a hostile bitch. [*Projection.*] I can understand why he hates her." For mildly fragile patients, a moderate rise of feelings can trigger this process. In severely fragile patients, reality chronically activates feelings and anxiety over their threshold of anxiety tolerance. As a result, these patients chronically split and project. We see this sequence: (1) a reality stimulus, (2) mixed feelings, (3) rising anxiety, (4) splitting, and then (5) projection. We addressed the defense of splitting earlier. We can now address the defense that follows from it: projection.

When we project, we attribute to others our thoughts, feelings, and desires (A. Freud 1936). Most commonly, we try to get rid of aggressive or sexual feelings or thoughts. Those traits would trigger guilt if we recognized them in ourselves. We try to eradicate that conflict unconsciously through projection. We attribute to others the qualities that trigger anxiety and guilt within ourselves. Then we condemn those traits "over there."

A feeling perceived to be outside ("*You* are angry with me") replaces one experienced inside ("*I* am angry with you") (Freud 1938/1963b). The same thing happens with judgments ("*You* judge me" replaces "*I* judge myself") or desires ("*You* want me to work on my problem" replaces "*I* want to work on my problem"). The defense of projection relocates an inner truth in another person.

Everybody projects. Consider the ways husbands and wives project onto each other. How does this common projection differ from more severe forms? Fragile patients equate others with their projections. They lose the ability to see others and the world realistically. As a result, they cannot adapt to reality. Rather than relate to people, they interact with their projections. When we equate others with the projections we place upon them, we see our projections, not the people themselves. Then we become scared, mistrustful, and unable to enjoy closeness with others. It is tempting to believe our projections. Why? Because each projection contains a piece of truth (A. Freud 1936; Searles 1965/1986a).

Whatever we project is an aspect of our shared humanity. As the ancient Roman poet Terentius said, "Nothing human is alien to me." Anything a patient attributes to me will be, in part, true. However, the fragile patient does two more things that make projection distorted. First, he assumes that his idea is the entire truth about me. That is not true. Second, he believes that what he projects onto me is not true about him (Green 1986). That is also not true. Thus, denial makes projection pathological.

He denies that what he projects onto others is true of himself. He appears not to be conscious of these aspects of his inner life. For instance, a man who lied claimed others were liars. He lied about his wealth but accused others of being fake. He verbally attacked people yet claimed others attacked him. His projections, designed to obscure truths about himself, disclosed those very truths. Correspondences between the inner life and projections suggest that we unconsciously perceive our inner world when we project.

The fragile patient can tolerate only a certain amount of a feeling or impulse. So he gets rid of the excess and "periodically expels what [he] cannot master" (Green 1986, 95). For instance, whatever anger I cannot face in myself I will project onto another person. Then I will misperceive him as if *he* is angry. The less anger I can bear inside, the more I have to attribute to him. Therefore, the more distorted my image of him becomes and the more dangerous the relationship appears. Yet, in reality, there is no danger. Likewise, I may project the excess I cannot bear and create a delusion that becomes so filled with feelings that it seems real because it *feels* real.

Once the patient projects his excess feelings, thoughts, or impulses onto others, he fears his projections. But he is convinced he is scared of people. Why? He cannot differentiate real people from the unreal projections he has placed upon them.

Meanwhile, other people wonder why he fears them and seems angry. He is interacting with his projections. Paranoia is not the irrational fear of people; it is the irrational fear of projections he has placed on people.

When projection becomes the lens of perception, knowledge becomes distorted. The patient's conception of you is an experience of himself. The feeling he cannot bear is projected upon you, and he experiences you as that feeling. "Just as God made man in his image, the paranoiac makes [another person] resemble him" (Green 1986, 94). You become the screen upon which the paranoid sees his internal screenplay. The more he perceives in you, the less he sees in himself. And the less he sees in himself, the less real he feels. Then projection creates the sense of derealization (Guntrip 1968/1993).

When he projects, the fragile patient lives in a fantasy world he equates with the real world. He imagines that his feelings, impulses, and wishes no longer dwell within him. He has placed them on another person (Green 1986, 97). He pays attention to his fantasy (the projection onto the other person) and ignores reality. What aspects of their inner world do fragile patients project onto the outer world?

EXAMPLES OF WHAT IS PROJECTED: THE AREAS OF TRAUMA THAT TRIGGER UNBEARABLE ANXIETY

Most fragile patients have experienced traumas in which a feeling, thought, urge, or capacity triggered unbearable anxiety. That element is projected later in life when mixed feelings rise in relationships.

Projection of Anger

In the following vignette, the patient, unable to bear her anger inside, projects it outside onto the therapist. Then she interacts with her projection.

Pt: I think you are angry with me. [*Projection of anger. She is angry with the therapist but projects it onto the therapist.*]

Th: I'm not aware of that. What is giving you the idea that I'm angry? [*Contrast the projection with reality.*]

Pt: [*No sigh.*] It just feels that way. [*Absence of a sigh means that mixed feelings are not rising in her. That occurs if she projects one of them onto the therapist.*]

Th: Since it feels that way, what is the evidence to support that idea? [*Encourage her to reflect on reality to counter her projection. The therapist does not use the word anger. It might trigger a rise of feelings and more projection. Instead, he refers to the patient's idea. Invite her to reflect on projection as an idea about reality, not reality itself.*]

Pt: I don't know.

Th: Okay. A thought about anger comes up. You thought it might be over here, but we don't have any evidence for that. There's something about an idea about anger that comes up inside you. Then it travels over here. And then you had the thought that anger might be over here. [*Describe the process of projection so she can observe it.*] But we don't have any evidence for that. If you let this anger thought be inside you for a moment, was there something that happened here that might have triggered an anger thought? [*Invite her to bear her anger inside rather than project it outside.*]

Pt: I didn't like that you rescheduled my time. [*The trigger to her anger.*]

Th: Of course not. When you were angry about the change in time, something about that felt risky. And then the anger traveled over here, and you thought I was angry. [*Describe the process of projection so she can observe it.*] What happens as you let yourself feel a little of that anger inside you right now? [*Invite her to bear her anger inside without projecting it outside to build her affect tolerance.*]

Pt: [*Sighs.*] It's weird. [*Her anxiety has returned to the striated muscles. She can tolerate this level of feelings without projection. Affect tolerance has increased. If she is moderately fragile, she might experience cognitive/perceptual disruption now. If the patient is severely fragile, she might split or project right away to avoid the rise of anxiety in cognitive/perceptual disruption.*]

Some have proposed that we push the patient's feeling back in. That is impossible. Projection is a fantasy that we can relocate our inner life into another person. We can only remind the patient where her inner life has always been: inside herself. We cannot relocate her experience because it never left her. This is why it has been said that if we don't heal our wounds, we may bleed onto those who never cut us.

Projection of a Wish

Suppose a patient was beaten and attacked for having particular desires as a child. Since his longings "caused" the abuse, he might project them onto others.

Pt: What are you wanting from me? [*Projection of his wants onto the therapist.*]

Pt: You keep trying to get at what is inside me. It's like you are an intruder! [*Projection of his wishes to know himself onto the therapist.*]

Pt: I can see in your eyes that you want to have sex with me. [*Projection of his sexual wishes onto the therapist.*]

Pt: You don't answer my questions. You are constantly holding back from me. Why? [*Projection of his wish to withhold from the therapist.*]

Projection of Responsibility

A child who was beaten for a deed learns that being "responsible" led to a beating. The fragile patient may know he acted but projected the responsibility for his action: "*You* made me do it." He does not view himself as responsible. Instead, he attributes his responsibility to others. We call this kind of projection *externalization* (Novick and Kelly 1970).

A disheveled man who externalizes might say, "Your office is a mess." Since he views himself as a messy person, now *you* have the nasty trait—not him. He uses you "to externalize an unpleasant aspect of himself" (Novick and Kelly 1970). Patients who project their feelings outside need help to bear them inside. In contrast, patients who externalize need help to accept themselves and their responsibility for their actions. (For examples on working with the defense of externalization, see pp. 308–311 in *Co-Creating Change* [Frederickson 2013].)

When we externalize, we live a life on the run. We try to escape an inner judge that condemns us for failing to be ideal. We abandon our real, flawed humanity in a flight toward an unattainable ideal. However, to become "perfect," we must become not real, not ourselves. An ideal is an idea, and you are not an idea. Patients who externalize judge themselves and others for being real rather than ideal. They try to be an idea rather than accept their being. Thus, we help them accept the reality of themselves.

We have discussed projection and externalization as defenses patients use. But families use these defenses too. A parent might project onto a child, "*You* are always angry!" Then the child suffers from anxiety and guilt over his supposed anger. The parent's projections amplify the child's anger. You might say there are three angers in the pot: (1) the child's initial feeling, (2) the parent's anger projected onto the child, and (3) the child's anger for having to accept the parent's projection.

To hide his rage, the child usually identifies with his parents' defenses. For instance, if the child's parents beat him, as an adult, he beats himself up. If they judged him, he judges himself. If they verbally abused him, he verbally abuses himself.

A parent who externalizes may call the child "a loser." The parent tries to get rid of a devalued self-image, and the child has to accept it. In response, the child may become depressed. He cannot form an accurate picture of himself.

Projection of Will

In traumas, someone violates the fragile patient's will through verbal, physical, or sexual abuse. Since expressing their will triggered more cruelty, fragile patients frequently project their will onto others. As a result, when the therapist asks, "Is it your will to work on this problem?" fragile patients flood with anxiety. To ward off their anxiety, they project their will to do therapy, fearing the therapist as a potential invader.

Th: Is it your will to work on this problem?

Pt: If you think I should. [*Projection of will.*]

Th: Only you can know if working on this problem would be beneficial for you. [*Deactivate the projection: remind the patient of reality.*] That's why we have to find out if you want to work on this problem for your benefit. [*Invite him to declare what he wants without projecting it outside.*]

Principle: *Deactivate the projection onto the therapist by reminding the patient of reality that conflicts with her fantasy about the therapist. Then remind her of the original location of her experience.*

Remind the patient of her inner experience to build her capacity to recognize her will. Deactivating the projection of will increases her autonomy as she defines herself by expressing her will (Rank 1930/1936). (See chapter 3.)

Projection of the Superego

Fragile patients usually experienced mixed feelings toward an abuser whom they loved. How does an abused child deal with massive rage, if expressing it triggers more abuse? The more severe the abuse, the more rage the child feels, and the more he must judge it to control it. To get relief from his inner judge, the patient may project that others judge him (Wurmser 2000).

Pt: I feel like you are judging me. [*Projection of the superego.*]

Th: Would you like to accept yourself? [*Deactivate the projection by inviting the patient to accept rather than judge himself.*]

Pt: I'm feeling dizzy. [*Cognitive/perceptual disruption.*]

Th: Isn't that interesting? Something about accepting yourself makes you dizzy. What's it like to notice that? [*Bracing: remind him of what triggers his feelings while regulating his anxiety.*]

Projection of the Ability to Think about Reality

Parents can punish children for having a thought or revealing a secret. Perceiving and thinking about reality become areas of trauma. As a result, a patient may project her ability to see and think about reality. She acts as if she cannot think. And she invites the therapist to think the thoughts she fears to know (Bion 1957; Kernberg 1975, 1977b; M. Klein 1975b; E. Marcus 1992/2017; Rosenfeld 1965, 1977, 1987).

Pt: I like cutting my wrists and watching the blood flow down my arms. It makes me feel alive.

Th: [*The therapist feels terrified, but the patient does not because he projects his ability to think and feel about reality. Thus, the therapist mirrors the patient's wish to die to see if this induces conflict within him. If the therapist voices the patient's wish to live, the conflict will be between the therapist and patient, not within the patient.*] It makes you feel alive to watch the blood flow down your arms.

Pt: Yeah. [*Looks expectantly at the therapist.*]

Th: Well, it's great you have a way to feel alive. [*By incarnating the patient's insane defense, the therapist helps the patient observe and think about it.*]

Pt: Aren't you supposed to convince me not to cut my arms? [*The patient projects his wish to live onto the therapist.*]

Th: It's not my job to convince you not to cut your arms. You have a right to cut yourself if you want. And if it makes you feel alive, it makes sense you would do what makes you feel alive. [*Mirror the toxic introjection (Coleman-Nelson 1962, 1968).*]

Pt: [*The patient becomes anxious.*]

Th: You seem to be feeling something. What do you notice feeling?

Pt: I'm feeling dizzy. [*Cognitive/perceptual disruption.*]

Th: That's a sign of anxiety. So, something about letting yourself cut yourself to feel alive makes you feel anxious for some reason. [*Help the patient see causality. Remind the patient of the trigger to keep her feelings up, while regulating anxiety.*]

Pt: So, you're okay with me cutting myself? [*Projection.*]

Th: You are okay with cutting yourself. [*Remind the patient of reality to block the projection: she is okay with cutting herself.*] And if cutting yourself makes you feel alive, why would you stop cutting yourself?

Pt: I'm, uh, I don't know what to say. [*The patient's speech has slowed. And she appears to be having trouble thinking, a sign of cognitive/ perceptual disruption. Perhaps the intervention of challenge triggered too much anxiety.*]

Th: You don't know what to say about being okay with cutting yourself. [*Help her bear her conflict, even though anxiety is high. Mirroring her splitting brings together the wish to cut herself (conscious) and not wanting to cut herself (dissociated).*]

Pt: Aren't you supposed to convince me to stop cutting myself? [*Projection of her healthy wishes, which are now conscious, albeit within the defense of projection.*]

Th: People have already tried that, and that didn't work. Why should we do what doesn't work? [*Remind her of reality.*] After all, if cutting yourself makes you feel alive, why should you stop doing what makes you feel alive? [*Mirror her destructive defense so her healthy wishes can rise in only one place: her.*]

Pt: That sounds crazy. [*Progress: she is thinking about her destructive urge. If the therapist agrees, the patient might split off and project her awareness onto the therapist. Instead, the therapist maintains a stance as if he does not see what is crazy. Then there is only one place where awareness can rise: in the patient.*]

Th: How so? What sounds crazy about cutting yourself? [*Incarnate the patient's defensive stance of the nonthinker (Coleman-Nelson 1962, 1968). Then the patient can differentiate from, observe, and think about this defense.*]

Pt: It's crazy for a therapist to say I should cut myself to be alive. [*The patient increasingly recognizes her previously dissociated capacity to think and reflect upon his destructive defense.*]

Th: But if cutting yourself makes you feel alive, what is crazy about that? [*Incarnate the patient's defensive stance of the nonthinker (Brandt 1968; Coleman-Nelson 1962, 1968; Spotnitz 1976, 1986). Then the patient can differentiate from, observe, and think about her defense.*]

Pt: It just doesn't make sense. [*The patient accepts the previously dissociated capacity to think and reflect. If the therapist agrees, the patient might split off this capacity again.*]

Th: If you say so. [*Keep mirroring the patient's defense of not thinking. Then the patient continues to be the location where thinking occurs. Patients do not get better because the therapist thinks about their defenses. They get better because they reflect on their defenses. When the therapist avoids enacting the thinking role, all thought rises within the patient, which she has denied and dissociated.*]

Through projective identification, the therapist becomes worried and starts to act as if she must be the patient's sanity to overcome the patient's defenses (T. Ogden 1982). Then the patient can defy or even mock the disavowed sanity now located in the therapist (Bion 1957). The patient presents as if he has no reality testing or self-observing capacity. These capacities are still intact, but he denies and dissociates them. Out of his awareness, they become nonfunctional.

In this situation, the therapist might play the role of "the one who has the patient's self-knowledge" or self-interest, or even the one who is "responsible" (Hinshelwood 2004, 21). The therapist takes omnipotent responsibility for the patient's life and becomes burned out. If the therapist enacts the patient's disavowed sanity, it never rises within him. No longer in conflict with his destructive defenses, the patient's pleasure and comfort with them increases.

What causes the patient to split off, project, and even attack the capacity to see reality and think about it? If he lacks the affect tolerance to bear a painful reality, through cognitive/perceptual disruption and severe splitting he can lose his mind (Bion 1957), our greatest fear (M. Klein 1975b). Fearing the avalanche of overwhelming feelings and anxiety if he faces reality, he may project his sanity (the ability to see reality) onto another person and argue with it there. This pattern occurs frequently in anorectic, suicidal, and addicted patients. Or the patient may project his disavowed sanity onto someone else and then attack it.

The severely fragile patient splits apart his capacities for perceiving reality and projects those functions onto others (Bion 1957, 47). He says things like "Other people are looking at me" or "My parents think I have a drug problem, but they don't know what they are talking about. They're crazy." He projects the capacities for attention, thinking, perceiving, and remembering reality to avoid the feelings the hated reality triggers. The patient sees reality (Katan 1954). But he projects his disavowed sanity onto others. Enacting his psychotic defenses, he can dismiss or argue with those who talk about reality. He claims not to see reality, or he asserts that the reality we see does not exist. He may even claim that the therapist is crazy.

Principle: *When a patient projects, (1) deactivate projections by reminding the patient of realities that conflict with his projection, and (2) invite him to bear his inner life inside without projecting it outside.*

When he accepts what he projected, feelings and anxiety will rise inside him. In response, he may do the following:

- Sigh, indicating that he can accept his will, reality, and mixed feelings without flooding with anxiety.
- Experience smooth muscle anxiety, fatigue, or muscle weakness from repression. This may appear in the form of self-attack.
- Experience cognitive/perceptual disruption, requiring anxiety regulation.
- Experience cognitive/perceptual disruption and a new projection. Deactivate the new projection. Then invite him to bear his will inside rather than project it outside.
- Become disorganized. For instance, he might hallucinate, become delusional and paranoid about the therapist, and then run out

of the room. Such patients have a psychotic level of character organization (Kernberg 1977a, 1977b; Kleiger and Khadivi 2015; E. Marcus 1992/2017).

THE SPECTRUM OF PROJECTIVE PROCESSES

When neurotic patients project, their reality testing remains intact. Their anxiety is in the striated muscles, and their resistance is in isolation of affect. Their projections function as tactical defenses to keep the therapist at a distance. When we block their projections and invite feelings toward the therapist, these patients tolerate the rise of feelings, sigh, and intellectualize. We address the neurotic patient's tactical defense of projection to undo a barrier to closeness.

Fragile patients with a borderline level of character structure lose their reality testing temporarily. Their anxiety goes into cognitive/perceptual disruption. To end that disruption, they rely upon splitting and projection. We can restore reality testing through inviting the consciousness of splitting and projection. (See chapters 10 on splitting and 12 on severe fragility.)

Patients with a psychotic level of character structure lose their reality testing permanently (Kernberg 1975, 1977b; Kleiger and Khadivi 2015; E. Marcus 1992/2017). Their delusions and hallucinations do not clear up when we address splitting and projection. However, some people with a psychotic level of character structure, while on medications, can respond to psychotherapy.

PROJECTIONS IN THE FRAGILE SPECTRUM

The range of affect tolerance correlates with a spectrum of projective processes. Verbal projections can be conscious or latent and unconscious. For instance, a conscious, verbal projection is revealed in the manifest content: "You want to hurt me. You don't care." An unconscious, verbal projection is revealed in the latent content: "People don't care. They just want to hurt you." More severe projections take the form of pseudodelusions, pseudohallucinations, and concrete speech. These projections can clear up when we address splitting and projection. (See chapter 12 on severe fragility.) We will now illustrate how to work with the continuum of projections in fragile patients.

Manifest Projections

Patients who project their anger often fear the therapist is angry with them. Or if they judge themselves, they fear the therapist's judgment. If not addressed, these projections can become the basis of persecutory pseudodelusions.

Pt: What are you trying to get at? [*Projection of will.*]

Th: Nothing. [*Deactivate the projection by reminding the patient of reality.*] The question is what you would like to get at that would be helpful to you. [*Invite him to become aware of his desire inside without projecting it outside.*]

Latent Projections

Severely fragile patients chronically project onto others. Fortunately, their conscious projections onto others reveal unconscious projections onto the therapist. If we can deactivate these unconscious projections about the therapist before they become conscious, we can more easily establish a therapeutic alliance. Once these projections become conscious, however, the patient may equate the therapist with the projection. He loses reality testing and is at higher risk for dropping out of therapy. That is why we do not interpret these projections, nor do we ask for evidence for them. Thus, identifying and deactivating unconscious projections is essential in the initial phase of treatment.

Pt: I just hate it when doctors are always telling me what to do. Take this medication! Take that one! None of them do any good. And then I've got all these side effects. [*Unconscious projection that the therapist will ask the patient to submit to his will.*]

Th: No one likes to be told what to do. And I have no right to tell you what to do in therapy. [*Deactivate the projection.*] So just to make sure that you are doing here what *you* want to do, could you tell me what the problem is that *you* want to work on that *you* think would be helpful for *you*? [*Invite the patient to be the one who tells the therapist where the therapy will go. Then she will acknowledge her will rather than project it onto a therapist who "tells her what to do."*]

Pseudodelusions and Pseudohallucinations

Patients at a borderline level of character structure sometimes have delusions or hallucinations. We can help them bear the feelings they project into their delusions or hallucinations. When these resolve, we call them pseudodelusions or pseudohallucinations (E. Marcus 2017). The following examples illustrate how these symptoms result from projection:

- Projection of the superego:
  - A woman hears a voice accusing her of having immoral sexual thoughts.
  - A woman complains of eyes watching her.

These patients judge themselves. When they cannot bear the severity of their inner judgment, they project it onto others or a voice.

- Projection of wishes and feelings:
  - An angry girl accuses her father of being sadistic. She is unable to face her sadism.
  - A teenage boy believes that his father is taking his strength away from him. He cannot face how he wants to take his father's power away.
  - An adolescent cannot tolerate his wish to become independent. Then he projects that his mother cannot tolerate his independence. He becomes furious and calls her a witch.

Once these patients project their wishes and feelings, they experience themselves as passive victims. They believe people persecute them with the desires they have disavowed.

Patients with psychotic symptoms have suffered a high rate of child abuse. The content of delusions and hallucinations often parallels past abusive behavior. Ross, Anderson, and Clark (1994) find that the following psychotic symptoms had the strongest relationship to a history of abuse: voices commenting on the patient, ideas of reference, thought insertion, paranoid ideation, and reading others' minds. For example, caretakers criticized some abused patients. This can be the origin of voices commenting on the patient. Parents told some patients that things referred to them that didn't. "It's your fault I am angry with you." This can be the origin of ideas of reference. The child was told to swallow the parent's idea of reference: "I demand that you believe something refers to you that does not." Abusive parents try to insert thoughts into patients through projection: "How many times do I have to beat this into you?" That is sometimes the origin of delusions of thought insertion. The parent tries physically to insert a thought into the child's mind. Or the abuser says, "I know what you are thinking." Here, the parent asks the child to accept a psychotic belief that she can read his mind. Thus, a delusion can be a compromise formation that reveals the history of abuse (mother claiming she can read his mind) while concealing it through displacement (people can read my mind).

Auditory hallucinations of severely maltreated children reveal details of the traumas they suffered (Famularo, Kinscherff, and Fenton 1992). A hallucination often contains the contents of traumas that triggered it (Raune, Kuipers, and Bebbington 1999). For instance, one incest survivor heard the voice of the perpetrator encouraging her to touch children. Psychotic incest survivors have high rates of sexual delusions (J. Beck and van der Kolk 1987). One survivor of childhood rape had delusions of being tortured by people inserting objects into her anus and vagina. (Examples are taken from Read et al. [2003].)

The risk of psychotic symptoms increases with exposure to trauma. The shocks of trauma cause neurodevelopmental abnormalities and heightened sensitivity to stressors that lead to schizophrenia (Read et al. 2001). The result is a chronically elevated level of anxiety and significant permanent changes to the brain and the body. (See chapter 1.) These elevated levels of anxiety triggered by traumas cause abnormalities in brain functioning. This suggests a trauma-based neurodevelopmental model for psychosis (Read et al. 2001; Read et al. 2014). (For a review of the literature on the relationship between trauma and psychotic symptoms, see Larkin and Read [2012].)

A hallucination can turn rage against the perpetrator back against the victim. For example, one victim heard the voice of the perpetrator telling him to jump off a bridge and kill himself. He had tried several times. To avoid his rage, he identified with the aggressor (A. Freud 1936). A man who had been raped by his uncle heard voices telling him he was "sleazy" and should kill himself (Heins, Gray, and Tennant 1990). He felt murderous rage toward his uncle, whom he wanted to kill. But he projected his rage into a hallucinated voice to avoid the guilt triggered by massive rage toward an uncle he loved. The hallucinations said to him what he felt toward his uncle, and he became the aggressor to be punished and killed. Thus, the hallucinations functioned as a form of self-punishment to ward off his guilt. In another case, the father had sexually assaulted the patient. She felt rage toward her father as a pervert. But she projected her rage onto a hallucinated voice that told her she was a pervert who did "dirty things" (Heins, Gray, and Tennant 1990). In both cases, the delusion and hallucination turned the rage and criticism toward the abuser back onto the patient. The defense, identification with the aggressor, also warded off unconscious guilt over the wish to murder people whom they loved.

While it is tempting to view these parents as all-bad, at times they loved their children who loved them. During abuse, the child feels the law of the talion. She wants to injure the other as she was injured. And since the abuser is killing the good relationship they had, the child feels the urge to kill the killer: the person she loves. To avoid those mixed feelings and the guilt they trigger, she may hallucinate. By viewing herself as the pervert, we see how she deals with loss—identifying with the abuser: "I haven't lost him; I became him" (Freud 1917/1961a). And by identifying with the abuser, she directs the rage upon herself: "I didn't want to hurt him; I hurt myself instead" (Freud 1917/1961a). She need feel no guilt over her wish to murder the abuser because the rage goes back onto her. But this self-punishment inflicts a horrific price: a lifetime of suffering.

Delusions and hallucinations not only ward off our guilt. When our pain is in someone else or a voice, it is no longer in us. The woman who hears a voice calling her a pervert does not have to remember that her father was dangerous. If the danger is inside her, she can have the illusion of controlling in the present what she could not control in the past (Guntrip 1993).

Bentall (2006) suggests that auditory hallucinations are ways we hear our disavowed inner speech in the outer world. This is just one way auditory hallucinations work. For instance, if I judge myself, I might hallucinate a judgmental voice outside me. The inner wish ("I want to kill my rapist") can become an outer defense ("The voice wants me to kill myself"). It is no longer my rage toward the rapist but the voice's rage toward me. The inner truth ("My rapist is horrible") becomes an outer voice ("You are sleazy"). My judgment of the rapist turns into the voice's judgment of me, as shown in table 11.1.

Table 11.1   The relationship between internal content and the content of hallucinations

Content	Hallucinated Inversion
"I judge my rapist."	"My voice judges me."
"I want to kill my rapist."	"The voice wants me to kill myself."
"My rapist was sleazy."	"The voice tells me that I am sleazy."

Hallucinations allow the history of abuse to become conscious while the perpetrators remain out of awareness. A patient's father called her a slut while raping her. Her memory can arise in the form of a voice snarling, "You are a slut." But there is no link to the father; thus, she feels no link to the fear, pain, grief, and guilt about the rage connected to him. Instead, the rage toward the father goes back onto her through a voice: "You are a slut."

A woman cared for a friend dying from cancer. Painful loss overwhelmed her. Her higher-level defenses collapsed, and a delusion took their place. She believed that time was going backward. Her friend would not die. Her magical fantasy replaced a cruel reality (Romme and Escher 2006).

A recovering drug addict in group therapy started to hear voices telling her she was an awful person.

Th: What else are the voices saying?

Pt: Don't take my voices away! They are helping me. [*Projection: the patient wants to be rid of her voices. But she thinks the therapist wants to take the voices away.*]

Th: There is no need to worry. I can't take your voices away because they are inside you. And even if I could, I have no right to. After all, if the voices are helpful to you, you have an obligation to hold onto anything that you think will help you in your recovery. [*Deactivate the projection that the therapist wants to take away her voices, and mirror her denial.*]

Pt: I think you and the group are trying to control me. [*Projection of her wish to have more control over her out-of-control life.*]

Th: I don't have any control over you. And even if I could control you, I have no right to. [*Deactivate the projection onto the therapist.*] Does anyone in the group want to control Jane? [*The group agrees that they do not want to control her.*] I wonder, would you like to see what feelings are going on inside you so that you are more in control of your life, so you know what is driving your addiction so you can be the one in the driver's seat? [*Invite her to bear her wish to know herself inside without projecting it outside.*]

Pt: [*Crying.*] I feel like you really understand me. [*The voices stopped in that session. Since she could acknowledge her wish for control over her life, she did not need to project it onto the voices or the group.*]

Principle: *Since pseudodelusions and pseudohallucinations result from the defenses of splitting and projection, they respond to interventions that deactivate those defenses.*

Pseudodelusions and pseudohallucinations result from a temporary loss of reality testing in patients with a borderline level of character structure. Therapists can misdiagnose a person as psychotic based only on the symptoms, not on the character structure generating them. As a result, some patients diagnosed as psychotic may actually have a borderline level of character pathology and respond well to treatment.

If we focus on the defenses and the meaning of the symptoms, we can help patients face what is inside rather than project it outside. Assess responses to intervention to see whether patients have a psychotic or a borderline level of character structure.

ACTING OUT AS A REACTION TO A PROJECTION

A man in a bar sees a guy glance at him, and he yells, "What are you looking at? Huh? Huh? Want to fight?" He projects his inner judgment onto the guy, believes his projection, and then interacts with his projection by provoking a fight.

Such patients are often referred to an anger management group. But they don't need anger management; they need help with projections.

They do not rage at real triggers in the real world. They rage at projections they place on people. Once they project, they interact violently with their projections. They need projection deactivation so they will not attack the projections they place on people.

It takes only a small amount of feeling for a fragile patient to resort to projection. Thus, we explore feelings at very low levels initially. We want the patient to be aware of his anger while still able to think and reflect. Repeated experiences of high levels of rage that lead to projection only promote regression in session and acting out. Do not invite such patients to beat pillows. That encourages acting out. And worse, any guilt not processed in session will rise afterward, leading patients to get depressed or act out to get punished. Instead, help them bear feelings without discharging through yelling, cursing, or moving. One therapist invited an adolescent to beat his punching bag when he was angry with his mother. Unfortunately, he merely became better at battering his mother.

NONVERBAL FORMS OF PROJECTION

Through projection, we try to put our inner world into the outer world. The previous projections we have viewed do this through words. However, patients can also attempt to expel their experience through nonverbal forms of projection we call *discharge*. They try to get it out by yelling, cursing, or moving: "I just need to vent." Unable to tolerate a feeling inside, they try to yell their experience out of their mouths. Venting offers temporary relief but it doesn't deactivate the projection. The patient perfects the art of discharging split-off rage rather than experience mixed feelings toward the people he loves. Patients are always getting better. The question is, what are they getting better at? Venting?

They shout, curse, or get up out of the chair. Or they walk around to walk away from their feelings.

Pt: [*Waving her arms and raising her voice.*] And that son of a bitch thought he could tell me what to do!

Th: And obviously, you had some feelings toward him. When you yell, feelings become unavailable to us because they get blown out of your mouth. If you let the feelings be inside you without talking for a moment and if you let your arms rest on the chair, notice how you experience this anger toward your boss. Just notice for a moment without saying anything and without moving. What do you notice feeling inside your body now? [*Block the defenses so the experience of feelings can rise in the body.*]

Pt: Are you angry with me? [*Projection framed as a question: her reality testing is still intact.*]

Th: You are angry with your boss. [*Block the projection.*] If you let the anger be inside you, how do you experience this anger toward your boss as you let it be in your body? [*Encourage her to experience her anger internally without projecting it externally.*]

Pt: What did you say? [*Cognitive/perceptual disruption. When a patient accepts a projected feeling, cognitive/perceptual disruption may occur. Regulate anxiety immediately. Otherwise, she will need to project in the next second.*]

Th: Notice how you are having trouble hearing me right now? That can be a sign of anxiety. Are you aware of feeling anxious right now? [*Assess anxiety.*]

Pt: No. [*Patients with cognitive/perceptual disruption early in therapy often cannot pay attention to or observe their anxiety.*]

Th: How is your thinking right now? [*Assess cognitive/perceptual disruption.*]

Pt: I'm just thinking. Are you angry with me? [*Projection. She just experienced cognitive/perceptual disruption, so the therapist restructures the projection.*]

Th: No. I'm not angry. But when we noted that you are angry with your boss, you got anxious. And then your mind conked out on you, and you had trouble hearing. Do you see that sequence now? [*Block the projection. Point out the triangle of conflict to help her understand the sequence of events.*]

Pt: I didn't, then.

Th: Of course. Acknowledging anger toward your boss made you anxious. Then your anger traveled over here as if I was angry with you. But it turns out you were angry with your boss. Does that make sense? [*Point out the triangle of conflict: anger, anxiety, and the defense of projection.*]

Pt: I see what you mean.

Th: Shall we help you with your anger toward your boss so you can keep your head clear no matter how high the anger goes? [*Mobilize her will to engage in the therapeutic task by proposing a positive goal.*]

Yelling, cursing, racing speech, and impulsive movements are primitive defenses. Do not encourage them. Helping patients regress does not build affect tolerance or impulse control. Nor does it develop self-reflective functioning.

Self-reflective functioning refers to the patient's ability to observe, pay attention to, and then understand her intentions, feelings, thoughts, desires, and beliefs. The better she can understand herself, the better she can understand others (Fonagy et al. 2002). Thus, we help patients pay attention to their feelings so they know what they want and have the motivation to pursue it. We help them pay attention to their anxiety to regulate it. And we help them pay attention to the defenses that create their suffering. When they understand their inner life and actions, they can better understand the inner life of others.

Patients who yell sometimes hope their shouting will make facts go away, or they believe a scream will force a different opinion to disappear. Ordinarily, when faced with a frustrating situation, we bear and experience our feelings. Then we use them to figure out a useful way to respond. If we cannot tolerate these feelings, we might try to get rid of them by yelling or acting out. But discharge never works. It destroys relationships, and it prevents the patient's opinion from being heard. Although we try to get rid of the feelings life triggers, reality never goes away.

By experiencing reality and our feelings about it, we can begin to think (Bion 1962). And through thought, we can engage in trial action. We can imagine different options for dealing with reality (Freud 1911/1958f). For a fragile patient, an impulsive reaction becomes a substitute for a thoughtful response. A patient acts before she thinks. As soon as acting out causes pain, she acts out again to ward it off. Unable to bear that pain, she wards it off through another wave of discharge and acting out. Thus, she cannot learn from experience and think about it (Bion 1957).

Let's look at a common form of discharge: explosive rage. Patients suffering from drug addiction or severe personality disorders frequently have aggressive outbursts. They yell, threaten family members or therapists, and punch walls and tables. We may see a combination of defenses:

- "I do not love him. I hate him." [*Denial.*]
- "He hates me." [*Projection.*]
- "I hate him because he persecutes me." [*Rationalization to justify acting out toward his projection.*]

Suppose a patient starts the session calmly. But after five minutes, he rants about people and institutions that have done him wrong. He raises his voice and waves his arms wildly. After twenty minutes, he deflates and calms down again. He has a history of crime-related violence. If we let him yell in sessions, he gets better at yelling. He will discharge his feelings rather than experience them in his body and keep acting out.

Principle: *Interrupt discharge immediately. Help the patient build his affect tolerance to increase his impulse control.*

First, block the defense of acting out.

Th: When you pound the chair like that, it's a way to get rid of feelings so they won't be available to our work. And it's also a way you might hurt yourself. Would you be willing to let your arms rest on the chair so we can help you be in control instead of the impulses being in control of you? [*The patient usually acts out to avoid the experience of being out of control (helplessness). Link the therapeutic task to a positive goal: being in control.*]

Principle: *Encourage the patient to be in control so his impulses no longer control him.*

Then, build his affect tolerance.

Th: As you let your arms be on the chair, just notice the feelings inside you without speaking or moving. Just let yourself notice this power rising in you. Wouldn't it be nice to feel this power so you could be in control instead of the impulses taking control of you? So, as you take back control, how do you experience this feeling in your body?

Help him intellectualize rather than act out at this level of feeling.

Th: As this feeling rises in you, you notice some heat coming up. It makes you anxious, and you get a bit tense. Then you notice this thought of wanting to hit something. [*Describe the triangle of conflict.*] How would you put that in your own words? [*Encourage him to observe and intellectualize while feeling.*]

Principle: *Encourage the patient to put his feelings into words rather than actions.*

Following are the steps in addressing acting out.
1. Block acting out in session.
2. Build the patient's ability to bear feelings without moving or yelling.
3. Encourage the patient to put his feelings into words rather than actions.

Impulsivity results from very low affect tolerance. Thus, we use the graded format to build affect tolerance and reduce impulsivity. We block discharge and encourage higher-level defenses such as intellectualization. The more feelings he can bear without resorting to action, the more affect tolerance he will have. That will increase his impulse control and self-reflective functioning.

Discharge can be a defense or result from one. For instance, the patient can use discharge to get rid of a feeling. Or he might project and use discharge in response to that projection. For instance, if he believes the therapist wants to criticize him, he might want to beat her up.

Discharge to Ward Off Feelings

In the following vignette, a patient, angry with his wife, yells and waves his arms to get rid of the experience of anger rising within him. The therapist intervenes to block the defense and build the patient's capacity for bearing mixed feelings.

Pt: [*Ranting and shaking his arms. Defense of discharge.*]

Th: Do you notice you are yelling right now and waving your arms?

Pt: Yes!

Th: That's often a way to get rid of feeling. Any feeling you yell away or shake out we won't be able to help you with. [*Point out the price of the defense in therapy.*] Would you be willing to speak quietly right now and put your arms on the armrests? [*Block the defense.*] Let's see what you feel in your body now when you let the feeling be inside you. [*Encourage him to experience his feeling instead of getting rid of it by acting out.*]

Discharge as a Response to a Projection

A police officer, after a scuffle, was put on probation and referred by his superiors for therapy. It was a sweltering summer afternoon, yet he sat in my office with his police jacket, hat, and sunglasses on, glaring at me suspiciously. He talked rapidly, barely giving me a chance to get a word in. He spoke angrily as if I was working with the police department to fire him. I did not explore the split-off rage toward me. Instead, I deactivated the projection triggering that rage.

Pt: [*Raised voice and pressured speech.*] I don't know why I should be here. The higher-ups have it in for me. I think they're just setting me up and trying to collect evidence on me. [*Projection: the therapist will collect evidence to get me fired.*]

Th: That sounds really stressful. Just to be clear: our conversations are confidential. No one can have access to my notes unless you give written permission. Even if they ask, I can't give them anything. [*Deactivate the projection.*]

Pt: They are always asking me questions, nosing around, trying to get into my stuff. [*Projections onto the therapist.*] And I'm really getting fed up with it. But I've got to get my job back.

Th: Of course. Now, even though you are here, I don't have the right to ask you questions about anything, unless there are questions you have that you want answered in therapy. I have no right to stick my nose in any of your business. The question is whether there is something you want to look into that you think would be helpful to you. I am here to serve you, so I have no right to get into your stuff. The only question I have for you is whether you have stuff you want to get into that would be helpful to you. If you do, I'll help you explore only what you want to explore. [*Deactivate each projection.*]

Pt: [*Takes his hat, jacket, and sunglasses off.*] That sounds okay to me. [*Drop in projective anxiety and rise in the alliance.*]

Principle: *Do not explore feelings based upon projections. Instead, restructure the projections, which create the patient's defensive affect of rage. Find out the projection he wants to attack.*

When patients express their rage toward a projection, there is no relief because projection remains: an imaginary unchanging obstacle. That's why they present as hopeless. If they continually project, they feel surrounded by a seemingly hostile world.

Therapists may hesitate to interrupt the patient's ranting. Several options are available:

Example One

Pt: [*Yells.*]

Th: When you yell, I find it hard to think. And when I find it hard to think, I'll be less useful to you. Would you be willing to talk in a lower voice so I can be more helpful to you? [*Calmly remind him the price of his defense: you can't think.*]

There is no rule that you should work under all conditions. If you can't reflect while the patient yells, let him know. If he insists that he has to yell, you can continue, "That may be. But if you need to yell, we need to find you another therapist who can think while you yell. That's not something I'm able to do."

Example Two

Pt: [*Rants. There is no reason for the patient to yell at the therapist. Find out the projection the patient is yelling at.*]

Th: May I ask a question? [*Block the defense of ranting.*]

Pt: Yes.

Th: You mention that you are angry at people you feel are really critical of you.

Pt: That's for sure.

Th: Given that you think many people have been critical of you, I wonder how that may be in operation here with me. [*Invite him to explore the projection in therapy so it can get deactivated.*]

Pt: I don't know if you will help me or not.

Th: That's true. We can't know yet if I will help you or not. Given that you think a lot of people are critical of you, how is that in operation here with me?

The fragile patient may try to control you to control the projection he has placed upon you. That's why we restructure projections to increase his reality testing.

Th: You are talking almost nonstop, so I have trouble getting a word in. I wonder what thoughts and ideas you are having about the therapy that make you talk so quickly? [*Invite him to describe his projections. Then deactivate his projections to bring down the projective anxiety. Then he will not need to talk over the projections he placed on you.*]

Another patient projected his anger onto people who became "dangerous." To control those dangerous people, he had a secondary defense: a delusion. The delusion "I can read minds" provides imaginary control over the people upon whom he projects. Since projection is the primary defense and delusion is the secondary defense, we deactivate his projection first. Then the delusion is no longer necessary.

Patients may perceive other people and events through the spectacles of their projection. As a result, their descriptions of current and past relationships can be distorted. If we try to restructure projections outside the room, the patient can ask, "How do you know? You weren't there!" Instead, we focus on feelings between the patient and therapist to examine projections and evidence in the room. Restructuring his projections will increase his affect tolerance and decrease his acting out.

The therapist may have to set limits on acting out to protect the patient from self-injury. Both the patient and the therapist need a calm space where they can think together. Then we can help the patient put his feelings into understandable thoughts rather than discharge them into incomprehensible actions (Lotterman 2015, 43).

The patient who acts out impulses can sabotage his therapy in several ways. First, he splits apart his mixed feelings of rage and love. And he may act out of pure hatred with no awareness of mixed feelings. He can find the experience of acting out pure rage so gratifying that he feels no motivation to explore it (Kernberg 1975). For instance, he may avoid his mixed feelings toward the therapist through verbal attacks or threats of physical harm. Or he may use drugs while threatening suicide in the session. Whatever he acts out, he cannot put into words.

Acting out prevents us from translating impulses into words and feelings that we can explore and understand together.

Explosions of rage toward the therapist do no good. They trigger more guilt and prevent self-knowledge. Then the patient will punish himself for the guilt he cannot face or provoke others to punish him. The more he acts out, the more guilt he feels, thus the more punishment he seeks. He has to escalate until the therapist sets a limit. It's as if the therapist let a criminal loose so he can act out more, but then he will have to be imprisoned longer (Bychowski 1954).

Acting out can prevent the patient from attending therapy. For instance, patients can destroy the preconditions for therapy through drug abuse, getting put into jail, spending long periods in the hospital, alienating family members so they won't pay for treatment, lying, or letting insurance plans lapse.

Pt: I told my parents off last night. They're such assholes, so I let them have it. We ended up just screaming at each other, and my father said to me, "Get the hell out of this house." Can you believe it? [*Calling parents "assholes" is splitting: viewing them as all-bad. By yelling at them, he invites them to punish him.*]

Th: Let's take a look at this. When you yell at your parents, who are paying for your therapy, you encourage them to kick you out, cut off your finances, and stop paying for your therapy. That would sabotage our chances to work together. I wonder what feelings you might be having here toward me that would make you try to destroy our relationship? [*The patient invites his parents to punish him and stop paying for the therapy. Ask about feelings toward the therapist that lead the patient to hurt himself this way.*]

PSYCHOTIC CHARACTER STRUCTURE: PERMANENT LOSS OF REALITY TESTING

Patients at a borderline level of character pathology can have psychotic symptoms that respond to interventions addressing splitting and projection. However, patients at a psychotic level of character pathology do not respond to those interventions. Instead, they become more disorganized. Their reality testing does not improve and remains permanently suspended. However, some psychotic patients, while medicated, can respond to psychotherapy.

Pt: Why are you asking me these questions? [*Projection of the patient's wish to have answers to her questions about her life.*]

Th: These aren't my questions. The question is, would you like answers to your questions so that you have better information and can make better decisions for yourself? [*Deactivate the projection by reminding her of reality that conflicts with her projection. Then invite her to recognize her will.*]

Pt: [*Patient's eyes start darting around the room.*]

Th: What are you looking at?

Pt: The devil is in the room, tempting me. [*Hallucination. When I invite her to get answers to her questions, she feels like she is being tempted by the devil to do something forbidden.*]

Inviting the patient to recognize her will did not lead to a rise in reality testing. Instead, she became more disorganized. She projects her inner wish outward into a hallucination. Further assessment would be necessary. But her initial response suggests that exploratory work might not be advisable for her.

Delusions and hallucinations can be markers of psychosis. But "the commonest presenting symptom of psychosis is not delusions or hallucinations, which are found in some 60 percent of cases, but lack of insight manifesting as denial and rationalization, which is found in over 90 percent of cases" (Lucas 2003, 36). This lack of insight into the difference between fantasy and reality is the key marker of a psychotic level of character structure. These patients do not use rationalization to detach from feelings but to justify their projections.

When the psychotic patient projects, she pays attention to her projection, not to reality. She pays attention to what is not real: what she projects upon you. (We call her projection her *positive hallucination*: she creates a fantasy that substitutes for reality.) At the same time, she is blind to what is real in you. She does not see you. (We call that her *negative hallucination*: she does not see what is here. Imagine a patient who could see all the objects in a room but you.) Therefore, the positive hallucination and the negative hallucination require one another. "To project my fantasy upon you requires that I deny what is real in you. I don't see you [*negative hallucination*]; I perceive what I project onto you [*positive hallucination*]." When a patient projects violently, she denies that any good qualities exist in you, and she interacts with her fantasy instead.

THE SPECTRUM OF PROJECTION AS ILLUSTRATED WITH THE SAME CONTENT

The following examples illustrate how the same content in projection looks across the spectrum of reality testing.

Isolation of affect: [*Sighs.*] "You may think this was not a good idea." [*Remains detached. Anxiety is in the striated muscles. "May think" shows that reality testing is good. It's an idea about the therapist. The patient projects a healthy conscience, not a severe superego.*]

Repression: "You will think I was bad for doing this." [*Becomes weepy. The weepiness and absence of tension suggest that anxiety is in the smooth muscles or motor conversion or depression/fatigue. The patient projects that the therapist judges her, and she becomes depressed.*]

Mild fragility: "I can see that you are judging me. I can't do anything right." [*Looks scared of the therapist. Thus, a sign of a loss of reality testing and anxiety discharged into cognitive/perceptual disruption.*]

Borderline level of character pathology: "There you go judging me again. And then you call yourself a therapist! I thought you were supposed to support me! Why do you hurt me like this?" [*Oscillating projection. First, she believes the therapist judges her. Then, she judges the therapist. Work on splitting and projection may restore her reality testing. Her anxiety is in cognitive/perceptual disruption.*]

Psychotic level of character pathology: "Extraterrestrials are trying to kill me through radio waves entering my fillings." [*Permanent loss of reality testing. The projected superego is very severe: meting out a death sentence.*]

The content of the projection can be the same across the spectrum of reality testing (a superego). But the pathway of anxiety discharge can be in the striated muscles, the smooth muscles, motor conversion/weakness, or cognitive/perceptual disruption. The same projection can occur within the systems of resistance: isolation of affect, repression, or splitting and projection. And the superego can be mild in isolation of affect, severe in repression, or murderous in the psychotic patient. Reality testing can be intact in isolation of affect and repression, temporarily suspended in the borderline patient, or permanently lost in the psychotic patient. Therefore, check the context within which projection occurs.

PROJECTION AND DENIAL OF NEED: THE MANDATED PATIENT

Patients mandated for treatment by the legal system often deny having a problem. Instead, they project awareness of a problem onto a judge, lawyer, or caseworker. They say they came to treatment to meet legal requirements or to qualify for housing. But without a problem, we have no basis for doing psychotherapy. So we address projection and denial to establish an alliance.

If we wait for him to see a problem he denies, we are in denial. Instead, we actively address treatment-destructive defenses.

Th: What is the problem you would like me to help you with?

Pt: I don't have a problem. [*Denial.*]

Th: And yet you are here. [*Note the contradiction between what he says (no psychological problem) and what he does (comes to a psychologist's office).*]

Pt: I have to come to get housing. [*Denial of a psychological problem.*]

Th: I see. You have a housing problem. You may have to come to therapy to get housing. But there would be no reason for us to work with you unless you have a psychological problem. That's why I'm checking with you, what is the psychological problem you would like help with?

Pt: Can't we just talk about stuff? [*Invitation to act out.*]

Th: No. That's not what we do in therapy. [*Set a limit on acting out.*] That's why we have to find out what the psychological problem is you would like me to help you with.

Pt: I don't have a problem. [*Denial.*]

Th: You're a lucky man. [*Mirror denial.*]

Pt: Well, my caseworker thinks I have a problem with anger. [*Projection.*]

Th: Just because she thinks you have a problem doesn't mean you have one. [*Block the projection.*] So, what is the problem you would like me to help you with?

Pt: What problem do you think I have? [*Projection.*]

Th: I have no idea since I'm not you. [*Block the projection by reminding him of reality.*] That's why I have to ask you.

Pt: I have a problem on jobs. I'm feeling dizzy now. [*As soon as he presents a problem, he suffers cognitive/perceptual disruption.*]

Th: Something about having a problem makes you anxious and dizzy. Do you notice that too?

Block defenses and keep the focus on an internal emotional problem. Do not explore a problem until the patient has declared one he wants to explore. Until then, we have no right to do therapy.

Pt: Can't we just talk? [*Invites the therapist to engage in chitchat rather than psychotherapy. This devalues the therapy and avoids emotional closeness with the therapist.*]

Th: You can talk anywhere. [*Block the defense.*] The question here is, what is the problem you would like me to help you with here in psychotherapy?

Pt: Look! I know other people who come in here, and they chitchat to get their housing. What's the big deal? [*He tests to see if the therapist is corrupt. "Will you go through the motions of pretending to do therapy so I can get some housing?"*]

Th: If we did that, we would just be pretending to do therapy. But both of us would know it was just a lie. Why do that? [*Point out the defense.*]

Pt: You would still get paid.

Th: Yes, I would get paid to be a liar. And you are asking me to be a liar to you, to offer you pretend therapy rather than real therapy. But then I would be absolutely no good to you at all. [*Point out the defense and the price.*]

Pt: I think therapy is a bunch of crap. [*Defense of devaluation.*]

Th: If I agreed to give you pretend therapy and just engage in chitchat, this would definitely be a bunch of crap. Why do you ask me to give you crap? [*Point out the price of the defense.*]

Pt: I hadn't thought of that before!

Mandated patients may also offer nonproblems for him but problems for others. He provides a pseudoproblem that, if explored, would result in a pseudotherapy.

Pt: Okay. I've been depressed before. You want to look at that? [*Projection of will.*]

Th: Depends on whether depression is a problem for you. [*Block the projection of will.*]

Pt: It's not a problem for me. I'm not depressed now. [*Denial.*]

Th: That's great. [*Mirror denial.*] So what is the problem you would like me to help you with?

Pt: I could tell you about my history. My previous therapist said it is quite traumatic. [*Switches topics to avoid declaring an internal emotional problem to work on in therapy.*]

Th: I have no right to hear anything about your history unless there is a problem you would like me to help you with. [*Block the defense.*] So, what is the problem you would like me to help you with?

Pt: I feel like you are pushing me. [*Projection of will.*]

Th: That's not possible. Only you can push yourself to do therapy. I have no right to do therapy unless you have a problem you want to work on. And right now, we don't know if there is a problem you would like to work on. And if you have no problem, why work on a problem you don't have. [*Deactivate the projection of will.*]

Pt: But doesn't everyone have problems? [*Projection of his awareness of his problem.*]

Th: That doesn't mean that you have one that requires therapy. [*Block the projection of awareness.*]

Pt: Is hospitalization a problem? [*Projection of awareness.*]

Th: I have no idea. Some people like being in hospitals. [*Block the projection.*]

Pt: I don't like being in them. [*Hint of a problem about to emerge.*]

Therapy requires two people working together to resolve the patient's difficulties. You can't do therapy by yourself, but that's what the patient asks you to do. Instead, block his denial and projection. And maintain your focus on an internal emotional problem. If he continues to insist he has no problem, you can refer him to another therapist. Otherwise, you agree to be a corrupt therapist who lies to himself and the patient, pretending to do therapy when no therapy can be done. When he asks you to see him when he supposedly has no problem, he asks you to collude with his lie. He invites you to be corrupt together. If you agree, you prove to him you are corrupt and, thus, not worth depending upon. Under the best of circumstances, therapy is difficult. When the patient maintains that he has no problem, treatment is impossible.

At the same time, all too often, therapists claim, "This patient is not motivated!" But is it true? If the patient is in your office, there must be some motivation. Assess his desire to do therapy by asking, "Where has he located his motivation?" "What is so frightening about depending that he denies a wish to depend?"

The statement "This patient is not motivated" is not an assessment. It is a description. But a description is not an explanation (Bateson 1969/2000). Why does the patient declare that he is not motivated to do therapy when he shows up in a therapist's office? If he were not motivated, he could have done what seven billion people do every day: not go to a therapist's office.

Th: What's the problem you would like me to help you with?"

Pt: I don't have one. [*Denial.*]

Th: A man without a psychological problem finds himself in a psychologist's office. [*Reflect the contradiction between what he says and does.*]

Pt: My wife thinks I have a problem. [*Projection of awareness of his problem. He locates his motivation in his wife.*]

Th: Just because she thinks you have a problem doesn't necessarily mean you have one though. That's why I have to ask you, what is the problem you would like me to help you with? [*Block his projection.*]

Pt: Aren't you supposed to tell me what my problem is? [*Projection of his awareness and motivation onto the therapist.*]

Th: I have no right to tell you what your problem is because I'm not you. Only you can know if you have a problem and whether you want help with it. [*Remind the patient of reality to block his projection.*]

Pt: I think I have everything under control. [*The defense of omnipotence. No one has everything under control.*]

Th: Wonderful. A lot of people would like to be in your position. [*Mirror his position as if it is a fact. Meet him exactly where he is. This blocks his projection that you will argue with him and be the representation of reality in conflict with his denial.*]

Pt: Maybe I have a problem. But no, I don't think so. [*Splitting. Contradictory statements side by side without awareness of the contradiction.*]

Th: You think maybe you have a problem and also don't think so. [*Invite him to be aware of contradictory thoughts and feelings within himself.*]

Is he unmotivated? No. He is highly motivated. But he splits off his motivation and relocates it onto other people. The wish to depend triggers his anxiety, so his wish to declare a problem is split off and expelled to avoid the dangers of depending. Perhaps he was not supposed to depend or have problems as a child, and he learned to hide his needs from his caretakers. Every defense enacts the history of the human heart. He hid his longings to avoid loss. His current relational behaviors may represent his childhood attachment strategies. Our job is to figure out how his reactions depict the history of his suffering. If you study his denials and projections, you will find his disavowed desire.

Let's look at the evidence for his motivation.

- He is in a therapist's office.
- *Response one:* "I don't have one [a problem]" means "I do have one." The defense of negation reveals and conceals his problem. He can disclose a difficulty only if he denies it.
- *Response two:* "My wife thinks I have a problem" means "Since it makes me anxious to admit that I have a problem, I relocate my awareness and desire for help onto my wife."
- *Response three:* "Aren't you supposed to tell me what my problem is?" means "Since it makes me anxious to admit that I have a problem, I relocate my awareness and desire for help onto my therapist."
- *Response four:* "I think I have everything under control" means "I am not supposed to depend on you but only on myself. I learned this rule as a child."
- *Response five:* "Maybe I have a problem. But no, I don't think so" means "I can admit I have a problem only if I hide it right away."

That's a lot of motivation for therapy. Why don't we see it? We want a patient to say, "Yes, I really want to do therapy!" But fragile patients were hurt in relationships. The current location for healing was the past source of harm. Thus, the patient who comes to therapy is always motivated. But he is guided by conflictual motivations: "I want help, and I fear harm." The more he was hurt, the more he will hide his needs. Denial and projection show us where his desires and needs are hidden.

The therapist who assumes the patient is not motivated to do therapy becomes blind to the patient's inevitably conflictual motivations. The therapist thinks the patient's responses are "wrong." What if they are right? *In what kind of relationship would these defenses be adaptive?* Who does the therapist represent in a relationship where hiding needs and desires would be wise? Does the therapist represent an abusive father, or a mentally ill mother? When the patient claims not to be motivated, he is protecting you. It is how he learned to love. At the moment you think he is hostile and unmotivated, he is loving you the way he had to love others. As Lorna Smith Benjamin (1993) says, "Every defense is a gift of love."

Principle: *Through defenses, the patient protects others from his wish to depend. The moment you think, "This patient isn't motivated," look for the patient's conflictual motivations (the desire to depend and the fear of doing so).*

Every patient who denies his needs or projects his desires onto others suffers from the need/fear dilemma (Burnham, Gladstone, and Gibson 1969). Where does the patient locate his needs and desires? What does he fear you would do if he shared his needs with you? If he's in your office, his motivation is too. Look for it. His lips deny his needs. But his projections tell you where his motivation has been located. He always provides you with clues, if you know where to look—in his projections and denial. You expected them to be your enemies. What if they are your secret confidantes?

SUMMARY

When mixed feelings rise, leading to cognitive/perceptual disruption, fragile patients split those feelings apart to stop that anxiety symptom. And they project a thought, feeling, impulse, or capacity onto other people. This way, they can avoid a feeling inside by placing it outside. Thus, projections in fragile patients result from a lack of ability to tolerate mixed feelings inside. The less affect tolerance the patient has, the more primitive the projection becomes, and the less reality testing he has. For instance, a mildly fragile patient may project a feeling onto another person. But a severely fragile patient may project a feeling onto a hallucination, a delusion, or a split-off personality. And a psychotic patient may project feelings and impulses onto inanimate objects.

The origin of these forms of severe projection is usually trauma. The child who was beaten not just for expressing a feeling but for even having one learns to empty himself of forbidden feelings to be the empty child who does not trigger a violent parent. The little girl was sexually abused while being told her parents would be killed if she told anyone about the abuse. She silenced herself by projecting her screams into a hallucinated voice. Thus, the area of trauma is the content that needs to be projected out. For many children, having a need or desire led to punishment or banishment. Thus, they projected their needs and desires outward. Such a child is allowed to be in a disorganized attachment if she projects out of that relationship the feelings, thoughts, impulses, and capacities that would lead to abandonment. The less affect tolerance parents have, the more of herself the child must project out of that relationship to be allowed within it: "I must lose my feeling or lose you."

Through projection, the patient tells the history of her suffering: "How much of me do you need to be absent so I can be present with you?" When inviting a secure attachment, we invite the patient to accept within herself the feelings, thoughts, and impulses she relocated elsewhere. We help her experience her right to be present in a relationship. Frustration of the desire to be loved and to have one's love accepted is the greatest trauma a child can experience (Fairbairn 1952/1969, 39–40). In therapy, the patient learns that she can be accepted with her mixed feelings. And through our acceptance, she learns to accept herself.

Projections talk to us about the past, restoring to us the aspects of trauma we forever keep forgetting. Haunted by projections, the patient does not recognize how every projection is her shadow, rising from the darkness of the past, running silently to meet her. Rather than run, she can learn to turn around, face, and embrace her shadow that has always longed for her love. The orphans, the feelings the patient rejected and sent off to live in exile in other people, can finally come home and be embraced.

CHAPTER TWELVE

Severe Fragility

Pseudohallucinations and Pseudodelusions

There are consolations that the strongest human love is powerless to give.

—RICHARD POWERS, *THE OVERSTORY*

Fragile patients at a borderline level of character pathology suffering from delusions and hallucinations can respond well when we address their projections and splitting. Their reality testing improves, anxiety returns to the striated muscles, isolation of affect returns, and their psychotic symptoms diminish and disappear. This group has been called "near-psychotic" (Berner, Gabriel, and Schanda 1980; E. Marcus 2017).

Patients with a psychotic level of character structure respond differently. When we address their splitting and projection, their reality testing does not improve. They continue to use splitting and projection, and they become more disorganized. Their loss of reality testing is permanent (Gunderson and Kolb 1978; Kernberg 1977a, 1977b; Kleiger and Khadivi 2015; E. Marcus 1992/2017). To assess patients with psychotic symptoms, we evaluate their responses to interventions that address splitting, projection, and primitive denial. This differential diagnostic assessment is essential for treatment planning.

Some believe psychotic symptoms are genetically caused and unlinked to environmental factors. As a result, those suffering from these symptoms often receive little if any psychological treatment. Yet the data do not support these two premises. (See Bentall [2006] and

Read et al. [2006].) A dose-response relationship between trauma and psychosis is suggested by research. In one study, people who had suffered five traumas in childhood were 193 times more likely to suffer from psychosis (Shevlin, Dorahy, and Adamson 2007).

We call delusions and hallucinations *psychotic*. But in treatment, we need to differentiate near-psychotic from psychotic patients. When a patient loses reality testing about a perception, we call it a hallucination. Psychotic patients can describe a hallucination in great detail—they are experiencing it. When a person knows that is a hallucination—for example, due to medication—we call it *hallucinosis*. A hallucination where reality testing can be restored is a pseudohallucination (E. Marcus 2017). Patients refer to a pseudohallucination as a "voice" or a "strong thought."

The more disturbed the patient, the lower his reality testing will be. And decreased reality testing distorts how he sees himself and others. As a result of these distortions, the patient suffers from more intense affects toward the therapist, loved ones, and the treatment unit.

To build affect tolerance in the near-psychotic patient, we must understand psychotic symptoms. Psychotic symptoms usually arise following an interpersonal stressor. Experiences in relationships trigger more feelings than the patient can bear (Federn 1952). To avoid them, he uses the defenses of splitting, projection, and denial (Freeman, Cameron, and McGhie 1966; Kernberg 1975; Searles 1965/1986a). He relocates his inner life into the outer world in the form of hallucinations or delusions, no longer seeing his feared feelings, thoughts, or impulses inside himself. He perceives them inside other people or the external world. But, before all else, when pain and the resulting rage are too much, the patient's "psychosis is the partially rationalized containment of the affect, the sacrifice of reality to preserve life" (Semrad 1969, 23).

DECODING PSYCHOTIC COMMUNICATIONS

When the near-psychotic patient comes in crisis or has suddenly regressed, he has lost something. Ask, "Whom did he lose? What did he lose?" (Post and Semrad 1965). Overwhelmed by painful feelings and anxiety, he must either deny that painful reality or replace it with a delusion or hallucination.

These patients often organize their projected feelings, thoughts, impulses, or conflicts within delusions. In these delusions, they describe their plight through metaphors that they treat concretely. For instance, everyone has had the experience of feeling like a stranger or an alien. We know we are not aliens from outer space. Yet the word *alien* symbolizes how estranged we may feel. A near-psychotic patient, however, may treat his metaphor as a concrete fact. He may believe that he was sent down to Earth by mistake. We can help him if we listen to the metaphorical meanings in his words. The metaphor wards off and points toward a painful truth in his life. Let's examine some common delusions and hallucinations and how they might be understood.

Delusion: "I am an alien from outer space."

> *Metaphor:* The patient feels like an alien, as if he doesn't belong in his closest relationships.

> *Defense:* Denial: "I do not have a relational problem; I have an outer space problem."

> *Implicit communication:* "My psychiatrist, family, and social worker try to control what I think, feel, and say. They believe that I am crazy and need drugs instead of understanding. Since humans can't understand me, I must be an alien from outer space."

Delusion: "I am being poisoned."

> *Metaphor:* Poison is often a metaphor for the lies the patient has been fed.

> *Defense:* Denial. Who poisons him is erased from his awareness.

> *Implicit communication:* "My mother's criticism poisons my life." "My family feeds me lies (poison)." "When you tell me how crazy I am, you feed me despair. This lie is killing me."

Delusion: "I am a great spiritual leader chosen to save the world."

> *Metaphor:* The patient seeks to feel great.

> *Defense:* Manic denial to ward off grief and shame over dropping out of school.

> *Implicit communication:* "I failed at my greatest ambition. Being a great leader will erase the shame and humiliation of my life."

Delusion: "Someone is watching me."

Metaphor: In therapy, the patient learns to observe his inner life.

Defense: Projection. Since he fears what he will see in himself, he projects that others want to look inside him.

Implicit communication: "When I look in myself, I fear what I will find. Now I accuse you of that wish and fear what you will see." "When I watch myself, I judge myself, so I fear you will judge me too."

Delusion: "I am dead."

Metaphor: The patient no longer feels alive, as if the life he had had died.

Defense: Self-attack: "I have tried to kill something in myself." *Denial:* "I am not alive."

Implicit communication: "If I'm dead, my anger can't explode and kill everyone." "If I am dead, I am in my dead father's grave and do not have to grieve his loss."

Delusion: A hospitalized patient said he was "living multiple parallel lives."

Metaphor: We present different personas with different people, yet we remain aware of ourselves as a living person who lives behind those personas.

Defense: Fusion: "If you can't love me as I am, I will try to be who you want me to be."

Implicit communication: "I have to present a different image to each person who can't bear to meet the rest of me."

Delusion: "I'm being followed."

Metaphor: All of us wish we were being followed by those we love.

Defense: Projection: "I fear my wish for closeness, so I relocate it in someone else and then I fear my wish in that person."

Implicit communication: "I long for closeness. But since getting close has hurt me, I have to place that wish in someone else to make sure I don't try to be close and get hurt again."

Principle: *Assess how a concrete statement symbolizes a painful truth in the patient's life and wards off a truth too painful to be said in any other way.*

Karon and Whitaker (1996) suggest four ways to understand delusions:

1. They can symbolize the patient's experience of other people and the therapist. Thus, the delusion may help us understand how she experiences her relationships. They can contain an important historical truth (Waelder 1951).

2. Delusions can also satisfy the desire to create a coherent meaning for one's life. It is a normal process to deal with abnormal problems.

3. Some hallucinations try to realize a wished-for relationship. They satisfy relationship needs that are not attainable in reality (Havens 1962). For instance, delusions of being pursued often represent disavowed longings for closeness. Other delusions try to deny loss by bringing back a lost relationship. Hallucinatory voices can represent memories of meaningful relationships (Havens 1962; Modell 1958). The delusion restores a loss, but what is lost? The sense of safety, meaning, and hope found within a secure attachment (Freud 1896/1958b). Within the apparent nonreality of a delusion or hallucination lies a more profound reality: a lost relationship and the longing for it. But the loss and longing, so painful or forbidden, need to be denied, reversed, or projected. Thus, hallucinated voices become a substitute for human relationships the patient wants yet fears and, thus, avoids (Gibson 1966).

4. Bizarre ideas shared within a family can also be a source of delusions.

WORKING WITH PSEUDODELUSIONS TO RESTORE REALITY TESTING

Fragile patients often lose their reality testing while projecting. So we need to identify the content of the projection to deactivate it. Now we will show how reality testing was restored in some pseudodelusions.

Vignette One: Pseudodelusion of Being Poisoned

A paranoid man had a delusion that people were trying to poison him. As a result, he always argued with people at his drug rehabilitation unit. When the treatment team became angry, they reinforced his delusion. By arguing, they tried to put ideas (poison) into him.

Such a person has trouble tolerating mixed feelings inside himself. As a result, he views himself as good. Then he projects everything bad onto others (M. Klein 1975b). Since he fears that people are trying to shove "badness" into him, he argues to keep their ideas (poison) out.

He may experience statements as attempts to poison him. Therapist statements reinforce his projection. Instead, ask questions. Then he is the only person making statements. By asking questions, you deactivate his projection: "You want to put something in me." (See Havens [1976, 1986] for more on counterprojective maneuvers.)

Pt: The staff here are trying to put ideas in my head. [*Projection: he thinks but does not want to recognize the thoughts as his. He does not accept his wish to recover from addiction. As a result, he believes the staff is trying to push that idea onto him.*]

Th: I have no right to tell you what to think. [*Deactivate the projection by reminding him of reality.*] That's why we need to find out what <u>you think</u> would be <u>good for you</u> to work on. What is the problem <u>you want</u> to work on that <u>you think</u> would be <u>good for you</u>? [*Invite him to notice his desire. I did not use the word explore because it would reinforce his projection that I want to "get into" him. Instead, we invite him to recognize his problem and his will as indicated by the underlined words.*]

Pt: Everyone here is always trying <u>to tell me what to do</u>. [*Projection: he wants to do something (recover from drugs). When he attributes that wish to others, he will have a misalliance with the staff.*]

Th: I have no right to <u>tell you what to do</u>, because I'm not you, and your choices are yours. [*Deactivate the projection by reminding him of reality. I use the underlined words in his projection to deactivate the exact projection active in this moment.*] That's why we need to find out, what do <u>you</u> want to work on that <u>you</u> think would be good for <u>you</u> and would help <u>you</u> achieve <u>your</u> goals? [*Help him recognize his thoughts and desires by emphasizing the word* you. *Make sure the therapy achieves his desires, no one else's. The more he projects, the more yous I will use.*]

Pt: You keep asking me what I want. I feel like you are trying to push something onto me. Like this is one of those therapist agendas. [*Projection: he has an internal agenda to get well. It arouses anxiety. So he projects: other people have agendas for me.*]

Th: I have no right to push any agenda onto you because this is your life. Only you have the right to set the agenda for your life. And only you have the right to set the agenda for what you want to do here in rehab that you think would be good for you. [*Deactivate the projection by reminding him of reality.*] That's why we have to find out: what is the agenda *you want* to set *for yourself* here that *you think* would be *good for you* and *help you* achieve the results *you want* for yourself? [*Invite him to accept his desires.*]

Pt: Well, I don't want to be homeless again. [*Negative desire, what he doesn't want, primes avoidance (Grawe 2006). Invite a positive desire to prime approach.*]

Th: Of course. That's what you don't want. What do *you* want instead, so we are working toward a goal that *you* want, that *you* think is good for *you*? [*Invite him to declare a positive goal that he wants to work toward.*]

Pt: I need to hold onto a job. [*He still has not stated a positive desire.*]

Th: And is that what you want? To be able to hold a job? [*Invite him to declare a positive goal for therapy.*]

Pt: Yes.

Th: And is that the goal, the agenda you want the therapy to help you with? [*Invite him to set the agenda for the therapy.*]

Pt: Yes. But I don't know if I can. [*He has set a positive goal for the therapy. Now we can work with defenses that arise as soon as he declares this goal.*]

Since this patient projects that you want to put something into him, the therapist's behavior countered his projection. Suppose the therapist had interpreted, "You think I want to put my thoughts into you." The interpretation would have "proven" to the patient that his projection was accurate. Since the therapist cannot interpret the projection, he can counteract it through a counterprojective maneuver (Havens 1976,

1986; Sullivan 1953b). The patient acts according to his projection. The therapist acts in ways that counter the projection.

In this case, the patient fears you want to put something into him. Another patient might experience your questions as trying to pull something out of him. In that case, you can deactivate his projection by making statements since they cannot pull anything out of him. Let him pull his thoughts and feelings out of himself. You can invite him to explore his inner life, but only he can go inside himself and explore it. The therapist who remembers this can avoid trying to pull anything out of the patient. We don't have the right to do that.

Pt: I'm not going to do it.

Th: Obviously, if you don't want to do it, you shouldn't. [*Remind him of reality to deactivate the projection driving his defiance.*]

Pt: I don't want to.

Th: It's good you know what you don't want.

Pt: I'm not going to listen to another therapist. [*If the therapist might poison him with thoughts, naturally, he doesn't want to listen.*]

Th: Why listen to someone you don't want to listen to? Would you like us to help you get better at listening to yourself? [*Avoid a battle of will with him. Do not ask him to listen to you. That would reinforce his projection that you want to poison him. Ask him if he wants to listen to himself. Remind him: there is no interpersonal conflict with you. The internal conflict is between his wish to listen to himself and his fear of doing so. The therapist avoids being in conflict with him so the patient can experience the conflict within himself.*]

Pt: So what am I supposed to do here? [*Projection of his desire. The phrase "supposed to do" suggests that the therapist wants something from him. The therapist can remind him of reality: he needs nothing from the therapy.*]

Th: Nothing. I have no right to tell you to do anything. [*Remind him of reality to deactivate the projection.*] The question is what you want to do here that you think would be good for you. [*Invite him to become aware of the desire inside himself that he imagines is in the therapist.*]

Remind him of reality: his solution can come only from him, not from you. Patients will not get better because you offer *your* answer.

They get better because they figure out *their* answers. Your job is not to answer their questions but to help them live their questions so they become the answer. In the previous case, since the patient feared that the therapist was going to put thoughts in his head, the therapist asked questions instead of making statements. In the second case, the patient was afraid the therapist was trying to pull thoughts out of him. Then we offer statements instead of questions.

Principle: *Your words and deeds either feed or starve a projection. Do not feed the patient's projection. Act the opposite of it. A counterenactment allows you to interpret within his language of enactment (Bass 2000; Havens 1976, 1986; Loewald 1989; Nelson 1962, 1968; Spotnitz 1986).*

Fragile patients frequently come from backgrounds of soul blindness (Wurmser 1989) where parents were blind to the child's inner life. They did not develop the child's capacity to think for herself. Instead, they told the child to accept their projections as substitutes for her thinking. Our task is not to think for her but to help her think for herself.

Make sure that neither your language nor your actions feed the projection. Do not enact the role the patient fears you will play. If he is afraid that you want to poison him, do not attribute feelings to him, argue with him, or try to convince him that he is wrong. That feeds the projection.

Feeding the projection: "Do you feel angry?"

Blocking the projection: "I have no idea what you are feeling. Only you would know."

Feeding the projection: "Do you notice how you are controlling?"

Blocking the projection: "I have no right to try to control you. That's not the purpose of therapy. Some people use therapy to get greater control over their lives, and some don't."

If the patient believes the therapist wants something out of him, asking about his will feeds the projection. Instead, the therapist can offer will and goal in the displacement.

Th: Some people use therapy to get greater control over their lives, and some don't.

This statement makes no demand that he take in anything. But it's there for him to reflect upon. The statement "Some people use therapy to get greater control over their lives" could trigger defiance. The therapist deactivates the defiance by anticipating it: "and some don't." Offer statements that make no demands so he can decide what, if anything, he will pick up and how much. And whatever he picks up may be in the displacement. For instance, he might ask, "Why wouldn't they have control in their lives?" You could talk about why "other people" don't have control in their lives. Then you could explore his concerns about control within the displacement.

Vignette Two: Pseudodelusion That People Are Listening to the Therapy through Hidden Microphones

A woman said I should complain to the management about the people in my office building. She believed that they were listening to our sessions through microphones hidden in the bookcases. How do we understand and work with a delusion like this?

Most delusions are projections. So, first, we figure out what she is projecting.

Delusion/projection: "Other people are listening in on our sessions."

What is projected? "I want to listen to myself."

In therapy, the patient learns to listen to her inner life. But what if listening to herself got her in trouble? Many fragile patients have been told, "Shut up! Stop listening to yourself; listen to me instead." They were criticized, beaten, or sexually attacked when they listened to themselves. Since listening to themselves was dangerous, they project that wish onto others. Consider a projection as an aging photo of the patient's history of suffering.

To deactivate the projection, we can help the patient bear inside what she projected outside.

Th: Let me ask you what might seem like an odd question. Do you want to listen to yourself? [*Invite her to recognize inside what she projected outside.*]

Pt: That makes me anxious. [*She becomes anxious because the will to listen to herself arises.*]

Th: Isn't that interesting? That just listening to yourself makes you anxious, as if it's against the law to listen to you. Are you sure you want to listen to yourself? [*Point out causality. Listening to herself triggers anxiety. Anxiety is triggered by an urge within herself, not by an urge in someone else.*]

Pt: Yes. [*She becomes physically anxious again, thus indicating that will has risen.*]

Th: What do you notice feeling when you say you want to listen to yourself? [*Invite her to see causality: her wish to listen to herself triggers anxiety.*]

Pt: I get anxious.

Th: Isn't that interesting? [*Invite her to see that her wish to listen to herself causes her anxiety.*]

I continue to ask about her wish to listen to herself so she can see how her wish triggered her anxiety. Then she can feel her desire inside without projecting it outside. Once we regulate her anxiety and she can own her wish to listen to herself, a memory arises into awareness. During a disagreement, her drunk father once held a gun to her head. No wonder she projected her wish to listen to herself! Now we can process the feelings related to that memory. As affect tolerance rises, increasingly powerful memories emerge.

Vignette Three: Pseudodelusion of Being Judged

A woman wanted to buy food for her parents using her food stamps. But once she stood in front of the meat counter, she became afraid and ran out of the store. She feared that customers in the store were judging her. This was a projection of her conscience: it is illegal to use your food stamps to feed other people.

Pt: When I'm alone in an aisle, I'm okay. But when I see another person, I have to leave the aisle. [*She tries to avoid people to avoid the projection she has placed on them. To resolve her social phobia, deactivate her projections.*]

Th: I wonder what thoughts are you having about that person? [*Invite her to intellectualize about her projection to learn what she projects. Then we know what thoughts, feelings, or impulses she does not recognize within herself.*]

Pt: I was afraid of what they were thinking about me.

Th: What were you afraid they were thinking? [*Explore the content of the projection. If we know the judgments she fears in others, we can help her recognize these judgments as hers.*]

Pt: That I was doing something wrong with my food stamps. [*This was a projection of her conscience: it is illegal to use your food stamps to feed other people.*]

Th: You had a thought about what you were doing with your food stamps. [*Invite her to accept her conscience inside without projecting it outside.*]

Pt: Yes. [*Becomes uncomfortable.*]

Th: Do you notice how you become uncomfortable as soon as we notice that you had a thought about what you were doing with your food stamps? [*Invite her to recognize her thoughts inside without projecting them outside. Since the word* guilt *might trigger too much anxiety, we grade the exploration by referring to thoughts. Thoughts* triggers a lower amount of feeling, so she can engage in self-reflection.*]

Pt: Yes.

Th: Isn't that interesting? Just knowing that you have a thought about your food stamps makes you anxious. [*Help her see the sequence and tolerate the anxiety of recognizing her projection.*]

Pt: [*Calms down.*] Yes.

Th: Having a thought about using your food stamps for your parents makes you uncomfortable.

Pt: Are you saying I did something wrong? [*Projection.*]

Th: Who just had that thought? [*Remind her of the thought inside her so she doesn't project it outside herself.*]

Pt: I did, but—

Th: [*Interrupt before projection increases.*] I'm just noticing that when you have a thought about your food stamps, you get anxious. Then you imagine I'm having a thought about your food stamps. But this is your thought. [*Remind her of reality: she has thoughts.*]

Pt: [*Momentarily dizzy. Cognitive/perceptual disruption. Regulate anxiety so projection and reality testing do not worsen.*]

Th: Notice how you get a little anxious right now as soon as you notice this thought inside you? Something about thinking about what you were doing makes you anxious and gets you dizzy. Do you see that too? [*Describe the sequence in this moment: becoming aware of her thoughts inside herself triggers her anxiety.*]

Pt: Yes.

Th: Something about thinking about using the food stamps for your parents makes you anxious. [*Slightly increase the dosage of language to test whether she can accept more of her inner life: (1) "something about thinking about what you were doing," (2) "thinking about using the food stamps."*]

Pt: I felt a little guilty. [*Sign of increased affect tolerance: the word* guilt *comes to mind. As affect tolerance increases, higher dose words will emerge.*]

Th: When you felt guilty, you worried that other people thought that too. But this guilt was something inside you. What do you notice feeling as you let the guilt be inside you right now? [*Build her capacity to bear a feeling inside without projecting it outside.*]

Here is a later example with the same patient involving another projection.

Pt: I was in a meeting, but I had to leave. I got too freaked out by all those people. [*She is not freaked out by other people but by the projections she places on them.*]

Th: What thoughts did you have about those people? [*Invite her to intellectualize about her projections.*]

Pt: I was afraid of what they were thinking about me. [*She begins to intellectualize about her projections.*]

Th: What did you think they were thinking? [*Invite her to reflect on her projections.*]

Pt: I was afraid they would think I wasn't doing the steps in rehab. [*Projection: she judges herself but fears they would judge her.*]

Th: Why would they think that? [*Invite her to describe in the displacement why she doesn't think she is doing the steps.*]

Pt: The other day, I wondered where Jim was getting his heroin. And they would think I wasn't doing the steps. [*Projection of self-judgment.*]

Th: You had a thought about getting heroin, but did you get it? [*Differentiate a thought from action.*]

Pt: No. But I thought about it.

Th: Sure. A thought came up. And you are aware of that thought. So, I wonder: since you didn't get heroin, why would they have trouble telling the difference between a thought and an action? [*Help her see the difference between a thought and an action.*]

Pt: I don't know.

Th: The reason I ask is that it sounds like you were afraid they would judge you for having a thought even though you didn't act on it. You still did the steps and stayed sober. [*I interpret her difficulty, but within the projection she has provided.*]

Pt: It's true. I didn't do anything. [*As she sees this difference, her self-judgment and anxiety drop. Next, I can ask about the feelings toward me under her self-judgment.*]

Use the graded approach (table 12.1) when inviting the patient to accept inside what she projected outside. First, we help her recognize that a thought she attributed to someone else is a thought inside her. We help her bear her thought that she did something wrong, and we help her feel her guilt. Rather than project her conscience onto others, she gradually learns to bear it inside.

Table 12.1   Steps in projection deactivation

1. Invite the patient to intellectualize to discover the content of the projection: "What thoughts come up about those people?"
2. Explore the content of the projection: "What were you afraid they were thinking?"
3. Invite her to accept what she projected: "So you had a thought."
4. Invite her to see causality—accepting inside what she projected outside triggers anxiety: "Having a thought about food stamps made you uncomfortable."
5. Invite her to accept a higher dose of what she projected: "You had a thought about doing something wrong." Throughout the process, regulate anxiety as needed.
6. She accepts what she projected (her conscience): "I felt guilty."
If she projects onto one person, she has one projection. But in a group of twelve people, she has twelve projections. Interacting with those projections, she "freaks out," acts out, argues, or runs away. She does not relate to the group; she interacts with projections she regards as real.

Here's a later exchange with the same patient:

Pt: When I heard the voices, I had trouble knowing if they were real or not.

Th: You didn't know if they were voices from the outside or thoughts from inside yourself. [*Build reality testing by differentiating inside from outside.*]

Later, she heard voices outside her home and believed people were talking about her.

Pt: The people outside were all against me because they knew I had been in the hospital. [*She judges herself for having been hospitalized. Then she projects her inner judgment onto others.*]

Th: There's a thought that other people would be against you for having been in the hospital. Since you have that thought about them, I wonder what thoughts you might be having about the therapy? [*Bring a projection onto the therapist in the open. Then it won't silently defeat the therapy, leading to premature dropout.*]

Since all delusions and hallucinations involve splitting and projection, we use the same principles of projection deactivation to build affect tolerance. Table 12.2 lists those principles.

Table 12.2   Principles of projection work

1. Invite the patient to intellectualize about the projection to find what she is projecting.
2. Invite her to become aware inside of what she projected outside.
3. Use the lowest affect dosage word to activate the least amount of feeling possible in a patient who projects.
4. When she bears inside what she projected, invite her to bear a higher dose inside to increase her affect tolerance.
5. When anxiety is too high, invite the patient to pay attention to bodily signs of anxiety to regulate it.

Vignette Four: Pseudodelusion of People Looking at Her

A patient entered the office, peered out the window, and asked the therapist to draw the curtains.

Th: [*Draws the curtains.*] Sure. I'm just wondering, what thoughts you're having that make you want them closed?

Pt: I don't want people in the office building over there looking at me.

In therapy, we invite the patient to look at her inner life with compassion. But fragile patients often learned not to look inside, for what they saw they might share, and what they share might endanger the relationship. To avoid speaking from the heart, they learned not to look in it. Instead, they sent the dangerous wish away to live in others. Then they feared what others might see. And that fear never leaves because the wish to look, to see, to become at one with the truth is inherent in our being (Bion 1970).

After closing the blinds, the therapist can help the patient become aware of her projected wish.

Th: I notice you were afraid that people might be looking into the office at us. This might seem like an odd question, but do you want to look at yourself in therapy? [*Invite her to become aware of her wish to look inside herself rather than project it.*]

Pt: Yes. [*Said tentatively.*]

Th: Do you want to look at yourself so you know more about yourself than anyone else?

Pt: Yes. But I'm wondering what you are looking for. [*Projection.*]

Th: Nothing. The question is what you are looking for out of the therapy. [*Block the projection.*] Do you want to look at yourself so you have better information about yourself? After all, let's not forget, just because you look inside and learn more about yourself doesn't mean you have to tell me what you learn. That's why we need to find out if you want to look inside yourself so you have better information to work with. [*Invite her to recognize her will to look inside so she doesn't project it onto others.*]

These invitations help her become aware inside of what she projected outside. But once she observes her inner wish, she may become anxious. Keep cognizing about her anxiety to help her remain aware of her wish to look at herself. Once she accepts her wish, she will no longer project it onto others. Then we can establish a therapeutic alliance based on her desire to look into her depths.

PSEUDOHALLUCINATIONS

Hallucinations and pseudohallucinations result from splitting and projection. Most auditory hallucinations occur right after a trauma or after an event that triggers memories of a trauma (Honig et al. 1998; Romme 2012). Romme and Escher (2006) find that 77 percent of schizophrenic patients and 100 percent of dissociative patients related their voices to traumatic events. Explore the event that triggered a hallucination. Find out what feelings and conflicts were evoked (Katan 1950). Then we know what the patient projects into the hallucination and why.

Pseudohallucinations refer to real people and situations, and the patient is not extremely withdrawn. The pseudohallucination expresses some internalized relationship in the patient's life (Freeman, Cameron, and McGhie 1966, 125–130). Hallucinations in psychotic character structure, however, try to establish a new psychic reality to substitute for the real world. And they do not respond to interventions.

Content of Hallucinations

Hallucinations have varied contents such as fragments of childhood experiences (Freud 1912/1958c). Find out what the patient projects into a hallucination so we know what to invite.

Hallucination of one's projected inner judgment:

- The patient hears a voice accusing her of having committed a terrible deed. [*She cannot bear her self-accusations.*]
- "I can hear through the wall that people are talking about me." [*She cannot bear the critical thoughts she has about herself.*]
- "This voice keeps telling me to kill myself." [*Unable to tolerate her wish to kill someone else, she gives herself a death sentence.*]

Hallucinations of one's projected anger:

- "A voice keeps telling me to kill people."
- "When I don't express my anger, my voices get angrier with me."

Hallucination as a split-off memory:

- A woman heard a child's voice reciting a nursery rhyme. Later in therapy, it was discovered that as a child she recited a nursery rhyme to blot out her pain while being abused.

Hallucination as a split-off conflict:

- A young man was angry with his roommates but could not let himself say anything. Later he hallucinated two voices: an outraged voice and a calm, rational voice. Now, his inner conflict occurred between two voices outside of him.
- A psychotic patient was trying to decide whether to leave the hospital. She felt better but wanted to stay. Since she could not tolerate her conflict, she hallucinated her former therapist's voice: "You are taking the easy way out." In this way, she could express the wish to stay while her voice judged it (Schulz 1980, 184).

Hallucination as split-off reasoning:

- Romme (2012) describes a woman who had recently moved into a larger apartment. However, she heard a voice: "I will get you; I will break you down; you are not worthy of living in such a beautiful apartment." The voice pointed out that the apartment was too expensive, given that she had no job. In fact, she had taken on too big a financial burden, denying her capacity for reasoning and self-care. Understanding her voice enabled her to seek a job and keep her apartment.

Hallucination as a defensive flight into fantasy:

- A patient's husband had an affair and left her. Later, she heard a voice telling her to fly to a foreign country where she would find a new husband. Her hallucination offered a fantasy husband to deny the loss of a real one.

Hallucination as a form of denial:

- A patient heard a voice telling him to blind himself (Romme 2012). The therapist asked, "What do you not want to see?" He described severe conflicts between his parents.

Hallucination as a form of identification with the aggressor:

- Sexually abused patients may hear voices repeating the abuser's words. The voices can share characteristics of the abuser, such as sex, age, or tone of voice. One patient's mother said, "I wish you were dead." His voices said, "You deserve to die."

Delusion that relies on manic self-inflation to avoid the shame for one's failure:

- "The Nazis are trying to destroy me because they know I will give birth to the Messiah."

Delusion as a defense against loss:

- A man who had lost his mother had a delusion that he could create a time machine. He collected materials to build one. Thereby, he could magically rewind time to the period before her funeral and never have to face his grief.

Exploring Voices to Build Affect Tolerance

We listen to voices to learn about the patient's disavowed inner life. When she sees the links between her life experiences and her voices, they make sense (Romme and Escher 2000, 16). To explore voices, do the following:

Find out the triggering event.

Th: When did you start to hear the voices?

Th: When did the voices become louder?

Th: What was happening in your life when the voices started?

Find out the content.

Th: What do the voices say to you?

Find out who the voices represent.

Th: Whom does the voice sound like?

Th: Who said things like that to you?

Find out what problems the voices represent.

Th: What occurred in your life that would make sense of this voice?

Th: How do these things the voices say make sense in your life?

The patient may not be able to answer these questions directly right away. Due to low levels of affect tolerance, her answers may be indirect and obscure. Thus, patience is essential. As she bears higher levels of feelings, her communication can become clearer.

Find out where the voice's content fits. Voices may represent patient's disavowed feelings, thoughts, or urges.

Th: Why is the voice angry? What happened at that time that would have made your voice angry? [*If the patient believes the voice, we may need to explore within the defense of projection: "Why was the voice angry?" Later we could ask, "What did you feel?" Graded exploration can start within the defense, then proceed directly within her.*]

Th: Why would the voice have that thought? What happened at that time that would have made the voice have that thought? Why is the voice afraid of that thought? [*Since the patient projects her conflict onto the voice, we can explore her conflict there. Help her think about her conflict without having to recognize it as hers yet.*]

Th: Why does the voice accuse you of that urge? Why does the voice judge that urge? Why is the voice afraid of that urge? [*Invite her to explore why the voice judges and fears this urge. Later, we can explore why she does.*]

First, we can explore conflicts the voice has to help her bear what she attributes to the voice. Grade exposure to ideas and feelings within the hallucinations to build her affect tolerance until she can accept her inner life.

Grading the Invitation to Bear Projections Inside

When reality testing is good and affect tolerance high, patients can accept their projections readily. However, when reality testing and affect tolerance are low, patients cannot. If we invite them to recognize projections too quickly, anxiety will spike again. This can lead to more projection and a loss of reality testing. See the following spectrum of interventions.

Direct invitation to bear the projection:

Pt: I feel like you can see inside me. [*Projection of the wish to look inside herself with a slight loss of reality testing.*]

Th: No. I can only see what you reveal to me. So, you are in control of what I can see. [*Deactivate the projection by reminding her of reality.*] The question here is, would you like to look inside yourself so you have the information you need to make better decisions for yourself? [*Invite her to bear her wish to look at herself.*]

Exploration within the projection (voices with greater loss of reality testing):

Pt: The voices are screaming at me, telling me to use drugs.

Th: Why do they want to punish you? [*Invite her to explore her superego within the projection. She cannot bear it inside, which is why she projects it so violently into a voice. Exploring within the defense of projection helps her think about her difficulties at a manageable level of feeling.*]

The lower the reality testing, the lower the affect tolerance. Thus, the lower the dose of feelings we invite her to bear inside.

Reflection as an Initial Phase in Exploring Hallucinations

Reflection can help patients who believe their hallucinations and have lost reality testing (Prouty 1994; Prouty, Van Verde, and Portner

2002). In Prouty's example (1994, 73–89), he reflects the patient's comments statically, not dynamically, without adding anything more than what the patient has said. The patient says the voice is evil and later says it is strong. Prouty replies, "It's evil and strong." Later, the patient says the voice is orange, square, and hates him. Prouty replies, "It's orange and it's square and it hates you." He continues to reflect the patient's experience exactly as the patient provides it. Eventually, the patient remembered a traumatic event that made sense of the hallucination.

In this constant invitation to feeling, the therapist reflects back the patient's words exactly, working within the defense of hallucination. He adds nothing that would trigger more feeling and anxiety to further disrupt the patient. Static reflection builds the patient's affect tolerance until his experience emerges in a higher form of symbol, in this case, a memory. For instance, a patient might hallucinate. You might reflect what he says without adding anything for some time. Later, he might talk in metaphors. You might interpret or explore within his defense of metaphor. And later, he might talk directly about a memory. Each of these steps in symbol formation represents a higher level of affect tolerance.

Principles for Deactivating Projections in Voices

Do not try to control the symptom. Listen to the feelings underneath that make the symptom necessary. Voices express emotions the patient cannot hold inside. Explore the origins, context, and history of the voices. Voices allow us to listen to what the patient cannot listen to within himself. They enable us to hear his split-off emotional life. Whatever he cannot bear inside, calls to him from the outside.

Therapists may become afraid when a patient hears voices or shares delusions. Instead, we should welcome voices. They reveal outside what he cannot bear inside. When therapists fear voices, they may try to control what the patient hears or thinks. That is impossible. Instead, focus on his relationship to those beliefs and voices.

Th: How does the voice treat you?

Th: Why does the voice criticize you?

Th: What does the voice think the criticism will achieve?

Th: How is the voice trying to help you?

Th: What does the voice think your problem is?

Accept that voices are real; after all, patients hear them. Do not argue about whether the voices are real. Listen to the deeper realities the voices reveal. By listening more deeply to your patient, she can listen more deeply to herself. Your interest may spark her hope for a better life outside the confines of her projections.

Help her experience the voices as personal messages about her inner life. Then, the truths that only her voices could speak, she can give voice to openly. Voices calling her names may be memories of verbal abuse. You might regard voices as memories in plain view. Help her face the mixed feelings toward parents who loved her and abused her. Then she can integrate her understanding of them and herself.

In psychotherapy, we face what we have avoided. The voices say what she could not. Once she can face her feelings and express them, she can speak rather than her voices speak for her. She is in charge rather than the voices being in charge of her. She can face her inner life without locating it in a hallucination.

In the following example, a patient hears a voice telling her not to trust the therapist. She cannot bear internal conflict. "I want to trust, and I do not want to trust." By projecting her distrust upon the voice, she remains a "good" trusting person with a "good" trustable therapist. But she still distrusts and projects and, as a result, remains anxious. Since she projects her distrust onto the voice, the therapist invites her to accept her distrust. This builds her capacity to bear internal conflict.

> Th: There must be some good reasons not to trust the therapy. [*I use the word* therapy *rather than* me. *Grading the invitation helps her reflect on the process.*] If we trust your mistrust [*Invite her to become aware of her distrust*], what does the mistrust say about the therapy? [*The therapist introduces the higher-level defense of displacement. Focus on what the voice says about the therapy, not what she says. This graded use of language allows her to talk about mistrust before she recognizes it as hers.*]

Here is another intervention that builds her capacity to bear internal conflict.

> Th: Why should you trust someone you don't trust? What if this distrust is trying to protect you? Sometimes, we have not listened to our distrust enough. [*This is always true for traumatized patients. They trusted someone who hurt them.*] Can we help you listen to

your distrust so that you can protect yourself better? [*Invite her to recognize a positive goal and to accept her distrust. Help her bear the conflict between her wish to trust and her fear of doing so.*]

When such a patient projects her distrust into the voice, she tries to be a "good" person with a "good" therapist. Just as she had to pretend not to be frightened with a frightening parent. If you point out that her mistrust functions as a barrier, she may "agree" to please you as she pleased her abuser. Instead, accept her mistrust and encourage her to explore it. This builds her capacity to tolerate inner conflict: her wish to trust and her defense of not trusting. In a secure attachment, we accept conflictual thoughts and feelings. The therapeutic task is not to get rid of the voice. Instead, we help her accept her inner life inside until she no longer needs to relocate it in a voice.

A SPECTRUM OF INTERVENTIONS FOR DISTRUST

We can address distrust in many ways. Reality testing correlates with the degree of affect tolerance. The following interventions illustrate that spectrum.

Example One: Isolation of Affect—Moderate Resistance

Pt: [*Sighs.*] How do I know if I can trust you? [*Anxiety in the striated muscles, reality testing is fine.*]

Th: You can't yet because we haven't worked together. If you like, we could explore a problem you would like help with. And as we work together, you can find out whether or not I am trustworthy.

Example Two: A Fragile Patient with Cognitive/Perceptual Disruption and Projection

Pt: I'm not sure I can trust you. [*Projection. "Not sure" indicates that reality testing has not been entirely lost in the moment.*]

Th: Thank you for trusting me enough to say that. What thoughts are you having about the therapy that make it seem untrustworthy? [*Find out the projections she is not trusting. Patients trust the therapist. They don't trust the projections they place on the therapist. But they often cannot differentiate the therapist from their projections.*]

Pt: I'm just afraid you will make me talk about things I don't want to talk about. [*Projection.*]

Th: I have no right to ask you to talk about things you don't want to talk about. [*Remind her of reality to deactivate the projection.*] That's why we have to find out what you want to talk about that you think would be good for you and help you achieve your goals. [*Invite her to declare her desire and goal.*]

She has stated the specific projection she distrusts, and she is aware of it. The therapist can deactivate it and invite her to recognize her desire. Rather than distrust the therapist's supposed desire, she can begin to trust her own.

Example Three: A Fragile Patient with Cognitive/Perceptual Disruption and Projection

Pt: I can't trust you yet. [*Projection. "Yet" indicates that although reality testing is impaired, she could trust the therapist if we clear up the projection.*]

Th: There must be a good reason for that. What thoughts come up about the therapy that make it seem untrustworthy? [*Find out the projections she is not trusting. Refer to thoughts that "come up," not thoughts she "has." This differentiates her from the thoughts so she can observe and reflect on them.*]

Pt: I've been hurt by too many people. And my last therapist said I had to trust her if the therapy was going to work. [*Projection: she fears that the therapist will try to control her distrust rather than explore it.*]

Th: Since you've been hurt by people, naturally you wonder if someone will hurt you or help you. [*Validate the origin of her distrust.*] I have no right to ask you to trust me if distrust is protecting you right now. [*Remind her of reality and deactivate the projection that you will try to control her.*] Could we listen to your distrust now, honor it, and see what it has to say? [*Deactivate the projection.*] What other thoughts occur to you about the therapy that generate this distrust reaction? [*Find out other projections that could be causing her distrust.*]

The patient starts by saying, "I can't trust you yet," not realizing that this is an automatic reaction. The therapist helps her differentiate herself from the defense. He doesn't refer to anything she "does." Instead, he refers to a "distrust reaction" that protects her. And he invites her to respect and reflect on the reaction. She and the therapist can look at and observe it. The therapist listens to and values the defense, thus deactivating the projection that he wants to control her distrust.

A SPECTRUM OF INTERVENTIONS WITH A HALLUCINATED VOICE

A therapist was working in a clinic with a patient described as "psychotic." In the initial session, she had declared a problem to work on.

> Th: And is this the problem you would like us to work on? [*Invite her to recognize her will without projecting it outside.*]
>
> Pt: Yes. [*Pauses.*] But the voice says, "No." [*She splits off her defense and projects it onto a voice.*]

The following interventions for projection illustrate a spectrum of graded invitations. The amount of feelings we invite her to bear depends on her affect tolerance. Clues to affect tolerance include the language the patient uses.

Inviting the patient to bear the projection inside: high-dose invitation

> Pt: [*Sighs.*] My mother thinks I shouldn't.
>
> Th: Since your mother says, "no," I wonder if you also are hesitant. Could you say a bit about your hesitance to work on this problem? [*She projects her wish not to work on a problem onto her mother. Although projected onto her mother the wish to resist is conscious and her reality testing is fine, so we can invite her to describe her hesitance.*]

Inviting consciousness of splitting

> Th: And is this the problem you would like us to work on? [*Invite her to recognize her will without projecting it outside.*]
>
> Pt: Yes. [*Pauses.*] But the voice says, "No." [*Projection of one side of her conflict (resistance) onto a voice.*]
>
> Th: An urge to work on this problem and an urge not to work on this problem. [*Mirror splitting. She says she wants to work on her problem, but she splits off her resistance and projects it onto a voice. Since she can accept her wish, we mirror the split to build her consciousness of splitting.*]

Inviting the patient to bear some of the projection inside: siding with the defense

> Th: And is this the problem you would like us to work on? [*Invite her to recognize her will without projecting it outside.*]

Pt: The voice says, "No." I mustn't listen to you. [*She looks afraid—a sign of decreasing reality testing. She projects one side of her conflict (resistance) onto a voice ("No"). And she projects the other side of her conflict (her wish to listen) onto the therapist. "Don't listen to him" is a form of negation. If we take out the "not," her statement is "do listen to him." Her preconscious wish to listen to the therapist can emerge as long as it is negated.*]

Th: Can we listen to that voice? It must have a very important reason not to work on this problem. If we honor and respect that voice, why do you suppose the voice doesn't want to work on this problem yet? [*The therapist encourages her to listen to her resistance, thus deactivating her projection that he wants her to listen to him.*]

The therapist could continue by asking, "Why do you suppose the voice doesn't want you to work on this problem?" The therapist invites her to think about and reflect on the voice's resistance. She does not have to accept it yet as hers, and she can describe why the voice doesn't want to work on a problem and the voice's fears. Intellectualizing about the voice builds her affect tolerance. Once her affect tolerance increases enough, she can talk about her own wishes and fears.

She believes the voice, and she splits off and projects both sides of her conflict. She projects resistance onto the voice, and she projects the wish to listen onto the therapist. Thus, the therapist invites her to describe her resistance within the defense of projection. He invites her to talk about the voice's resistance. She projects her wish to listen to herself onto the therapist: "*You want me to listen* to you." The therapist deactivates the projection by inviting her to listen to her voice to help the patient bear the conflict between her wish to connect and her fear of doing so.

Exploring the resistance by working within the defense of splitting: lowest dose

Suppose these interventions triggered cognitive/perceptual disruption. Then the therapist can deactivate the projection ["*You want me to work*"] by inviting the patient to say out loud what the voices say.

Th: Can we listen to that voice? It must have a very important reason not to work on this problem. If you sit in this other chair, would you be willing to say out loud what the voice is saying so we can hear its side of the story?

The therapist can explore what the voice thinks and fears without needing the voice to change in any way. After the patient has spoken as the voice, the therapist invites her to sit back in the other chair.

> Th: What do you understand about this voice that you didn't understand before?

At this lowest level of reality testing, we can converse with the voice to discover its motivations in its relationship with the patient. Accept everything the voice says without expressing any desire to change the voice. Find out how the voice relates to her, regards her, and protects her. Help the patient express the voice's point of view: exploring within the defenses of splitting and projection. At the end of the session, you can ask the voice what advice it has for her. Thank the voice and invite the patient to sit in the other chair. Then the two of you can reflect on what you have learned. This dialogue allows her to observe and think about what the voice says. Exploring within the defense builds her affect tolerance. When it builds enough, she will spontaneously talk about issues as her own.

Oscillating Projected Voices

Since a paranoid patient was very hesitant in her initial therapy session, the therapist asked what thoughts she had about the therapy. She reported hearing voices that were telling her to quit and stop talking to the therapist.

Like every patient, she wanted help. But her wish to form a healing connection triggered anxiety. As a defense, she wanted to resist the therapy, but she could not bear her internal conflict. She wanted help and did not want help. When she projected her resistance onto the voices, she could seem like a "good" girl with "bad" voices.

The therapist can help her become aware of the conflict inside herself. Otherwise, she might have to obey the voice and quit the therapy. To help build her capacity, the therapist mirrored her conflict:

> Th: Sounds like you're having a struggle inside: you want help, and the voices tell you to quit and not get help. [*Mirroring the conflict builds her awareness of it while bearing the feelings conflict triggers.*]

The therapist maintained this stance until she broke down crying.

> Pt: I hate myself.

This was a marked piece of progress. Instead of projecting that the voices hated her, she acknowledged how she hated herself. But recognizing her internal conflict caused a rise of feelings, anxiety, and the next projection.

> Pt: I don't want to let that go. I don't know who I would be without it. I'm not letting it go right now. [*Projection. She accuses the therapist of wanting her to give up her self-hatred. In fact, she would like to let go of it, but she cannot bear the feelings triggered by that wish.*]

Before, she projected her resistance onto the voices. Now she accepts her resistance but denies her wish to get well. So the therapist mirrors the patient's resistance and denial.

> Th: I will honor your wish to hate yourself. I will not ask you to stop your self-hatred and criticism if that is something you feel is helpful for you. I can't take your self-hatred away from you, and I will never try to push you or make you look at something you're not ready to look at.

> Pt: [*Becomes dizzy. Cognitive/perceptual disruption. Progress: she disrupts with anxiety rather than project to avoid conflict.*]

The therapist avoids being in conflict with the patient's wish to hate herself. As a result, she is in conflict with her self-hatred. This triggers anxiety. The therapist helps her regulate her anxiety and see its cause. She wants to get well, and she wants to hate herself. Once she can bear her internal conflict, the therapist can help her look at the feelings toward the therapist that the self-hatred is covering.

To understand this complex sequence, let's spell it out:

1. The therapist invites the patient to form a healing relationship.
2. Anxiety rises in the patient.
3. She projects her wish to resist. "The voices don't want me to do therapy, and they attack me." (*By projecting her wish to resist onto the "bad" voices, she remains a "good" girl who wants to collaborate.*)
4. The therapist mirrors the conflict: "You want therapy, and the voices don't want you to do therapy." The patient becomes aware of her internal conflict.
5. Anxiety rises in the patient.

6. She projects her wish to get well. She experiences conflict, becomes anxious and projects: "You want me to be healthy. You want to take my self-hate away."

7. The therapist deactivates the projection: "I can't take it away. Only you can do that. If self-hate helps you, you should do it as long as it is useful to you."

8. The patient bears a higher degree of conflict. She becomes dizzy. Now she sees her wish to get well and her self-hatred. The complex mixed feelings inside trigger anxiety without projecting, self-attack, or acting out.

The patient alternates between projecting her resistance and projecting her wish to get well. She has trouble tolerating both inside at once. If the therapist tries to stop her self-hatred, the patient might hate herself more freely. Her healthy wish will be in the therapist, not her. She will be in conflict with the therapist, not within herself.

Assessing Latent Projections

Up to this point, we have evaluated projections in pseudodelusions and pseudohallucinations. Now we will examine another form of unconscious projection. Patients may not tell you directly when they fear you. Instead, they describe how they fear other people. They portray their projections within the defense of displacement.

The following patient had suffered a brain injury, and he had gone to prison after he shot a stranger. He had called for the session, but he arrived a half-hour late and spoke aggressively to the therapist. The quotes in italics reveal his latent projections onto the therapist.

Pt: My father is really controlling. I built a house, and he tried to take it. ["*You will try to control me and take something from me.*"] When I'm gone, my dogs howl until I return. ["*I will feel tremendous grief when you leave me.*"] I was afraid you would be like my previous therapists, who were all assholes. ["*I project my rage on you and expect you to hurt me. That's what happened with my previous therapists.*"] I get so frightened that I crawl under my bed [*loss of reality testing*]. ["*I am afraid of you. I equate you with my projection, and I behave accordingly.*"] It's hard to be around other people, so I stay away from them. I prefer to live alone. ["*It's hard for me to be with you when I equate you with my projection, so I will stay away from you. That's what I did today for the first thirty minutes."*] It's a hard thing in prison because you can't do that. There was a guy I was attracted to, but he is distancing from me, and I don't know what I did wrong. He won't talk to me. I have no idea what he is thinking about me. [*"It's hard for me to avoid you when I'm here. I want to work with you, but when I project my anger upon you, I assume you don't like me and won't talk to me. When you are silent, I assume you don't like me and won't talk to me. Your silence proves that you don't like me."*]

He has suffered a brain injury and shot someone. That suggests that he equated someone with a projection and lost his reality testing. He came late to the session, which may indicate that he was already projecting upon the therapist. In the transcript, we see latent projections onto the therapist. The patient's defense of displacement is a higher-level defense we do not want to weaken. Therefore, we do not address his projection directly (e.g., "I wonder if you are afraid I will try to control you as your father did."). A direct interpretation could weaken his higher-level defenses, causing a regression. Instead, we can address his projections indirectly within the defense of displacement. That way, we do not weaken his higher-level defense. The following examples illustrate how to address projections within the defense of displacement.

Example One

Pt: My father is really controlling. I built a house, and he tried to take it.

Th: Nobody likes being controlled. [*Counterprojective maneuver: I won't try to control you.*] So just to be clear, what would you like to work on here so you could feel in more control in your life? [*Invite his will and remind him of the therapeutic goal: to be more in control. This counters his projection that the therapist wants to control him.*]

Example Two

Pt: When I'm gone, my dogs howl until I return.

Th: Dogs get attached to us, and they miss us. It's hard for them to remember that we'll come back. It's like they forget. [*Interpretation within the defense of displacement. Describe his attachment, grief, and fear of abandonment: the loss of evocative memory (Adler 1993).*]

Example Three

Pt: I was afraid you would be like my previous therapists, who were all assholes.

Th: Nobody likes an asshole. [*Counterprojective maneuver.*] What do you think we need to do differently this time so you could have a better result? [*Before, the projection was unconscious. Now it is conscious: "I was afraid you. . . ." As a result, the therapist can address his projection consciously: "What do you think we need to do differently?" This places him in control, thus deactivating his projection.*]

Example Four

Pt: I get so frightened that I crawl under my bed [*loss of reality testing*].

Th: It can be scary when we have a thought and we can't tell the difference between the thought and what is actually happening. [*Interpret his loss of reality testing and how it increases his anxiety. By saying "It can be scary" instead of "You were afraid," the therapist offers the defense of displacement. This helps the patient think about feelings and problems without having to recognize them yet directly. A statement in the displacement can test whether he can reflect on the difference between reality and a nightmare.*]

Example Five

Pt: It's hard to be around other people, so I stay away from them. I prefer to live alone.

Th: It's hard to be around people if we think they would be controlling. Would you like us to help you feel more in control of yourself so that your fear would no longer be in control of you? [*Deactivate the projection onto the therapist. Then mobilize his will to the task.*]

Example Six

Pt: It's a hard thing in prison because you can't do that. There was a guy I was attracted to, but he is distancing from me, and I don't know what I did wrong. He won't talk to me. I think he has it in for me.

Th: It's hard to know what people are thinking if they are silent. And then sometimes we can imagine they are thinking one thing, but they are thinking something else. [*Without information, he projects. Therefore, do not allow much silence. Otherwise, projections will fill the silence, he will lose his reality testing and drop out of treatment. Be active so your presence counters his unconscious projections.*]

Principle: *When a severely fragile patient reveals latent projections in the displacement, explore issues within the displacement. Do not interpret through the defense. Build affect tolerance within the displacement. As affect tolerance increases, his language will shift from indirect to direct references to the therapy. Then you can invite him to bear higher levels of feelings and conflict.*

Example Seven

A patient said she was afraid that if she talked about spirits, she would see them again (hallucinate). This occurred when her feelings rose toward the therapist. The therapist understood how rising feelings triggered her anxiety and hallucinations.

Pt: My husband wants me to talk about the spirits. [*Projection of her desire onto her husband.*]

Th: Why does he think you should do that? [*Explore her desire within the projection onto her husband.*]

Pt: I know he thinks it would help me, but I think it would be too much.

Th: If you respect your wish not to talk about it right now [*deactivate projection onto the therapist*], why does he think it would help? [*Explore her desire within the defense of projection.*]

We explore within the defense of projection to build her capacity to talk about her desire. When her capacity to bear her desire has increased, projection will drop. Eventually, she can acknowledge her wish to talk about the spirits.

All-good therapy supports patients' highest functioning by building the capacity for bearing internal conflict and feelings (Federn 1952; Pinsker 2015; Rockland 1989, Werman 2015; Winston, Rosenthal, and Pinsker 2015). We help fragile patients bear experience inside without flooding with anxiety and suffering from projecting so they can observe and think about their internal experience.

Reality Testing

Losses of reality testing occur across a spectrum:

1. The psychotic patient cannot test reality and has no awareness of this problem.

2. Another group of psychotic patients has lost reality testing and knows it (E. Marcus 2017).

3. A severely fragile, near-psychotic patient can tell the difference between his emotional experience and reality. But he does not care because he partly believes the emotional experience. It overwhelms his conscious experience of reality. He may superficially agree that his emotional experience and reality are different. But the patient's comments show that he equates his emotional experience with reality. For instance, he may think his therapist doesn't care about him, and he wants to quit therapy (E. Marcus 2017).

4. A moderately fragile patient can tell the difference between his emotional experience and reality, and he cares. However, he still wants the therapist to change, but not just to avoid frustration. He wants the therapist to change today to change a memory of a person in the past.

5. Neurotic patients can test reality even when distorted perceptions arise. Though frustrated, they feel no great urge to change the therapist.

Actively question the patient about the relationship between his emotional experience and reality experience (E. Marcus 2017). Help him see contradictory statements, actions, and feelings. Point out the missing steps in logic in descriptions of a relationship or event. Active questioning helps the patient see either defenses or their results. Help the patient observe how his defenses work. Denial, projection, and splitting can prevent the patient from seeing specific facts, emotions, or perceptions. Thus, the resulting story has gaps in logic or content. Help the patient look at these contradictions, holes, and gaps.

Therapists may try to convince the patient that his psychotic point of view is wrong. Instead, help him think about his psychotic point of view. Don't contradict him. Remind him of contradictions in what he has said, or remind him of inconsistencies between what he has said and done. Help him see his contradictory thinking and perceptions. Do not ask him to take on one side or the other (splitting). Build the preconditions for reality testing. Help him observe and think about contradictory realities. To test reality, we compare our fantasy and our perception of reality so we can change our conclusions about reality. If we bypass that step, the patient cannot test reality.

Some psychotic patients who cannot reality test may use your words to support their delusion. They twist facts in reality into evidence for their delusions, which are not bizarre. Since they misuse reality to justify their delusions, their lack of reality testing may not be apparent. Many patients with a psychotic level of character structure do not have a diagnosis of schizophrenia or schizoaffective disorder. Lucas (2003) finds that only about 30 percent of psychotic patients had overt delusions or hallucinations. Only careful inquiry revealed their permanent loss of reality testing.

Exploring the projections:

Th: What thoughts and ideas are you having about the therapy? [*We ask "about the therapy," not "about me." Help the patient differentiate you from the therapy. Differentiate his ideas from the therapy so he can reflect upon his thoughts rather than equate them with reality.*]

Sometimes the patient's distrust is higher, however:

Pt: I don't want to talk about it.

Th: Let yourself not talk about it then. [*Side with his defense (Nelson 1962, 1968).*] Take all the time you need. It may be important not to talk about the therapy until you feel ready. [*Deactivate the projection that you will make him talk.*]

Differentiating reality from the projection:

Th: What is the evidence that I want to judge you?

Patient with reality testing: I know there isn't. [*Good reality testing.*]

Patient with impaired reality testing: I can't think of any, but I feel that way. I sense it. [*Impaired reality testing: "I regard my feelings as the same as reality."*]

Th: Although there is a feeling that I'm judging you, there isn't any evidence to support that feeling. [*Point out the difference between fantasy and reality.*]

Patient who has lost reality testing: "I can see it in your eyes." [*Loss of reality testing. Positive hallucination: seeing what is not there.*]

Th: We see there is an image of judgmental eyes that comes in here between you and me. [*The therapist places a book in front of his face and moves it back and forth so that the patient alternately sees and doesn't see his face. This helps him differentiate an image in his mind from the therapist.*] And when you see those judgmental eyes, it becomes difficult to see mine. It must be very upsetting to you to have these judgmental eyes coming in here to interfere with the relationship you and I are trying to form. [*Cognitive restructuring of the projection.*]

Restoring Reality Testing

When the patient projects, can he maintain doubt about his emotional experience? Can he use logical thinking to compare his emotional experience with his reality experience? And can he change his conclusions about reality? (E. Marcus 2017) If so, he can maintain a boundary between reality and his emotional experience.

Suppose a patient is disappointed that her boyfriend didn't bring her flowers. In response, she becomes enraged and decides to dump him. At this moment, she cannot compare her past reality experience of him with her current emotional experience. As a result, she cannot change her conclusions about him. Rather than dump her conclusions, she dumps him.

The loss of reality testing in personality-disordered patients is rarely global but confined to a particular area. A sexually abused woman hears a voice telling her that she is "dirty." She temporarily lacks reality testing in this area yet functions well at work.

We can help restore reality testing through the following steps:

1. Explore the content of delusions and hallucinations to discover their meaning.
2. Deactivate projections onto the therapist.
3. Invite the patient to become aware of her inner life inside so she doesn't project it outside.

4. Identify and regulate the anxiety triggered by taking in the projection.

5. If denial occurs, remind him of reality. If she engages in splitting, mirror splitting. And if another projection happens, invite her to bear that part of her inner life inside herself.

6. Continue steps three, four, and five until she sighs and intellectualizes. Then she can hold a higher level of feeling inside without projecting it outside. We have built a new threshold for affect tolerance.

COMMENTARY

Defenses such as projection, splitting, and denial ward off feelings based on past relationships (Freud 1917/1961a; M. Klein 1975a, 1975b). Our memories of relationships show us how to make sense of the world and other people. These memories are not always photographic, however. Experience, feelings, defense (Dorpat 1985; Loewald 1989), genetics (Smoller et al. 2013), temperament (Kagan 1994; Parens 1979), neurocognitive development (DeGangi 2017; Greenspan 1992; Piaget and Inhelder 1969), neurocognitive deficits resulting from trauma (Almas et al. 2012; Bos et al. 2009), and brain injury (van Reekum et al. 1993) work together to create memories of and fantasies about our past relationships. Thus, although these affective memories may not be veridical, we work with these feelings since they are the results with which the patient struggles.

When interventions restore reality testing, we know that these were pseudodelusions and pseudohallucinations. The fragile patient's reality testing was temporarily suspended. However, if delusions and hallucinations persist, he has a permanent loss of reality testing (Kernberg 1977a, 1977b). He suffers from a psychotic level of character structure.

Psychotherapy of psychotic character structure lies outside the scope of this book. However, for readers interested in psychotherapy with these patients, see Alanen et al. (2012); Arieti (1974); Bak (1954); A. Beck et al. (2009); Benedetti (1987); Boyer and Giovacchini (1980); Breggin and Stern (1996); Brody and Redlich (1952); Burton (1961); Bychowski (1952); Chadwick, Birchwood, and Trower (1996); Chiland and Bequart (1977); Downing and Mills (2017); M. Evans (2016);

Federn (1952); Feinsilver (1983, 1986); Freeman (1973); Freeman, Cameron, and McGhie (1966); J. Frosch (1983); Garety and Helmsley (1997); Garfield (1995); Garrett and Turkington (2011); Gunderson and Mosher (1975); Hagen et al. (2011); L. Hill (1955); Hinshelwood (2004); Karon and Vandenbos (1981); Kingdon and Turkington (2008); Levin (2018); Little (1981); Lotterman (2015); Mace and Margison (1997); Marcus (1992/2017); P. Miller (2016); Milner (2010); T. Ogden (1982); Pao (1979); Rosenfeld (1965); Schwing (1954); Searles (1960, 1979, 1965/1986a); Sechehaye (1951); Semrad (1966, 1969); Semrad and Buskirk (1969); Silver (1989); Silver and Cantor (1990); Spotnitz (1976, 1986); Strauss et al. (1980); Stone et al. (1983); Sullivan (1953a, 1956, 1962); Wexler (1952); and Wright et al. (2014).

SUMMARY

Severely fragile patients use three defenses or variants of them: (1) splitting, (2) denial, and (3) projection. When they use the defense of splitting, we invite consciousness of splitting. The therapist reminds them of contradictory thoughts or urges to build the capacity to bear mixed feelings. When they use the defense of projection, we deactivate the projection. Then we invite them to bear inside what they formerly projected onto others. When they use the defense of denial, we remind them of realities that conflict with their denial. This builds their capacity to bear reality and the mixed feelings it triggers.

As we build affect tolerance, anxiety moves out of cognitive/perceptual disruption into the striated muscles. And defenses shift into the resistance systems of repression and isolation of affect.

CHAPTER THIRTEEN

Projective Identification and Countertransference

Learning to Bear What Is Inside Ourselves

We know the truth, not only by reason, but also by the heart.

—PASCAL, *PENSÉES*

Just as the patient has unconscious patterns of expectations and relating (transference), so too does the therapist (countertransference). They arise "as a result of the patient's influence on his unconscious feelings" (Freud 1910/1957a, 144–145). And they serve as a possible pathway for deeper understanding of the patient (Heimann 1950). The client's inner life mobilizes the therapist's inner life (Cohen 1952; Heimann 1950; Reich 1951; Sullivan 1949). Every therapist struggles between accepting and rejecting the patient's inner life since it reverberates in the therapist's depths. This led some to conclude that countertransference might include all the therapist's responses to the patient (Alexander 1948).

In a "totalistic" definition of countertransference, all therapist responses to the patient can be divided into three categories (Kernberg 1965): (1) *objective countertransference,* an objective response, such as anger when a patient flicks cigarette ashes on your furniture, (2) *subjective countertransference*, a subjective response to the patient based on your own past and conflicts, and (3) *communicative countertransference*, a response based upon the patient's projective identification and your ability to contain that induced experience. Our ability to identify with the patient will depend on our resistance to accepting what is mobilized within us.

PROJECTIVE IDENTIFICATION

Countertransference always occurs because we always have feelings in relationships. The question is how to become aware of the thoughts, feelings, and impulses we have with patients and how to recognize the roles we enact. But before we go into the process of self-analysis, we need to understand how the defense of projective identification can induce those feelings.

In projection, a person attributes an aspect of himself to you. Projective identification is a primitive form of projection where a person attributes to you what he cannot tolerate in himself. *Then he induces that experience in you* (Kernberg 1975; M. Klein 1975a, 1975b; T. Ogden 1982). He sees it in you, judges it in you, or fears it in you. In any case, he feels a connection with this aspect of his inner life but in you. He tries to control you so that you remain the residence of his dangerous feeling or impulse. Let's review the steps in this defense:

1. *Projection* of a feeling, thought, or impulse that triggers guilt, shame, or anxiety
2. *Empathic* connection with the projection
3. *Induction* of that experience into the therapist or another person
4. *Control* of the other person to keep the projection there and prevent it from returning to the patient

In projection, the patient can attribute something to the therapist, and that is enough. When feelings are more intense, however, projection by itself is not enough. The feeling must be induced in the therapist so the patient can experience it *in* the therapist. Then the patient tries to control that experience to ensure it stays in the therapist and does not come back to "attack" the patient.

Suppose a patient experiences powerful anger, is very sensitive and defensive, and has destroyed his relationships. At the same time, he feels overwhelming guilt he cannot face. In treatment, he might accuse the therapist of feeling angry. Initially, the therapist may see the projection and be able to think and reflect. However, the patient interrupts the therapist, talks over him, and repeatedly accuses him of being controlling. After a while, the therapist realizes, "I really am angry!" Maybe the anger comes out in his withdrawal, his tone of voice, an irritated facial expression, or a critical comment. Now the patient has proof: "See, you *are* angry!" The patient denies that he is angry. Instead, he says, "You are angry. Look at what you said!" And any anger he feels now he believes is in response to you. He can judge you as angry, sensitive, defensive, and destructive—the traits in himself that triggered so much guilt and shame. He interacts with his projection, judging you for the feelings and qualities he cannot bear in himself. But this anger he perceives in you is merely the anger he projected there and then induced through interruptions, criticisms, and cutting you off. "This just proves that *you* are causing my difficulties."

Under the impact of the interruptions, talking over, and criticisms, the therapist may lose his sense of who he is. He may feel so caught up in the patient's fantasy that he begins to wonder if his anger is destroying the therapy. He is so identified with the projection that he temporarily can't function as a therapist.

While we have described the defensive function of projective identification, it is also a pathway to healing. Insofar as the therapist can bear the projection and think about it, his experience of the patient's disavowed feeling will give him a deeper understanding. We might call it "not-so-vicarious introspection" (Frederickson 1990).

Projective identification can be confusing. While the patient tries to control the location of the projection, he thinks the therapist is trying to control him. He does not know that he acts in a controlling manner. He sees the therapist as controlling. Thus, he views his behavior as a reaction to the therapist, the therapist's fault. Projective identification relocates a feeling in others so he won't feel it in himself. The truth won't matter because the purpose is to project inner truths to live in other people, the truths too painful to bear. Projective identification, by provoking experiences in the other person, can be a self-fulfilling prophecy. Inducing disavowed feelings in others can provoke them to enact the projection.

SELF-ANALYSIS

How can we analyze and understand these feelings, attitudes, and reactions that therapy arouses in the therapist? We understand them within a context: a relationship unconsciously enacted by the therapist and patient (E. Levenson 1991). The first question becomes, "What is this relationship?" Then we ask, "Which role am I enacting?"

Suppose the answer to the first question is that the relationship involves a judge and the judged. The patient judges you as she was judged in the past. To analyze the second question, Racker (1968) suggests two possibilities: (1) *a concordant identification*, or (2) *a complementary identification*. In a concordant identification, I am identified with an aspect of the patient. For instance, I might feel angry at the judge or depressed as if I am a hopeless failure. Thus, I would feel what the patient may have felt in the past with a judging parent.

In a complementary identification, I am identified with the other person in the patient's life. I might find myself feeling judgmental of the patient, tempted to talk about how her defenses are destructive or perhaps even wanting to make moralizing remarks. Thus, I would judge the patient as she experienced someone judging her in the past.

Whether we identify with the patient or someone in her past, our reactions can take two forms (Racker 1968): (1) *countertransference thoughts, feelings, or fantasies*, or (2) *countertransference positions*, roles we adopt that become persistent enactments by the therapist. For instance, if you view your patient as a suffering victim, this partial truth may ward off your awareness of how the patient victimizes others. It may also be your defense, joining with the patient as a fellow victim vis-á-vis other people who are victimizers. Then you and the patient can enjoy the comfort of being "all-good" people in an "all-bad" world.

Likewise, if you find yourself being active with a passive patient, what does your active stance ward off? Does it ward off irritation when the patient remains underinvolved? Why don't you comment on his passive stance? Does his passivity enact your own passive longings that you gratify as you wish others would do for you? When you are so active, what are you trying to control in the patient?

If you find yourself taking a passive stance with an aggressive patient, what is your passivity warding off? Are you afraid to set a limit? Does the patient's aggression enact your own aggressive urges? Does letting the patient aggressively attack you allow you to secretly judge and feel superior to him?

Let's examine how to analyze your countertransference.

Content

- What thoughts, feelings, and reactions do you notice having toward your patient?
- What kind of behavioral pattern do you notice having with your patient: passive, active, seductive, detached, critical, fearful, aggressive, erotic? If unsure, how would you describe the patient's habitual behavioral pattern? Whatever that pattern is, you probably enact the same behavior and the opposite. Examine how you are enacting each of those behaviors.

Enactment

- How would you describe the two roles in your relationship: critic/criticized, attacker/attacked, avoider/pursuer, hopeless/hopeful, passive/active, withholder/beggar, seducer/seduced, nonthinker/thinker, accuser/accused, and so on?
- Which role do you enact? What feelings do you have in that role?
- In an enactment, you ward off the other role and feelings that the patient is enacting. What role or wish and feelings is the patient enacting for you? For instance, is the patient enacting your wish to dominate, to criticize, to take a superior stance, or to be passive? If you accept an idealizing relationship, what aspects of your humanity do you fear the patient cannot accept? Those are the aspects of yourself you do not accept. Who did not accept those qualities in you in the past? Whom did you judge in the past for having those qualities? What do you feel as you accept these qualities in yourself? Anything you cannot receive in yourself, you cannot heal in the patient.
- Find three ways you have enjoyed the disavowed feeling or role and enacted it in your life. Accept and identify with the patient's inner life so she can as well. For instance, if you have tolerated hostile abuse from a patient, you are also warding off your own hostile wishes. How is that true with the patient? How has that been true in your past? Who was hostile and abusive to you?

Remember the law of the talion. If someone abused the patient, she felt an equal urge to retaliate, but she had to hold back this urge to keep the relationship. Likewise, if the patient attacks you, the urge to attack will arise in you. This is not a problem. It is information about yourself and your patient. It only becomes a problem if you are not aware of it, cannot tolerate it, and then act out the urge or invite the patient to act out the urge on you so you can get punished for having it. Many fragile patients enact abuser/abused dynamics to tell the story in actions when they can't say it in words. The patient accepts abuse, triggers abuse, abuses herself, and sometimes abuses others. The therapist may unwittingly also accept abuse, trigger abuse, or want to abuse the patient. If the therapist accepts abuse, he remains pure, while the patient remains the repository of disavowed rage. If the therapist invites abuse, the patient will only feel more guilt. As a result, she will either have to punish herself or invite the therapist to do it. If the therapist wants to abuse the patient, he begins to split and view the patient as all-bad. For instance, the therapist might sit in a peer supervision group where colleagues agree on how "pathological" and "destructive" the patient is, thus confirming the therapist's splitting and projection. These identifications with the patient, however horrifying and painful they may be, can become the pathway to healing. By accepting these inevitable urges in ourselves we help the patient embrace her explosive feelings—the affective memories of her traumas.

Process

- Since projective identification is a defense, when did it occur? What took place before the defense? What feelings did your interaction stir up that made this defense necessary? If you stirred up excessive feelings in the patient (empathy failure), what led you to do so?

Examine the roles enacted in therapy. See the role you are in. Notice the feelings you ward off and how the roles shift. The less affect tolerance the patient has, the more powerful the projective identification, and the more intense the countertransference will be. Likewise, the greater the therapist's resistance to bearing these feelings, the more the patient will have to rely on projective identification to be felt and understood. When we are no longer identified with a feeling, thought, or impulse, we gain the ability to think about it, its function, and the patient's plight.

INDICATIONS OF COUNTERTRANSFERENCE ENACTMENTS

The following list (Mills 2005, 222–224) offers common signs of countertransference.

- *Therapeutic enactments:* Accepting what the patient says at face value, boundary problems with fee or time or inappropriate self-disclosure, not addressing defenses, taking a passive or masochistic stance, attempting to provoke the patient's feelings, taking an authoritarian stance, continuing therapy when goals are achieved.

- *Passivity:* Inattentive or distractible, problems concentrating or remembering, inability to identify with the patient, drowsiness, disinterest, aloofness, daydreaming.

- *Anxiety:* Laughing readily or out of context, talking more than the patient, confusion, helplessness, avoiding issues, feeling intimidated, premature reassurance, dread of seeing the patient, masochism (letting the patient abuse you), paranoid attitudes.

- *Aggressiveness:* Criticizing or invalidating the patient, overly directive, disapproval or contempt, frustration, scorn, hatred for the patient or self-hatred, feeling trapped, feelings of revenge, cruelty, death wishes.

- *Eroticism:* Attention and compliments paid to the patient's body, initiating self-disclosures about one's personal life, flirtation, idealization of the patient, initiating discussions of sexuality, encouraging detailed description of sexual fantasies, suggesting contacts outside of therapy, sexual fantasies, falling in love with the patient.

- *Narcissistic vulnerabilities:* Talking about oneself and one's accomplishments, seeking to impress the patient, jealousy/envy, feelings of competition, feelings of superiority, need to see the patient as special and be seen as special, using the patient for mirroring, intolerance of the patient's self-assertion, encouraging illusions about the therapist's powers, belief that the patient's recovery reflects on the therapist's prestige.

These behaviors indicate that therapy is blocked by the counter-transference, pointing toward the need to analyze it. When we do, we can see what the patient is projecting, what she cannot bear, *and what the therapist cannot bear.* Then we can accept inside ourselves what we are rejecting in the patient. Since the patient cannot bear both sides of her conflict, she enacts one side and projects the other onto the therapist. To help the patient, the therapist must bear both sides. If the patient criticizes him for being aggressive, can he bear his aggression and accept it as a universal, human capacity? Can he bear inside himself his wish to criticize, attack, and dominate (the urge the patient is enacting)? Through this inner act of self-unification, the therapist regains the capacity to think, feel, and reflect. And from this enhanced level of inner unity, responses will arise that reflect this deeper empathy with the patient.

Since we do not usually see our role-responsive behaviors, supervision can help us see our blind spots. And since no one has ever made the entire unconscious conscious, our capacity for unconscious countertransference is ever present. Having blind spots is human.

The most common blind spot results from the victim/victimizer polarity of the roles fragile patients enact. If abused as a child, the patient may enact either the abuser role or the victim role. But *you* may be perceived as that abuser. Why? We internalize relationships. We can't take in only the good or bad qualities in our parents. We take them in as a whole. Our best strategy is to absorb everything they do. Since they have survived, this must be how to be to survive.

But when the patient enacts the abuser role, this triggers massive anxiety and guilt that must be exported. To export the guilt, the patient induces the therapist to think, feel, or act in some way like the abuser. Perhaps you find yourself tuning out, feeling critical, or even getting angry. Then the patient can criticize you for being an abuser. This defense is multidetermined. The patient may express rage toward you that belongs to a past abuser. She may judge you as she judges herself. She may judge you the way her mother judged her. She may blame you for her suffering to avoid the pain, grief, and guilt over how her behavior destroyed her life long before she met you. As one patient said to me, "I was fine until I met you." For the previous ten years, she had been chronically suicidal, cutting herself.

In the victim/victimizer dynamic, the patient cannot bear her guilt over her wish to victimize others. Her aggressive criticism of you (victimizing you) may induce anger in you so you can be judged for the victimizing feeling and urge. Likewise, you can easily feel "victimized" by a "victimizing" patient. In this way, the therapist remains the "innocent" victim of a "cruel" patient. That is splitting.

The patient can mobilize in us the urge to victimize, an urge difficult to accept and metabolize. As a result, rather than face our own cruel, sadistic urges that can be mobilized, we may rely on defenses. For instance, we may become passive and masochistic to hide our rage under a facade of pure love and pseudoneutrality. Or we may rely on denial and reaction formation, claiming to feel only positive feelings, while explaining away the patient's aggressive attacks. Or we may act out aggressive feelings through interpretive attacks, withholding, or premature confrontations.

For instance, a therapist may complain about an insensitive, narcissistic patient. But further inquiry reveals that the therapist takes the patient's phone calls at all hours of the day and night and has let the patient fall behind on his bill. Here we can help the therapist see how *he* has induced the patient to act in this way. By not keeping track of the bill, he *invited* his patient to exploit him. Perhaps he invited the patient to act out his own greedy wishes so he could gratify them while resenting the patient for exploiting him.

If an enactment continues for weeks, we are in some way supporting it. To find out what you project, make a list of your complaints or make a list of what you hate about your patient.

Let's examine a complaint. Each complaint about a patient may describe your unconscious behavior.

Complaint: "This patient is controlling."

Fact: Through projective identification patients try to control who has the projected feeling. However, when you defend yourself or argue, you try to control how the patient thinks and feels. You enact the conflict rather than observe or describe it. This may reflect the patient's history—for example, her longing to argue with a controlling mother. However, if you argue, you enact her past rather than help her have a new experience in the present.

We can also discover our countertransference through the patient's complaints. A patient may complain about her spouse, whom she perceives as highly irresponsible and dependent, and the therapist may unwittingly explore anger toward the husband, which goes nowhere. Upon reflection, the therapist may recognize how he supported the patient's victim stance. Rather than examine her externalization, he listened to her blaming and complaining. With this understanding, he could encourage the patient to work in therapy by addressing her defenses of complaining, blaming, and externalizing.

COMMON COUNTERTRANSFERENCE PATTERNS

A suicidal patient may claim he wants to die, and the therapist wants her to live. The patient, to avoid her inner conflict between wanting to live and punishing herself through a death sentence, sends her wish away to live in the therapist. The therapist might accept omnipotent responsibility for the patient's life, become frantic, encourage the patient to live, and reassure her about a future neither of them can know. When the therapist accepts all responsibility for the patient's life, the patient often argues with the therapist. Now the conflict is between them rather than in the patient.

A fragile eating-disordered patient advocates for self-starvation, and the therapist encourages healthy eating. The patient invites the therapist to try to control her. The battle between her wish to live (control over self-destructiveness) and her wish to die is enacted between the patient and therapist. As a result, the therapist and staff become more controlling and the patient more identified with her wish to die.

A drug-addicted patient may claim he has no problem with drugs or no desire to let go of his addiction. Through his responses, he often induces in the therapist the urge to convince him to let go of drugs or to comment on how destructive drugs are or to remind the patient that he nearly died from an overdose the week before. Here, the patient invites the therapist to be the voice of sanity while the patient can give voice to his insane defenses. The therapist often feels like a secret hero, "fighting the good fight," but all to no avail. Why? If the therapist gives voice to the patient's disavowed sanity, it never has to rise *in the patient*.

A severely disturbed patient may present as if he has no hope for his life or for therapy. Over time, the therapist may start to feel an urge to reassure the patient that there is hope. As the therapist takes on the role of a "cheerleader," oddly, the patient becomes even more adamant about his hopelessness, and his depression worsens. Rather than help the patient with his conflict between hope and despair, the therapist becomes the voice of hope, which empties the depressed patient of his conflict. A severely depressed patient may be unable to bear his conflict between the wish to live and the wish to die. Thus, hope may be projected into the therapist. And if the therapist enacts that disavowed hope, it no longer lives in the patient.

Countertransference takes many forms. Here, I emphasize the pattern of projecting sanity and the wish to live because it is one of the most common in the fragile spectrum. If the therapist does not see this pattern, he may take on the omnipotent responsibility for being the voice of hope, sanity, and the wish to live. The therapist may consciously enjoy this heroic role, but it is a defense against the anxiety of facing the patient's wish to die. The patient's wish to die is, in turn, a defense against murderous rage toward the therapist and anyone who tries to help him. Only if the therapist sees this countertransference and avoids the omnipotent role can he help the patient face the rage toward the therapist, who represents all failed helpers in the patient's past. Then his rage, now felt toward the therapist and past abusers, will not kill him through eating disorders, drug abuse, or suicide.

The greater the patient's affect tolerance, the less she needs to project, and, thus, the less violent the projective identifications. As a result, less primitive forms of projective identification have less of a defensive and more of a communicative function, serving as a bridge to empathy. And this leads us to a central question when we consider projective identification.

According to M. Klein (1975a, 1975b), the patient who uses projective identification projects some aspect of her inner life *into* the therapist. However, if the poet Terentius is correct, "Nothing human is alien to me." Therefore, the patient does not have to "put" anything "into" the therapist. If everything human is already within us by virtue of being human, then the patient only has to *evoke* these universal potentials, whether they be hatred, love, envy, helplessness, hope, despair, or erotic feelings. Thus, what makes projective identification pathological, as with projection, is that the patient denies that she shares these feelings by locating them exclusively in the therapist. Location is what the patient tries to control. This recognition allows us to avoid the paranoid view implicit in the patient "putting a feeling into" us. Instead, can we bear this universal human experience in ourselves that the patient cannot bear now? And through our bearing, can she learn to bear it as well (Bion 1962)? Perhaps we might imagine each of us as a gamelan orchestra of gongs. And when those gongs are hit and vibrate in the patient, those same tones start to vibrate in us as well. Humanity resonating with humanity.

When the patient tries to ensure that her feelings stay in the therapist, she may also be enacting her history. She fears that the therapist will try to place those feelings back into her—replicating the past trauma, overwhelming her, and, thus, attacking her—for the parental rejection of feelings always involves, to a degree, the pushing of feelings back into the child, and controlling the location of those feelings so they remain in her. Verbal abuse, beatings, and sexual molestation are all forms of parental projective identification. As one mother said, "How many times do I have to beat this into you?" She has a fantasy that she can beat some thought or feeling into the child. Whether the abuse is obvious or obscure, the issue remains the same: control over the location of pain.

Whatever the patient is most guilty or ashamed of, she will project onto other people, and she will react strongly to the projections she places on those people. She will attract those people into her life, and she will keep them in her life because she needs them as the filing drawers for everything she rejects in herself. She will act provocatively to evoke her disavowed urges in them, which is how she reenacts her childhood drama. Everything in this paragraph applies to the therapist as well.

When you feel strong feelings or urges, do not act on them. Simply feel them and try to see what they may be telling you about the patient's internal experience. For instance, a patient thought her therapist was conducting an experiment on her and criticized her severely. In response, the therapist felt the urge to argue the patient into submission. Pause and reflect: "Ah, I am wanting to defend myself as if I need her to agree with me if I'm going to survive. I am feeling as if her opinion is a threat to my survival. Okay. This is a paranoid transference: she fears that my ideas will threaten her survival. She fears there cannot be two minds in the same room. Maybe she is afraid that I want to control her and what she thinks."

Now the therapist can listen to the patient's criticisms and intervene: "I appreciate your letting me know your point of view. I'm not aware of this being the case, but I could be wrong. At any rate, it's important for us to accept that there are two different perspectives on this. And would it be okay with you if we agree for there to be two minds in this room at this time?"

The therapist models an openness where she is not threatened by another mind. At the same time, without interpreting the transference, she addresses it by asking the patient if it is okay if there are two minds in the room at the same time. This can deactivate the patient's projection and reduce her anxiety.

Projective identification is often the primary means of communication for patients at a borderline level of character pathology. Patients who project their violent urges upon the therapist will fear for their lives. Thus, these patients may threaten to be violent with the therapist. In response, we may feel frightened, violated, or sadistic. Yet we need to start first with the patient's fear and help him see the projection generating his fear. Then we can find ways to help him gradually accept the massive rage inside that he sends outside to live in others.

> Th: You wouldn't have made that statement unless you felt frightened here with me. Could you let me know what I said or did that frightened you?

When working with sexually perverse patients we will feel corrupted, seduced, or disgusted, while the patient is speaking calmly about child pornography, for instance. We cannot stop here. Instead, we can inquire into the meaning. If we feel corrupted or seduced, that suggests that the patient may be testing to find out if he can corrupt us. Then he doesn't have to trust us. If we feel disgusted, that hints at a conscience inside himself that he has relocated onto you. If we can hold our limits and pass his test and manage not to act out his conscience, his conflict can arise within him, leading to change.

Pt: I bet you feel disgusted when you hear about these pictures. [*Projection of his conscience.*]

Th: Perhaps you are comfortable with those pictures. [*Block the projection of the patient's conscience while being aware of a feeling of disgust inside you.*]

Pt: [*Squirms in his chair with anxiety as he experiences internal conflict.*]

A patient who was referred to therapy following his arrest for theft offered to give me a nice sweater from a store where he could steal it. I noticed myself feeling anxious, a clue to what he was feeling.

Th: On the one hand, I appreciate that you have positive feelings and want to give me something. On the other hand, if I accepted something you stole, I would be an accomplice in your crime. We would be criminals together. But then I would just be another corrupt person in your life, someone who couldn't be trusted. I would become useless to you. Is it possible that it makes you anxious to let me know who you really are behind this facade of the criminal?

When we work with traumatized patients, we may feel abused, omnipotently indulgent, hostile, or dismissive. If we feel abused, we may be learning about the patient's early abuse and the loss of limits in her early life. If we feel omnipotently indulgent, we may be engaging in a perverse denial of aggression, perhaps enacting the patient's past. But all of these feelings are to be expected (Gordon and Kirtchuk 2008, 95). We should expect violent projective identification from patients who experienced violence. Violence was inflicted to induce feelings in children and to control the location of those feelings.

SUMMARY

Projective identification is a more primitive form of projection in which the patient not only projects but induces the feelings and urges inside the therapist, who then embodies that projection. Then the patient acts and speaks in ways to control the location of those feelings so that the therapist, not the patient, struggles with these painful experiences.

Just as a mother digests the inchoate distress of her baby's non-verbal cries, the therapist digests the inchoate distress of the patient's nonverbal emotional induction (Bion 1962). Through this induced emotional experience, the therapist feels what the patient could not say. However, by bearing this experience without reacting, the therapist's experience leads to a kind of empathic knowing that flavors any later responses, as we help the patient leave his fantasy world for the real world.

The more violent the patient's early experiences, the more violent the projective identifications and the more disturbing the experiences the therapist is asked to bear. In response, the therapist, temporarily unable to bear those feelings, may ward them off by detaching, judging, or trying to push those feelings back into the patient. The therapist may try to control the location of the patient's feelings just as the patient is trying to do. This only replicates the patient's past where a parent could not bear feelings and threw them back at the patient. Thus, the therapist's acting out triggers the patient's implicit fears of being attacked.

"A therapist and a patient are each struggling with the same problem, the patient's shattered experience, and each has the opportunity to examine his way of dealing with related areas of anxiety and conflict. Emotional interchange indeed becomes an affective coming together in which the two participants realign their meanings for each other and see life anew" (Semrad 1969, 35). The therapist inevitably picks up the patient's pain, and by bearing it, becomes part of the patient's process of integration (Semrad 1969). By bearing the experience and living through the enactment (Fiscalini 2004), the therapist can contain (Bion 1962) the patient's pain. And out of bearing his being, the therapist will respond with an understanding that may manifest in silence, a new bearing, words, or a new interaction.

Conclusion

Inside us there is something that has no name, that something is what we are.

—JOSÉ SARAMAGO, *BLINDNESS*

We are born into relationships we need for survival. If our feelings make our mothering ones anxious, an endangered relationship could lead to death. To reduce the anxiety of our caretakers, we protect them from our feelings by using the defenses they offer. For some patients, the universal relational traumas of life are small and the defenses that are offered mature. For most fragile patients, however, the traumas of life were early and large, and the defenses offered were denial, splitting, and projection. For some fragile patients, the intersection of traumas, genetics, temperament, and neurocognitive deficits overwhelmed their capacities. Bearing the unbearable, they had to send what could not be endured onto others through splitting and projection. These defenses became their system of self-protection and other-protection. For by emptying themselves of feelings, they became the absence their parents could bear. And by sending their feelings away to live in others, they could avoid the overwhelming anxiety those feelings evoked in themselves.

Yet these strategies that solved a problem in the past create the patient's problems in the present. The patient's anxiety, remaining unrecognized and unregulated, makes her body feel unsafe today. And her feelings, relocated in other people, create a cosmos populated by projections. Thus, she feels unsafe in her body and in danger with everybody.

The therapist must help her feel safe by recognizing and regulating her anxiety. The therapist and patient must then co-create a safe place by identifying and deactivating the projections that make therapy feel insecure. When the patient feels safe in her body and secure with her therapist, together they can face the feelings that were too much to bear in the past.

Just as the full impact of those feelings was too much for the child, they are often too much for the patient's capacity today, a capacity that never had the chance to develop within a relationship. Our task is to explore those feelings gradually, according to the patient's current capacity, so we can increase it over time. Whenever the patient's ability for bearing her feelings is broached, her anxiety will shift into cognitive/perceptual disruption, and the defenses of denial, splitting, and projection will appear. Then we regulate anxiety while helping her bear feelings inside that she previously placed outside. Little by little we help her bear together what was formerly too much to bear alone. In the past, she had to rely on defenses instead of a relationship. In therapy, she learns to depend on a person instead of her defenses. She has the right to depend, to declare her will, and to share her feelings.

The patient learns in therapy that she has a right to be seen. When parents abuse the child, they do not relate to her but to the projection they have placed upon her. Parents, overwhelmed in the moment by the history of their own suffering, become temporarily blind to the soul of the child they love and pass on their own trauma to the one they hoped to spare. In that instant of blindness, they project some thought, feeling, or intent of their own onto the child. Then they attack, judge, or punish that projection placed in her.

What they call discipline crosses the line into cruelty. And once that line is annulled, the child lives in a voiceless hell. Having looked into blind eyes to find herself, instead she sees her parents' projections and becomes blind to who she really is, even if her anxiety and symptoms silently direct us to her essence. For not only does the patient pursue the truth, but the feelings, anxiety, and projections are the secret truths pursuing her. Truths rejected by others seek acceptance from us. And in therapy we help the patient accept what she rejected in herself, for self-hatred leads to madness, and self-acceptance reveals our sanity.

Everyone knows how the conflicts of needing love and acceptance while fearing pain and rejection can become the sources of suffering, lost life, and a crippled potential. Yet we have also seen how learning to bear our mixed feelings, urges, and desires leads to healing. Every person is a universe filled with universal feelings, thoughts, and longings. No longer looking at herself through soul-blinded eyes of the past, the patient begins to experience her ever-present wholeness in the moment. Through grief, the communion with the truth, she feels her tears, songs of unborn potentials rising to the surface. And each time, filled by another truth, she can never return to her former imaginary limits. Looking to others to give her the answers, by bearing her inner darkness she becomes the answer she was seeking.

The patient's inner world is no longer relocated onto others. Instead, she discovers an inner world, mysterious, never fully plumbed, always unknowable. No longer drowned out by the noise of the world, she learns to hear the silence inside from which all arises. Rather than distract herself with ideas about people in the external world, she becomes still, silently listening to her being, previously hidden underneath the opinions of others.

When others projected onto her, they gave her a name: "bad girl," "slut," or "evil." When she projected onto others, she gave them names too. Yet now, she realizes that all these names, whether for her or for others, could only point to the nameless. All those who claimed to see her saw their belief. And when she perceived people through her beliefs, she became blinded as well. Together, she and the therapist looked behind the names, beliefs, and projections only to discover the unknowability of the patient, the inherent mystery of her being—for the therapist's task is to learn to see what has been invisible to others, hidden behind these ideas. All those previously concrete identities as "bad" or "evil" are revealed as concepts. And now the therapist and patient recognize that she is not a concept, a name, or even an identity but that nameless, wordless something toward which words can only point.

References

Abbass, A. (2004). *Treatment of fragility* [Presentation]. Washington School of Psychiatry, Washington, DC.

Abbass, A. (2007). Bringing character changes with Davanloo's intensive short-term dynamic psychotherapy. *Ad Hoc Bulletin of Short-Term Dynamic Psychotherapy, 11*(2), 26–40.

Abbass, A. (2015). *Reaching through resistance: Advanced psychotherapy techniques.* Seven Leaves Press.

Abbass, A., Lovas, D., and Purdy, A. (2008). Direct diagnosis and management of emotional factors in chronic headache patients. *Cephalagia, 28*(12), 1305–1314. https://doi.org.10.1111/j.1468-2982.2008.01680.x

Abbass, A., Town, J., and Driessen, E. (2012). Intensive short-term dynamic psychotherapy: A systematic review and meta-analysis of outcome research. *Harvard Review of Psychiatry, 20*(2), 97–108.

Adam, E., Klimes-Dougan, B., and Gunnar, M. (2007). Social regulation of the adrenocortical response to stress in infants, children, and adolescents. In D. Coch, G. Dawson, and K. Fischer (Eds.), *Human behavior, learning, and the developing brain: Atypical development* (pp. 264–304). Guilford Press.

Adler, G. (1993). The psychotherapy of core borderline psychopathology. *American Journal of Psychotherapy, 47*(2), 194–205.

Ainslie, G. (2001). *Breakdown of will.* Cambridge University Press.

Alanen, Y., Rakkolainen, V., Laakso, J., Rasimus, R., and Kaljonen, A. (2012). *Towards need-specific treatment of schizophrenic psychoses.* Springer.

Aleksandrowicz, D. (1962). The meaning of metaphor. *Bulletin of the Menninger Clinic, 26*(2), 92–101.

Alexander, F. (1948). *Fundamentals of psychoanalysis*. Norton.

Alexander, F., and French, T. (1946). *Psychoanalytic psychotherapy*. Ronald Press.

Almas, A., Degnan, K., Radulescu, A., Nelson, C., Zeanah, C., and Fox, N. (2012). Effects of early intervention and moderating effects of brain activity on institutionalized children's social skills at age 8. *Proceedings of the National Academy of Sciences, 109*(Suppl. 2), 17228–17231. https://doi.org/10.1073/pnas.1121256109

Andersen, S., Reznik, I., and Glassman, N. (2005). The unconscious relational self. In R. Hassin, J. Uleman, and J. Bargh (Eds.), *The new unconscious* (pp. 421–484). Oxford University Press.

Anderson, M. (2012). Concretisation, reflective thought, and the emissary function of the dream. In A. Frosch (Ed.) *Absolute truth and unbearable psychic pain* (pp.1–16). Karnac.

Anzieu, D. (2016). *The skin ego* (C. Turner, Trans). Yale University Press. (Original work published 1985)

Arieti, S. (1974). *The interpretation of schizophrenia*. Basic Books.

Arnsten, A. (1997). Catecholamine regulation of the prefrontal cortex. *Journal of Psychopharmacology, 11*(2), 151–162.

Arnsten, A. (1998). The biology of being frazzled. *Science, 280*(5370), 1711–1712.

Arnsten, A. (1999). Development of the cerebral cortex: XIV. Stress impairs prefrontal cortical function. *Journal of the American Academy of Child and Adolescent Psychiatry, 38*(2), 220–222.

Austin, J. (2006). *Zen-brain reflections: Reviewing recent developments in meditation and states of consciousness*. MIT Press.

Azzi-Lessing, L. (2017). *Behind from the start: How America's war on the poor is harming our most vulnerable children*. Oxford University Press.

Bacal, H. (Ed.). (1998). *Optimal responsiveness: How therapists heal*. Jason Aronson.

Bak, R. C. (1954). The schizophrenic defence against aggression. *International Journal of Psychoanalysis, 35*(2), 129–133.

Bargh, J., and Chartrand, T. (1999). The unbearable automaticity of being. *American Psychologist, 54*(7), 462–479.

Basch, M. (1983). The perception of reality and the disavowal of meaning. *Annual of Psychoanalysis, 11*, 125–154.

Bass, A. (2000). *Difference and disavowal: The trauma of eros.* Stanford University Press.

Bateman, A., and Fonagy, P. (2004). *Psychotherapy for borderline personality disorder: Mentalization based treatment.* Oxford University Press.

Bateson, G. (2000). *Steps toward an ecology of mind: Collected essays in anthropology, psychology, evolution, and epistemology.* University of Chicago Press. (Original work published 1969)

Beauchaine, T. (2001). Vagal tone, development, and Gray's motivational theory: Toward an integrated model of autonomic nervous system functioning in psychopathology. *Development and Psychopathology, 13*(2), 183–214.

Beauchaine, T., and Thayer, J. (2015). Heart rate variability as a transdiagnostic biomarker of psychopathology. *International Journal of Psychophysiology, 98*, 338–350.

Beck, A., and Emery, G. (1985). *Anxiety disorders and phobias: A cognitive perspective.* Basic Books.

Beck, A., Rector, N., Stolar, N., and Grant, P. (2009). *Schizophrenia: Cognitive theory, research, and therapy.* Guilford Press.

Beck, A., Rush, A., Shaw, B., and Emery, G. (1979). *Cognitive therapy of depression.* Guilford Press.

Beck, J., and van der Kolk, B. (1987). Reports of childhood incest and current behavior of chronically hospitalized psychotic women. *American Journal of Psychiatry, 144*(11), 1474–1476.

Beebe, B., Jaffe, J., Markese, S., Buck, K., Chen, H., Cohen, P., Bahrick, L., Andrews, H., and Feldstein, S. (2010). The origins of 12-month attachment: A microanalysis of 4-month mother-infant interaction. *Attachment and Human Development, 12*(1–2), 3–141. https://doi.org/10.1080/14616730903338985

Benedetti, G. (1987). *The psychotherapy of schizophrenia.* Jason Aronson.

Benjamin, L. (1993). *Interpersonal diagnosis and treatment of personality disorders.* Guilford Press.

Benjamin, L. (1995). Good defenses make good neighbors. In H. Conte and R. Plutchik (Eds.), *Ego defenses: Theory and measurement* (pp. 53–78). Wiley.

Bentall, R. (2006). The environment and psychosis: Rethinking the evidence. In W. Larkin and A. Morrisson (Eds.), *Trauma and psychosis* (pp. 7–22). Routledge.

Berdyaev, N. (1944). *Slavery and freedom*. Scribners.

Berner, P., Gabriel, E., and Schanda, H. (1980). Nonschizophrenic paranoid syndromes. *Schizophrenia Bulletin, 6*(4), 627–632.

Berney, S., de Roten, Y., Beretta, V., Kramer, U., and Despland, J. (2014). Identifying psychotic defenses in a clinical interview. *Journal of Clinical Psychology, 70*(5), 428–439.

Berntson, G., Cacioppo, J., and Quigley, K. (1991). Autonomic determinism: The modes of autonomic control, the doctrine of autonomic space, and the laws of autonomic constraint. *Psychological Review, 98*(4), 459–487.

Berntson, G., Cacioppo, J., and Quigley, K. (1994). Autonomic cardiac control: I. Estimation and validation from pharmacological blockades. *Psychophysiology, 31*, 572–585.

Bettelheim, B. (2010). *The uses of enchantment: The meaning and importance of fairy tales*. Vintage.

Bion, W. (1957). Differentiation of the psychotic from the non-psychotic personalities. *International Journal of Psycho-Analysis, 38*(3–4), 266–275.

Bion, W. (1959). Attacks on linking. *International Journal of Psychoanalysis, 40*, 308–315.

Bion, W. (1962). A theory of thinking. *International Journal of Psycho-Analysis, 43*(4–5), 306–310.

Bion, W. (1965). *Transformations*. William Heinemann.

Bion, W. (1970). *Attention and interpretation*. Jason Aronson.

Birnbaum, S., Gobesske, K., Auerbach, J., Taylor, J., and Arnsten, A. (1999). A role for norepinephrine in stress-induced cognitive deficits: Alpha-I adrenoceptor mediation in the prefrontal cortex. *Biological Psychiatry, 46*(9), 1266–1274.

Blackman, J. (2004). *101 defenses: How the mind shields itself.* Routledge.

Blair, C., Granger, D., and Razza, R. (2005). Cortisol reactivity is positively related to executive function in preschool children attending Head Start. *Child Development, 76*(3), 554–567.

Blatt, S., and Wild, C. (1976). *Schizophrenia: A developmental analysis.* Academic Press.

Bloch, E. (1995). *The principle of hope* (N. Plaice, S. Plaice, and P. Knight, Trans.; Vol. 1). MIT Press. (Original work published 1954)

Bos, K., Fox, N., Zeanah, C., and Nelson, C. (2009). Effects of early psychosocial deprivation on the development of memory and executive function. *Frontiers in Behavioral Neuroscience, 3,* 16. https://doi.org/10:3389/neuro.08.016.2009

Bowlby, J. (1969). *Attachment and loss: Vol. 1. Attachment.* Basic Books.

Bowlby, J. (1973). *Attachment and loss: Vol. 2. Separation: Anxiety and anger.* Basic Books.

Bowlby, J. (1980). *Attachment and loss: Vol. 3. Loss: Sadness and depression.* Basic Books.

Boyer, B., and Giovacchini, P. (1980). *Psychoanalytic treatment of schizophrenic, borderline, and characterological disorders.* Jason Aronson.

Bradley, S. (2000). *Affect regulation and the development of psychopathology.* Guilford Press.

Brandt, L. (1968). The unobserving participant. In M. Coleman-Nelson, B. Nelson, B. Sherman, and H. Strean (Eds.), *Roles and paradigms in psychotherapy* (pp. 120–149). Grune and Stratton.

Breggin, P., and Stern, E. (Eds.) (1996). *Psychosocial approaches to deeply disturbed persons.* Haworth Press.

Bremner, J., Narayan, M., Anderson, E., Staib, L., Miller, H., and Charny, D. (2000). Hippocampal volume reduction in major depression. *American Journal of Psychiatry, 157*(1), 115–127.

Bremner, J., Randall, P., Scott, T., Bronen, R., Seibyl, J., Southwick, S., Delaney, R., McCarthy, G., Charney, D., and Innis, R. (1995). MRI-based measurement of hippocampal volume in patients with combat-related posttraumatic stress disorder. *American Journal of Psychiatry, 152*(7), 973–981.

Brody, E., and Redlich, F. (1952). *Psychotherapy with schizophrenics.* International Universities Press.

Brown, J. (1972). *Aphasia, apraxia, and agnosia: Clinical and theoretical aspects.* Chas. C. Thomas.

Burnham, D., Gladstone, A., and Gibson, R. (1969). *Schizophrenia and the need-fear dilemma.* International Universities Press.

Burton, A. (Ed.) (1961). *Psychotherapy of the psychoses.* Basic Books.

Bychowski, G. (1952). *Psychotherapy of psychosis.* Grune and Stratton.

Bychowski, G. (1954). On the handling of some schizophrenic defenses and reaction patterns. *International Journal of Psychoanalysis, 35*(2), 147–153.

Bychowski, G. (1956). The ego and the introjects. *Psychoanalytic Quarterly, 25*(1), 11–36.

Cain, A. C., and Maupin, B. M. (1961). Interpretation within the metaphor. *Bulletin of the Menninger Clinic, 25*(6), 307–311.

Caruth, E., and Ekstein, R. (1966). Interpretation within the metaphor: Further considerations. *Journal of the American Academy of Child Psychiatry, 5*(1), 35–45.

Cassidy, J. (2004). Emotional regulation: Influences of attachment relationships. *Monographs of the Society for Research in Child Development, 59*(2–3), 228–249.

Chadwick, P., Birchwood, M., and Trower, P. (1996). *Cognitive therapy for delusions, voices, and paranoia.* Wiley.

Chaudhuri, H. (1987). *The philosophy of love.* Routledge and Kegan Paul.

Chiland, C., and Bequart, P. (Eds.). (1977). *Long-term treatments of psychotic states.* Human Sciences Press.

Clyman, R. (1992). The procedural organization of emotions: A contribution from cognitive science to the psychoanalytic theory of therapeutic action. In T. Shapiro and R. Emde (Eds.), *Affect: Psychoanalytic perspectives* (pp. 349–382). International Universities Press.

Cohen, M. (1952). Countertransference and anxiety. *Psychiatry*, *15*(3), 231–243.

Coleman-Nelson, M. (1962). Effect of paradigmatic techniques on the psychic economy of borderline patients. *Psychiatry*, *25*(2), 125–134.

Coleman-Nelson, M. (1968). Prescriptions for paradigms. In M. Coleman-Nelson, B. Nelson, H. Sherman, and H. Strean, *Roles and paradigms in psychotherapy*. Grune and Stratton.

Coleman-Nelson, M., Nelson, B., Sherman, H., and Strean, H. (1968). *Roles and paradigms in psychotherapy*. Grune and Stratton.

Cooper, A., and Guynn, R. (2006). Transcription of fragments of lectures in 1948 by Harry Stack Sullivan. *Psychiatry*, *69*(2), 101–106.

Cornelissen, K. (2005). Understanding and undoing projection: The alien. *Ad Hoc Bulletin of Short-term Dynamic Psychotherapy*, *9*(3), 24–50.

Coughlin, P. (1996). *Intensive short-term dynamic psychotherapy: Theory and technique*. Wiley.

Coughlin Della Selva, P., and Malan, D. (2006). *Lives transformed: A revolutionary method of dynamic psychotherapy*. Karnac.

Cramer, P. (1991). *The development of defense mechanisms: Theory, research and assessment*. Springer-Verlag.

Cramer, P. (1998). Coping and defense mechanisms: What's the difference? *Journal of Personality*, *66*(6), 919–946.

Cramer, P. (2003). Defense mechanisms and physiological reactivity to stress. *Journal of Personality*, *71*(2), 221–244.

Cramer, P. (2006). *Protecting the self: Defense mechanisms in action*. Guilford Press.

Damasio, A. (1994). *Descartes' error: Emotion, reason, and the human brain*. Putnam.

Damasio, A. (1999). *The feeling of what happens: Body and emotion in the making of consciousness*. Harcourt Press.

Darwin, C. (1998). *The expression of the emotions in man and animals* (3rd ed.). Harper Collins. (Original work published 1872)

Davanloo, H. (1987). The unconscious therapeutic alliance. In P. Buirski (Ed.), *Frontiers of dynamic psychotherapy* (pp. 64–88). Brunner Mazel.

Davanloo, H. (1990). *Unlocking the unconscious: Selected papers of Habib Davanloo, M.D.* Wiley.

Davanloo, H. (2000). *Intensive short-term dynamic psychotherapy: Selected papers of Habib Davanloo, M.D.* Wiley.

Davanloo, H. (2001). Intensive short-term dynamic psychotherapy: Extended major direct access to the unconscious. *European Journal of Psychotherapy, 2*(2), 25–70.

Davidson, R. (2004). Well-being and affective style: Neural substrates and biobehavioral correlates. *Philosophical Transactions of the Royal Society of London Series B, 359*(1449), 1395–1411.

DeGangi, G. (2017). *Pediatric disorders of regulation in affect and behavior: A therapist's guide to assessment and treatment.* Academic Press.

DePrince, A., and Freyd, J. (2014). Trauma-induced dissociation. In M. Friedman, T. Keane, and P. Resick (Eds.), *Handbook of PTSD: Science and practice* (2nd ed., pp. 219–233). Guilford Press.

DeRijk, R., Kitraki, E., and De Kloet, E. (2009). Corticosteroid hormones in stress and anxiety: Role of receptor variants and environmental inputs. In H. Soreq, A. Freidman, and D. Kaufer (Eds.), *Stress—From molecules to behavior* (pp. 119–150). Wiley-VCH.

Donnelly, J. (1966). Short-term therapy of schizophrenia. In G. Usdin (Ed.), *Psychoneurosis and schizophrenia* (pp. 141–154). J. B. Lippincott Company.

Dorpat, T. (1985). *Denial and defense in the therapeutic situation.* Jason Aronson.

Downing, D., and Mills, J. (2017). *Outpatient treatment of psychosis: Psychodynamic approaches to evidence-based practice.* Karnac.

Dozier, M., Stovall, K., and Albus, K. (1999). Attachment and psychopathology in adulthood. In J. Cassidy and P. Shaver (Eds.), *Handbook of attachment: Theory, research, and clinical applications* (pp. 497–519). Guilford Press.

Duffy, C. (1997). Implicit memory: Knowledge without awareness. *Neurology, 49*(5), 1200–1202.

Eigen, M. (1998). *The psychoanalytic mystic.* Free Association.

Eisenstein, V. (1952). Differential psychotherapy of borderline states. In G. Bychowski and J. Despert (Eds.), *Specialized techniques in psychotherapy* (pp.303–322). Basic Books.

Eissler, K. R. (1954). Notes upon defects of ego structure in schizophrenia. *International Journal of Psychoanalysis, 35*(2), 141–146.

Ekstein, R. (1966). *Children of time and space, of action and impulse: Clinical studies on the psychoanalytic treatment of severely disturbed children.* Appleton-Century-Crofts.

Erdelyi, M. (1974). A new look at the new look: Perceptual defense and vigilance. *Psychological Review, 81*(1), 1–25.

Etkin, A., Gyurak, A., and O'Hara, R. (2013). A neurobiological approach to the cognitive deficits of psychiatric disorders. *Dialogues Clinical Neuroscience 15*(4) 419–429.

Evans, F. B. (1996). *Harry Stack Sullivan: Interpersonal theory and psychotherapy.* Routledge.

Evans, M. (2016). *Making room for madness in mental health: The psychoanalytic understanding of psychotic communication.* Karnac.

Fairbairn, R. (1954). *An object relations theory of the personality.* Basic Books.

Fairbairn, R. (1969). *Psychoanalytic studies of the personality.* Routledge and Kegan Paul. (Original work published 1952)

Famularo, R., Kinscherff, R., and Fenton, T. (1992). Psychiatric diagnoses of maltreated children: Preliminary findings. *Journal of the American Academy of Child and Adolescent Psychiatry, 31*(5), 863–867.

Fanselow, M., and Gale, G. (2003). The amygdala, fear, and memory. *Annals of the New York Academy of Science, 985,* 125–134.

Federn, P. (1952). *Ego psychology and the psychoses.* Basic Books.

Feinsilver, D. (1983). Reality, transitional relatedness, and containment in the borderline. *Contemporary Psychoanalysis, 19*(4), 537–569.

Feinsilver, D. (1986). Pao's telescopic overview of treatment. In D. Feinsilver (Ed.), *Towards a comprehensive model for schizophrenic disorders: Psychoanalytic essays in memory of Ping-Nie Pao, MD* (pp. 237–258). Analytic Press.

Feinsilver, D. (1999). Counter-identification, comprehensive countertransference, and therapeutic action: Toward resolving the intrapsychic-interactional dichotomy. *Psychoanalytic Quarterly, 68*(2), 264–301.

Fenichel, O. (1945). *The psychoanalytic theory of neurosis*. Norton.

Ferenczi, S. (1988). *The clinical diary of Sandor Ferenczi* (J. Dupont Ed.; M. Balint and N. Jackson, Trans.). Harvard University Press. (Original work published 1932)

Ferenczi, S. (1994). Confusion of tongues between the adult and the child. In M. Balint (Ed.), *Final contributions to the problems and methods of psycho-analysis* (pp. 156–167). Karnac. (Original work published 1933)

Fink, B. (1999). *A clinical introduction to Lacanian psychoanalysis: Theory and technique*. Harvard University Press.

Fiscalini, J. (2004). *Coparticipant psychoanalysis: Toward a new theory of clinical inquiry*. Columbia University Press.

Folkow, B. (2000). Perspectives on the integrative functions of the "sympatho-adrenomedullary system." *Autonomic Neuroscience, 83*(3), 101–115.

Fonagy, P., Gergely, G., Jurist, E., and Target, M. (2002). *Affect regulation, mentalization, and the development of the self*. Other Press.

Fox, N., and Hane, A. (2008). Studying the biology of human attachment. In J. Cassidy and P. Shaver (Eds.), *Handbook of attachment: Theory, research, and clinical applications* (2nd ed; pp. 811–829). Guilford Press.

Franchini, K., and Cowley, A. (2004). Autonomic control of cardiac function. In D. Robertson, I. Biaggioni, G. Burstock, and P. Low (Eds.), *Primer on the autonomic nervous system* (2nd ed.; pp. 134–138). Elsevier Academic Press.

Frankfurter, D. (2008). *Evil incarnate: Rumors of demonic conspiracy and satanic abuse in history*. Princeton University Press.

Frankl, V. (1959). *Man's search for meaning*. Beacon Press. (Original work published 1946)

Frederickson, J. (1990). Hate in the countertransference as an empathic position. *Contemporary Psychoanalysis, 26*(3), 479–496.

Frederickson, J. (1991). From delusion to play. *Journal of Clinical Social Work*, *19*(4), 349–362.

Frederickson, J. (2000). There's something "youey" about you: The polyphonic unity of personhood. *Contemporary Psychoanalysis*, *36*(4), 587–617.

Frederickson, J. (2003). The eclipse of the person in psychoanalysis. In R. Frie (Ed.), *Understanding experience: Psychotherapy and postmodernism* (pp. 204–224). Routledge.

Frederickson, J. (2005). The problem of relationality. In J. Mills (Ed.), *Relational perspectives in psychoanalysis: A critique* (pp. 71–96). Jason Aronson.

Frederickson, J. (2013). *Co-creating change: Effective dynamic therapy techniques*. Seven Leaves Press.

Frederickson, J. (2016). Overcoming unconscious forces in treatment-resistant depression. *Psychiatry*, *79*(2), 190–198.

Fredriksen, K., Schoeyen, H., Johannessen, J., Walby, F., Davidson, L., and Schaufel, M. (2017). Psychotic depression and suicidal behavior. *Psychiatry 80*(1), 17–29.

Freedman, N., and Lavender, J. (1997). On receiving the patient's transference: The symbolizing and desymbolizing countertransference. *Journal of the American Psychoanalytic Association, 45*(1), 7–103.

Freeman, T. (1973). *A psychoanalytic study of the psychoses*. International Universities Press.

Freeman, T., Cameron, J., and McGhie, A. (1966). *Studies on psychosis: Descriptive, psychoanalytic, and psychological aspects*. International Universities Press.

Freud, A. (1936). *The ego and the mechanisms of defense*. International Universities Press.

Freud, S. (1955). Notes upon a case of obsessional neurosis. In J. Strachey (Ed. and Trans.), *The standard edition of the complete psychological works of Sigmund Freud* (Vol. 10, pp. 151–318). Hogarth Press. (Original work published 1909)

Freud, S. (1957a). The future prospects of psychoanalytic therapy. In J. Strachey (Ed. and Trans.), *The standard edition of the complete psychological works of Sigmund Freud* (Vol. 11, pp. 1–249). Hogarth Press. (Original work published 1910)

Freud, S. (1957b). Totem and taboo. In J. Strachey (Ed. and Trans.), *The standard edition of the complete psychological works of Sigmund Freud* (Vol. 13, pp. 1–164). Hogarth Press. (Original work published 1913)

Freud, S. (1957c). On narcissism: An introduction. In J. Strachey (Ed. and Trans.), *The standard edition of the complete psychological works of Sigmund Freud* (Vol. 14, pp. 69–102). Hogarth Press. (Original work published 1912)

Freud, S. (1957d). Repression. In J. Strachey (Ed. and Trans.), *The standard edition of the complete psychological works of Sigmund Freud* (Vol. 14, pp. 141–158). Hogarth Press. (Original work published 1915)

Freud, S. (1957e). The unconscious. In J. Strachey (Ed. and Trans.), *The standard edition of the complete psychological works of Sigmund Freud* (Vol. 14, pp. 159–215). Hogarth Press. (Original work published 1915)

Freud, S. (1957f). The loss of reality in neurosis and psychosis. In J. Strachey (Ed. and Trans.), *The standard edition of the complete psychological works of Sigmund Freud* (Vol. 19, pp. 181–188). Hogarth Press. (Original work published 1924)

Freud, S. (1957g). Negation. In J. Strachey (Ed. and Trans.), *The standard edition of the complete psychological works of Sigmund Freud* (Vol. 19, pp. 235–239). Hogarth Press. (Original work published 1925)

Freud, S. (1958a). Further observations on the defense-neuropsychoses. In J. Strachey (Ed. and Trans.), *The standard edition of the complete psychological works of Sigmund Freud* (Vol. 3, pp. 162–185). Hogarth Press. (Original work published 1912)

Freud S. (1958b). The neuro-psychosis of defence. In J. Strachey (Ed. and Trans.), *The standard edition of the complete psychological works of Sigmund Freud* (Vol. 3, pp. 43–70). Hogarth Press. (Original work published 1896)

Freud, S. (1958c). The dynamics of transference. In J. Strachey (Ed. and Trans.), *The standard edition of the complete psychological works of Sigmund Freud* (Vol. 12, pp. 97–108). Hogarth Press. (Original work published 1912)

Freud, S. (1958d). Formulations on the two principles of mental functioning. In J. Strachey (Ed. and Trans.), *The standard edition of the complete psychological works of Sigmund Freud* (Vol. 12, pp. 218–226). Hogarth Press. (Original work published 1911)

Freud, S. (1958e). Observations on transference love: Further recommendations on the technique of psychoanalysis III. In J. Strachey (Ed. and Trans.), *The standard edition of the complete psychological works of Sigmund Freud* (Vol. 12, pp. 157–171). Hogarth Press. (Original work published 1915)

Freud, S. (1958f). Psychoanalytic notes on an autobiographical account of a case of paranoia. In J. Strachey (Ed. and Trans.), *The standard edition of the complete psychological works of Sigmund Freud* (Vol. 12, pp. 1–82). Hogarth Press. (Original work published 1911)

Freud, S. (1958g). Remembering, repeating and working-through: Further recommendations on the technique of psycho-analysis II. In J. Strachey (Ed. and Trans.), *The standard edition of the complete psychological works of Sigmund Freud* (Vol. 12, pp. 145–156). Hogarth Press. (Original work published 1914)

Freud, S. (1961a). Mourning and melancholia. In J. Strachey (Ed. and Trans.), *The standard edition of the complete psychological works of Sigmund Freud* (Vol. 14, pp. 239–258). Hogarth Press. (Original work published 1917)

Freud, S. (1961b). Inhibitions, symptoms, and anxiety. In J. Strachey (Ed. and Trans.), *The standard edition of the complete psychological works of Sigmund Freud* (Vol. 20, pp. 75–175). Hogarth Press. (Original work published 1926)

Freud, S. (1961c). The ego and the id. In J. Strachey (Ed. and Trans.), *The standard edition of the complete psychological works of Sigmund Freud* (Vol. 19, pp. 3–66). Hogarth Press. (Original work published 1923)

Freud, S. (1961d). *Beyond the pleasure principle (The standard edition)* (J. Strachey, Trans.). Liveright Publishing Corporation. (Original work published 1920)

Freud, S. (1963a). Constructions in analysis. In J. Strachey (Ed. and Trans.), *The standard edition of the complete psychological works of Sigmund Freud* (Vol. 23, pp. 255–270). Hogarth Press. (Original work published 1937)

Freud, S. (1963b). Splitting of the ego in the process of defense. In J. Strachey (Ed. and Trans.), *The standard edition of the complete psychological works of Sigmund Freud* (Vol. 23, pp. 271–278). Hogarth Press. (Original work published 1938)

Freud, S., and Jung, C. (1994). *Freud/Jung letters.* (W. McGuire, Ed.). Princeton University Press. (Original work published 1906–1914)

Freyd, J., and Birell, P. (2013). *Blind to betrayal: Why we fool ourselves we aren't being fooled.* Wiley.

Fromm, E. (1973). *The anatomy of human destructiveness.* Henry Holt.

Frosch, A. (Ed.). (2012). *Absolute truth and unbearable psychic pain.* Karnac.

Frosch, J. (1983). *The psychotic process.* International Universities Press.

Fry, T. (Ed.). (1980). *RB 1980: The rule of St. Benedict in English.* Liturgical Press.

Garety, P., and Helmsley, D. (1997). *Delusions: Investigations into the psychology of delusional reasoning.* Psychology Press.

Garfield, D. (1995). *Unbearable affect: A guide to the psychotherapy of psychosis.* Wiley.

Garrett, M., and Turkington, D. (2011). CBT for psychosis in a psychoanalytic frame. *Psychosis, 3*(1), 2–13.

Gaynor, D., and Egan, J. (2011). Vasovagal syncope (the common faint): What clinicians need to know. *Irish Psychologist, 7*(37), 176–179. http://hdl.handle.net/10147/135366

Geleerd, E. (1965). Two kinds of denial: Neurotic denial and denial in the service of the need to survive. In M. Schur (Ed.), *Drives, affects, behavior* (Vol. 2; pp.118–127). International Universities Press.

Gellhorn, E. (1967). *Principles of autonomic-somatic integrations: Physiological basis and psychological and clinical implications.* University of Minnesota Press.

Gibson, R. (1966). The ego defect in schizophrenia. In G. Usdin (Ed.), *Psychoneurosis and schizophrenia* (pp. 88–97). J. B. Lippincott Company.

Goldberg, L. (1979). Remarks on transference-countertransference in psychotic states. *International Journal of Psychoanalysis, 60,* 347–356.

Goldstein, D. (2004). Merging of the homeostate theory with the concept of allostatic load. In J. Schulkin (Ed.), *Allostasis, homeostasis, and the costs of physiological adaptation* (pp. 99–112). Cambridge University Press.

Goldstein, D. (2006). *Adrenaline and the inner world: An introduction to scientific integrative medicine.* Johns Hopkins University Press.

Gordon, J., and Kirtchuk, G. (Eds.). (2008). *Psychic assaults and frightened clinicians: Countertransference in forensic settings.* Karnac.

Grawe, K. (2006). *Neuropsychotherapy: How the neurosciences inform effective psychotherapy.* Psychology Press.

Green, A. (1977). Negative hallucination: A note as an addendum to a treatise on hallucinations. *L'Evolution Psychiatrique, 42,* 645–656.

Green, A. (1986). *On private madness.* International Universities Press.

Greenspan, S. (1992). *Infancy and early childhood: The practice of clinical assessment and intervention with emotional and developmental challenges.* International Universities Press.

Grotstein, J. (1985). *Splitting and projective identification.* Jason Aronson.

Grotstein, J. (2004). The seventh servant: The implications of a truth drive in Bion's theory of "O." *International Journal of Psychoanalysis, 85*(5), 1081–1101.

Grotstein, J. (2009). Foreword. In A. Reiner, *The quest for conscience and the birth of the mind* (pp. 1–11). Karnac.

Gunderson, J., and Kolb, J. (1978). Discriminating features of borderline patients. *American Journal of Psychiatry, 135*(7), 792–796.

Gunderson, J., and Mosher, L. (Eds.). (1975). *Psychotherapy of schizophrenia.* Jason Aronson.

Guntrip, H. (1993). *Schizoid phenomena, object relations and the self.* Routledge. (Original work published 1968)

Haan, N. (1977). *Coping and defending: Processes of self-environment organization.* Academic Press.

Hagen, R., Turkington, D., Berge, T., and Gråwe, R. (Eds.). (2011). *CBT for psychosis: A symptom-based approach.* Routledge.

Hamill, R., and Shapiro, R. (2004). Peripheral autonomic nervous system. In D. Robertson, I. Biaggioni, G. Burnstock, and P. Low (Eds.), *Primer on the autonomic nervous system* (2nd ed.; pp. 20–28). Elsevier Academic Press.

Hartke, R. (2009). Notes for a theory of generalized splitting. In T. Bokanowski and S. Lewkowicz (Eds.), *On Freud's "Splitting of the ego in the process of defense"* (pp. 134–154). Karnac.

Hartmann, H. (1958). *Ego psychology and the problem of adaptation.* International Universities Press. (Original work published 1939)

Hartmann, H. (1964). *Essays on ego psychology.* International Universities Press.

Hassin, R., Uleman, J., and Bargh, J. (Eds.). (2005). *The new unconscious.* Oxford University Press.

Havens, L. (1962). Replacement and movement of hallucinations in space: Phenomenology and theory. *International Journal of Psychoanalysis, 43,* 426–435.

Havens, L. (1976). *Participant observation.* Jason Aronson.

Havens, L. (1986). *Making contact: Uses of language in psychotherapy.* Harvard University Press.

Heimann, P. (1950). On countertransference. *International Journal of Psychoanalysis, 31,* 81–84.

Heins, T., Gray, A., and Tennant, M. (1990). Persistent hallucinations following childhood sexual abuse. *Australian and New Zealand Journal of Psychiatry, 24*(4), 561–565.

Herman, J. (1992). *Trauma and recovery: The aftermath of violence— From domestic abuse to political terror.* Harper Collins.

Hill, L. (1955). *Psychotherapeutic intervention in schizophrenia.* University of Chicago Press.

Hill, P. (2002). *Using Lacanian clinical technique—An introduction.* Press for the Habilitation of Psychoanalysis.

Hinshelwood, R. (2004). *Suffering insanity: Psychoanalytic essays on psychosis.* Brunner-Routledge.

Hinsie, L., and Campbell, R. (1970). *Psychiatric dictionary* (4th ed.). Oxford University Press.

Honig, A., Romme, M., Ensink, B., Escher, S., Pennings, M., and deVries, M. (1998). Auditory hallucinations: A comparison between patients and non-patients. *Journal of Nervous and Mental Disease, 186*(10), 646–651.

Howell, E. (2005). *The dissociative mind.* Routledge.

Jacobson, E. (1953). The affects and their pleasure/unpleasure qualities in relation to the discharge processes. In R. Lowenstein (Ed.), *Drives, affects, behavior* (Vol. 1; pp. 38–56). International Universities Press.

Jacobson, E. (1957). Denial and repression. *Journal of the American Psychoanalytic Association, 5*(1), 61–92.

Jacobson, E. (1967). *Psychotic conflict and reality.* International Universities Press.

Jacobson, E. (1971). *Depression: Comparative studies of normal, neurotic, and psychotic conditions.* International Universities Press.

Jänig, W. (2003). The autonomic nervous system and its coordination by the brain. In R. Davidson, K. Scherer, and H. Goldsmith (Eds.), *Handbook of affective sciences* (pp. 135–186). Oxford University Press.

Jänig, W. (2006). *The integrative action of the autonomic nervous system: Neurobiology of homeostasis.* Cambridge University Press.

Jaremka, L., Glaser, R., Loving, T., Malarkey, W., Stowell, J., and Kiecolt-Glaser, J. (2013). Attachment anxiety is linked to alterations in cortisol production and cellular immunity. *Psychological Science, 24*(3), 272–279.

Joels, M., and Karst, H. (2009). Effects of stress on the function of hippocampal cells. In H. Soreq, A. Friedman, and D.

Kaufer (Eds.), *Stress—From molecules to behavior* (pp. 53–70). Wiley-VCH.

Jung, C. (1965). *Memories, Dreams, Reflections* (A. Jaffe, Ed.; R. Winston and C. Winston, Trans.). Vintage.

Kagan, J. (1994). *Galen's prophecy: Temperament in human nature.* Basic Books.

Kahneman, D. (2011). *Thinking, fast and slow.* Farrar, Straus and Giroux.

Karon, B., and Vandenbos, G. (1981). *Psychotherapy of schizophrenia: The treatment of choice.* Jason Aronson.

Karon, B., and Whitaker, L. (1996). Psychotherapy and the fear of understanding schizophrenia. In P. Breggin and E. Stern (Eds.), *Psychosocial approaches to deeply disturbed persons* (pp. 23–40). Haworth Press.

Katan, M. (1950). Structural aspects of a case of schizophrenia. *Psychoanalytic Study of the Child, 5*(1), 175–211.

Katan, M. (1954). The importance of the non-psychotic part of the personality in schizophrenia. *International Journal of Psychoanalysis, 35*(2), 119–128.

Kaufmann, H. (2004). Evaluation of the patient with syncope. In D. Robertson, I. Biaggioni, G. Burnstock, and P. Low (Eds.), *Primer on the autonomic nervous system* (2nd ed.; pp. 217–220). Elsevier Academic Press.

Keats, J. (1958). *The letters of John Keats, 1814–1821* (H. E. Rollins, Ed.). Harvard University Press.

Kennard, M. (1947). Autonomic interrelations with the somatic nervous system. *Psychosomatic Medicine, 9*(1), 29–36.

Kenny, A. (1998). *Action, emotion, and will.* Routledge. (Original work published 1963)

Kernberg, O. (1965). Notes on countertransference. *Journal of the American Psychoanalytic Association, 13*(1), 38–56.

Kernberg, O. (1975). *Borderline conditions and pathological narcissism.* Jason Aronson.

Kernberg, O. (1976). *Object-relations theory and clinical psychoanalysis.* Jason Aronson.

Kernberg, O. (1977a). The structural interview. In P. Hartcollis (Ed.), *Borderline personality disorders* (pp. 87–122). International Universities Press.

Kernberg, O. (1977b). Clinical observations regarding the diagnosis, prognosis, and intensive treatment of chronic schizophrenic patients. In C. Chiland and P. Bequart (Eds.), *Long-term treatments of psychotic states* (pp. 332–360). Human Sciences Press.

Kernberg, O. (1980). *Internal world, external reality: Object relations theory applied.* Jason Aronson.

Kernberg, O. (1984). *Severe personality disorders.* Yale University Press.

Kernberg, O. (2001). Object relations, affects, and drives: Toward a new synthesis. *Psychoanalytic Inquiry 21*(5), 604–619.

Kernberg, O., Selzer, M., Koenigsberg, H., Carr, C., and Appelbaum, A. (1989). *Psychodynamic psychotherapy of borderline patients: Psychotherapeutic strategies.* Basic Books.

Kingdon, D., and Turkington, D. (2008). *Cognitive therapy of schizophrenia.* Guilford Press.

Kleiger, J., and Khadivi, A. (2015). *Assessing psychosis: A clinician's guide.* Routledge.

Klein, G. (1959). Consciousness in psychoanalytic theory: Some implications for current research in perception. *Journal of the American Psychoanalytic Association, 7*(1), 5–34.

Klein, G. (1976). *Psychoanalytic theory: An exploration of essentials.* International Universities Press.

Klein, M. (1975a). *The writings of Melanie Klein: Vol. 1. Love, guilt and reparation and other works 1946–1963* (R. Money-Kyrle, Ed.). Delacorte Press.

Klein, M. (1975b). *The writings of Melanie Klein: Vol. 3. Envy and gratitude and other works 1946–1963* (R. Money-Kyrle, Ed.). Hogarth Press.

Korzybski, A. (1994). *Science and sanity: An introduction to non-Aristotelian systems and semantics* (5th ed.). Institute of General Semantics.

Lacan, J. (2007). *Ecrits* (B. Fink, Trans.). Norton. (Original work published 1966)

Laing, R. D. (1965). *The divided self: An existential study in sanity and madness* (Rev. ed.). Penguin. (Original work published 1959)

Landers, M., and Sullivan, R. (2012). The development and neurobiology of infant attachment and fear. *Developmental Neuroscience, 34*(2–3), 101–114.

Larkin, W., and Read, J. (2012). Childhood trauma and psychosis: Revisiting the evidence. In M. Romme and S. Escher (Eds.), *Psychosis as a personal crisis* (pp. 62–73). Routledge.

LeDoux, J. (1998). *The emotional brain: The mysterious underpinnings of emotional life.* Weidenfeld and Nicolson.

LeDoux, J. (2000). Cognitive-emotional interactions: Listen to the brain. In R. Lane and L. Nadel (Eds.), *Cognitive neuroscience of emotion* (pp. 129–155). Oxford University Press.

LeDoux, J. (2002). *The synaptic self: How our brains become who are.* Viking Penguin.

Levenson, E. (1991). *The purloined self: Interpersonal perspectives in psychoanalysis* (A. Feiner, Ed.). Contemporary Psychoanalysis Books.

Levenson, R. (2003). Autonomic specificity and emotion. In R. Davidson, K. Scherer, and H. Goldsmith (Eds.), *Handbook of affective sciences* (pp. 212–224). Oxford University Press.

Levin, R. (2018). *Successful drug-free psychotherapy for schizophrenia.* Routledge.

Levine, P., and Frederick, A. (1997). *Waking the tiger: Healing trauma.* North Atlantic Books.

Lewin, B. (1950). *The psychoanalysis of elation.* Norton.

Lindner, R. (1999). *The fifty minute hour.* Other Press. (Original work published 1955)

Linehan, M. (1993). *Cognitive-behavioral treatment of borderline personality disorder.* Guilford Press.

Liotti, G. (1992). Disorganized/disoriented attachment in the etiology of the dissociative disorders. *Dissociation 4,* 196–204.

Liotti, G. (2004). Trauma, dissociation, and disorganized attachment: Three strands of a single braid. *Psychotherapy: Theory, Research,*

Practice, Training, 41(4), 472–486. https://doi.org/10.1037/0033-3204.41.4.472

Little, M. (1951). Countertransference and the patient's response to it. *International Journal of Psycho-Analysis, 32*, 32–40.

Little, M. (1981). *Transference neurosis and transference psychosis.* Jason Aronson.

Loewald, H. (1989). *Papers on psychoanalysis.* Yale University Press.

Lotterman, A. (2015). *Psychotherapy for people diagnosed with schizophrenia: Specific techniques.* Routledge.

Lucas, R. (2003). Risk assessment in general psychiatry: A psychoanalytic perspective. In R. Doctor (Ed.), *Dangerous patients: A psychodynamic approach to risk assessment and management.* Karnac.

Lupien, S., de Leon, M., de Santi, S., Convit, A., Tarshish, C., Nair, N., Thakur, M., McEwen, B., Hauger, R., and Meaney, M. (1998). Cortisol levels during human aging predict hippocampal atrophy and memory deficits. *Nature Neuroscience, 1*(1), 69–73.

Lyons-Ruth, K. (1998). Implicit relational knowing: Its role in development and psychoanalytic treatment. *Infant Mental Health Journal, 19*(3), 282–289.

Mace, C., and Margison, F. (Eds.). (1997). *Psychotherapy of psychosis.* Gaskell.

Mahler, M. S. (1972). On the first of three subphases of the separation-individuation process. *International Journal of Psychoanalysis, 53*, 295–306.

Mahler, M., Pine, F., and Bergman, A. (1975). *The psychological birth of the human infant.* Basic Books.

Main, M. (1995). The organized categories of infant, child, and adult attachment: Flexible vs. inflexible attention under attachment-related stress. *Journal of the American Psychoanalytic Association, 48*(4), 1055–1096.

Main, M., and Solomon, J. (1990). Procedures for identifying infants as disorganized/disoriented during the Ainsworth Strange Situation. In M. T. Greenberg, D. Cicchetti, and E. M. Cummings (Eds.), *Attachment in the preschool years* (pp. 121–160). University of Chicago Press.

Malan, D. (1979). *Individual psychotherapy and the science of psycho-dynamics.* Butterworths.

Maltsberger, J., and Buie, D. (1974). Countertransference hate in the treatment of suicidal patients. *Archives of General Psychiatry 20*(5), 625–633.

Marcus, E. (2017). *Psychosis and near psychosis: Ego function, symbol structure, treatment* (3rd ed.). Routledge.

Marcus, J. (1973). The experience of separation-individuation in infancy and its reverberations through the course of life: 2. Adolescence and maturity. *Journal of the American Psychoanalytic Association, 21*(1), 155–167.

McEwen, B., Bulloch, K., and Stewart, J. (1999). *Parasympathetic function.* Research Network on SES and Health. http://macses .ucsf.edu/research/allostatic/parasym.php

McEwen, B., and Lasley, E. (2002). *The end of stress as we know it.* Joseph Henry Press.

McEwen, B., and Sapolsky, R. (2000). Stress and cognitive function. In L. R. Squire and S. Kosslyn (Eds.), *Findings and current opinions in cognitive neuroscience* (pp. 173–184). MIT Press.

Meltzer, D. (1992). *The claustrum: An investigation of claustrophobic phenomena.* Karnac.

Meltzer, D. (2009). *Studies in extended metapsychology: Clinical applications of Bion's ideas.* Karnac.

Menaker, E. (1986). *Otto Rank: A rediscovered legacy.* Columbia University Press.

Merzenich, M., and deCharmes, R. (1996). Neural representations, experience, and change. In R. Llinás and P. Churchland (Eds.), *The mind-brain continuum: Sensory processes* (pp. 62–81). MIT Press.

Miller, A. (1990). *For your own good: Hidden cruelty in child-rearing and the roots of violence* (3rd ed.). Farrar, Straus and Giroux.

Miller, P. (2016). *EMDR therapy for schizophrenia and other psychoses.* Springer.

Miller, W., and Rollnick, S. (2002). *Motivational interviewing* (2nd ed.). Guilford Press.

Mills, J. (2005). *Treating attachment pathology*. Jason Aronson.

Milner, M. (2010). *The hands of the living god*. Routledge.

Miłosz, C. (2011). *Selected and last poems: 1931-2004* (A. Miłosz, Trans.). Penguin Books.

Modell, H. (1958). The theoretical implications of hallucinatory experiences in schizophrenia. *Journal of the American Psychoanalytic Association, 6*(3), 442–480.

Nathanson, D. (1996). *Knowing feeling: Affect, script, and psychotherapy*. Norton.

Nelson, M. C. (1962). Effect of paradigmatic tactics on the psychic economy of borderline patients. *Psychiatry, 25*(2), 119–134.

Nelson, M. C. (1968). Prescriptions for paradigms. In M. Coleman-Nelson, B. Nelson, B. Sherman, and H. Strean (Eds.), *Roles and paradigms in psychotherapy*. Grune and Stratton.

Neruda, P. (1988) *Late and posthumous poems: 1968-1974* (B. Belitt, Ed.). Grove Weidenfeld.

Newcomer, J., Selke, G., Melson, A., Hershey, T., Craft, S., Richard, K., and Alderson, A. (1999). Decreased memory performance in health humans induced by stress-level cortisol treatment. *Archives of General Psychiatry, 56*(6), 527–533.

Nijenhuis, E. (2004). *Somatoform dissociation: Phenomena, measurement, and theoretical issues*. Norton.

Novick, J., and Kelly, K. (1970). Projection and externalization. *Psychoanalytic Study of the Child, 15*(1), 65–96.

Nunberg, H. (1955). *Principles of psychoanalysis*. International Universities Press.

Ogden, P., Minton, K., and Pain, C. (2006). *Trauma and the body: A sensorimotor approach to psychotherapy*. Norton.

Ogden, T. (1982). *Projective identification and psychotherapeutic technique*. Jason Aronson.

Ohman, A., and Wiens, S. (2003). On the automaticity of autonomic responses in emotion: An evolutionary perspective. In R. Davidson, K. Scherer, and H. Goldsmith (Eds.), *Handbook of affective sciences* (pp. 256–275). Oxford University Press.

O'Keefe, J. and Nadel, L. (1978). *The hippocampus as a cognitive map.* Clarendon Press.

Palombo, S. (1999). *The emergent ego: Complexity and coevolution in the psychoanalytic process.* International Universities Press.

Panksepp, J. (1998). *Affective neuroscience: The foundations of human and animal emotions.* Oxford University Press.

Panksepp, J. (2009). Brain emotional systems and qualities of mental life: From animal models of affect to implications for psychotherapeutics. In D. Fosha, D. Siegel, and M. Solomon (Eds.), *The healing power of emotion: Affective neuroscience, development, and clinical practice* (pp. 1–26). Norton.

Panksepp, J., and Biven, L. (2012). *The archaeology of mind: Neuroevolutionary origins of human emotions.* Norton.

Pao, P. (1979). *Schizophrenic disorders: Theory and treatment from a psychodynamic point of view.* International Universities Press.

Parens, H. (1979). *The development of aggression in childhood.* Jason Aronson.

Pascal, B. (1995). *Pensées.* (A. Krailsheimer, Trans.). Penguin. (Original work published 1670)

Perris, C. (1989). *Cognitive therapy with schizophrenic patients.* Guilford Press.

Perry, B. D. (2004, September 23). *Maltreatment and the developing child: How early childhood experience shapes child and culture* [Lecture]. The Inaugural Margaret McCain lecture (abstracted). The Centre for Children and Families in the Justice System, London, ON, Canada.

Piaget, J., and Inhelder, B. (1969). *The psychology of the child.* Basic Books.

Pickett, K., and Wilkinson, R. (2009). Greater equality and better health. *British Medical Journal, 339,* b4320. https://doi.org /10.1136/bmj.b4320

Pinsker, D. (2015). *The practice of supportive psychotherapy.* Routledge.

Plato (1998). *The symposium* (R. Waterfield, Trans.). Oxford University Press.

Porges, S. (1997). Emotion: An evolutionary by-product of the neural regulation of the autonomic nervous system. *Integrative Neurobiology of Affiliation, 807*(1), 62–77.

Porges, S. (2001). The polyvagal theory: Phylogenetic substrates of a social nervous system. *International Journal of Psychophysiology, 42*(2), 123–146.

Porges, S. (2011). *The polyvagal theory: Neurophysiological foundations of emotions, attachment, communication, self-regulation.* Norton.

Porges, S., and Bazhenova, O. (2006). Neurophysiological aspects of communication and learning disorders: Evolution and the autonomic nervous system: A neurobiological model of socio-emotional and communication disorders. In *The polyvagal theory: Neurophysiological foundations of emotions, attachment, communication, self-regulation.* Norton.

Post, J., and Semrad, E. (1965). The psychosis-prone personality. *Journal of Hospital and Community Psychiatry: Mental Hospitals, 16*(2), 81–84.

Powers, R. (2018). *The overstory.* Norton.

Prins, A., Kaloupek, D., and Keane, T. (1995). Psychophysiological evidence of autonomic arousal and startle in traumatized adult populations. In M. Friedman and D. Charney (Eds.), *Neurobiological and clinical consequences of stress: From normal adaptation to post-traumatic stress disorder* (pp. 291–314). Lippincott-Raven.

Prochaska, J., and Norcross, J. (2007). *Systems of psychotherapy: A transtheoretical analysis* (6th ed.). Thompson/Brooks/Cole.

Prouty, G. (1994). *Theoretical evolutions in person-centered/experiential therapy: Applications to schizophrenic and retarded psychoses.* Praeger.

Prouty, G., Van Verde, D., and Portner, M. (2002). *Pre-therapy: Reaching contact impaired clients.* PCSS Books.

Racker, H. (1968). *Transference and countertransference.* International Universities Press.

Rank, O. (1936). *Will therapy* (J. Taft, Trans.). Norton. (Original work published 1930)

Rank, O. (1978). *Truth and reality* (J. Taft, Trans.). Norton. (Original work published 1929)

Rapaport, D. (1953). On the psychoanalytic theory of affects. *International Journal of Psychoanalysis, 34,* 177–198.

Rauch, S., van der Kolk, B., Fisler, R., Alpert, N., Orr, S., Savage, C., Fischman, A., Jenike, M., and Pitman, R. (1996). A symptom provocation study of posttraumatic stress disorder using positron emission tomography and script-driven imagery. *Archives of General Psychiatry, 53*(5), 380–387.

Raune, D., Kuipers, E., and Bebbington, P. (1999, September 23–24). *Psychosocial stress and delusional and verbal auditory hallucination themes in first episode psychosis: Implications for early intervention* [Paper presentation]. Psychological Treatments of Schizophrenia, Oxford, United Kingdom.

Read, J., Agar, J., Argyle, N., and Aderhold, V. (2003). Sexual and physical abuse during childhood and adulthood as predictors of hallucinations, delusions, and thought disorder. *Psychology and Psychotherapy: Theory, Research, and Practice, 76,* 1–22.

Read, J., Fosse, R., Moskowitz, A., and Perry, B. D. (2014). Traumagenic neurodevelopmental model of psychosis revisited. *Neuropsychiatry, 4*(1), 65–79.

Read, J., Perry, B., Moskovitz, A., and Connolly, J. (2001). The contribution of early traumatic events to schizophrenia in some patients: A traumagenic neurodevelopmental model. *Psychiatry, 64*(4), 319–345.

Read, J., Rudegeair, T., and Farrelly, S. (2006). The relationship between child abuse and psychosis: Public opinion, evidence, pathways, and implications. In W. Larkin and A. Morrisson (Eds.), *Trauma and psychosis* (pp. 23–57). Routledge.

Reber, A. (1993). *Implicit learning and tacit knowledge: An essay on the cognitive unconscious.* Oxford University Press.

Reich, A. (1951). On countertransference. *International Journal of Psychoanalysis, 32,* 25–31.

Reiner, A. (2010). *The quest for conscience and the birth of the mind.* Karnac.

Reller, M. (2005). Fragile Ich-Struktur. I. Fratilitat bei Patientem mit regressive Abwehrstruktur. II. Fragilitat bei Patientem mit Obsessive Abwehrstruktur. Weiterbildungsseminare der Schweizerischen Gesellschaft fur Intensive Dynamik Kurzpsychotherapie. In P. Troendle, *Psychotherapie: Dynamisch-intensiv-direkt: Lehrbuch zur Intensiven Dynamischen Kurzpsychotherapie.* Psychosozial-Verlag.

Robertson, D., Biaggioni, I., Burstock, G., and Low, P. (Eds.). (2004). *Primer on the autonomic nervous system.* Elsevier Academic Press.

Rockland, L. (1989). *Supportive psychotherapy: A psychodynamic approach.* Basic Books.

Romme, M. (2012). Personal links between traumatic experiences and distorted emotions in those who hear voices. In M. Romme and S. Escher (Eds.), *Psychosis as a personal crisis* (pp. 86–100). Routledge.

Romme, M., and Escher, S. (2000). *Making sense of voices.* Mind.

Romme, M., and Escher, S. (2006). Trauma and hearing voices. In W. Larkin and A. Morrisson (Eds.), *Trauma and psychosis* (pp. 162–191). Routledge.

Rosen, J., and Schulkin, J. (2004). Adaptive fear, allostasis, and the pathology of anxiety. In J. Schulkin (Ed.), *Allostasis, homeostasis, and the costs of physiological adaptation* (pp. 164–227). Cambridge University Press.

Rosenbaum, B., Harder, S., Knudsen, P., Køster, A., Lajer, M., Lindhardt, A., Valbak, and Winther, K. (2012). Supportive psychodynamic psychotherapy versus treatment as usual for first-episode psychosis: Two-year outcome. *Psychiatry, 75,* 331–341.

Rosenfeld, H. (1965). *Psychotic states.* Hogarth Press.

Rosenfeld, H. (1977). Notes on psychoanalytic treatment of psychotic states. In C. Chiland and P. Bequart (Eds.), *Long term treatments of psychotic states* (pp. 200–217). Human Sciences Press.

Rosenfeld, H. (1987). *Impasse and interpretation: Therapeutic and anti-therapeutic factors in the psychoanalytic treatment of psychotic, borderline, and neurotic patients.* Routledge.

Ross, C., Anderson, G., and Clark, P. (1994). Childhood abuse and positive symptoms of schizophrenia. *Hospital and Community Psychiatry, 45*(5), 489–491.

Rothschild, B. (2003). *The body remembers casebook*. Norton.

Rottenberg, J., Wilhelm, F., Gross, J., and Gotlib, I. (2003). Vagal rebound during resolution of tearful crying among depressed and nondepressed individuals. *Psychophysiology, 40*(1), 1–6.

Rukeyser, M. (1996). *The life of poetry*. Wesleyan University Press. (Original work published 1949)

Safran, J. (Ed.). (2003). *Psychoanalysis and Buddhism: An unfolding dialogue*. Wisdom Publications.

Safran, J., and Muran, C. (2003). *Negotiating the therapeutic alliance: A relational treatment guide*. Guilford.

Sanders, K., and Akiyama, T. (2018). The vicious cycle of itch and anxiety. *Neuroscience and Biobehavior Reviews, 87*, 17–26. https://doi.org/10.1016/j.neubiorev.2018.01.009

Sapolsky, R. (2004). *Why zebras don't get ulcers*. Henry Holt.

Sapolsky, R., Uno, H., Rebert, C., and Finch, C. (1990). Hippocampal damage with prolonged glucocorticoid exposure in primates. *Journal of Neuroscience, 10*(9), 2897–2902.

Scaer, R. (2001). *The body bears the burden: Trauma, dissociation, and disease*. Haworth Medical Press.

Scaer, R. (2005). *The trauma spectrum: Hidden wounds and human resiliency*. Norton.

Schneider, S. (2009). *You are what you hate: A spiritually productive approach to enemies*. A Still Small Voice.

Schore, A. (1991). Early superego development: The emergence of shame and narcissistic affect regulation in the practicing period. *Psychoanalysis and Contemporary Thought, 14*(2), 187–250.

Schore, A. (1994). *Affect regulation and the origin of the self*. Lawrence Erlbaum.

Schore, A. (2002). Dysregulation of the right brain: A fundamental mechanism of traumatic attachment and the psychopathogenesis of posttraumatic stress disorder. *Australian and New Zealand Journal of Psychiatry, 36*, 9–30.

Schore, A. (2003a). *Affect dysregulation and disorders of the self.* Norton.

Schore, A. (2003b). *Affect regulation and the repair of the self.* Norton.

Schore, A. (2009). Right brain affect regulation: An essential mechanism of development, trauma, dissociation, and psychotherapy. In D. Foshan, D. Siegel, and M. Solomon (Eds.), *The healing power of emotion: Affective neuroscience, development and clinical practice* (pp. 112–144). Norton.

Schulkin, J. (Ed.). (2004). *Allostasis, homeostasis, and the costs of physiological adaptation.* Cambridge University Press.

Schulkin, J. (2007). *A behavioral neuroscience perspective on the will.* Lawrence Erlbaum.

Schultz, C. (1980). All-or-none phenomena in the psychotherapy of severe disorders. In J. Strauss, M. Bowers, T. Downey, S. Fleck, S. Jackson, and I. Levine (Eds.). (1980). *The psychotherapy of schizophrenia* (pp. 181–190). Plenum Press.

Schwartz, J., and Begley, S. (2002). *The mind and the brain: Neuroplasticity and the power of mental force.* Harper Collins.

Schwing, G. (1954). *A way to the soul of the mentally ill.* International Universities Press.

Searles, H. (1960). *The non-human environment in normal development and schizophrenia.* International Universities Press.

Searles, H. (1979). *Countertransference and related subjects: Selected papers.* International Universities Press.

Searles, H. (1986a). *Collected papers on schizophrenia and related subjects.* Karnac. (Original work published 1965)

Searles, H. (1986b). The differentiation between concrete and metaphorical thinking in the recovering schizophrenic patient. In H. Searles (1986), *Collected papers on schizophrenia and related subjects* (pp. 560–583). Karnac. (Original work published 1962)

Sechehaye, M. (1951). *Autobiography of a schizophrenic girl.* Grune and Stratton.

Segal, H. (1981). *The work of Hannah Segal.* Jason Aronson.

Semrad, E. (1966). Long-term therapy of schizophrenia. In G. Usdin (Ed.), *Psychoneurosis and schizophrenia* (pp. 155–173). J. B. Lippincott Company.

Semrad, E. (1969). Comments on psychotherapy of the psychoses. In E. Semrad and D. Buskirk (Eds.), *Teaching psychotherapy of psychotic patients: Supervision of beginning residents in the "clinical approach"* (pp. 31–44). Grune and Stratton.

Semrad, E., and Buskirk, D. (Eds.). (1969). *Teaching psychotherapy of psychotic patients: Supervision of beginning residents in the "clinical approach."* Grune and Stratton.

Sheline, Y., Gado, M., and Kraemer, H. (2003). Untreated depression and hippocampal volume loss. *American Journal of Psychiatry, 160,* 1516.

Sheline, Y., Wang, P., Gado, M., Csernansky, J, and Vannier, M. (1996). Hippocampal atrophy in recurrent major depression. *Proceedings of the National Academy of Sciences of the United States of America, 93*(9), 3908–4003.

Shengold, L. (1991). *Soul murder: The effects of childhood abuse and deprivation.* Ballantine Books.

Sherman, M. (1968). Siding with resistance rather than interpretation: Role implications. In M. Coleman-Nelson, B. Nelson, B. Sherman, and H. Strean. (Eds.), *Roles and paradigms in psychotherapy* (pp. 74–107). Grune and Stratton.

Shevlin, M., Dorahy, M., and Adamson, G. (2007). Trauma and psychosis: An analysis of the National Comorbidity Survey. *American Journal of Psychiatry, 164*(1), 166–169.

Siegel, D. (1999). *The developing mind: How relationships and the brain interact to shape who we are.* Guilford Press.

Silver, A. (Ed.). (1989). *Psychoanalysis and psychosis.* International Universities Press.

Silver, A., and Cantor, M. (Eds.). (1990). *Psychoanalysis and severe emotional illness.* Guilford Press.

Sledge, W. H. (1977). The therapist's use of metaphor. *International Journal of Psychoanalytic Psychotherapy, 6,* 113–130.

Smoller, J. (2013). Disorders and borders: Psychiatric genetics and nosology. *American Journal of Medical Genetics Part B Neuropsychiatric Genetics 162*(7), 559–578.

Southwick, S., Rasmusson, A., Barron, J., and Arnsten, A. (2005). Neurobiological and neurocognitive alterations in PTSD: A focus on norepinephrine, serotonin, and the hypothalamic-pituitary-adrenal axis. In J. Vasterling and C. Brewin (Eds.), *Neuropsychology of PTSD* (pp. 27–58). Guilford Press.

Spotnitz, H. (1976). *Psychotherapy of preoedipal conditions: Schizophrenia and severe character disorders.* Jason Aronson.

Spotnitz, H. (1986). *Modern psychoanalysis of the schizophrenic patient: Theory of the technique.* Human Sciences Press.

Sroufe, A. (1989). Pathways to adaptation and maladaptation: Psychopathology as developmental deviation. In D. Cicchetti (Ed.), *Rochester Symposium on developmental psychopathology: Vol. 1. The emergence of a discipline* (pp. 13–40). Lawrence Erlbaum.

Sroufe, A. (1996). *Emotional development: The organization of emotional life in the early years.* Cambridge University Press.

Sroufe, A., Egeland, B., Carlson, E., and Collins, W. (2005). *The development of the person: The Minnesota study of risk and adaptation from birth to adulthood.* Guilford Press.

Stern, D. (2003). *Unformulated experience: From dissociation to imagination in psychoanalysis.* Routledge.

Sternberg, E. (2010). *My brain made me do it: The rise of neuroscience and the threat to moral responsibility.* Prometheus Books.

Stone, M., Albert, H., Forrest D., and Arieti, S. (1983). *Treating schizophrenic patients.* McGraw Hill.

Strauss, J., Bowers, M., Downey, T., Fleck, S., Jackson, S., and Levine, I. (Eds.). (1980). *The psychotherapy of schizophrenia.* Plenum Press.

Sullivan, H. S. (1949). The theory of anxiety and the nature of psychotherapy. *Psychiatry, 12*(1), 3–12.

Sullivan, H. S. (1953a). *Conceptions of modern psychiatry* (2nd ed.). Norton.

Sullivan, H. S. (1953b). *The interpersonal theory of psychiatry.* Norton.

Sullivan, H. S. (1956). *Clinical studies in psychiatry.* Norton.

Sullivan. H. S. (1962). *Schizophrenia as a human process.* Norton.

Sullivan, H. S. (1966). *Conceptions of modern psychiatry.* W. W. Norton. (Original work published 1947)

Suttie, I. (1960). *The origins of love and hate.* Pelican Books. (Original work published 1935)

Symington, J. and Symington, N. (1966). *The clinical thinking of Wilfred Bion.* Routledge.

Symington, N. (2002). *A pattern of madness.* Karnac.

Symington, N. (2006). *A healing conversation: How healing happens.* Karnac.

Tomkins, S. (1962). *Affect, imagery, consciousness. Vol. 1. The positive affects.* Spring.

Trunnell, T., and Semrad, E. (1967). Object anxiety and primitive defenses in schizophrenia. *Journal of Nervous and Mental Disease, 114*(2), 101–110.

Usdin, G. (Ed.). (1966). *Psychoneurosis and schizophrenia.* J. B. Lippincott Company.

Vaillant, G. (1992). *Ego mechanisms of defense: A guide for clinicians and researchers.* American Psychiatric Publishing.

Van der Hart, O., Nijenhius, E., and Steele, K. (2006). *The haunted self: Structural dissociation and the treatment of chronic traumatization.* Norton.

Van Reekum, R., Conway, C., Gansler, D., White, R., and Bachman, D. (1993). Neurobehavioral study of borderline personality disorder. *Journal of Psychiatry Neuroscience 18*(3), 121–129.

Verhaeghe, P. (2004). *On being normal and other disorders: A manual for clinical psychodiagnostics.* Other Press.

Waelder, R. (1951). The structure of paranoid ideas: A critical survey of various theories. *International Journal of Psychoanalysis, 32*(3), 167–177.

Waelder, R. (1960). *Basic theory of psychoanalysis.* International Universities Press.

Wegner, D. (2002). *The illusion of conscious will.* MIT Press.

Wehrenberg, M., and Prinz, S. (2007). *The anxious brain: The neurobiological basis of anxiety disorders and how to effectively treat them.* Norton.

Weinberger, J. (1995). Common factors are not so common: The common factors dilemma. *Clinical Psychology, 1*, 45–60.

Weiner, I. (1996). *Psychodiagnosis in schizophrenia*. Routledge.

Weiss, J., and Sampson, H. (1986). *The psychoanalytic process: Theory, clinical process, and empirical research*. Guilford.

Werman, D. (2015). *The practice of supportive psychotherapy*. Routledge.

Werner, H. (1948). *Comparative psychology of mental development*. Follett.

Wexler, M. (1952). The structural problem in schizophrenia: The role of the internal object. In E. Brody and R. Redlich (Eds.), *Psychotherapy with schizophrenics* (pp. 179–201). International Universities Press.

Wexler, M. (1975). The evolution of a deficiency perspective on schizophrenia. In J. Gunderson and L. Mosher (Eds.), *Psychotherapy of schizophrenia* (pp. 161–174). Jason Aronson.

Whittemore, J. (1996). Paving the royal road: An overview of conceptual and technical features in the graded format of Davanloo's ISTDP. *International Journal of Short-Term Dynamic Psychotherapy, 11*, 21–39.

Willick, M. (1983). On the concept of primitive defenses. *Journal of the American Psychoanalytic Association, 31*, 175–200.

Winnicott, D. W. (1965a). Ego distortion in terms of true and false self. In D. W. Winnicott, *The maturational process and the facilitating environment: Studies in the theory of emotional development* (pp. 140–157). International Universities Press. (Original work published 1960)

Winnicott, D. W. (1965b). The mentally ill in your caseload. In D. W. Winnicott, *The maturational processes and the facilitating environment* (pp. 217–229). International Universities Press. (Original work published 1963)

Winnicott, D. W. (1965c). *The maturational processes and the facilitating environment*. International Universities Press.

Winnicott, D. W. (1971). *Playing and reality*. Penguin Books.

Winnicott, D. W. (1975). Hate in the countertransference. In D. W. Winnicott, *Through paediatrics to psychoanalysis* (pp. 194–203). Basic Books. (Original work published 1947)

Winnicott, D. W. (1977). *The piggle: An account of the psychoanalytic treatment of a little girl*. Penguin.

Winston, A., Rosenthal, R., and Pinsker, H. (2015). *Learning supportive psychotherapy: A clinical guide*. American Psychiatric Association.

Wishnie, H. (1977). *The impulsive personality: Understanding people with destructive character disorders*. Plenum Press.

Wojtyla, J. (1993). *Love and responsibility*. Ignatius Press. (Original work published 1960)

Wolberg, A. (1973). *The borderline patient*. Intercontinental Medical Book Corporation.

Wright, N., Turkington, D., Kelly, O., Davies, D., Jacobs, A., and Hopton, J. (2014). *Treating psychosis: A clinician's guide to integrating acceptance and commitment therapy, compassion-focused therapy, and mindfulness approaches within the cognitive/behavioral tradition*. New Harbinger Publications.

Wurmser, L. (1984). The role of superego conflicts in substance abuse and their treatment. *International Journal of Psychotherapy, 10*, 227–258.

Wurmser, L. (1989). Blinding the eye of the mind. In E. Edelstein, D. Nathanson, and A. Stone (Eds.), *Denial: A clarification of concepts and research* (pp. 175–201). Plenum Press.

Wurmser, L. (2000). *The power of the inner judge: Psychodynamic treatment of the severe neuroses*. Jason Aronson.

Yeats, W. B. (1989). *The collected poems of W. B. Yeats* (R. Finneran, Ed.). MacMillan Publishing Company.

Ziegler, M. (2004). Psychological stress and the autonomic nervous system. In D. Robertson, I. Biaggioni, G. Burnstock, and P. Low (Eds.), *Primer on the autonomic nervous system* (2nd ed.; pp. 189–190). Elsevier Academic Press.

Index

About the Author

Jon Frederickson, MSW, is on the faculty of the Intensive Short-Term Dynamic Psychotherapy (ISTDP) Training Program at the Washington School of Psychiatry. He is also on the faculty of the Laboratorium Psychoedukacji in Warsaw and teaches at the Ersta Sköndal Bräcke Högskola in Stockholm. Jon has provided ISTDP training in Sweden, Norway, Denmark, Poland, Italy, India, Iran, Australia, Canada, the United States, and the Netherlands. He is the author of over fifty published papers and three books, *Co-Creating Change: Effective Dynamic Therapy Techniques*, *Psychodynamic Psychotherapy: Learning to Listen from Multiple Perspectives*, and *The Lies We Tell Ourselves: How Face the Truth, Accept Yourself, and Create a Better Life*. His book *Co-Creating Change* won the first prize in psychiatry in 2014 at the British Medical Association Book Awards. It has been published in Farsi and Polish and is forthcoming in Spanish and Slovak. His book *The Lies We Tell Ourselves* has been published in Polish, Farsi, Danish, and Norwegian.

Jon has DVDs of actual sessions with patients who previously failed in therapy at his websites www.istdpinstitute.com and www.deliberate practiceinpsychotherapy.com. There you will also find skill-building exercises designed for therapists. He writes posts on ISTDP at www .facebook.com/DynamicPsychotherapy. His forthcoming skill-building book for therapists, *Healing through Relating*, will be published in 2021.

Also by Jon Frederickson

Co-Creating Change
Effective Dynamic Therapy Techniques

"This book is a brilliant master class. It demonstrates how to work collaboratively with patients safely, compassionately, and effectively to achieve successful outcomes."
—**David Malan, DM, FRCPsych**, author of *Individual Psychotherapy and the Science of Psychodynamics*

"An incredibly useful book . . . Offers crystal clear and highly practical therapy techniques with plenty of transcript examples. Good for new and advanced practitioners of any therapeutic orientation."
—**Leslie Greenberg, PhD**, author of *Emotion-Focused Therapy*

Written for therapists, *Co-Creating Change* shows what to do to help "stuck" patients—those who resist the therapy process—let go of their resistance and self-defeating behaviors and willingly co-create a relationship for change instead. It includes clinical vignettes that illustrate hundreds of therapeutic impasses taken from actual sessions, showing how to understand patients and how to intervene effectively. The book provides clear, systematic steps for assessing patients' needs and intervening to develop an effective relationship for change.

Co-Creating Change, which won First Prize in Psychiatry at the British Medical Association Book Awards, presents an integrative theory that uses elements of behavior therapy, cognitive therapy, emotion-focused therapy, psychoanalysis, and mindfulness. This empirically validated treatment is effective with a wide range of patients.

Paperback, ISBN 978-0-9883788-4-1
Ebook, ISBN 978-0-9883788-5-8

The Lies We Tell Ourselves

How to Face the Truth, Accept Yourself, and Create a Better Life

THE LIES WE TELL OURSELVES

How to Face the Truth, Accept Yourself, and Create a Better Life

JON FREDERICKSON, MSW

"This book is a revelation—a gift to all who come across it. I can't recommend this book highly enough!"
—**Patricia Coughlin, PhD**, author of *Intensive Short-Term Dynamic Psychotherapy*

"I wholeheartedly recommend this book to everyone who wants to see what therapy is really about or who wants to increase the value of the psychotherapy they engage in or offer to others."
—**Peter Fenner, PhD**, author of *Radiant Mind* and *Natural Awakening*

Do you feel stuck in your life? Do you wonder why? Does something seem wrong, but you can't put your finger on it? In *The Lies We Tell Ourselves*, psychotherapist Jon Frederickson reveals the ways we fool ourselves and how to get unstuck.

Through dozens of stories and examples, he demonstrates that the *apparent* cause of our problems is almost never the *real* cause. In addition, he reveals what we really fear and how to face it. Frederickson shows how to recognize the lies we tell ourselves and face the truths we have avoided—and stop saying yes when we really mean no.

Although we may use falsehoods to escape pain, clinging to our fantasies actually becomes the source of greater suffering. This book shows how to create a better life by letting go of our lies and facing reality. It also demonstrates that therapy is not merely a chat; it is a relationship between two people devoted to facing the deepest truths of our lives so we can be healed.

Paperback, ISBN 978-0-9883788-8-9
Ebook, ISBN 978-0-9883788-9-6